THE LAND OF
PROMISE

Abdelwahab M. Elmessiri has had a distinguished career as an educator, author, and journalist. He is Associate Professor of English at Ain Shams University, Cairo, and at present holds the position of Advisor on Cultural Affairs in the Office of the Permanent Observer of the Arab League to the United Nations. His scholarly interest in Zionism, as a political movement, dates back to his appointment in 1972 as head of the Zionist Ideology and Literature Section in the Center for Political and Strategic Studies, an affiliate of Cairo's authoritative daily, *Al-Ahram*. In that capacity, he published a number of articles and studies, among them *The End of History: An Introduction to the Study of the Structure of Zionist Thought*.

Dr. Elmessiri's extensive research during his tenure with the Center led to the publication in 1975 of *The Encyclopedia of Zionist Concepts and Terminology*, acknowledged to be the only work of its kind in the Arabic language. Two books in Arabic, comprising his lectures at the Nasser War Academy, the Institute of Diplomacy, and the Institute of Arab Studies, were published in 1976. The first book focuses on the Zionist "imagination"; and the second provides an outline for an economic history of Western Jewry. Dr. Elmessiri also edited *A Lover from Palestine and Other Poems* (1971), a bilingual anthology of Palestinian resistance poetry.

Elmessiri is a graduate of Alexandria University and has a Ph.D. in English and American Literature from Rutgers University. He has lectured widely on Middle East affairs in the United States. Several of his articles on the Arab-Israeli conflict have been published both in the Arab world and the United States.

THE LAND OF
PROMISE

A CRITIQUE
OF POLITICAL ZIONISM

Abdelwahab M. Elmessiri

with a Foreword by John Davis
former Commissioner General, UNRWA

NORTH AMERICAN
New Brunswick, New Jersey

Published by North American, Inc.
P.O. Box 65
New Brunswick, N.J. 08903
U.S.A.

DS
149
.E594
1977
Mar.1977

Library of Congress Cataloging in Publication Data

Elmessiri, Abdelwahab M   1938–
    The land of promise.

    Bibliography: p.
    Includes index.
    1. Zionism. 2. Jewish-Arab relations—1917–
I. Title.
DS149.E594   956.94'001   77-11057
ISBN 0-930244-02-8 (cloth)   0-930244-01-X (paper)

To my friends
Rabbi Yosef Becher, member of Neturei Karta and a lover of Zion,
and
Marwan Kanafani, an Arab from Acre and a lover of Palestine

And I knew that both Yahia Effendi and Mussa Alami were telling the truth. And the facile Zionism, the verbose fuss, appeared to be more ridiculous than ever.

David Ben Gurion (1966)

CONTENTS

FOREWORD BY JOHN DAVIS xi

PREFACE xiii

1. JUDAISM AND ZIONISM 1
   Zionism and Religious Belief 1
   A Physical and Spiritual Zion 6
   The Messiah with a Flag 10
   A Metaphysic of Peoplehood 13

2. THE QUINTESSENTIAL JEW 19
   The "Danger" of Assimilation 19
   Corporate Identity 21
   A Racial Definition 21
   An Ethnic and a Religious Definition 23
   Dual or Multiple Loyalties? 27

3. ZIONISM AND DIASPORA JEWRY 31
   The Status 31
   The Forcible Redemption 36
   The Negation 41
   Zionist Anti-Semitism 43
   Population Transfer I 48

4. THE JEWISH RESPONSE 55
   Jewish Anti-Zionism 55

The Centrality of the Diaspora 66
Who Is a Zionist? 74

5. ZIONIST SETTLER COLONIALISM: ORIGINS AND SPECIFIC TRAITS 83
Restoring the Jews 83
Pro-Anti-Semitism 89
The Zionist Strategy I 93
A Vassal Jewish State 95
Specific Traits 101

6. ZIONIST SETTLER COLONIALISM: APOLOGETICS 109
The White Jew's Burden 109
The Pure Jew's Burden 119
The Socialist Jew's Burden 124

7. A LAND WITHOUT A PEOPLE 127
Intentions 127
The Zionist Strategy II 129
Population Transfer II 136
What Is to Be Done? 143

8. ISRAELI-ZIONIST RACISM 147
In Captivity: The Laws of Return and Nationality 147
Jewish Land and Hebrew Labor 153
Body and Soul, Past and Present 156
Christians and Druzes 162
A Form of Racism and Racial Discrimination 163

9. THE RESPONSE OF THE ORIENT 171
Eternal Arab Hostility? 171
Afro-Asian Solidarity 177

10. TROUBLE IN THE PROMISED LAND 187
The Israeli Question 187
A Complex of Legitimacy 196
The Road Away from Massada 201

NOTES 211

BIBLIOGRAPHY 241

INDEX 249

FOREWORD

The Land of Promise by Dr. Elmessiri warrants a careful reading by everyone who wants to understand the complex nature and far-reaching implications of Zionism and the Arab-Israeli conflict. Because the book is well written, logical, and factual, it is likely to appeal not only to scholarly readers but also to large elements of the public.

The author is uniquely qualified to make such a study. Born and reared in Egypt, he holds Masters and Ph. D. degrees from Columbia and Rutgers, respectively. He has resided for long periods in Egypt and the United States and has traveled extensively throughout the Middle East. Among his many published works, this book deserves special praise for its scholarship and objectivity in treating an extremely sensitive subject.

The reader is challenged to make a critical examination of political Zionism, rather than Judaism, as the force that has generated and sustained the Arab-Israeli conflict. In analyzing political Zionism, the author discussed aspects that are not apparent to the public or perhaps not even to policymakers in general. He delineates the antecedents of Zionism, its motivation, its power base, its claim to the land of Palestine, and the far-reaching repercussions of the creation of the State of Israel on both Jews and Arabs. A critical result of this has been the twofold transfer of people— the Jews immigrating into Israel and the native Arabs being ejected from it. This transfer of people has been brought about by political Zionist action—the Jewish influx by invitation and persuasion and the Arab exodus by coercion and expulsion. The Western countries, the United States in particular, apparently have failed to recognize the true nature of political Zionism and have accepted the ambiguities and mythicism that blur the differences between Zionism and Judaism. This accommodation which facilitates the rationalization of, and support for, a Zionist-dominated Israel also helps conceal the mistreatment of the native Arab population.

The situation is not without hope, Dr. Elmessiri concludes, and he suggests which aspects of Zionist policy and practice could be changed or eliminated so that peace and justice could be realized. None of these changes would do violence either to the basic tenets of Judaism or to the individual human rights of the Israelis and diaspora Jews.

I recommend this book as essential reading by all persons interested in the Middle East and in the important related subjects. In view of America's growing involvement in the Middle East, Dr. Elmessiri's book is most timely.

JOHN H. DAVIS
International Consultant
Former Commissioner General
of UNRWA

PREFACE

Books dealing with the Arab-Israeli conflict either steer away from the issue of Zionism or relegate it to a perfunctory background chapter. The conflict is generally dealt with in the familiar terms of territories, refugees, or sovereignty. Scholars and laymen in the West are reluctant to see the link between the Arab-Israeli conflict on the one hand and Zionist theory and practice on the other. It is not hard to account for this reluctance. Politicians interested in quick results and laymen keen on knowing what is "really happening" have no patience with historical considerations. Most writers prefer to deal with the familiar and the customary, and Zionism, at least in its rhetoric and its rationalizing myths, is *sui generis.* Dealing with the conflict in familiar terms is the best means of circumventing that problem.

Moreover, scholars in the Western world feel understandably uneasy about dealing with the issue of Zionism, with its carefully advertised Jewish credentials. For one thing, it was only three decades ago that Nazism almost succeeded in destroying European Jewry. Besides, the whole issue of Zionism in the Western world is riddled with ambiguities and shrouded in religious mystery. The term itself is linked with Judeo-Christian eschatology and evokes a religious concept that has central significance in the Occidental religious imagination.

I, however, do not share these assumptions, nor do I suffer from such inhibitions. It is my contention that the Zionist state and Zionism, in its nationalistic political variety, are the primary causes of the Arab-Israeli conflict. My central argument in this study is that Judaism and political Zionism have very little in common and are actually two *conflicting* outlooks. Zionism is a political movement seeking to recast the spiritual and religious concepts of Judaism in ethnic and materialistic terms. As such, it cannot claim any religious sanctity.

Zionism not only recasts Judaism in ethnic terms, but it also reinterprets the historical experience of Jewry in terms of the same ethnicity. In lieu of the assimilationist image of the Jew as a complex personality, the Zionists set forth the view of the quintessential Jew who lives "in exile," in perpetual alienation, always longing to be "ingathered" into a Jewish homeland. The theme of "the negation of the diaspora" and its worthlessness and the view of the Jew as a marginal personality dominate Zionist literature. In its definition of Judaism and Jewry, Zionism echoes in many respects the literature of anti-Semitism, as many of the Zionist leaders and theoreticians themselves have realized. The Jewish response to Zionism, as the present study attempts to demonstrate, has not been one of mere acquiescence, for the Jews, resisting reductionist formulas that relegate them to a marginal status, have asserted the centrality of the diaspora and the richness of its historical experience.

Rather than trace Zionism to Judaism or to the historical experience of Jewry, the present study argues that the history of the movement is traceable to the anti-Semitism and colonialism of nineteenth-century Europe. Indeed a form of unorganized gentile colonial Zionism predated later Jewish Zionist formulations. The Jews, according to the gentile Zionist plan, were to be "restored" to Palestine in order to rid Europe of their presence and to turn them, simultaneously, into agents of their colonial sponsors.

The first part of this study examines the intellectual and political setting of Zionism and its power base. Later chapters deal with the various rationalizations of the Zionist project, the expulsion of the majority of the Palestinian Arabs from their homeland, the discrimination against those who remained, and the active resistance of the dispossessed Palestinians and of the Afro-Asian peoples as a whole.

The final chapter deals with the core of the Israeli question, namely, the problem of the new settlers. It is argued that all solutions lie outside the political Zionist *status quo*. One alternative is to reconstitute Israel so that it becomes a state for its actual citizens rather than a state and a potential home for world Jewry. It is hoped that in this way the new state and its citizenry, comprising Jews, Christians, and Muslims, can be integrated into the pattern of Middle Eastern culture and politics.

Because I take my stand against political Zionism primarily as a humanist, and only secondly as an Arab, the specific Arab case against Zionism is given only secondary importance. Even though this study is an exploration and a definition of an ideology and its political structure, it is also, and primarily, a reminder—at a time when some form of settlement may be near—that no permanent and just resolution of the Middle East question is feasible or attainable without first addressing the issue of

Zionism. In claiming to be a state for *all* Jews, regardless of time and place, Israel is an anomaly that has little chance of a permanent peaceful existence. This is the lesson of the past quarter-century, a lesson that some would now like to ignore.

The present study, a general critique of political Zionism, posits a minimum definition of that ideology, namely: It is a belief in Jewish people-hood in a political sense which endows the Jews, as Jews, with specific political rights in a state of their own. That definition subsumes almost all Zionist schools and thinkers, whether they are rightist or leftist, human-istic or terroristic, theistic or atheistic. The definition also encompasses Zionist practice in the past 80 years, reaching to the underlying unity be-tween a gentle Theodor Herzl asking for a Jewish state on pragmatic grounds, and a spiritual Martin Buber asking for the same on the basis of a highly mystical view of Jewish history. The term "political Zionism" (with small "p") as used in this study has a wider implication than the same term (sometimes spelled with a capital "P") as used in studies on Zionism. The words "Zionism" and "political Zionism" in the wider sense are some-times used interchangeably in this study. I try to explain the reasons for this usage in various parts of this study, mainly in Chapters 1 and 4. This usage, however, is not in any sense unique, for after the establishment of the Zionist state, Zionism came to be identified in the media and even in scholarly writings with that state and with the efforts made on its behalf.

Given the relatively wide scope of this study, it proves at times diffi-cult to maintain a balance between generalities and specifics. On some occasions, complex issues are simplified for the sake of comprehensiveness. For instance, the ambiguity of Ahad Ha'am's position and his cultural Zionism are merely mentioned rather than fully explored. The political developments in the Middle East have led to the hegemony of the Zionist state and to the dominance of political Zionism over Jews, reducing cultural Zionism to marginal significance. One may even argue that many of the premises of cultural Zionism are now put in the service of the political Zionist objectives.

Given this point of departure and level of analysis, I have abandoned chronology in favor of a thematic approach. As a rule, I have overlooked developments and divisions *within* the Zionist movement, unless they have had some impact on the lives of diaspora Jewry and the destiny of Pales-tinian Arabs and unless they portend some serious restructuring of the premises of political Zionism.

In order to keep details that are unrelated to the structure of Zionist thought down to a minimum, very little is said here about the biographies of Zionist leaders and thinkers. Theodor Herzl's and Max Nordau's per-sonal experiences undoubtedly had some bearing on the evolution of their thought regarding the Jewish question, and even on Zionist thought in general. Nevertheless, for the purposes of this study it was deemed advisable to deal with the wider political and historical contexts of Zionism. After all, it was in various European colonial capitals and on the land of Palestine—not in Herzl's psyche—that the history of Zionism was shaped.

I did not concern myself much with what Zionist thinkers claimed, hoped for, or intended, but rather I addressed myself to those statements that guided actual practice and had direct bearing on the history of the Arab-Israeli conflict. Other statements might be of great psychological interest but of little political value. However, I devote the whole of Chapter 6 to Zionist apologetics and touch briefly on the issue of intentions in Chapter 7. Whenever possible, an attempt has been made to base the analysis on a reading of the works of Zionist authors or on Jewish critiques thereof, confining the study almost exclusively to books and other works published in English. Only on very few occasions are Arabic translations of Israeli or Zionist texts cited. The exact words of the sources are given, though on several occasions the punctuation and the spelling have been changed for purposes of standardization. For the sake of simplicity, phrases or terms that carry Zionist overtones or which have been redefined along Zionist lines (Jewish people, Jewish nation) are not placed between quotation marks. Such terms have been used in this study because they have become part and parcel of the debate concerning Zionism. They are employed with a great deal of reservation, and only in order to redefine them by discussing the complex totality of Jewry's religious and historical experience.

In writing this study, it is my hope to provide the serious reader and anyone interested in understanding the Middle East conflict with a critical view of political Zionism. In so doing, my main concern is to generate in the reader's mind a sense of receptivity that might enable him to reject the simplistic and lopsided definitions and terms that he encounters in the press and in countless books and other publications.

ACKNOWLEDGMENTS

For their valuable comments and advice, I am deeply indebted to Clement H. Henry of the University of Michigan at Ann Arbor; Stephen Miller of the National Endowment for the Humanities, Washington, D.C.; Ibrahim Abu-Lughod of Northwestern University, Illinois; Ayman El-Amir of the Egyptian delegation to the United Nations; Elsayid Hussein and Ossama Tawfik of the Egyptian Foreign Ministry; and Richard Stack of the State University of New York at Purchase. For intellectual stimulation of a high order, I thank my good friends Kevin Reilly of Somerset Community College and David Weimer of Rutgers University. I am particularly

grateful to Ambassador Amin Hilmy II, Permanent Observer of the Arab
League delegation to the United Nations and Ambassador Abdalla Bishara,
Permanent Representative of Kuwait to the United Nations, for their encouragement of this study from its inception. It is a pleasure to acknowledge the advice and assistance of Dr. Burhan Hamadi, Legal Advisor to
the Permanent Mission to the United Arab Emirates to the United Nations.
I have also been helped by a number of Jewish-American organizations in
my efforts to present a well-documented study. I wish to extend thanks to
all of them and particularly to the Neturei Karta, the American Council for
Judaism, and American-Jewish Alternatives to Zionism.

Special gratitude is due to Margaret Pennar, who read the manuscript,
edited it, and made several suggestions concerning style and content, all
of which were incorporated into the final text. I would also like to thank
Jane Tonero and Maria Alvarez for their help and assistance. I would like
to express my appreciation to Nasra Hassan and Ernestine Franco for
patiently transforming my messy handwriting into typed text. My special
thanks go to Hoda Hegazy and Nur Elmessiri for their research and secre-
tarial work; they, together with Yasser Elmessiri, provided the support so
necessary for an author from those nearest to him.

New York   ABDELWAHAB M. ELMESSIRI
August 1977

THE LAND OF
PROMISE

1

JUDAISM AND ZIONISM

ZIONISM AND RELIGIOUS BELIEF

It is difficult to think of a political phenomenon that generates more controversy and elicits more violent reaction than Zionism. Many political movements and institutions have been described over the years as progressive or counterrevolutionary, nationalist, or settler-colonialist. But, unlike Zionism, very few such movements in the twentieth century have been described as being "much more than a political entity."[1] It is doubtful whether any political outlook has ever been classified as a "sacred word and concept" and as "a legitimate religious belief."[2] Some Zionists and Zionist sympathizers even view the establishment of a state in the land of Palestine by a 1947 United Nations resolution as being a fulfillment of biblical prophecy and an event of apocalyptic significance.

It is this aspect of the controversy surrounding Zionism that makes it necessary to begin the study of this ideology by asserting the self-evident, namely, that Zionism *is* a political movement, and is *not* a religious doctrine. Perhaps the hue and cry in the West, following the 1975 United Nations resolution equating Zionism with racism, is a timely reminder of the need to emphasize once more the difference between the religious belief and the political program.

Far from being sacred, Zionism is a political ideology of complex European origins, rooted primarily in the socioeconomic realities of the Eastern European Jewish ghettoes and in European society of the late nineteenth century. The movement embraced a wide variety of schools and trends (General, Socialist, Religious, Revisionist, Labor, and others). The common denominator among these schools was the conviction that, since their early history, the Jews have constituted a nation, or a people, and that this peoplehood confers on them certain timeless national rights. This people, according to the Zionist argument, has existed continuously since

1

the time of the destruction of the Second Temple (63 B.C.). The state of exile in which the Jews found themselves, following their dispersion by the Romans, had made foreigners of them around the globe, ever yearning to return to the land of their forefathers, or at least to have a land of their own. The proponents of Zionism believed that the Jews, without waiting for divine intervention, should achieve "autoemancipation" by taking matters into their own hands and terminating their state of perpetual alienation and deep longing. The Jews must, said the new leaders, create a Jewish state of their own or, to use the more precise phrase of Theodor Herzl, "the Jews' state *(der Judenstaat)*."[3] The Jewishness of this state lay neither in its religious orientation nor in its commitment to Judaism and its values; it lay in its presumed national (ethnic) Jewish character.

Many of the founders of Zionism had little concern with Judaism, and even evinced a marked hostility toward its precepts and practices. During his visit to the Holy City, Theodor Herzl (1860–1904), the Austro-Hungarian journalist and founder of Political Zionism, consciously violated many Jewish religious practices in order to emphasize his new nonreligious outlook as distinct from a traditional religious stance.[4] Max Nordau (1849–1923), the German writer and Zionist leader, and Herzl's close friend, was a self-avowed atheist who believed that the Torah was "inferior as literature" compared "to Homer and the European classics," and that it was "childish as philosophy and revolting as morality."[5] He even suggested that the day would come when Herzl's *Jewish State* would be given equal status with the Bible, even by its author's religious opponents.[6] And Chaim Weizmann (1874–1952), the Russian chemist who became the first president of Israel, took pleasure at times in "baiting the Rabbis about kosher food."[7]

The Zionist settlers in Palestine, the first to implement this new philosophy of political Zionism, were unusually careful to emphasize the nonreligious and untraditional nature of their endeavor so that there would be no misunderstanding of their philosophy. It was probably with that in mind that the pioneers dropped the name "Jew," calling themselves "Hebrews" instead. They used this more modern term in their campaigns in the 1930s and in the early 1940s, calling for a "Hebrew" rather than a "Jewish" state. The current term, "Jewish state," originally coined as a nonreligious concept, was revived in the 1940s, again with no intended religious connotation.

A typical group of Zionist *halutzim* (pioneers), deliberately irreligious, and militantly atheistic, marched in defiance of Jewish dietary laws in the early 1920s to "the Wailing Wall on the Day of Atonement munching ham sandwiches."[8] Melford Spiro, in his scholarly study of a group of Eastern European Zionists who formed a kibbutz in Palestine (Israel), described their Zionism not as "an expression of Judaism," but rather as "an escape from it,"[9] for the members of this group proved more responsive to a European national nonreligious ideal and showed no pride in their religious or cultural traditions.

Most of the Zionists have seen themselves in nonreligious terms. Their ideology, patterned after nineteenth-century European nationalism, was intended to replace traditional religious beliefs. As in other nationalistic movements, especially pan-Germanism and pan-Slavism (both of which had great influence on the Zionists and the idea of pan-Jewish nationhood), religious symbols and forms that had been stripped of moral content were made to serve the nationalist cause.

Jacob Klatzkin (1882-1948), a Zionist Russian thinker, drew a distinction between the Jewish religion and what he termed "the spirit of our ethic," suggesting that the former divorced from the latter could help "crystallize" the national ethos. Religion interested him neither in its spiritual nor in its "abstract" ethical aspects, as he put it. Rather, what he valued most in his faith were the rich forms of Judaism that imply "national apartness," and which therefore can "fashion and protect a national life."[10] Guided by this Zionist viewpoint, many Israeli Zionists view with alarm any decline of the Jewish religion in the diaspora because of its cohesive ethnic value. However, in Israel, so they claim, "a person may discard his religion since it is merely an external form of nationality."[11]

Such an amoral outlook, replacing deep religious commitment while making full use of it, has always proved to be a more or less sure way for recruiting the masses. This was particularly so in the case of Zionism, in view of the fact that a large sector of the Eastern European Jewish communities was deeply religious (even in a mystical sense). The fusion of the nationalist outlook with religious fervor was achieved by turning authentic religious doctrine into a national myth.

The perceptive Lubbavitcher Rebbe, Rabbi Schneersohn, was fully aware of that process. Writing at the beginning of this century, he indicated that the Zionists viewed the Torah and the commandments merely as a convenient means "to strengthen collective feeling."[12] Max Nordau, as described by his biographer Meir Ben-Horin, was enough of a realist "to give proper weight to both the rational and the irrational elements in human civilization." This shrewd realism alerted Nordau, the nonbeliever, to the fact that religion could serve the nationalist drive if it were turned into "a source of potential reconstructive energy."[13]

The transference of religious themes, terms, and concepts from the religious onto the political plane is hardly noticeable in the modern world. Total secularization of perception has absorbed the religious dimension of man's experience, reducing it to the level of the natural and material. A quasi-religious secular terminology is accepted by many Jews and gentiles alike, owing to the modern trend of using religious terms to describe historical and human phenomena. Terms such as "prophetic vision," "messianism," and the "millennium"—all denoting strictly religious concepts—are commonly used to describe ideas and attitudes that are substantially political. Zionism benefits greatly from this tendency to confuse the religious with the quasi-religious terms.

Eliezer Ben Yehuda (1858-1923), the founder of the modern renaissance of the Hebrew language, had the sense to distinguish between the religious meaning of the term "redemption" and its more mundane designation. He emphasized that "redemption" for him was the restoration of the Jewish nation to the land of its fathers, and the restoration of the Hebrew language as a national tongue. He perceived this in a "clear and literal" sense. Any talk about a spiritual people or a religious community was, for him, merely a "veiled and over-subtle substitute"[14] for the real national, nonreligious sense, which the Zionists had evolved.

Intolerance of subtlety and complexity, so evident in Ben Yehuda's writings and similar works, can be traced back to the scientism of many Zionist thinkers who were contemptuous of religious modes of perception and impatient with truly religious ideas based on a nonmaterialistic point of reference. Many of the Zionist theorists and founding fathers either came from nonreligious backgrounds or held unfavorable views of Judaism and the Jews, and often of all religions for that matter. Given this outlook and state of mind, Zionists experienced genuine difficulty in trying to understand the full significance of some Jewish religious concepts, grappling in vain with some of the central tenets of Judaism. However, they were familiar with the folklore of the Eastern European Jewish ghetto and they considered Jewish religious practices and beliefs as part of this folklore. It is only in this limited "ethnic" sense that Zionism can claim to be "Jewish." The ethnicity, needless to say, is not in the least universal, for it is largely of Eastern European origin.

There are, however, some "religious" Zionists who believe that there is not only compatibility but also a necessary relationship between the political ideology and the faith. However, if a movement or a state is to be identified as Jewish or Christian, it must be judged by Jewish or Christian criteria. In order to assess the Jewishness of Religious Zionism, we should follow the same procedure. The initial Zionist theoretical formulation, it should be remembered, was avowedly nonreligious. It was evolved and implemented by atheists; only later was it sanctioned by religious apologists. Rabbi Isaac Kook (1865-1935), a Russian cabalist mystic and first Ashkenazi chief rabbi in Palestine, was one of the first religious apologists who asserted that the Zionist settlers, even though heretical and irreligious, were implementing the dictates of Judaism by physically settling in Palestine. He gave his unqualified support for Zionist settlement and issued several *responsa*, written replies to questions about Jewish law, in order to bestow religious legitimacy upon the Zionist project, probably in the vain hope of eventually converting the future Zionist state into a full-fledged theocracy.

It is true that a quasi-religious orthodoxy is quite influential in the Zionist state, especially in matters pertaining to the laws governing personal affairs, such as marriage, divorce, and death, but not those governing national or foreign policies. It is, however, an orthodoxy devoid of any universal moral content, and it never betrays any signs of religious transcendence. A clear manifestation of this "orthodoxy" is the system of "files and informers" set up to ascertain the "Jewishness" of an individual or his lack of it, in order to determine his eligibility for marriage. This process has produced a unique "blacklist of unmarriageable Israelis."[15] The concern here is more with racial purity and religious segregation than with moral and religious values.

But this religious orthodoxy also dabbles in politics—foreign and domestic—as is evident in the case of the Gush Emunim, the small annexationist group whose emotionalism does not demonstrate any piety or charity. It is difficult for a detached observer to recognize anything Jewish, in a religious sense, in the activities of this group. It is even more difficult to detect anything ennobling in the words of Rabbi Moshe Ben-Zion Uspizai of Ramat-Gan. His Religious Zionist interpretation of the Talmud has led him to call for the destruction of the Palestinians and the colonization of all the biblical Land of Israel.[16] Many would agree that it is almost impossible to detect anything "religious" or "Jewish" in the words of Rabbi Abraham Avidan (Zamel), Chaplain of the Israeli Central Command, when he counseled mistrust of the Arabs because, as he claimed, "we should not, according to religious law, trust a gentile." When he told the Israeli soldiers that "they are allowed—and they are obliged, according to the law—to kill . . . good civilians, or rather civilians who appear to be good," and when he quoted the saying, " 'The best of the gentiles you should kill,' "[17] we know he was not speaking in the name of any religious or ethical code, but was merely repeating words out of context in order to rationalize acts of brutality.

It is quite evident that the ideology and practice of this Religious Zionism is nationalistic, in the narrowest sense, and that its literalist interpretations and exegeses are as incompatible with Judaism as those of the nonreligious Zionists. Mahatma Gandhi, India's great philosopher and leader, arrived at the same conclusion in 1938. Commenting on Zionist settlement in Palestine and the violence that accompanied it, he declared that "a religious act cannot be performed with the aid of the bayonet or the bomb."[18]

Moshe Menuhin, in his *Jewish Critics of Zionism*,[19] pointed out that the Jewish prophets always warned against the rabid nationalists who try

to build "up Zion with blood and Jerusalem with iniquity." Therefore, it
comes as no surprise to learn that the Neturei Karta (guardians of the city),
the Jewish orthodox sect, characterizes the Zionist rabbis as "the clericals
of the false Israel," who "teach a false doctrine." According to them, true
Israel is based on a commitment to God and Torah,[20] going beyond the
established order (or disorder) of nature and history. This Religious Zionism, therefore, is better understood if we view it not as a serious religious
commitment or as a willingness to shoulder the moral burdens attendant
on religious belief, but rather as a nationalism defended with religious zeal.
It is largely a variety of political Zionism assuming a religious form.

If one were to take the literalist and nationalist interpretations of the
Torah and the Talmud as the "right" ones, and assume that a reading of
these religious texts demonstrates, for instance, that the Jews of Russia,
Rumania, Berlin, and Brooklyn have the right to emigrate and settle in
Palestine, then one would argue (as does Dr. Mohamed Mehdi, Secretary
General of the American-Arab Relations Committee) that this aspect of
the Jewish faith (which the Jewish religionists themselves deny) "should
be condemned."[21]   One can also add that if Christianity encourages the
occupation of the Holy Land, as it did in the Middle Ages, or if the call is
sounded for the "return" of Arab "exiles" to Andalusia (as southern Spain
was called during Arab rule), then those aspects of Christianity and Islam
should be viewed as equally aggressive.   But, in fact, these literalist interpretations used to justify military aggression and territorial expansion
have very little to do with authentic religious doctrine.

A PHYSICAL AND SPIRITUAL ZION

One can detect the falseness of Religious Zionist apologetics by com-
paring them with genuine religious doctrine. The cardinal trait of religious
conviction, in contrast with other human ideologies or creeds, is the concept of transcendence, based not on emotional experience but rather on a
firm belief in something beyond nature and matter. Love of Zion is an
excellent example of a Jewish religious concept suffused with this sense of
transcendence; it sets the land of Palestine, or *Eretz Yisrael,* apart from the
rest of the world as a holy land, God's own. Consequently, the concrete
history of the peoples actually living there is rightly and legitimately overlooked. Zion is thus an ideal, and the believer is urged to develop a pious
attachment to it. Such belief imbues him with the spiritual strength, particularly in this age of increasing materialism and positivism, to transcend
his surroundings and to establish a link with the ideal. Dwelling in the
land was indeed considered a *mitzva,* a good deed in the religious sense.
Throughout history many religious Jews have gone to dwell in the Holy

Land. Viewed in this light, love of Zion is not radically different from the attachment that the followers of many religions have for their respective "holy places"—their "Zions," so to speak.

Many religious Jewish thinkers believe that to dwell in Zion (the Land and/or the City) is a religious duty; yet, to them, their understanding of this concept of their faith is in direct contradiction with the political Zionist interpretation of it. Nathan Birnbaum (1864-1937), the Austro-Hungarian Jewish writer, wrote that for religious Jews *Eretz Yisrael* is not a new country, but an entity they have never ceased to love, to yearn for, and to remember. The religious, with their keen desire to fulfill the *mitzva,* wanted to dwell in Palestine "for the sanctification of the land."[22] These sentiments, as expressed by Birnbaum, are unmistakably and deeply religious. Followers of any religion who are able to transcend some of the limits of their own dogma can comprehend Birnbaum's feelings and relate them to their own. Birnbaum, however, contrasts the dwelling "for the santification of the land" to the dwelling, or rather settlement, that results in "its desecration."[23] The first takes place within a commitment to religious values and beliefs, the second is nationalistic and political, and therefore has a completely different content and goal.

It is of some interest to note that Gandhi, expressing his opposition to Zionism, used words remarkably similar to Birnbaum's: "The Palestine of the Biblical conception is not a geographical tract. It is in [the Jews'] hearts."[24] The same distinction was made recently by Nancy Fuchs-Kreimer, a rabbinical student and member of the Board of Directors of Breira, who faults an American Zionist on his use of "the word 'Israel' in two different ways"—to refer "to the dream of Zion restored—a Zion which would represent all the highest values of the Jews," and to identify "the nation-state Israel, population: 3 million; Prime Minister: Yitzhak Rabin."[25]

Such a subtle distinction between the physical reality and the religious concept is not in keeping with the tenets of political Zionism and the Zionist outlook. Nordau, for instance, was somewhat bewildered when he discovered that the rabbis were opposed to the Zionist call for a "physical" return to Zion. "After all," he protested, "it should be their principal function to keep alive the love of the Jews for their people and for *Eretz Yisrael.*"[26] The Zionist fundamentalist could not comprehend the fact that the rabbis were indeed urging the Jews to love Zion in the full religious sense, for when they thought of *Eretz Yisrael,* the pious had enough clarity of vision to see it as a religious concept rather than a geographical reality.

The absence of genuine religious "love of Zion" on the part of the Zionists was noted in 1903 by Rabbi Schneersohn .[27] Even Nordau himself, when not posturing as a nationalist mystic, was forthright enough to recognize his convictions for what they were. For instance, addressing the

Fourth Zionist Congress (1900), he declared that in developing their ideology, the Zionists were not motivated by any "mystical yearning for Zion." "Of that," he assured everybody, "most of us are free."[28]

To Herzl, similarly, the vision that the Promised Land offered was not one of salvation and redemption, but of opportunities for settlement and investment. That is why he believed that "the location" was to be determined in a positivist way as a "purely scientific" issue. "We must have regard," he wrote, "for geological, climatic, in short, natural factors of all kinds with full circumspection and with consideration of the latest research."[29] The whole question of the territory of the Zionist state was deliberately left open, for Herzl was neither against Palestine nor for Argentina. He wrote in his *Diaries* that his interest was focused on a territory that had "a varied climate for the Jews who are used to colder or to warmer regions." Other economic considerations were equally important. Anticipating a bright future in world trade for his proposed state, he wrote that "we have to be located on the sea, and for our large-scale mechanized agriculture we must have wide areas at our disposal." As a nonreligious Jew, his approach to his own proposal was correctly materialistic, for he advised the Zionists to turn to "the scientists . . . to provide us with information."[30]

Leo Pinsker (1821–1891), a Russian Zionist thinker whose writings predate Herzl's, was not overly concerned with the actual location of the territory selected for Jewish settlement. He believed it could take place in any of "the two hemispheres. . . . This piece of land might form a small territory in North America, or a sovereign pashalik in Asiatic Turkey."[31] Pinsker even suggested that the Jews must not attach themselves to Palestine and should "not dream of restoring ancient Judea." The goal, as he defined it, "must not be the 'Holy Land,' but a land of our own."[32] Like Herzl, Pinsker had harbored diverse pragmatic notions. The land finally chosen had to be "productive and well-located." Its area was to be such as "to allow the settlement of several millions." The selection, Pinsker insisted, should not be based on "offhand decisions"; a "commission of experts" was to weigh and evaluate the options.[33]

Even when Palestine was considered as an alternative, Herzl was at great pains to emphasize the nonreligious nature of the choice. He told Pope Pius X, on January 26, 1904, that the Zionists were "not asking for Jerusalem" or such holy places; it was "only the secular land" which interested him.[34] He was even more emphatic when he assured Cardinal Merry del Val that he was not looking for *Eretz Yisrael,* but that he was "asking only for the profane earth."[35]

The East Africa (Uganda) project of which Herzl and Nordau approved and which the Sixth Zionist Congress (1903) did *not* reject, is a good case in point. The Congress voted, 295 to 17, to appoint a committee of inquiry "to investigate possibilities of Jewish settlement there." When some of the delegates withdrew in protest, another vote was taken which still yielded a majority in favor of the proposal.[36] The delegates representing the Zionist settlers in Palestine (Ben Yehuda among them) were among the supporters of the Uganda scheme. In the Seventh Zionist Congress (1905), the Uganda scheme was rejected by the delegates "after the commission of inquiry sent by the Sixth Congress to examine the proposed territory presented a negative report in their findings." The settlement plan was also opposed both by British settlers in East Africa and assimilated Jews in Britain.[37]

The whole nonreligious trend represented by these early Zionist leaders could be termed "Zionism without Zion"—"Zion" being a place clearly interchangeable with any other. As a matter of fact, the interchangeability of the territory of the Zionist state is the main premise of the Territorialist Zionism of Israel Zangwill (1864-1926), the British Zionist novelist.

Notwithstanding these historical facts, religious symbols and imagery were often prudently adopted in the drive to recruit religious Jews and to endow a political ideology with sanctity. Among the more revealing alternatives considered as possible for Jewish settlement was Iraq. One of the proponents of this settlement scheme believed that in calling upon the Jews to settle in Iraq, the Zionist movement could "make use of the mystic elements"[38] associated with the Jewish experience in that ancient land. Probably that factor, together with equally cynical ones, such as support for an "English policy in the Orient,"[39] led the Zionists to opt for Palestine, also known in Zionist literature as Zion and later as Israel. In favor of Palestine, as Herzl indicated, was "the mighty legend—the very name."[40] It would be, the playwright said, "a marvelously effective rallying cry."[41]

The confusion between Zion of the heart and Palestine has created problems of a tragic nature for the Palestinians. Paradoxically, the Zionists themselves have had to deal with some unpleasant problems. For instance, if Palestine is Zion, then some of the biblical injunctions concerning the soil of the Holy Land should be applied to it. One such injunction enjoins the Jews to let the land lie "fallow on the seventh year." Interpreted literally, this would, of course, spell economic disaster. However, a "dispensation on technical grounds,"[42] issued by Rabbi Kook, provides that *Eretz Yisrael* be *sold* every six years to a gentile at a nominal price.[43] Thus, Zionist settlers can continue to work the land, which has ostensibly fallen once more into gentile hands, without any pangs of conscience. Once the seventh year is over, the land is duly bought back. This ceremony still takes place in Israel, without much publicity.

THE MESSIAH WITH A FLAG

Love of Zion is linked to a concept probably unique to Judaism, though not without analogues in some Christian (Protestant) and Islamic (Shiite) eschatological doctrines; that is, the concept of the messianic restoration of Zion and the messianic return. This concept clearly implies a form of "religious Zionism," which, according to Rabbi Elmer Berger, a leading American anti-Zionist scholar, "many Jews do profess, as do many Christians." Rabbi Berger, who does not himself share this belief, states that "this Zionism holds that, in *God's own time* and in *His own way,* when man is ready for the millenium, Jews will be returned to Palestine and Zion shall shine forth again as the place from where all mankind shall hear the word of the Lord."[44]

The messianic message in Judaism generates a creative tension in the life of the believer, for he can live in this world without being entirely absorbed in it. He is constantly expecting the arrival of the Messiah, who will dispense absolute justice and spread harmony among all the peoples. At the moment of discord, there is always the hope of harmony; in the midst of chaos, there is the expectation of order. In the here-and-now is implied another time and another place.

Although such a belief includes a definite concept of the "ingathering of the exiles," the emphasis is undoubtedly on the divine agency of the return. The restoration of Zion is not to be achieved through the medium of individuals or groups who would preempt the divine will, and would themselves decide that history ends here and now and that the present moment is the long awaited messianic epoch. The Talmud, in some passages, even considers anyone "returning" to Palestine as positively breaking a biblical commandment.[45] That much was expressed in a letter sent to Herzl by a Jewish editor, whose purpose was to remind Herzl that Talmudic teachings "forbade the Jews from taking Palestine by force or establishing a state there."[46] Discussing "Jewish nationalism" in an American publication, Rabbi Philip Sigal touched on the question of the "ingathering of the exiles," declaring that "there is no article of faith among all medieval attempts to formulate a Jewish creed which includes as one dogma or principle, immigration to Israel."[47]

Theodor Herzl clearly disavowed any link or sympathy with the messianic concept. When asked by King Victor Emmanuel III of Italy whether he expected the coming of the Messiah, the Zionist leader, with obvious embarrassment, assured the king that in religious circles they still did, but "in our own, the academically trained, and enlightened circles, no such thought exists, of course."[48]

But, since the messianic idea is central to Judaism, the Zionists, like the false messiahs, tried to exploit it for their own ends. One cardinal trait of the fraudulent messianic movements in Judaism, as Rabbi Jacob Bernard Agus indicated in *The Meaning of Jewish History,* is impatience with the divine will and emphasis on man's initiative.[49] Zionism, with its emphasis on autoemancipations, proved to be no exception to the pattern. Ambassador Chaim Herzog, Israel's representative to the United Nations, declared, in describing the rise of Zionism, that "the Jewish people organized the Zionist movement in order to transform a dream into reality."[50] This pseudo-messianic impatience is manifest in the thoughts and writings of Ben Gurion, who characterized the concept of the coming of the Messiah as too "passive" from his Zionist standpoint.[51]

Another trait of false messianism is its absolute certainty concerning "the identity of the Redeemer," for it conceives this divine personality as a "concrete person, a specific plan or organization. It is here and now, certain and irresistible."[52] In Zionist literature, the traditional Messiah of Jewish religious lore practically disappears, to be replaced by a series of literal surrogates. At times, he becomes an impulse that expresses itself through the Jewish people; at others, he becomes "a messianic epoch," which starts on May 1948, or the First Zionist Congress, or at this or that point *in* time. Ben Gurion identified Jewish messianism with "the messianic longings of the Jewish people for national redemption in the land of their fathers."[53] Herzl even flirted with the idea that the Messiah could be the "electric current."[54] An Israeli secularist has shrewdly observed that "the Messiah, who is supposed to appear and redeem his people at the Millennium, when the dead will rise from the grave and the Almighty will sit in judgment on the world, has been identified by some with the personalities of leaders of the State."[55]

Reminiscing at a banquet in 1927, Weizmann said that when he held the Balfour Declaration in his hands, he thought for a fleeting second that he had heard the steps of the Messiah. But knowing better, he checked himself and recalled the quietism of the religious tradition: "The true Redeemer is said to come silently like a thief in the night."[56] Having realized that the Balfour Declaration was not exactly a form of divine mediation, Weizmann stated on another occasion that the twentieth-century return to Zion "would not take place without the assistance of a Great Power."[57]

Herzl, despite his protestations to the Italian king, experienced some messianic illusions about himself and his role. But he had the good sense not to pose as the true Redeemer, identifying himself instead with the fraudulent messiah Shabbetai Tzvi, drawing comparisons between himself and his seventeenth-century predecessor. He even contemplated composing an opera about him, to be performed in the Zionist state.[58]

Herzl's messiah would return not to Zion but to any territory. He would not take with him the Jewish people as a religious community but only "those Jews who are unable to assimilate."[59] Nor would he take the rich West side Jews of Berlin, but the Jews of North or East Berlin, the poor ones.[60] In other words, those "returning" would do so for various true or imaginary socioeconomic reasons, which had little to do with Judaism. The Zionist "messiah" was so aware of the power of political motivation that he believed that "with a flag one can lead men wherever one wishes, even into the Promised Land."[61]

The "messiah with a flag" was deeply influenced by the pan-Germanic nationalist thought of his time and its pervasive pantheism. Perhaps it is the Germanic origins of Zionist thinking which account for the centrality of the idea of the state in the Zionist scheme and for the Zionist postulation of the state as a categorical imperative for the fulfillment of Judaism and Jewishness. This idea is, of course, quite distinct from the millennial rule of the Messiah. Any reader of Herzl's diaries will perceive how Germanic adulation of the state, as an abstraction, has been made to replace Jewish commitment to moral values. "The foundation of a State lies in the will of the people for a state, yes, even in the will of one sufficiently powerful individual. . . . Territory is only the material basis; the State itself, when it possesses a territory, is always something abstract."[62]

Herzl was a devoted admirer of this Germanic abstraction. "Look at the plan called 'The Unification of Germany,' " he wrote in his diary on August 22, 1895. It was created "out of ribbons, flags, songs, speeches, and finally, singular struggles." Pursuing this theme, the father of Zionism admonished his readers not to "underestimate Bismarck! . . . he forced [the Germans] to wage wars"—one war after another. Writing admiringly of the beneficial effects of these wars on Germany, he declared: "A nation drowsy in peacetime jubilantly hailed unification in wartime."[63]

Waiting one day for one of his many colonial sponsors, Herzl saw from his window several groups of German officers marching in the Flag Festival. "And up the street came cadets," he wrote in his diary, "littler and littler ones, the future officers of this inexhaustible Germany, which wants to take us under its protection."[64] He had been entertaining the thought that the return could be effected, not through divine mediation, but "under the protection of this strong, great, moral, splendidly governed, tightly organized Germany," which is certain to "have the most salutary effect on the Jewish national character."[65] This surely has very little to do with Judaism or any religion.

In more recent times, General Ariel Sharon asserted in *Marriv* of January 25, 1974, that "the first and the most supreme value is the good of the State. The State is the supreme value."[66] We are once more reminded, not of Jewish religious traditions, but rather of the great tragedy that this kind of state adulation brought upon humanity not long ago in Europe.

A METAPHYSIC OF PEOPLEHOOD

What has been said of the misuse of the terms "love of Zion," "the return" or "the Messiah" applies equally to the concept of "Jewish peoplehood." Jewish religious tradition has a rich vocabulary referring to the Jewish people variously as the Chosen People, the Holy People, the Spiritual People, Israel (he who strives with the Lord) and God's treasure. Like Israel (the land), Israel (the people) is set apart from the rest of mankind as a community having a special relationship with a transcendent God, a claim made by all the devout in almost all religions.

But this sense of chosen-ness is defined and limited by other concepts and images in Judaism. The majestic story of the creation of Adam and Eve implies a common origin for all people and therefore a basic equality between them. God in Judaism is universal, the God of all who blesses all nations and who considers the Jews "as the Children of Ethiopians unto me."[67] Therefore, the vision of salvation includes all nations. When Isaiah prophesies about peace, he conjures up an image of universal peace for *all* nations:

> Nation shall not lift up sword against nation,
> Neither shall they learn war any more. (Isaiah 2:4)

Peace will envelop all, for all peoples are His children. "Blessed be Egypt my people, and Assyria the work of my hands, and Israel mine heritage" (Isaiah 19:25).

Regardless of one's interpretation of the idea of chosen-ness, one thing should be remembered—the term "Jewish people" in Judaism is a religious one, signifying a community of true believers who put their faith in One True God, and whose membership in that community, as British historian Arnold Toynbee wrote, is conditional on their obeying God's commands.[68] The traditional peoplehood is a community of believers, whose faith is based on a religious covenant between God and His people. This peoplehood is still being so defined. Emile L. Fackenheim, a contemporary Jewish theologian, believes that if the Jew wants to survive as a Jew, he must accept "as authentic the ancient encounter of his people with the living God." This people is "constituted by an encounter with the Nameless and [is] still extant as a people only because it continues to be committed to that encounter."[69]

Given the fact that the Jews are the people of the Torah and not the people of a certain land or soil, political or national allegiance is of little importance. The Jew is counseled by his sages and prophets to make his peace with the earthly city like any other citizen. Over 2,500 years ago the prophet Jeremiah said, "Seek ye the welfare of the city . . . and pray in its

behalf unto the Lord; for in its welfare shall ye fare well."[70] This same
theme is detected in the words of Robert Loeb in the "Breira Report," in
which he discusses unity among the Jewish communities "through spiritual,
moral, cultural, historical and 'peoplehood' ties *outside the political framework.*"[71]

But such a spiritual outlook was not popular with Zionist leaders and
thinkers who took a different view of the matter. For instance, Micah
Berdichevsky (1865–1922), the Russian Zionist writer, declared emphatically that the Jews should "cease to be Jews by virtue of an abstract Judaism and become Jews in their own right, as a living and developing nationality."[72] Arthur Hertzberg, in his anthology *The Zionist Idea,* refers to
Eliezer Ben Yehuda as reiterating the Zionist "messianic theme" that the
"Jews must end their peculiar history [as a religious community] by becoming a modern secular nation."[73]

Repeating the same Zionist theme, Max Nordau declared that "we do
not want to be a mere religious community; we want to be a nation like all
other nations."[74] Having been told that "the Jews are different from the
other inhabitants of their native lands only by virtue of their religion and
definitely not by virtue of their nationality," Nordau replied that it would
be the business of Zionism to "turn the Jews into a distinct people in the
national sense of the term."[75] Jacob Klatzkin believed in a nationhood
based on land and language, and therefore any talk of "spiritual uniqueness" was for him "a mark of the diseased abnormality of an un-nation."[76]
In keeping with the nationalist definition, a Zionist periodical once claimed
"that even one who transgressed all the commandments of the Torah, even
one who denied the existence of God, was a Jew provided that he was a
nationalist."[77]

The pattern of appropriating a religious idiom to describe a secular
phenomenon is again very much in evidence here. The sanctity attached to
the Jewish people in the religious sense is transferred to the Jewish people
in the ethnic sense and, accordingly, to the people's history, to their land,
and finally, to their state. This is achieved through a relative de-emphasis
of the transcendence of the God of Israel and through a concurrent emphasis on the sanctity of Israel, the nation, until God and the people become
more or less identical.

In Zionist literature, the pantheistic interchangeability between the
sacred and timeless, on the one hand, and the profane and temporal on the
other is such that the effort to define the boundaries between these two
distinct categories is almost futile. In seeking the source or the basis of
sacredness in Zionist writings, one finds it virtually impossible to determine
whether it is the Lord or the *Volk,* for the dialogue between the two is so
intimate and casual that it turns out, under close scrutiny, to be a mono-
logue. A French anti-Zionist aptly described the Zionists as *"adorateurs de*

leur sang"[78] (worshipers of their own blood), something coiled around itself in rapt self-satisfaction.

The theology of Martin Buber (1878-1965), the mystic Zionist thinker, manifests a similar transference of sacredness, which inevitably leads to confusion. Buber used the term "Israel" in both a national and a religious sense, Israel being a "people like no other . . . both a nation and a religious community." This unique religio-national people experiences "history and revelation as one phenomenon, history as revelation and revelation as history . . . here humanity is touched by the divine."[79]

While Rabbi Kook's writings are not as subtle or complex as Buber's, he and other religious Zionists dwell in their own fashion on this theme. Rabbi Kook asserted that the Jewish people are "different from all nations, set apart by a historical experience that is unique and unparalleled,"[80] the reason being, according to him, that "the spirit of Israel is so closely linked to the spirit of God." But the especially "close link" is transmuted a few lines later by a radical form of pantheism, for all national possessions of the Jewish people—land, language, history, and even customs—are said to be "vessels of the spirit of the Lord."[81] In such a context, Rabbi Kook described nationalism or religion "as merely elements of the spirit of Israel," an implied identity between the nationalist ideology of the people and divine dictates. Such an interpretation led him to adopt the deterministic position that "a Jewish nationalist, no matter how secularist his intention may be, must, despite himself, affirm the divine."[82]

Even a supposedly level-headed pragmatist such as Horace Mayer Kallen, the American Zionist educational thinker, accepts this mystical view of Israel. He believes that the memories, hopes, and fears, the creeds and codes, and the works and ways of the Israelis invest their national struggles with sacredness. The mysticism transvalues "the brute stuffs" of their daily lives, "even as the Christian doctrine of the Real Presence transforms the vapid stale wafer of his Holy Communion for the true believer."[83]

The sanctity or divinity of the Jewish people, or its "naturalistic supernaturalism," if we may borrow one of Kallen's terms,[84] is the common ground on which nonreligious and Religious Zionists meet. It forms the basis for a facile adoption of a religious language that both can use. Both groups can think in terms of a holy people (and a holy land), but whereas the religious see the source of this holiness as divine, for the nonreligious it is self-begotten. This religio-national pantheism made it possible for Vladimir Jabotinsky (1880-1940), the Russian Zionist leader, to speak of himself as "one of the masons building a new temple for my God—whose name is Jewish people."[85] It is also equally legitimate for Reform Rabbi Eugene B. Borowitz to claim that what was on trial in the Arab-Israeli war on June 5, 1967, was "in very earnest God Himself," and

therefore any question concerning the outcome of the war "was not military . . . it was theological."[86] Given this transvalued divinity and sanctity,
it became perfectly natural for General Moshe Dayan to refer to the *eretz*
as his only God. He could also ask for the military occupation of the Land
of the Torah, and then receive a cable from Rabbi Isaac Nissim, Israel's
Sephardic chief rabbi, congratulating him on his correct interpretation of
the Torah.

Possibly such thinking lies behind the decision to replace the traditional phrase "God of Israel" by the vague term "tsur Israel" (the rock of
Israel) in the Israeli Declaration of Independence. It is a vague term,
traditional enough to satisfy the orthodox and godless enough to satisfy the
atheist.

If history is revelation and revelation is history, as Buber claimed, then
it is possible to agree with Yigal Yadin, Israel's scholarly retired general
and active politician, that for young Israelis a "belief in history" has come
to be a substitute for religious faith. Thus, the young consider their religious values not through a creative rediscovery of their Holy Book or
religious tradition and values, but through the science of archaeology.
Through this science and in a respectable positivistic way, they "learn that
their forefathers were in this country 3,000 years ago. This is a value."[87]
But they will undoubtedly learn these national values as if they were religious absolutes, for these Israeli youngsters learn their history from their
Holy Book. The Torah for them, as it was for the early Zionists, is "a
historical record testifying to [the Jews'] ancient nationhood."[88] An
Israeli writer, Boaz Evron, commenting on this situation said, "If you
substitute nationalism for religion, *raison d'état* becomes the sole absolute
value."[89]

Buttressed by their belief that their earthly nationhood stems from
"divine" origins or that it has certain innate holiness, the Zionist Israelis
see their acts not only as legitimate but also as invested with sanctity.
Israel can thus be described as a godless theocracy. It is godless insofar as
it is based on a metaphysic of the national self and on rights that may not
be questioned; godless insofar as the collective conscience of its leadership
is undisturbed by any of the traditional ethical values that ordinarily follow
from a belief in the Almighty.

The Zionist attempt at replacing Judaism or recasting it in national
ethnic terms did not go unchallenged by religious or humanist Jewish
thinkers. In an astute characterization of the new national religion, Rabbi
Judah Magnes (1877-1948), a Religious Zionist who turned into a critic of
the movement and who opposed the creation of the Zionist state, wrote of
the "new Jewish voice" that "speaks from the mouth of guns." That is the
"new Torah," he lamented, coming from the land of Israel. But it is not
the true Torah of Judaism, he argued, for it tries to shackle Judaism and

the people of Israel to "the madness of physical force." He even described this new religion as "pagan Judaism."[90]

Israel Shahak, an Israeli dissenter who is a professor at the Hebrew University in Jerusalem, argued that Jewish idealization of the state of Israel is "both immoral and against the mainstream of Jewish tradition and must bring disaster to Israel." In words that almost echo those of Magnes, he declared that "it seems to me that the majority of my people has left God, and has substituted an idol in His place," exactly as when "they were so devoted to the Golden Calf in the desert. . . . The name of this modern idol is the State of Israel."[91]

Zionism was regarded by many Eastern European religious Jews as the latest and least reputable "catastrophic pseudo-messianic" heresy, for it confuses superficially similar elements: one from the physical world (the natural cult of people, language, and soil), and the other from the world of religious transcendence (the Holy Land and the fulfillment of the divine precepts connected with the soil).[92] To these religious Jews, the false parallelism between the indigenous traditional Jewish precepts and the imported nonreligious concepts made Zionism "the most confusing and therefore the most dangerous of all the Satanic ordeals that the Community had ever to face."[93] Even though superficially similar to Judaism, according to some Jewish critics of the movement, Zionism represents "*the direct opposite* of all that constitutes"[94] authentic religious belief.

The debate between Zionist, non-Zionist, and anti-Zionist Jews concerning the religious legitimacy of Zionism is still raging, assuming at times violent forms, as in the case of Rabbi Jacob De Haan, who is believed to have been felled by Zionist bullets on June 30, 1924.[95] The Arabs, regardless of whether they are Muslims or Christians, find themselves involved in this controversy. The transposition of religious concepts from the religious plane to the political plane has led to two demographic changes, as historical events clearly demonstrated: transferring Jews from the diaspora to Israel; and expelling the Palestinians from Palestine to their own present diaspora. Consequently, what might appear as a strictly theological discussion has a direct bearing on the destiny of the Arabs. They understandably lend their support to those who are interested in keeping spiritual precepts and political concepts apart and distinct.

2

THE QUINTESSENTIAL JEW

THE "DANGER" OF ASSIMILATION

Even though the Zionists do not accept a religious definition of the Jew, it should be pointed out that their position on this issue is not a rigid one. As already noted, they do not hesitate to make full use of the "mystic elements" in Judaism. Even Herzl, who was neither a believing nor a practicing Jew, gave his blessing to the creation of a religious Zionist party.[1] "Religious" parties in Israel have joined government coalitions, and the state has granted countless concessions to some of the formalities of orthodoxy. The main Zionist goal was, and still is, to gain the allegiance of *all* Jews to the national ideal. To the Zionists, a religious definition of the Jew, provided it is placed within a "nationalist" context, is perfectly acceptable.

Given this possible accommodation, the espousal of a nationalist view of the Jew, therefore, does not necessarily pit the Zionists against the religious Jews. It is the assimilationists, whether religious or nonreligious, who represent the most serious and fundamental challenge. The assimilationist outlook views the Jew as a complex personality, belonging to whatever country he may be living in, contributing to whatever cultural tradition he may have evolved from, without necessarily overlooking his specific religious and/or cultural heritage. Zionist theoreticians, on the other hand, denounce assimilation, characterizing it as a form of alienation from what they conceive to be a true and pure national Jewish identity.

The writings of Joseph H. Brenner (1881–1921) and Berl Katzenelson (1887–1944), the Russian Zionist writers, are replete with references to assimilation as a poisonous and destructive force. In their eyes, the assimilated Jew was an unnatural and negative being. Arthur Ruppin (1876–

1943), a Zionist theoretician and one of the early planners and promoters of Zionist settlement in Palestine, described absorption as an "imminent danger,"[2] threatening Jewish life. Klatzkin characterized assimilation as a disease, "infecting" the Jewish communities and "disfiguring" and "impoverishing" them.[3] Chaim Weizmann had nothing but unqualified contempt for assimilation,[4] even making reference in his writings to the "assimilationist taint."[5]

In keeping with this anti-assimilationist outlook, a 1964 joint meeting of the Israeli cabinet and the executive committee of the World Zionist Organization issued an official communique that described "the danger of assimilation" as a major problem facing the Jewish people in the diaspora. The fear of assimilation as a "threat" to Jewish survival, even more detrimental to the Jews than "persecution, inquisition, pogroms and mass murder," was the theme of the Twenty-Sixth Zionist Congress (1964–1965).[6] In 1958, Dr. Nahum Goldmann, president of the World Jewish Congress and former president of the World Zionist Organization, went so far as to claim that the emancipation of the Jews might become identical with their disappearance.[7]

Among those who spoke out against the Zionist stance was Rabbi Moritz Gudemann, the chief rabbi of Vienna, Herzl's birthplace, who asked in a pamphlet on "Jewish nationalism": "Who is indeed more 'assimilated,' the nationalist Jew who ignores the Sabbath and dietary laws, or the believing and practicing Jew who is a loyal and full citizen of his country?"[8]

As was to be expected, the attack on assimilation in the name of a higher, autonomous Jewish nationalism did not always meet with universal jubilation among the majority of the Jewish people in the diaspora. In the hope of pacifying those who felt they were being placed in untenable positions in the lands of their birth, reassuring noises are sometimes made by Israeli spokesmen. To cite an example, on August 23, 1950, Ben Gurion declared that the state of Israel "represents and speaks only on behalf of its own citizens." He then drew a sharp distinction between the "people of [the state of] Israel" and the Jewish communities abroad. In no way, said Ben Gurion, did the Zionist state presume "to represent or speak in the name of the Jews who are citizens of any other country."[9] In its lead editorial of May 10, 1964, the *Jerusalem Post* asserted "the right of every Jew . . . to have as much or as little contact with Zionism and Israel as he personally pleases."[10]

Although such statements are duly quoted in the appropriate circumstances to appease diaspora Jewry, nevertheless the more persistent underlying premise in Zionist thought and practice is the concept of a universal pan-Jewish peoplehood. Ben Gurion's use of the phrase "the people of Israel," as applicable only to the Jewish citizens of Israel, is neither representative of the Zionist use of that term nor of the meaning usually attached to it, as this chapter will demonstrate.

CORPORATE IDENTITY

Zionism, shunning complex and dialectical interpretations, has advocated the concept of an abstract, quintessential Jew. Klatzkin, for instance, used the terms "unhyphenated Jew,"[11] and "pure national type."[12] Ben Gurion likewise talked of "the Jew who is one hundred percent Jewish."[13] What, one might ask, constitutes this pure Jewishness and peoplehood? What is the basis of this "new definition of Jewish identity," and of the new *"secular definition"*?[14] In attempting to answer this question, one encounters a curious fact: The anti-assimilationist Zionists sought to reconstitute the Jewish character and situation in order that the Jews might become a people "like any other," as they phrased it. To achieve that goal, they sought to "normalize" the Jew, deriving the norms not from the Jewish tradition but rather from the world of the gentiles,[15] of which the Zionists are at other times so critical.

Identifying one of the goals of Zionist vocational training, a speaker at a Histadrut convention referred to it as being "the self-preparation of the Jewish worker to become a gentile. . . . The Jewish village girl shall live like a gentile country lass."[16] Nathan Birnbaum sarcastically noted in his moving essay, "In Bondage to Our Fellow Jews," that the Zionists try "to remold" the Jews on the European model, 'to make men of us' . . . and drag our children away from our holy teachings, from our Judaism."[17]

To prove that their program for reform is not unrealistic, the Zionists developed their theory of a national Jewish identity, separate from all others, yet not different from them. The Jew, who is at the center of the Zionist program, is at times identified biologically. At other times, it is his culture or religious faith that identifies him as Jewish. But at all times he is identifiable by one or two exclusively "Jewish elements" in his existence.

A RACIAL DEFINITION

The view of a biologically or racially determined Jewish identity was first advocated by Moses Hess (1812–1875), the German proto-Zionist theoretician. Predicting that the race struggle was going to be the "primal one," Hess subscribed fully to the Semitic-Aryan distinction that was destined to serve as one of the main concepts discussed in later years by theoreticians of European racial thought.[18] Theodor Herzl, for a while at least, flirted with the idea of a corporate racial identity, freely using phraseology such as "Jewish race," or the "uplifting of the Jewish race."

Such terms were ambiguous at the time and remain so, for they acquire an interchangeable biological and cultural content. For instance, we know from Herzl's answer to Nordau, who was anxious about the anthropological fitness of the Jews to be a nation, that Herzl had in mind a form of biological determinism.[19] On his first visit to a synagogue in Paris, what struck Herzl most was the racial resemblance, "bold misshapen noses; furtive and cunning eyes," which he claims was common among Jews in Vienna and Paris.[20] Herzl was later to see evidence that refuted this observation.

It appears that the ranks of the Zionists were full of "scientists" interested in proving that the Jews were a distinct race. Klatzkin reported that some Zionists wanted to argue "the impossibility of complete assimilation" on the basis of a "theory of race."[21] Ruppin referred to the fact that "the literature of the Jewish race question is plentiful" and cited "many valuable authorities."[22] Karl Kautsky referred to one such Zionist thinker, Zollschan, who objected to some of the ideas contained in Joseph Chamberlain's racist classic, *The Foundations of the Nineteenth Century.* Nevertheless, he firmly subscribed to the central thesis of the book, that is, that humanity is moving from a "politically conditioned racelessness to a *sharper and sharper definition of race.*" Zollschan, like others, tried to prove that the Jews constitute a pure race. It was his intention to make the ghetto in Palestine, which the Zionists envisaged, a "necessary goal for all Jews."[23]

Relatively unknown today, Zollschan was an "authority" in his time on the subject of the "Jewish race." He is quoted several times by Arthur Ruppin in his book *The Jews of Today,* which purports to give a racial definition of Jewishness. The Jews, Ruppin argued, "have assimilated to a small extent certain foreign ethnical elements, though *in the mass*, as contrasted with the Central European nations, they represent a well characterized race."[24] The racial purity achieved instinctively throughout history should be perpetuated consciously now, Ruppin maintained. He asserted that a "highly cultivated race deteriorates rapidly when its members mate with a less cultivated race, and the Jew naturally finds his equal and match most easily within the Jewish people." Ruppin frowned on the whole process of "assimilation which begins in denationalization and ends in intermarriage."[25] Through "intermarriage the race character is lost," he said, and the descendants of such a marriage are not the "most gifted." Since intermarriage is "detrimental to the preservation of the high qualities of the race, it follows that it is necessary to try to prevent it to preserve Jewish separatism."[26]

Ruppin's study upheld the notion of racial purity and alleged Jewish racial superiority. These convictions are held by many other Zionists. As noted by Morris Cohen, the Jewish-American philosopher, the Zionists accept the racial ideology of the anti-Semite, but draw different conclusions. "Instead of the Teuton, it is the Jew that is the purer or superior race."[27] Ruppin is true to type, for on the basis of this claim of purity and superiority, he builds his ideological Jewish separatism. He argued, for instance, that races "less numerous and infinitely less gifted than the Jews" have established their right to a separate national existence, so why should the superior Jews be an exception? He also quoted Joseph Kohler, another racist theoretician, who declared that the Jews are "one of the most gifted races mankind has produced." Ruppin accounted for Jewish superiority on Darwinian grounds. "The Jews have not only preserved their great natural racial gifts, but through a long process of selection these gifts have become strengthened."[28]

Many Zionist theoreticians and functionaries who did not expound the racial theory nevertheless assumed it as a matter of fact in their statements. Norman Bentwitch, the British Zionist leader, in an interview in 1909, claimed that a Jew could not be a full Englishman "born of English parents and descended from ancestors who have mingled their blood with other Englishmen for generations."[29] Judge Louis D. Brandeis defined Jewishness, in a speech he gave in 1915, "as a matter of blood." This fact, he said, was accepted by the non-Jews who persecute those of the Jewish faith, and Jews themselves who take pride "when those of *Jewish blood* exhibit moral or intellectual superiority, genius, or special talent, even if they have adjured the faith like Spinoza, Marx, Disraeli, or Heine."[30] Nahum Sokolow (1859–1936), the Polish Zionist historian and thinker, "frequently referred to his people as a race," and, like the theoreticians of racism, believed that there were no pure races; however, he added, "[of those that existed] the Jews were the purest."[31]

In a speech given in 1920 at Heidelberg University, Germany, Nahum Goldmann asserted the eternal racial separateness of the Jews. According to his view, "the Jews are divided into two categories, those who admit that they belong to a race distinguished by a history thousands of years old and those who don't." He characterized the latter group as "open to the charge of dishonesty."[32]

Lord Balfour, a gentile Zionist, thought of the Jews in racial terms. Perhaps it is not entirely without significance to recall that one of the earlier drafts of the Balfour Declaration urged the establishment of a "national home for the Jewish race,"[33] a phrase that carried an unmistakable biological designation.

AN ETHNIC AND A RELIGIOUS DEFINITION

All these Zionist efforts notwithstanding, the argument for a corporate racial identity could not be sustained for long. Theories of race and racial superiority or inferiority are of dubious validity and have little scientific sanction. "By the 1930's the intellectual climate had swung clearly away from racism, and racism had lost its apparent scientific respectability."[34] We still hear statements about the "Jewish race" among political Zionists and racists, but such statements were far more frequent before the 1930s.

Simcha King observed in his book, *Nachum Sokolow: Servant of His People*, that "having lived through the era when the word 'race' has become identified with cruelty and barbarism, most people shy away from using the word. Moreover, anthropology has shown that the term cannot be correctly applied to the Jews."[35] However, the author pointed out that "it was very common to refer to the Jews as a race in pre-Hitler days and many believed that being a Jew was a matter of birth and physical relationships."[36]

Tight racial definitions are simply too mythical and therefore too readily challenged by reality. The Nazis, after evolving their "scientific" hierarchy of races, found themselves forming an alliance with the Asiatic Japanese, and were forced to reclassify the latter as "honorary Aryans." The biological determinism in the purely racist outlook is always moderated by reality and by the very complexities that racist ideas and practices attempt to minimize or ignore.

Perpetuating the biological definition of the self proved a difficult task for the Zionists because the argument was too simplistic. The Zionists, unlike the Nazis, had to contend with a widely dispersed diaspora, and consequently the racial definition initially alienated the diaspora Jews who were clearly not genetically homogeneous. Any single genetic definition would have excluded one or more of the Jewish communities.

Herzl, despite his flirtations with the racial theory, had his difficulties with Israel Zangwill. Zangwill was a Jew who was of the "long-nosed Negroid type, with very woolly deep-black hair." The father of Zionism remarked with good humor that so much as a glance at both Zangwill and himself would demolish the racial argument.[37] The Zionists therefore sought another definition of a corporate identity derived from ethnicity rather than from heredity or race.

During the United Nations debate concerning Zionism, Israeli Ambassador Chaim Herzog tried to argue from ethnic rather than racial affiliations. In one of his statements he pointed out that the Zionist ideal was based "on the unique and unbroken connection, extending for some 4,000 years, between the People of the Book and the Land of the Bible."[38]

The premise of ethnic permanence and immutability underlies Zionist terminology. The term "Israel" itself is intended to imply this idea of unbroken continuity. The Zionist state is referred to by some as the Third

Commonwealth (*Bayit sh'lishi*)—one link in a series that was begun by David, upheld by the Maccabees, temporarily dismantled by the Romans, only to surface again in A.D. 1948. To many Zionist historians and political scientists the society of the Zionist settler-colonists before 1948 is the new *Yishuv*, a term intended to suggest continuity with the old religious settlement and implying an unbroken existence in Zion. To give an illusion of the same continuity, some Israeli military commentators seriously compare David and Solomon's cavalry with the tanks of the Israeli army.

Ben Gurion is a prime example of this trend. In *Rebirth and Destiny of Israel* he wrote of the "third return to Zion"[39] and attempted to relate Middle Eastern realities of his time to what he conceived to be similar events in the past. He also referred to the Arabs of today as Assyrian and Babylonian Iraqis, Phoenician Lebanese, and Pharaonic Egyptians!

Others, not ideologues like Ben Gurion, were also committed to the notion of continuity. Following the 1967 Israeli victory, a professor of history at the Hebrew University declared that the Israeli soldiers were able to see the Red Sea for the first time since they crossed it with "General" Moses 4,000 years ago. Presumably, that was how General Dayan earned the title of Moshe II. At one time, an Israeli professor of international law who was engaged in a debate at the International Peace Academy in New York told his listeners that the return of the Jew to Palestine after an absence of 2,000 years is like the return of an American to his homeland from a short trip abroad. When congratulated on his sense of humor, he assured his bewildered audience that he was serious. The professor was plainly as oblivious to historical realities as Max Nordau was when he suggested that Palestine and Syria should be restored to their original owners.[40]

The ethnic argument, like the racist one, claims for the Jews ethnic continuity and purity as well as ethnic superiority. Herzl boasts in his diary of the "human material we possess in our people! They divine what one would have to hammer into other people's heads."[41] Ruppin acknowledged that other nations may have other points of superiority, but, he hastened to add, "in respect of intellectual gifts the Jews can be scarcely surpassed by any nation."[42] Believing that the traditional religious concept of "the people" was of central significance in the historical process of redemption, Ben Gurion transposed this spiritual concept to the ethnic plane by claiming that the Jews have a certain "moral and intellectual superiority," and that they can serve as a model of redemption for the human race.[43] In November 1975, Ambassador Chaim Herzog presented the United Nations with a list of Jewish thinkers who have excelled in many fields, implying that their Jewishness, not their concrete cultural surroundings, was the determining factor that explains their genius.[44]

Obviously, this same thesis is used by anti-Semites, who attribute to Jewishness any negative traits a Jew may have.

But even though the more subtle formula of culture or ethnicity has largely replaced the simplistic biological formula of race, the determinism is scarcely moderated. The Jew is seen as eternally "determined" by a unique historical and cultural structure to which he is reducible, outside of which he has no valid existence and over which he has no control. This slight shift in the source of determination is more apparent than real in view of the fact that many racists believe that culture itself is an expression of the *Weltanschauung* of a nation whose character is biologically determined. Race, nation, and culture overlap to such a degree that Sokolow's biographer observed that "when one reads the passages where Sokolow uses the word 'race,' one notices that he frequently uses it in the sense of nationality, in the sense of being born a member of a group which has a great heritage."[45]

The correlation, and at times implicit synonymity, of the words "nation," "race," and "culture" in Zionist literature is such that no reader can fail to detect that the categories of "nation" or "culture," in a religious or ethnic sense, overlap with the category of "race" in the genetic sense. Moses Hess, as we pointed out earlier, viewed world history as the arena for two world-historic *races.* "The final aim of history," he wrote, "is harmonious cooperation of all *nations*,"[46] that is, races. Ruppin correlated the racial and cultural more than once in his writing, asserting that "a nation's racial and cultural values are its justification for a separate existence,"[47] and he discussed Jewishness, a racial category according to his definition, as "a high type of human culture."[48]

The same correlation was implied in the writings of Joachim Prinz, a German-born Zionist rabbi, when he called for the replacement of integration by "an acknowledgement of the Jewish nation and the Jewish race."[49] More recently, Barnet Litvinoff, a historian of Zionism, described the Zionist view of "brotherhood" as founded "on a strictly nationalist or racial basis," for it "meant brotherhood with Jew, not with Arab."[50]

Unlike the French view of nationalism, which grew out of the Enlightenment and considered all men equal, Zionism grew out of German idealism and romanticism with its emphasis on the *Volk* and its organic ties with the Fatherland, or the *eretz.* According to Hans Kohn, in defining Jewish identity Zionism borrowed organicist and determinist terms, such as "blood, destiny and the organic folk community," from nationalist German thought. Kohn stated further that some of his Zionist friends believed that "a man of Jewish ancestry and cultural heritage could never become or be a true German, Italian, Frenchman, or Dutchman." He was bound to "remain an alien everywhere except on his own 'ancestral' soil." Hans Kohn was of the opinion that this concept of nationhood, based on "biological determinism," runs counter to the spirit of the Enlightenment.[51]

The same point is made by Hannah Arendt, the Jewish-American author, in her celebrated essay titled "Zionism Reconsidered." Tracing the "crazy isolationism" of the Zionists to an "uncritical acceptance of German-inspired nationalism," she finds it to be based on a belief in the nation as "an eternal organic body, the product of inevitable growth of inherent qualities." This view explains "peoples not in terms of political organizations, but in terms of biological superhuman personalities."[52] Reading Zionist literature, one perhaps ought to decode the term "Jewish people" into "Jewish race" and to remember that the terms "people," "nation," or "culture," given the organicist orientation of Zionist thought, imply a reductive determinism that is almost biological.

Zionist definitions and assumptions concerning Jewish identity were presumably taken from the "normal" world of the gentiles. The Religious Zionist definition, however, could be considered an exception. But while its claimed origins may be different from the racial and ethnic definitions, its purist national designation makes it indistinguishable from them, as indicated earlier. All definitions view the Jewish people as alien, unique, and sacred, and all endow all Jews with more or less the same "national" rights.

In sum, whether a Jew is a Jew by race, through cultural-historical heritage, religio-national tradition, or a combination of all, this construct of a "pure Jew" is at the core of Zionist ideology. The controversy surrounding the rationale of "claimed purity" is quite tangential in comparison. When Israel's former Prime Minister, Levi Eshkol, advocated a "corporate Jewish life" aimed at strengthening itself and Israel,[53] he did not see fit to clarify the source of this presumed unitary existence. This was quite prudent of him, for rather than stir ideological controversy among various Zionist groups, he limited himself to the area of Zionist consensus—the quintessential Jew.

DUAL OR MULTIPLE LOYALTIES?

The concept of a unitary Jewish existence forms the basis of a number of Zionist themes and notions such as the Jewish genius, the Jewish vote, and Jewish power. Above all, it underlies the Zionist view of the pure Jewish state as a *sine qua non* for the fulfillment of this undiluted Jewishness.

Ben Gurion emphatically stated that "only in a sovereign Israel is there the full opportunity for moulding the life of the Jewish people according to its own needs and values, faithful to its own character and spirit, to its heritage of the past and its visions of the future."[54] If this idea is already bewilderingly difficult to comprehend on the sociopolitical level, it becomes ridiculous when applied to inanimate objects. The latter, too, were viewed by Ben Gurion in Jewish terms: "the Jewish book, the Jewish laboratory and scientific research . . . the Jewish field, the Jewish road, the Jewish factory, the Jewish mine, and [naturally] the Jewish Army."[55] Barnet Litvinoff described the settlers as living "on Jewish bread raised on Jewish soil that was protected by a Jewish rifle."[56]

The concept of the pure Jew is the basis for the Zionist schematic division of the world into Jew and gentile. Division on a religious basis is common to other monotheistic religions, but it has been exaggerated by the Zionists, who often apply it outside a religious context. Even in sports, the Israeli-Zionist state clings tenaciously to this unalloyed purity. Two non-Jewish Norwegian sportsmen who were invited to participate in the Maccabiah, a kind of Zionist Olympiad, were prevented from participating when the American delegation objected, arguing that the Maccabiah was a strictly Jewish event,[57] for pure Jews only. In another tournament, in November 1975, as the United Nations was debating the Zionism-Racism Resolution, Jim Baatright, the American basketball professional player, had to convert to Judaism to participate in the Maccabiah. Baatright was so cooperative that he stumbled on the fact that his grandmother back in the Bronx was Jewish—a discovery that speeded up the process of conversion at the hands of one of Israel's chief rabbis.[58]

The same narrow outlook underlies Israeli tinkering with the International Women's Year symbol. The symbol was censored because it incorporates a cross, which happens to be the scientific sign for the female sex. For use in domestic activities promoting International Women's Year, Israel redesigned the United Nations symbol, creating one without a cross. The local Israeli symbol incorporates the Star of David, thereby giving full expression to pure Jewish identity.[59]

The term "Jewish national," not "Israeli national," is used in Israel to refer to Israeli citizens of the Jewish faith. The presumed loyalty on the part of Jews everywhere is to their true Jewish nation and homeland. Weizmann believed that every Jew was a potential Zionist and that those Jews "whose Jewish patriotism was qualified by any other national loyalty were to be pitied or despised"[60] as traitors to their one and only homeland and probably God.

Klatzkin, the most radical of all Zionists, sounding the theme of Jewish national consciousness, warned the German people that the boundaries of Germany could not in any way restrict the movement or loyalty of the Jewish people because Jewish unity is something that transcends national boundaries. "A loyal Jew," according to him, "can never be other than a Jewish patriot. . . . Not the slightest feeling of belonging to German nationality can be found in the Jewish consciousness."[61]

Ben Gurion gave us another illustration of this Zionist outlook when he drew an image of the purely Jewish lawyer in exile who is "in Jewish duty bound to oppose the state and its ordinances." In Israel the situation is different, for this very Jewish lawyer should "implant instincts of reverence and esteem for the State and the law."[62] The Jewish lawyer, according to this view of the Jew, owes allegiance only to the Jewish state.

The Jew who has the misfortune to live in the world of the gentiles finds himself surrounded by the all-powerful majority, which "controls the government, the economy, the law, the political parties and the dominant culture." This view of the gentiles is strikingly similar to the view of the Jews in the *Protocols of the Elders of Zion*. Whether he likes it or not, this Jew will be influenced by gentile culture even though he has "no roots" in it, and therefore will experience "a constant duality" in his life if he wants to preserve his purity.[63] He will be a *"split personality"* for he is a Jew who partakes of a "non-Jewish" environment.[64]

Dr. Nahum Goldmann might feel uneasy about some of the statements he made during his "purist" Zionist days. In the 1920s, while in Germany, Dr. Goldmann struck the same Klatzkin theme of Jewish loyalty to the Jewish homeland only. However, in New York City, on January 9, 1959, he moderated his stand; he exhorted Jews in the United States (and those in other countries) to declare courageously and openly that they have a dual allegiance. The Jews' loyalty, he said, should be evenly divided between the country in which they lived and the Jewish homeland. Goldmann went on to counsel the Jews not to "succumb to patriotic talk that they owe allegiance only to the country in which they live."[65]

Assumption of pure Jewishness and loyalty to the Jewish homeland can also be detected in Kallen's system of classification of Jews. Jews are not categorized by him as good or bad, unique or ordinary; they are not American, Moroccan, or French, or members of any such recognizable group. The pragmatic philosopher presents the following catalogue of Jews, compiled on the basis of their degree of purity and their relation with the pure Jewish homeland. According to him, Jews "may be distinguished as Undispersed and Ungathered, Dispersed and Ungathered, Undispersed and Ingathered, Dispersed and Ingathered, Undispersed and Ungatherable, and in addition there are Strangers and Aliens gatherable and ungatherable."[66] It might be of interest to the reader to try to unravel Kallen's allegorical catalogue by reading the chapter entitled "Of the Ingathered, the Ungathered and the Ungatherable" in his book, *Utopians at Bay*.

Zionist "corporate Jewish identity," whether racial, ethnic, or religious, is a doubtful formula, based on simplistic determination. It is an overlay of many concepts glued together and corresponding to no concrete reality. All of us as individuals have multiple identities and, as a result, conflicting loyalties. For instance, the problems encountered by Jews in a secular society founded on separation of church and state are not radically different from those faced by a believing Christian who wants to uphold and implement Christian values.

However, the Zionist definition rejects the complexity of the circumstances faced by the assimilated Jews, who are perceived as people with split personalities. According to the radical Zionist view, this "duality" must be cured by emigrating to Israel. On the other hand, the less radical diaspora Zionists feel that the duality has validity and that Jews, irrespective of their loyalty to the land of their birth, must recognize the centrality of Israel in their lives. Were the monism or the duality to be replaced by a complex, open-ended dialectics, the emerging image would be that of the assimilated diaspora Jew. In a rich assimilationist context, multiple loyalties can coexist within the psyche of each individual, be he Jew or gentile. Such loyalties can be organized according to each individual's existential situation and moral commitments. The "corporate national personality" offers us two alternatives: loyalty as advocated by the Ben Gurions, or the dual loyalty of the Goldmanns, which inevitably plays into the hands of the anti-Semites.

It is important to state, in conclusion, that the Arabs would not be so presumptuous as to inject themselves into the question of what constitutes Jewish identity were this a subjective matter lying outside their national interests. Such, however, is not the case. The Arabs are concerned with the Zionist definition of Jewish identity because it encroaches on their rights, impinges on their destiny, and has had an incalculable effect on their lives.

3

ZIONISM AND DIASPORA JEWRY

THE STATUS

From a theoretical standpoint, the Zionist premise concerning a Jewish unitary and corporate identity is superficial. In practice, however, it has had, and will continue to have, far-reaching consequences for both Arabs and diaspora Jews, putting their national and civil rights in jeopardy. For the Arabs it is discriminatory through *exclusion*, for as more and more Jews are "ingathered," Palestine Arabs, once a majority in Palestine, are squeezed out. The few who remain live as second-class citizens in a "restored Zion," which is distinctly "Jewish" in character and orientation. For the Jews, the concept of a Jewish corporate identity is discriminatory through *inclusion* because the "national" implications of that concept undermine the principle of equal status under the law for Jews in the diaspora. If carried to excess, the concept threatens to make Jews outside Israel potential aliens in their own homelands.

It is important to recall that the safeguard clauses in the Balfour Declaration, set forth as a precondition for the fulfillment of the Zionist plan, stated "that nothing shall be done which may prejudice" not only "the civil and religious rights of existing non-Jewish [that is, largely Arab] communities in Palestine," but also "the rights and political status enjoyed by Jews in any other country." The second clause was added under pressure from the Jewish community in Britain, which feared discrimination by inclusion. As Sir Edwin Montagu (1879–1924)—the only Jewish member of the British cabinet that issued the Balfour Declaration—put it: "When the Jew has a national home surely it follows that the impetus to deprive us of the rights of British citizenship must be enormously increased. Palestine will become the world's ghetto. . . . All Jews will be foreign Jews, inhabitants of the great country of Palestine."[1]

The Zionists had never intended to respect the safeguard clauses referred to above. They openly espoused the Jewish-people concept and worked energetically to promote it. Present-day Israel, the supreme manifestation of a purely Jewish nationalism, is *not* constituted solely as a state for the citizens living within its borders. Rather, it proclaims itself a state for the whole Jewish people, within *and* outside its still undetermined boundaries. The establishment of the Jewish state in 1948 was declared by a National Council representing the Jewish people both in Palestine and in the diaspora. Ben Gurion himself, in the August 1962 issue of *The Jewish Frontier*, described Israel as the "State of the whole Jewish people."[2] This was ten years after his conciliatory statement about the independence of diaspora Jewry.

The Zionist state has promulgated several laws and set up diverse institutions to translate into concrete terms the Jewish-people concept. One such law is the Law of Return, which, without taking into consideration the diversity of Jewish attitudes toward the issue, grants *all* Jews the "right" to leave the land of their birth and to "return" to their Jewish homeland. Both the Histadrut (General Federation of Labor) and kibbutz movement, which predate the establishment of the state, have as their declared objective the promotion of the rights and well-being of exclusively Jewish industrial and agricultural workers. The Jewish National Fund is yet another Zionist institution that acquires land from non-Jews in the name of the Jewish people. Only Jews can buy or lease such land. The World Zionist Organization is in the business of promoting Jewish unity beyond national borders. Its "covenant" defines its task as "the ingathering of the exiles in *Eretz Yisrael;* and the fostering of the unity of the Jewish people."[3]

Both the Zionist state and the World Zionist Organization espouse the same ideals and work for the same goals, operating within the same concept of Jewish peoplehood. Putting their ideal into practice has presented them with some difficulties, for the Zionist state is located geographically in the Middle East, with the vast majority of its "exiled" people scattered all over the world. Since the state cannot reach "its people," for its "power outside its frontier is scant," as Ben Gurion once explained,[4] the World Zionist Organization, which "has the occasion and the ability to do what the State neither can nor may,"[5] acts as a link between the state and diaspora Jewry.

Given this Zionist-Israeli objective and *modus operandi*, the Covenant of the World Zionist Organization (WZO) spells out "the various specific duties of the Organization toward the State," such as "the strengthening of the State of Israel," and "the mobilization of world opinion" in support of its aims. Reference is also made to "activities conducted outside

Israel."[6] The foundation of the state in 1948 "did not bring the reign of the Organization to a close,"[7] and WZO still continues to act as the long arm of the state in reaching Jewish communities in other lands.

To institutionalize this anomalous relationship between a state and an organization operating on its behalf in other sovereign states, Israel promulgated in 1952 the Law of the Status of the World Zionist Organization/ Jewish Agency, which recognizes the organization, *inter alia*, an an "authorized agency" working in the "State of Israel for the development and the colonization of the country."[8] An agreement between the state and the World Zionist Organization, aimed at clarifying the law, cited the following as some of the tasks entrusted to WZO: "The organizing of immigration abroad . . . the transfer of immigrants and their property to Israel," and "the mobilization of resources for financing these [Zionist] activities"[9] inside Israel. The Status Law, characterized by Ben Gurion as complementary to the Law of Return and of equal importance, is also based on the concept of the Jewish people.

The commitment to the Jewish-people concept in a political sense is not confined to laws and institutions, but takes more direct and less abstract forms, such as strong statements by Israeli spokesmen or even direct Israeli intervention in the affairs of diaspora Jewry. Various Israeli-Zionist statements have included references to an organic relationship tying Jews to the Jewish homeland and state. Yosef Tekoah, former Israeli ambassador to the United Nations, once declared that the future of American and Israeli Jews is "irrevocably interlocked."[10] Ben Gurion, with his predilection for blunt language, wrote of "an indestructible bond, a bond of life and death . . . a community of destiny and destination" indissolubly joining "the State of Israel and the Jewish people."[11]

Such statements are not without political significance when they are translated into concrete action. While prime minister of Israel, for instance, Ben Gurion told a Zionist Action Committee that "Zionists in other countries ought to have the courage to stand up for the state [of Israel] even if their governments are against it."[12] He indicated that when a Jew says "our government" to his fellow Jews, he usually means the government of Israel. Ben Gurion even claimed that the "Jewish public in various countries views the Israeli ambassador as their own representative."[13] Equally explicit was Golda Meir. When she occupied the post of foreign minister, she once emphasized that it was part of the responsibility of Israeli diplomats and officials to remain in permanent contact and to work closely with local Zionist organizations.[14] Perhaps it is with this in mind that Israeli consuls, on certain occasions, contact American rabbis directly, "either to assist in organizing regional meetings with congregational leaders or to locally disseminate statements prepared in the offices of the Consulate."[15]

In *Haaretz* of May 20, 1975, Zvi Yehuda Hacohen Kook, one of Israel's two chief rabbis, denounced former U.S. Secretary of State Kissinger as "the gentile's husband" who desecrated "the name of the God of Israel and the name of *his* people."[16] The rabbi was guided by the Jewish-people concept in a political, nationalist sense. Kissinger, accordingly, was seen not as an American secretary of state representing the interests of *his* country, but as a "Jew," who must always represent the interests of "his people."

Implicit in such statements is the premise that asserts the autonomy of the Jews and their *de facto* segregation. Rabbi Mordechai Kaplan, a leading American Zionist and founder of the Reconstructionist Movement, has even asked for "a *de jure* recognition" of world Jewry as a people, in order to restore their "corporate status,"[17] undermined by the Emancipation and the Enlightenment, both of which put an end to the segregation of Jews.

Such logic is dangerous and counterproductive, for the argument in defense of the civil and political rights of the Jews or any other minority in society can be advanced only in terms of individual liberty, not in terms of a presumed group autonomy. The Zionist assumption of corporate Jewish identity, reaching above and beyond one's society, is obviously not in the interest of Jews, for it makes them aliens and temporary residents in their own countries.

There is not a single country in the whole world, with the exception of Israel, that accepts the corporate definition of the Jew, as advanced by Ben Gurion, Klatzkin, and Zionist ideology in general, or as implied in the structure of Zionist laws and institutions. When he first began to lobby on behalf of Zionism, Chaim Weizmann tried to secure international recognition of the concept of the Jewish people because he assumed that this would guarantee a "juridical foundation for the establishment" of the Zionist state. But the inclusion of the two safeguard clauses concerning diaspora Jewry (and the Arabs) in the Balfour Declaration foiled his effort. The "objective was also frustrated in the League of Nations Mandate for Palestine of 1922," for the Mandate incorporated the same safeguard clauses. Even the Palestine Partition Resolution of 1947, despite its basic inequities, did not recognize that concept.[18]

As for the official American attitude, it is consistent with the American Constitution. A letter dated November 12, 1959, from the Department of State to Clarence L. Coleman, president of the American Council for Judaism, and signed by Parker Hart, acting secretary of state for Near East and South Asian Affairs, underlined the American position in the following words: "I believe there is . . . a common awareness inside and outside our country of the undivided loyalty which American Citizens, regardless of their race, color, or creed, possess for their country."[19] The letter undoubtedly implies a rejection of the concept of Jewish peoplehood as operative or valid under American law.

A similar rejection was made explicit in a letter dated April 20, 1964, from Assistant Secretary of State Phillips Talbot to Rabbi Elmer Berger. The letter stated that the Department of State "does not recognize a legal-political relationship based upon the religious identification of American citizens. It does not in any way discriminate among American citizens upon the basis of their religion."[20] The U.S. government's rejection of the Jewish-people concept, contained in the Phillips Talbot letter, is codified in *Digest of International Law* (edited by Marjorie M. Whiteman, Assistant Legal Advisor to the Department of State, Volume 8, September 1967, U.S. Government Printing Office, pp. 34-35).[21]

Similarly, Gandhi, in rejecting this concept, drew a distinction between concrete individual rights and group autonomy. The great Indian leader insisted on "a just treatment of the Jews, wherever they are born and bred. The Jews born in France are French precisely in the same sense that the Christian born in France is French." He underlined the inherent danger in the Zionist premise when he asked: "If the Jews have no home but Palestine, will they relish tht idea of being forced to leave the other parts of the world in which they are settled? Or do they want a double home where they can remain at will?" Finally, he pushed the Zionist premise to its logical and inescapable conclusion: "This cry for the national home affords a colorable justification for the German expulsion of the Jews."[22]

Gandhi's words did not constitute an exaggerated view of the situation, for the Nazis had made full use of Zionist claims and premises. In Nazi-dominated Europe the most anti-Semitic slogan was *"Juden raus* to Palestine"[23] ("Out with the Jews to Palestine"). As it turned out, the Nazis accepted the Zionist idea of a Jewish unity transcending mere frontiers and boundaries. From the very beginning, it seems, the Nazis wanted to accord the Jews "the status of protected foreigners," who were "to be allowed to practice as doctors, work as teachers." The rights of the Jews, as an alien national entity, would be protected,[24] the Nazis were saying, as long as they were on their way to their homeland.

The Haavra (Transfer) Agreement between the Third Reich and the Zionists, signed in August 1933, was a tangible interpretation of the Nazi and Zionist view of the Jew as a "temporary alien" residing outside his homeland. The Nazis were also quite anxious to turn the *de facto* segregation of the Jew into a *de jure* status, as was to be recommended later by Rabbi Kaplan.

Herzl anticipated many of the implied meanings that would later be read into his declaration that the Jews are "a people, one people" *(ein Volk)*. He realized that it might hinder the assimilation of the Jews, jeopardize their status wherever their assimilation was "already an accom-

plished fact," and even give "aid and comfort to the anti-Semites."[25] But
he was rightly convinced that this "oneness" of the Jewish people was the
very core and essence of Zionism.

THE FORCIBLE REDEMPTION

Zionist proclamations and allegations notwithstanding, the vast majority of world Jewry has in fact been assimilated. Given its view of Jewish
existence in the diaspora as temporary, and of assimilation as something to
be shunned, it is little wonder that Israel shows marked impatience with
the "failure" of Jews around the world to live up to Zionist expectations.

Describing the reluctance of diaspora Jews to be transplanted to
Palestine, an Israeli official at the Ministry of Absorption once complained
that "each new immigrant has to be dragged into Israel like an obstinate
mule." Then, in language that does not suggest love and affection, he
warned that Tel Aviv might eventually be forced to "resort to surgical
intervention."[26]

Immediately following the establishment of Israel, Ben Gurion expressed his disappointment at the failure of the "exiled" members of the
Jewish people to flock to the Jewish homeland. In markedly pseudo-
messianic terms, he declared it to be the duty of "the present generation
to redeem the Jews in the Arab and European countries."[27] This process
of redemption means in practice the establishment of political Zionist
hegemony over all the Jewish communities at any price, forcing on them a
view of life and history to which they do not necessarily subscribe. "To
redeem" the communities in Zionist parlance is another way of saying
"to coerce" or even "to conquer" them,[28] as indicated by Rabbi Jakob I.
Petuchowski.

It is in the name of Israeli centrality and Zionist hegemony that the
movement has taken the destiny of the communities into its own hands.
This fact has not always worked out in the Jews' favor. In June 1960,
when Golda Meir, in her capacity as foreign minister of Israel, sent formal notes to some Western governments protesting anti-Semitic incidents
taking place within their respective countries, the Israeli press hailed her
for an "historical act investing Israel with the authority to protect Jews
everywhere." Western Jewry, however, viewed these Israeli good offices
on its behalf with a great deal of skepticism. Some Jewish-American
circles were troubled, and the Jewish-British press expressed some dis-
content.[29]

Interference in the internal affairs of diaspora Jewry does not always
take such diplomatic form, as witness the case of Zionist intervention in
the affairs of Arab Jewry. Historically, Arab Jews have had their ups and

downs like any other minority in the world, and their situation has differed
from one Arab country to another, according to the prevailing economic
and cultural conditions, as indicated by Shlomo Avineri, former director
of the Israeli foreign ministry.[30] Given their outlook, however, the Zionists could not possibly have left Arab Jewry alone, for their "redemption"
had to be achieved.

To grasp fully the implications of Zionist activity in the Arab world, it
has to be viewed against its specific historical background. The colonial
powers, in keeping with their traditional policy and tactics, attempted to
enlist the minorities, including the Jews, under their banner. One tactic
was to open to these minorities various options closed to the rest of the
population. Under the Crémieux Decree of 1870, for example, the Jews of
Algeria were accorded French citizenship, and on the eve of the 1954
revolution the vast majority were French Jews. By 1947, only 20 percent
of Egyptian Jews were Egyptian citizens,[31] the rest preferring to remain
either European nationals or stateless. (A dramatic example of this
process of westernization is the case of the French Consul in a Syrian town
who was a Jewish Syrian.) What accelerated the process of westernization and alienation from the local communities was the influx of Ashkenazi
Jews from various European countries. In 1835 there were 5,000 Jewish
Egyptians, but by 1897 the number had risen to 25,000, owing mainly to
immigration from abroad. This process of westernization took place during
the western colonial onslaught on the Arab world and the Arab resistance
thereto.

The Zionists, oblivious to the complexities of the situation, launched
their activities on behalf of Arab Jewry, fully supported by the colonial
powers. In 1917, Britain gave colonial sanction to Zionism by issuing the
Balfour Declaration. A few years later, the British Mandate in Palestine
cooperated with the Zionist settlers at the expense of the Palestinian
Arabs. In Iraq, the Zionist society was granted legal recognition from
the British mandatory government there in 1921. The Zionist Federation
of Tunisia received the same recognition from the French authorities in
1922, that is, two years after its formation. Various British Zionist-spon-
sored Jewish Legions were established in Egypt, and elsewhere, counting
in their ranks Arab Jews from both the Ashkenazi and Sephardic communities. Finally, in 1948, a settler-colonial state, claiming to be a Jewish
state, was founded in the Arab world, against the will of the Arabs and at
a time when the Arab national liberation movement was becoming increasingly aware of itself.

It was within this frame of reference that Zionist emissaries traveled
throughout the Arab world, with the purpose of winning converts and
urging support for the future Zionist state. Training camps for prospective
emigrants were set up.[32] Fund-raising drives were mounted with varying
degrees of intensity. From 1920 to 1940, the Zionists raised about a quarter

of a million dollars in Baghdad alone. The campaign continued even after the establishment of Israel. Membership dues for the World Zionist Organization, according to Zionist sources, were clandestinely collected in Egypt in 1951 (that is, *after* the creation of Israel) in preparation for the Twenty-Third Zionist Congress, the main theme of which was immigration.[33] An analogous activity would be a fund-raising drive in the United States on behalf of Japan right after Pearl Harbor!

The situation became quite untenable as continuing Zionist agitation created a state of polarization between Jew and gentile—in this particular case between Arab Jews and their Muslim and Christian compatriots. In Libya, for instance, a country that the Zionists had eyed in 1908 as a potential territory for settlement, there was a "circolo Herzl," which raised funds for Jewish settlement in Palestine, as the report of the Twelfth Zionist Congress (1921) indicates. In Tunisia, many Jews acquired French citizenship and espoused Zionist ideology. In 1922, Tunisian Zionists, who even boasted of having a Revisionist (Zionist maximalist) faction among their ranks, organized a protest against the Palestinian uprising of 1921. The Zionist Federation in Tunisia printed its leaflets in Arabic for distribution to Zionist clubs all over the Arab world.

Zionism in Algeria played an equally negative and subversive role. It succeeded in driving a wedge between the Jewish community assimilated into French culture in Algeria and the rest of the population. By 1901, there were two Zionist unions in Algeria affiliated with the Zionist Federation of France. As in other Arab countries, Zionist efforts to recruit immigrants for Palestine were organized. A transit camp was set up in Algeria in the 1950s. During the revolutionary struggle of the Algerian-Arab people, two emissaries were sent by Israel, probably to contact Algerian Zionists and intensify Zionist activities, but they were executed by the revolutionaries. On the eve of independence and in the wake of the collaboration among Israel, Britain, and France in the 1956 war against Egypt, Algerian Zionists displayed remarkable insensitivity by celebrating the tenth anniversary of the establishment of Israel. Two years later in 1960, they celebrated the anniversary of Herzl's birth.

Morocco also witnessed some Zionist activity, such as periodic visits by French Zionists and the publication of Zionist literature advocating "the mass migration of Moroccan Jews to the Homeland," as the entry on "Zionism in North Africa" in the *Encyclopedia of Zionism and Israel* indicates, thus implying that Arab Jews were alien, temporary residents in that country. Zionist intervention in Morocco reached unusual proportions when some Jewish Moroccan youths, wearing white caps with the blue star of David, demonstrated and shouted against President Nasser during his visit there.[34]

Zionist sources have understandably always been reluctant to document the record of Jewish resistance to Zionist intervention in the affairs of diaspora Jews. Over the years, many Jewish Arabs informed their governments about Zionist activity, and in reality Zionists remained a small and unrepresentative minority. In the 1940s, Egypt, Iraq, and Tunisia witnessed a veritable war between the Zionists, whose origins were largely European, and the Arab Jews. Fist fights sometimes took place between the various Zionist elements, usually right-wing and procolonialists, and the anti-Zionists, usually leftists and anticolonialists. Many cases are known where Egyptian Zionists stormed the clubs of Egyptian assimilationists and beat them up. In a message to Elmer Berger from Elias Cohen, an Egyptian Jew, the anti-Zionist American rabbi was informed that another Jewish Egyptian, a Mr. Sutton who owned a tourist agency, was killed in 1950 in Italy by a Zionist terrorist for "expressing his opposition to Zionist policy."[35] Such Zionist activities, though mounted by small minorities, were at times effective because the groups were well organized and generously subsidized.

But far more sinister than all these Zionist activities were the espionage schemes of the Jewish Agency that recruited Zionist agents from the ranks of Arab Jewry. In the 1920s, the Jewish Agency set up an espionage network that had branches in the Arab world operating clandestinely behind legitimate front organizations, such as the Maccabee clubs or the numerous Jewish charity organizations. In the 1930s, the Haganah had an intelligence agency with an "Arab" section headed by Moshe (Shertok) Sharett (1894–1965). The Mossad established a center in 1937 to train Arab Jews in espionage activities against their own countrymen. The spies were called "the Arab boys."

Following the establishment of the State of Israel, the recruitment of Arab Jews for espionage activities continued unabated. The *Encyclopedia Judaica* informs us that a "highly developed underground Zionist movement" existed in Egypt, operating on behalf of Zionism.[36] A prominent figure was the Jewish-Egyptian citizen, Moshe Marzouk, born in Cairo in 1926. Rather then identifying with his country, Dr. Marzouk, as the *Judaica* says, was "convinced that the future of all Egyptian Jews lay in their migration to *Eretz Yisrael*." Accordingly, "he dedicated his life" not to the defense of the country he was born and raised in, but rather "to the realization of his Zionist ideals." He recruited "young Jews" to go to Israel. He himself could have left, but he decided "to stay at his post" at the Jewish hospital in Cairo and work for Israel. A friend of Marzouk's, Samuel Azzar, born in Alexandria, was "awarded a scholarship that enabled him to study electronic engineering. Like Marzouk, he [too] chose to stay in Egypt and carry out his mission."[37]

One of the most notorious "missions" undertaken by the Zionist underground in Egypt was the one that came to be known as the Lavon Affair. In 1955, 13 Jewish Egyptians, under instructions from the Israeli government, planted explosives in the library of the American Information Center in Cairo and in American- and British-owned establishments in

Cairo and Alexandria. These acts were designed to create tension between Egypt and the two Western countries. The tension, as Uri Avnery explains in his book, *Israel Without Zionists,* was supposed to enable the colonial reactionary elements in the British Parliament "to prevent an agreement providing for the evacuation of the Suez bases, and also provide ammunition for those parts of American public opinion that opposed arming Egypt." But above all, the sabotage activity was designed to undermine the prestige of the new revolutionary regime in Cairo and to demonstrate to the world its lack of stability.[38] Some of the Zionist agents were caught red-handed, a fact that led to the arrest of all involved in the plot. Those arrested were the ringleader, Max Bennet, Dr. Marzouk, Samuel Azzar, and ten others. During the trial, two managed to escape, and Max Bennet committed suicide. Of the remaining agents, two were acquitted and seven were sentenced to prison terms. Marzouk and Azzar, who headed the Cairo and Alexandria rings, were sentenced to death. Marzouk was accused of having organized the Cairo group, after a period of training in Israel, and of having arranged for wireless transmission to Israel. Azzar was accused of being the head of the Alexandria group, and of "operating an underground workshop to manufacture sabotage devices."[39] In the wake of the trial, the all-too-habitual accusations of Arab anti-Semitism and of an Egyptian frame-up were duly repeated.

The Lavon Affair continued to haunt the Israeli leadership long after the Cairo trials. Ben Gurion disavowed responsibility for issuing the orders for it, placing all the blame on Pinhas Lavon, Israel's minister of defense in 1953-1954. The latter, however, maintained his innocence to the very end. When an investigating committee absolved Lavon of any responsibility, Ben Gurion resigned from the ruling Mapai Party and, together with Peres and Dayan, formed the Rafi Party. Regardless of inter-Israeli politicking concerning personal responsibility, Israeli involvement was implicitly admitted when Dr. Marzouk, who had been executed by the Egyptian authorities, was later posthumously made a major in the Israeli Army.[40] He and Azzar were called "*Kedoshei Kahir*" (the martyrs of Cairo).[41] More than anything else, the Lavon Affair was instrumental in complicating the already difficult situation of Jewish Egyptians.

Attempts to redeem the people forcibly, in the name of the higher Zionist ideal, have on several occasions been marked by tragedy and great loss of life. One such example is the incident of the *S.S. Patria*. The ship, carrying Jewish refugees, was blown up in the port of Haifa on November 22, 1940, resulting in the death of 240 Jewish refugees and 12 policemen. The explosion was described at the time by the Jewish Agency as an act of "mass protest" and even "mass suicide," a Massada. The incident was a source of embarrassment to the British authorities, who, viewing the issue of Jewish refugees in humanitarian rather than in political terms, had planned to send the immigrants to a British colony, whereas the Jewish Agency insisted they must go to Palestine. A British commission of inquiry, established in January 1941, ruled that the sinking of the ship was "the work of a small determined group working from the shore, and not in consultation with the people on board." It was tentatively concluded that the destruction of the *S.S. Patria* was the work of Zionist extremists. In his *Crossroads to Israel*, however, Christopher Sykes says that the responsibility for the explosion lies with the "responsible-minded Jewish Agency acting through Haganah." The Haganah men had planned to blow up the motor and instead sank the whole ship with its human cargo. "To cover up the atrocity," the Jewish Agency hastily concocted the story of the "mass suicide."[42]

When the head of the German-Jewish community merely hinted that the "mass suicide story was propaganda nonsense," an attempt was made on his life on his way home from the meeting where he gave expression to his doubts.[43] It is significant that despite the findings of the investigating committee, the Zionist propaganda machine continued for some time to grind out its favorite Massada myth.

David Flinker, in the November 27, 1950, issue of the New York *Morning Freiheit*, wrote that the order to blow up the ship was conveyed to the Haganah members on the *S.S. Patria*,[44] who executed the orders. It is believed that the man who placed the bomb became "a well-known functionary of the Israeli port of Haifa." A similar incident took place when a refugee ship, the *S.S. Struma*, was blown up off the Turkish coast. Miraculously, there was only one survivor who was believed to be an ex-Haganah officer.[45]

THE NEGATION

Zionist activism and militancy on behalf of Jewry are motivated by a strong belief in the nationalist ideology of pure Jewishness. The presumed purity and superiority of the national ideal implies the impurity, inferiority, and worthlessness of the diaspora. One can even argue that just as the conquest of the national *eretz* implies that the cultural life of the Palestinians is of no significance, the conquest of the Jewish communities abroad implies that the cultural life of diaspora Jewry has no intrinsic worth. Nationalist Zionist "affirmation," in the words of Klatzkin, means the "negation" of the diaspora, which is not "worth keeping alive."[46]

This Zionist theme of the worthlessness of the diaspora is most pervasive and persistent. Quite recently, on March 4, 1977, Rabbi General Mordechai Piron, chief rabbi of the Israeli Defense Army, described the diaspora as a "curse forever and ever. . . . It is always a curse." He even did not make exception of the several golden ages of the diaspora.[47] In his letter of resignation as first prime minister of Israel (1953), Ben Gurion talked of the diaspora as "human dust, scattered and crumbled throughout the exile."[48] Thirty years earlier Klatzkin characterized the diaspora as nothing more than "deterioration and degeneration" and "eternal impotence."[49] The unnaturalness of the Jewish diaspora, according to Zionist ideology, is most evident in the occupational abnormality of the Jews—

their heavy concentration in trade and the professions, with little or no presence in the ranks of the peasantry or the proletariat.

To put an end to this state of affairs, Zionist education is designed to eliminate the negative aspects of diaspora existence, denying its achievements and presenting Jewish contributions on "foreign soil" as a mere betrayal of the pure Jewish spirit.[50] Levi Eshkol, in his official foreword to the 1965 *Israel Government Yearbook*, pictures diaspora creativity as drawing "sustenance from alien soil and to that soil [giving] back its fruit."[51] The happy alternative to this presumed abnormality is Zionist Israel as a growing, normal "center" replacing the diaspora, which is marginal and on the way to extinction.

Such a negative description of the diaspora is essential to the Zionist idea, for if the life of Jewry outside of Israel were presumed to be a healthy and vigorous one, with its ordinary quota of human suffering and joy, what then would be the *raison d'être* of the Zionist state? Why Zionism at all? One can perhaps outline the Zionist strategy concerning world Jewry and the Jewish question as operating in terms of two possible alternatives, with no middle ground—settlement and Jewish survival in the Jewish homeland for the select few who go there, and eventual disappearance, either through assimilation or pogroms, for those who remain in exile. Both alternatives are seen as leading to the "liquidation" of the diaspora.[52]

In his "The Imperatives of the Jewish Revolution," delivered in Haifa in 1944, Ben Gurion argued for a "radical break" with the deplorable dependence of the diaspora, "making an end of it."[53] Diaspora Jewry, according to Klatzkin, is to serve as "a source of supply" for the national renaissance, and any Zionist effort at delaying the total dismantling of the diaspora edifice is simply a matter of expediency, giving the Zionists "the time to salvage some bricks" for the new national structure.[54] This approach to the diaspora was at the root of Zionist strategy vis-à-vis the Nazis. The Zionists saw the Jewish communities as a "natural reservoir from which immigrants could be drawn to strengthen the key position of the Jewish community in Palestine."[55] As Klatzkin put it, in itself the diaspora does not deserve to survive, but as a means, it would be useful. "The transitional existence," he said in no uncertain terms, "is of significance, precisely because it is transitional."[56]

The mystical Russian Zionist, Aaron David Gordon (1856–1922), drew a picture of a Jewish Palestine acting as the mother country of world Jewry "with the Jewish communities in the diaspora as its colonies,[57] a curiously mixed metaphor of a colonial, exploitative mother. Interestingly enough, a half-century later, an American "Bundist," Chil Spiegel, found the metaphor of conquest and colonialism quite appropriate to describe Israel's "neo-colonial hold on world Jewry, drawing from it the material—dollars—to fuel her machinery."[58] Spiegel's metaphor is more precise, for he drops any talk about motherhood.

The Zionists, especially the radicals among them, were unable to comprehend the fact that negation of the diaspora was tantamount to negation of Judaism and Jewry. Neither has concrete existence outside of exile. Almost all Jewish religious books and literature—ranging from the Babylonian Talmud, that "portable homeland," to the *Shulhan Arukh*, to the Zohar, to Yiddish literature, to Philip Roth's and other Jewish-American novels—have been the work of Jews in the diaspora. "To reject all that had happened to the Jews in the last two thousand years," Simon Dubnow (1860–1940), the Russian Jewish historian noted, is "tantamount to rejecting Jewishness itself."[59] In that sense, the Zionist perception of the Jew not only runs counter to the Jewish religious experience, but is also at variance with the Jewish historical experience itself.

ZIONIST ANTI-SEMITISM

Political Zionism partly grew out of, and was undoubtedly conditioned by, one aspect of the historical experience of Jewry in the diaspora: anti-Semitism. In a real sense it should trace its origins not to the positive assertions of the religious Jewish tradition, nor to the complexity and diversity of the Jewish historical experience, but rather to the negative qualities of anti-Semitism. Herzl recorded in his diary that he and Nordau agreed that only anti-Semitism "had made Jews of us,"[60] and he specifically traced his recognition of Judaism or Jewishness to the days when he read Eugen Duhring's anti-Semitic classic: "The Jewish Question as a Question of the Racial Image for the Existence, Morals and Culture of the Nations."[61] The link between his sense of his own Jewish identity and anti-Semitism is so deep and organic that in the first entry of the *Diaries*, written for posterity, he recorded that "anti-Semitism has grown and continues to grow—and so do I."[62]

Any reader of Zionist literature cannot help but conclude that the Zionists attribute to anti-Semitism a certain inevitability and a degree of centrality in the Jewish experience. Herzl's *The Jewish State* is premised on the view that wherever Jews live, they are "persecuted in greater or lesser measure." There is a whole "sorry catalogue of Jewish hardships," which includes murder in Rumania and exclusion from clubs in France.[63] But regardless of time and place, "the fact of the matter is, everything tends to one and the same conclusion"[64]—anti-Semitism. Pinsker described the hatred of the Jew as a "hereditary," "psychic aberration," a kind of "incurable . . . disease transmitted for 2,000 years."[65] The description of anti-Semitism as an "organic" phenomenon is dramatically illustrated by a conversation between Weizmann and Richard Crossman, British Labour member of Parliament and Zionist sympathizer. When the Zionist leader asked Crossman whether he was an anti-Semite, the latter unhesitatingly replied, "Of course." To Weizmann, who became a life-long friend, Crossman's reply demonstrated his sincerity and honesty, for the Zionist leader was convinced that anti-Semitism was "a bacillus which every gentile carries with him."[66]

The determinism of the bacillus metaphor betrays the narrow and rigid reductionism of the Zionist view of life. It dehumanizes the gentile, reducing him to the level of a racist, actual or potential, nullifying the efforts of all those gentiles who fought and died for the political and civil rights of the Jews and other minorities. Zionism, however, cannot operate except in terms of abstractions: If the Jew is abstracted into a permanent victim or a permanent parasite, the gentile is equally abstracted into a permanent wolf.

If anti-Semitism has such permanence and persistence, if it is reducible to an organic aspect of gentile human nature, then it necessarily follows that it is the most *natural* of phenomena. Pinsker and Herzl not only assumed the impossibility of assimilation; they also assumed, as an inevitable and logical corollary to the premise, the naturalness of anti-Semitism— "the inseparable companion" of Judaism throughout history,[67] as Pinsker phrased it.

This assumption of the naturalness of anti-Semitism implies that it is a logical response to Jewish existence in the diaspora—one that actually makes the diaspora Jew partly or wholly responsible for anti-Semitic attacks on him. As a parallel to the bacillus metaphor, used by Weizmann to describe the anti-Semitism of gentiles, one can cite Nordau's equally pseudo-scientific deterministic metaphor in his characterization of the Jews. They, said the Zionist leader, are like certain kinds of "tiny organisms which are perfectly harmless, so long as they live in the open air, but become the cause of frightful disease when deprived of oxygen." Then the "scientific" racist goes on to warn governments and nations that the Jews might become just such a "source of danger."[68]

The figurative language partly conceals what it attempts to communicate. Therefore, Klatzkin's bluntness and forthrightness are helpful. The radical Zionist declared that he could understand perfectly well the legitimacy and "rightfulness" of anti-Semitism as "essentially . . . a defense of the integrity of a nation in whose throat" the Jews, another nation, are "stuck." Klatzkin then asserted the organic link between the two movements: "If we do not admit the rightfulness of anti-Semitism, we deny the rightfulness of our own nationalism."[69]

Herzl, the gentle liberal, shared this same view of modern anti-Semitism. He dissociated it from the "old religious intolerance," and characterized it as "a movement among civilized nations [*sic*] whereby they try to exorcise a ghost from out of their own past."[70] He also conceded that the Jewish state meant a victory for the anti-Semites, but this did not seem to bother him: "They will have turned out to be right because they *are* right."[71]

This justification for anti-Semitism is a cardinal theme in Herzl's *The Jewish State*. The author poses the question asked by all anti-Zionists: "Will not Zionism provide weapons for the anti-Semites?" His answer is ambiguous but suggestive: "How so? Because I admit the truth? Because I do not maintain that there are none but excellent men among us."[72] By expelling the Jews, the anti-Semites were simply liberating themselves, ridding themselves of Jewish dominance, as Herzl wrote in his *Diaries*. "They could not have let themselves be subjugated by us in the army, in government, in all of commerce."[73]

Since its inception, many Jews have objected to Zionism as anti-Semitic, and even a friend of Herzl's (jokingly, of course) told him that he would become "an honorary anti-Semite."[74] Apparently the joke impressed Herzl so much that he took good care to record it in his diary. A famous anti-Semite of Herzl's days, in a review of *The Jewish State*, expressed his satisfaction that finally anti-Semitism had been correctly and probably scientifically understood by the Jews, and that the anti-Semites were perceived by the Zionists not as maniacs or fanatics but as "*citizens who exercise the right of self-defense*."[75] As if reciprocating, Nordau expressed his deep gratification "to see that honest anti-Semites applaud our proposed [nationalist] solution for the Jewish question."[76]

The "naturalness" of anti-Semitism is predicated on a perception of the Jews' unnaturalness or abnormality, a basic premise of political Zionism that has already been dealt with briefly. It is important to point out here that to establish the abnormality of the diaspora, the Zionists based their critique of the Jewish character "on a rationale of charges"[77] taken over from the literature of anti-Semitism in the Western world. Zionist literature is indeed replete with discussions of the ways and means to "productivize" the Jews in order to make them less "parasitical," "marginal," or dependent. The Jews in Zionist literature are usurers, and "sick personalities," living like "dogs and ants," accumulating money, following the values of the marketplace.

The Zionist assumption concerning diaspora Jewry, as indicated earlier, is that Zionism will restore the Jews to normalcy. Brenner expressed himself in very gross terms when he urged the Jews "to recognize and admit" their "meanness since the beginning of history to the present day," and then went on to counsel them to make a fresh start.[78] He was surely an extremist, even by Zionist standards, but his views put in sharp focus an important aspect of the Zionist perception of the Jews.

Sometimes the Zionist critique spills over into direct anti-Semitic

caricature. Klatzkin, for instance, described Jews as a "rootless and rest-
less" people, "living a false and perverted existence."[79] The Jew, in
Pinsker's words, is "everywhere a guest," "nowhere at home," "moving
like a ghost from one country to another, an alien body; he is half-dead,
struck with the sickness of wandering."[80] A frankly anti-Semitic tone
distinguishes the writings of Israel Joshua Singer, the Zionist brother of
Isaac Bashevis Singer, the noted writer. For him, the Jews are a "stooped,
despondent" people, "living in filth." They are a "clump of Asia" in the
middle of Europe, and, as a separate body, they are "one big hunchback."[81]
In his article entitled "the Ruin of the Soul,"[82] Yehezkel Kaufman culled
his own collection from Zionist literature:

Frishman:	*Jewish life is a "dog's life" that evokes disgust.*
Berdichevsky:	*Not a nation, not a people, not human.*
Brenner:	*Gypsies, filthy dogs, inhuman wounded dogs.*
A. D. Gordon:	*Parasites, people fundamentally useless.*
Schawadron:	*Slaves, harlots, the basest uncleanliness, worms, filth, rootless parasites.*

The Zionist press has also described Jews in negative terms. *Davar,* the
Histadrut newspaper, once came out with a headline about the "regeneration of a parasitic people."[83]

This is a recurrent theme in the works of the "liberal" Herzl, as well
as in the unliberal Brenner. If the latter used extreme terms, Herzl too,
as an anti-Zionist Jewish writer indicated, drew certain stereotypes, which
if used by a gentile would undoubtedly be labeled as racist as the *Protocols
of the Elders of Zion.*[84]

The words of the Zionist Chaim Kaplan, who kept a diary during the
Warsaw ghetto uprising, further illustrate this variety of Zionist anti-
Semitism: "Every nation, in its time of misfortune, has conspirators who
do their work in secret. In our case an entire nation has been raised on
conspiracy. With others the conspiracy is political; with us it is religious
and national." He then referred to the exceptional case of the Marranos,
the Spanish crypto-Jews who, to defend their faith, ostensibly converted
to Christianity, maintaining a Christian facade to cover up their authentic
religious belief.[85] Kaplan applied an anti-Semitic stereotype to himself
and the Jews at large. Identification with the oppressor and his views is
a familiar phenomenon in the history of oppression.

Acceptance of certain premises of anti-Semitism led the Zionists to
think of anti-Semites as natural allies and a positive force in their nationalist struggle to liberate diaspora Jewry from its alleged captivity. Rather

than combat anti-Semitism, Herzl declared that "the anti-Semites will be our most dependable friends, the anti-Semitic countries, our allies."[86] From the very beginning he perceived the parallelism between Zionism and anti-Semitism and saw the potential for cooperation. In an 1895 diary entry, Herzl outlined a blueprint for his future Zionist activities. Indicating that the next step would be the "selling" of Zionism, he added between brackets that it would "cost nothing, for the anti-Semites will rejoice."[87] In another diary entry, he enumerated the elements of world public opinion that he could mobilize in the fight against the "imprisonment" of the Jews, and he included the anti-Semites as one element that could work in their behalf.[88]

Perception of the common outlook between Zionists and anti-Semites has been reiterated by later Zionist spokesmen. In 1925, Klatzkin proposed that "instead of establishing societies for defense against the anti-Semites, who want to reduce our rights, we should establish societies for defense against our friends who desire to defend our rights."[89] Nahum Goldmann, in his heady radical Zionist days, felt that the disappearance of anti-Semitism might benefit the Jewish community politically and materially, but it would have a "very negative effect on our eternal life."[90]

Again this abnormal sentiment is not unusual; it is inherent in Zionist ideology and practice and is repeatedly emphasized. The Zionist founding fathers were the first to propound it and their descendants in Israel perpetuate it with the same vigor. In his book *The End of the Jewish People?* the Jewish-French sociologist Georges Friedmann noted that the Ashkenazi Jews of Israel reacted negatively, and sometimes aggressively, to any information that Jews were leading a normal life in any country of the diaspora without being subjected to anti-Semitic harassment.[91] The same individuals showed a "positive" reaction when they heard of "any piece of news indicating anti-Semitism anywhere in the world."[92]

Anti-Semitism was so "positive" from the point of view of one Zionist settler before 1948 that he believed it to be more or less "divinely ordained and inspired."[93] He was unconsciously echoing Herzl, who claimed that "anti-Semitism . . . probably contains the Divine Will to Good because it forces us to close ranks."[94] In an exchange in the Hebrew press in Palestine between this settler and Kaufman, the former described himself as "an anti-Semitic Zionist," adding "that he failed to see how any Zionist could avoid a similar position."[95] Kaufman himself concurred, declaring that "many Zionists . . . are completely convinced that in order to become 'good Zionists' " they must "hate" themselves.[96] Zionist negation of self is ultimately a form of alienation and surrender to the oppressor.

POPULATION TRANSFER I

The Zionist themes of the worthlessness of the diaspora and the inevitability of anti-Semitism imply *a priori* need for the return of the Jews
to their "ancestral fatherland" as the only remedy for an innate sickness
and the only defense against external dangers. Zionism presupposes the
need for the demographic transfer of the Jews from the countries of the
diaspora to the national *eretz*. But the concrete, unfolding reality is not
always consistent with the Zionist scheme.

Toward the end of the nineteenth century, waves of Jewish and gentile
migrants left their homelands in Russia and Poland, in Italy, and in Ireland,
and settled in the New World and elsewhere. Millions of Jews settled in
the United States, particularly from the 1880s on, making the country one
of the largest spiritual centers of Judaism. Only a few thousands went to
Palestine, even after it was placed under the British Mandate.

When the Zionist state was established in 1948, following 60 years of
organized Zionist immigration, Israel had only about 800,000 Jews. About
one-fourth of these were survivors of concentration and displaced persons'
(D.P.) camps, many of whom had *not* necessarily wanted to settle in
Palestine. A *New York Times* poll in 1948 revealed that 80 percent of
the D.P.s quite expectedly, given the ordeals they had barely survived
and given the armed conflict in Palestine, wished to migrate to the United
States rather than to Palestine.[97] Loyal to their vision, the Zionists ex-
ercised maximum pressure "to convince" the D.P.s to settle in Palestine.
Methods of pressure included "confiscation of food rations and dismissal
from work." Dissidents and political opponents were denied "legal protection, . . . visa rights" and at times were expelled from the camps.[98]

Another and more recent illustration of the Zionist zeal for a negation of the diaspora and for the transfer of Jewry to the *eretz* is the campaign mounted on behalf of Soviet Jewry. The campaign for "rescuing"
Soviet Jewry, like other similar rescue efforts, overlooks many of the complexities of their situation. For one thing, Soviet Jews are citizens of a state
that despite détente, is still engaged in an ideological, economic, and sometimes military conflict with the United States and its allies. A campaign
mounted by American Zionists who are an integral part of American society is not necessarily in their best interest. That point was not lost on one of
the Soviet refugees, who described Soviet emigrants as "pawns in a game
between the USSR and the United States with Israel [and, one would add,
American Zionists] acting as the broker provocateur."[99]

In addition to these considerations of international politics, the internal, economic, and cultural factors inherent in the very structure of Soviet
society should be remembered. The Soviet Union is made up of several
nationalities existing in a precarious balance. Any strident nationalist

campaign would, at least in the view of Soviet officials and an important segment of the Soviet intelligentsia, unbalance the frail structure. Zionism represents such a threat. If continued, the Soviets argue that it could intensify divisive feelings and even spur anti-Semitism. One may agree or disagree with this Soviet argument, but it should be considered seriously because Soviet Jews exist in a society in which this view is accepted by many officials and private citizens.

Above all, however, many people forget that, in some very important aspects, the Soviet Union is still a "developing country" that needs all its human resources. The Jewish community there, having one of the highest ratios of specialists and experts among the national minorities, is an important asset. Soviet emigration policies, dictated by Soviet political and economic needs, apply equally to *all* Soviet citizens, regardless of religion, race, or "national affiliation." In the Soviet Union emigration is considered an act of betrayal. Those seeking to emigrate are seen as those who were willing to stay on in their society to earn a degree and acquire a skill, but when the time comes to serve their country, they head for the United States to buy a "better car." This perception of the skilled emigrant is quite common in the developing world. Probably this attitude explains why many of the emigrants "were not targets of persecution *prior* to their application for exit visas."[100]

Zionist agitation "on behalf" of Soviet Jewry, being ideological and nonhumanitarian, does not reckon with all such considerations. Had it been an expression of humane and genuine concern for Soviet Jews, both as individuals and as a cultural entity, the campaign would have called for the improvement of the situation of *all* Soviet minorities and nationalities *in* their homeland. However, the goal of the Zionist liberationist struggle is a population transfer. This has been the Zionist strategy from the outset. As Levi Eshkol put it, "We are not now struggling for Jewish rights in the diaspora, but for the diaspora's Jewishness."[101]

Nevertheless, the plan for the transfer of Soviet Jewry to Israel is gradually losing ground because almost 50 percent of Soviet emigrants head for the United States, foregoing the "privilege" of going to the national *eretz*[102] and thus earning the derogatory name "dropouts," a term imposed on them by the American press, which unconsciously adopts Zionist terminology. The rise of the dropout rate among Soviet emigrants has led to bickering and strained relations among the various Zionist and Jewish organizations. The bitter and emotional controversy centers on whether it is still legitimate to give aid to the Soviet emigrants who choose to settle in the United States rather than in Israel. In July 1976, a proposal was submitted to the Jewish Agency Assembly suggesting that the Hebrew Immigration Aid Society (HIAS) and the Joint Distribution Committee end "their administrative and financial aid to dropouts."[103] The extreme step of refusing to issue an Israeli visa to a Soviet Jew unless he guaranteed that he would go to Israel is at times mentioned as a way of turning the migration into an ideological transfer.[104] An Israeli lecturer at the Hebrew University has made the obvious point that such a course of action "would suggest that Zionism, as its opponents have long contended, does not treat the individual Jew as an end, but as a means."[105]

In the early days after the establishment of Israel, one of the most successful Zionist efforts to effect a Jewish population transfer involved Yemenite Jews. Through Operation Magic Carpet, a total of 48,818 Jews from Yemen and elsewhere were flown to Israel "at an over-all cost of $4,500,000, or roughly $100 a person," according to the *Encyclopedia of Zionism and Israel*.[106] No other "cost" is mentioned. After all, the Yemenite Jews, according to the Zionist view, were living, since the seventh century, "fortified . . . within the wall of [pure] Jewish existence,"[107] and not as an integral part of their society. The operation also included Jews from Aden, Dijibouti, and Asmara in Eritrea, as well as the entire Jewish community of Haban in Hadhramaut.

The transfer of Jews, if need be, can take a more activist form. A writer in the leading labor Zionist newspaper *Davar* once declared that if he were given a free hand, he would delegate a group of zealous young Israeli-Zionists to undertake the task of redeeming the ungathered diaspora Jews. The youngsters would disguise themselves and plague the Jews with anti-Semitic epithets and slogans such as "bloody Jews" and "Jews go to Palestine."[108]

I. F. Stone, characterizing a cardinal trait of Zionism, said that the movement "grows on Jewish catastrophe."[109] Experience has shown that when reality did not conform to the abstract Zionist view of it, it was cynically made to do so. Fantastic as it may sound, this is more or less what happened to Iraqi Jews.

The claim is not being made that Iraqi Jewry had been leading an ideal existence. In the 1940s, life in Iraq, a country undergoing a social transformation, had its drawbacks for all the religious or ethnic minorities, the Jewish minority included. In 1941, there were demonstrations against the Jewish community, "the first of its kind," as the *Encyclopedia of Zionism and Israel* indicates.[110] But, on balance, Iraqi Jewry had what may be considered a normal quota of joy and suffering. In December 1934, Sir F. Humphrys, British ambassador to Baghdad, sent a confidential dispatch to his Foreign Office describing the Jewish community in Iraq as enjoying "a more favorable position than any other minority in the country," and pointing out that there was no "natural antagonism between Jew and Arab in Iraq."[111] The Ambassador's experience and perception ran counter to those of Pinsker, who believed that there was a *"natural antagonism"* between Jew and gentile.[112] The report of the British ambassador seems largely accurate, for the Iraqi Jews believed themselves to be primarily Iraqis who traced their ancestry to the days of the Babylonian exile. Many of the members of the Jewish community enjoyed relative prosperity by Arab standards, the only standards relevant to them.

Enrollment of Jewish Iraqi youngsters at schools and colleges was proportionately much higher than the national average. Rafi Nissan, an Iraqi Jew who emigrated to Israel, pointed out that even though Iraqi Jews had left their property behind in Iraq, they had brought with them something "more important than money: our skills and education." One-third of all the emigres had had at least 11 years of education, "a higher percentage than even those newcomers [to the Zionist state] from Europe and America." He added that "over eighty percent of the immigrant householders were artisans, shopkeepers, officials, administrators, lawyers and teachers."[113] This was hardly typical of an oppressed minority.

As for the various institutional safeguards and participation in government, King Faisal of Iraq had proclaimed "freedom of religion, education and employment for the Jews of Baghdad who had played such an important part in its welfare and progress." There were six Jewish Iraqi delegates in the Iraqi Parliament,[114] "and there was at least one Jewish minister in nearly every Iraqi cabinet,"[115] in the late 1940s.

Given this relative peace and stability, it was not surprising that the Zionists made Iraq their prime target. Iraq, like Libya, Egypt, and Palestine, had been originally marked as a possible target for the Zionist settlement scheme, which in itself was enough to generate tension between the majority and the Jewish community. When Zionist territorial designs were narrowed down to Palestine (and vicinity), Zionist activities were directed away from the land of Iraq and focused on Iraqi Jewry. In 1919 Aharon Sasson of Baghdad founded a Zionist society bearing the fantastic name of Mesopotamian Zionist Committee.[116] The organization set up branches in several Iraqi towns (about 16 in all) and even sent a delegation to the Thirteenth Zionist Congress in 1923.[117] It also organized youth groups to prepare the young for immigration, printed and distributed two Hebrew and two Arabic mimeographed monthly bulletins to its members, and founded a Zionist library.[118]

To poison relations between Iraqi Jews and the rest of the Iraqi Arab people, the Zionists sometimes distributed leaflets in the synagogues, containing inflammatory slogans such as *Don't buy from Muslims*, with the express purpose of letting these pamphlets fall into the hands of the Muslims.[119] Zionist propaganda succeeded, up to a point, in sowing seeds of dissension and "bitterness," as the 1934 confidential dispatch of the British ambassador indicated. He further pointed out that the banning of Zionist literature might be in the "interests of the Jews themselves."[120]

It appears, however, that despite the Zionist efforts and the pessimism of the British ambassador, Iraqi Jews were not completely alienated from their country. After the prolonged Zionist activity and the unfortunate demonstrations in 1941, Iraqi Jewry, with deep roots in the country, resumed its normal life. It established a Jewish neighborhood, invested large sums in construction in the city of Baghdad, and lapsed into what the Zionists feared was "a kind of inertia."[121]

Bracha Habas, wife of Knesset member David Hacohen, reported in *The Gate Breakers* that the Zionist emissaries to Iraq "became aware 'that Zionist ideology would not be accepted in many, if not most, Jewish circles.' One of the emissaries 'tried to win converts among the intelligentsia, but failed.' "[122] Then came the establishment of the Zionist state and the Arab defeat, which expectedly complicated matters for everyone. Iraqi Jews, occupying positions that involved international contacts with one country or another, were relieved of their posts.[123] Apart from such incidents, the Iraqi response, given the situation, was quite restrained.

On the whole, despite intensive Zionist activity inside Iraq and the involvement of some prominent Iraqi Jews in such activity, there was no mass hysteria of the kind that uniformly grips the popular mind in wartime, especially in the wake of defeat. As the chief rabbi of Iraq told Rabbi Berger in 1955, "We hear that you in the United States did not treat your Japanese citizens so well in the emotionalism following Pearl Harbor,"[124] a reference to the internment of thousands of Japanese Americans during World War II.

The trouble could have ended then in 1948 and Iraqi Jewry could have resumed its life with varying degrees of tension and harmony. Time would have healed wounds and people would have necessarily made the new and necessary adjustments. But the Zionists had a different plan. Radical steps had to be taken to redeem "130,000 Jews while at the same time improving [Israel's] demographic situation."[125] We know from Zionist sources that an underground Zionist movement, similar to the one operating in Egypt, was founded in 1942. Given the name of The Babylonian Pioneer Movement, the organization began to instruct Jewish Iraqi youth in the use of firearms and the manufacture of explosives.[126] The underground formed a more or less autonomous enclave within Iraq with its own weapons and recruits. In 1947, Yigal Allon, commander of the Palmach, wrote a letter to Dan Ram, addressing him in a ridiculously inflated manner as "Commander of the Jewish Ghettos of Iraq."[127] Arms were smuggled into Iraq—rifles, ammunition, and hand grenades, all supplied by the Haganah.[128] These arms, Allon claimed in his letter to Dan Ram, were designed "to encourage *all forms* of immigration."[129]

What is this ambiguous phrase, "all forms"? What is the point of all these arms? As an irked Iraqi rabbi complained in 1955, "What did we want with them [the arms]? Were we going to fight all of Iraq—even if our loyalties were with Israel, which they were not?"[130]   The question, asked in 1955, was a justified one, and it has not yet been entirely answered, though several clues have since been revealed.

In 1950, Baghdad witnessed a number of incidents. An explosive was thrown into a coffee house where Jewish intellectuals habitually gathered. Then the United States Information Center was bombed. Again it was a place where "young people, especially Jews, used to sit and read." When a third bomb exploded in the Massauda Shemtov synagogue, casualties included a small Jewish boy and an Iraqi Jew who lost his right eye. The episode would have been classified by Zionist historians as yet another pogrom, but as chance would have it, a persistent Zionist pattern of provocation was eventually revealed.[131]

One Iraqi Jew, later an Israeli citizen and member of the Black Panther Party, was persuaded that the Arabs had bombed the big synagogue in Baghdad. However, he heard a rumor in Israel (after almost the entire Iraqi Jewish community had emigrated to the Zionist state) that the incidents had been caused by a Zionist agent. He remarked that when someone talks, "people investigate. Word of mouth brings the true story out. It was also published in the papers . . . and nobody denied it."[132] Kochavi was probably referring to the *Haolam Hazeh* story of May 29, 1966, and to the report published in *The Black Panther* magazine of November 9, 1972, which reconstructed the incidents of the Zionist pogrom and revealed the whole sordid truth.

In 1951, right after the mysterious explosion, a Palestinian refugee from Acre, while working in a department store in Baghdad, recognized among the customers the face of Yehuda Tagar, an officer in the Israeli Military Government in Acre. He reported his presence to the police, who arrested Tagar together with Shalom Tzalah and 15 others who were members of the Zionist underground. During the interrogation, Tzalah revealed the truth behind the Zionist plan and led the Iraqi police to arms caches in the synagogues.[133] The agents, members of the Zionist underground, were tried for their attempt "to frighten the Iraqi Jews, to drive them to emigrate to Israel." Two agents were sentenced to death and the rest were given long prison sentences. A Jewish-Iraqi lawyer, now a resident of Tel Aviv, said "the evidence was such that there was nothing to prevent the sentences from being passed." Kaduri Salim, the Iraqi Jew and now citizen of Israel, who lost his right eye during the Shemtov synagogue incident, is trying to obtain compensation from the Israeli government.[134] The Zionist establishment, which had called the disastrous espionage episode in Egypt the "Lavon Affair," described the Iraqi scheme as an "unfortunate affair."[135]

All of these "affairs," far from being exceptions to the rule, were part of the Zionist plan. If the Jews are indeed one people in the political sense, as Herzl asserted, and if Jewishness is a matter of "land and language,"[136] as Klatzkin claimed, then the leadership of this national liberation movement is in effect acting in the name of that peoplehood, whether the majority of the people approves or not. Only outside the context of Jewish peoplehood could the Lavon Affair be decried as a serious aberration, could the vituperative remarks of the Israeli chief rabbi about Mr. Kissinger be seen as pure hysteria, and could the Golda Meir message to Western countries be interpreted as interference in the affairs of sovereign states and their Jewish communities. Only outside the context of the national liberationist frame of reference could the forced exodus of the Iraqi Jews be seen as a pseudo-messianic tinkering with the destinies of other human beings and as an arrogant assumption of the divine role of redemption.

4

THE JEWISH RESPONSE

JEWISH ANTI-ZIONISM

When the Zionist movement first appeared on the international political scene, its proponents had to work hard to win the allegiance of Jews and the support of Jewish organizations around the world. But, as the *Encyclopedia of Zionism and Israel* points out, "*all* major Jewish organizations either opposed [Zionism] or, at best, took a non-Zionist position."[1] The American Jewish Committee (AJC) itself espoused an anti-Zionist position when it was founded in 1906. It then adopted a non-Zionist position that lasted until the late 1940s. Only a few years before the establishment of Israel, one of the AJC's leading members decried the Zionist project as undemocratic because it canceled out the rights of others.[2] Thus, contrary to widely accepted notions and impressions of Zionism, generally fostered by Zionist sources, Jewish communities in many countries have not only refused to support Zionist activities, but also have actually fought back.

Perhaps the oldest tradition of Jewish anti-Zionism that has maintained its momentum throughout the years is that of Jewish leftists, who have regarded Zionism as a counterrevolutionary movement—one that collaborated with the colonial powers in order to dominate the Arab world and to drive a wedge between Jewish revolutionaries and the world revolutionary movement. Many Jewish leftists were fully aware of the collaboration of Herzl and the Zionist leadership with the reactionary forces in Europe and the world. At a conference of the British Socialist Party in 1918, a British-Jewish socialist forecast that the Zionist project would turn the Jews into a tool of world capitalism. The conference passed a resolution condemning the Balfour Declaration as a "veiled attempt at the annexation of Palestine."[3] These premonitions were borne out by later events when the British Mandate was imposed on Palestine in 1923.

European Jewish revolutionaries also knew of Herzl's efforts to sell Zionism as the movement that would lure Jewish youth away from revolutionary organizations. Herzl, playing many roles, appeared at times to be assuming the part of the antisocialist and counterrevolutionary politician *par excellence.* He recounted how he once told a German official that the "Jews were not socialists at heart." "Pre-Mosaic Egypt was a socialist state," Herzl said, while Moses was a true democrat.[4] As he explained, "through the Decalogue Moses [had] created an individualistic form of society." It followed, therefore, that the Jews "are and will remain individualists."[5]

Many Jewish revolutionaries were strongly opposed to the Zionist-Ottoman negotiations, which lasted until 1898, on the grounds that the Ottoman government was persecuting the Armenians. But Herzl, well versed in the game of *realpolitik,* felt that he could profit from that issue and, in the manner of latter-day Zionists, he considered initiating "a little press campaign for the cooling of tempers in the Armenian question."[6]

The hostility of the Jewish socialists to the new movement continued unabated. One might say that to this day it remains strong and effective. Over the years it has included among its ranks an impressive number of eminent Jewish intellectuals, such as Rosa Luxemburg, Leon Trotsky, Grigory Zinoviev, Ilya Ehrenburg, and Karl Kautsky. In more recent times, the list has included Maxime Rodinson, Roget Graraudy, Isaac Deutscher, Noam Chomsky, and George Novak. A number of organizations with a large Jewish membership in Europe and the United States still maintain an anti-Zionist, anti-colonialist stand.

Opposition to Zionism has also come from the "diaspora nationalists," who advocate the development of a specific national Jewish character in the diaspora. Though they accept some Zionist premises concerning the nature of Jewishness, the diaspora nationalists do not share the Zionist view of Jewish history and experience. Simon Dubnow, a leading Jewish historian and chief theoretician of this trend, considered Zionism to be just another fraudulent messianic movement. He perceived that the current of Jewish migration since the end of the nineteenth century was running counter to simplistic Zionist logic. There was, he said, an "annual emigration of several hundred men to Palestine, at a time when tens of thousands were leaving for America." On the basis of such a reality, he concluded that the "hopes of transplanting the core of the Jewish people from the diaspora to the historical homeland appear groundless."[7] Dubnow based his own program on a concrete understanding of the Jewish experience, which disregarded the abstract claims and allegations of the Zionists. He devoted all his efforts to the betterment of the political and cultural life of

Jewish communities in their respective homelands, and even predicted that
the "major center of Judaism" would be the United States.[8] Later developments have undoubtedly proved him right.

Among the leading groups that espoused the "diaspora nationalist"
philosophy was the Bund, a Jewish socialist organization founded in
Poland in 1897. Emphasizing what they defined as *Do-igkeit* ("the here-
ness")[9] of the Jewish communities, the Bundists advocated the preservation of Yiddish, not the revival of Hebrew, as a diaspora national language
for Eastern European Jewry. They called for cultural-national autonomy
within socialist states. Though rejecting total assimilation as a solution
for the Jewish question, the Bund nevertheless denounced Zionism as a
bourgeois movement, seeking to achieve the impossible utopian objective
of the ingathering of all Jews into a Jewish state. The Bundists held that
such a goal would only lead to a long and agonizing conflict between Jews
and Arabs, the result of which could not but undermine the economic and
civil rights of Jews everywhere.

Major opposition to Zionism came also from the ranks of both Orthodox and Reform Jews, for despite their theological differences, both groups
reject a nationalist definition of the Jew. The Neturei Karta, a leading
Orthodox anti-Zionist group, in an advertisement published in *The New
York Times* of November 17, 1975, declared that "Zionism, from its very
inception, has been bitterly opposed by the greatest Rabbinical leaders as
being a complete denial of the spiritual and religious character of the Jewish people."

The attitude of the sage Zadok of Lublin (1828–1900) is fairly representative. In one of his letters he described the Zionists as "inciters and
seducers" who are trying to "cast Israel [in the religious sense] into the
infidelity which is destruction." Then, in moving words, he expressed his
deep love for Zion:

> Jerusalem is the height of heights to which the hearts of Israel
> are directed. Our soul too pants and yearns to breathe her pure
> and holy air. In Heaven are my witnesses that I would hasten to
> go there like an arrow from a bow, without fear of the perils of
> the roads, or of the misery and poverty in the country.

However, despite his overwhelming devotion to his faith, the Zadok of
Lublin refrained from "ascending" (departing) to Jerusalem for fear
that his "departure . . . might seem like a gesture of approval of Zionist
activity."[10]

A deep distrust of Zionism and Zionist leadership, and even downright hostility to them, is characteristic of Orthodox literature on the
subject. Rabbi Joseph Hayyim Sonnenfeld described Zionists as "evil

men and ruffians,"[11] referring to Herzl as a fraudulent messiah who came "not from the Lord but 'from the side of pollution.' "[12]

Nathan Birnbaum, credited with having coined the term "Zionism" in its modern political sense, represents an interesting example of Jewish anti-Zionism. Birnbaum was for some time a leading Jewish nationalist. In 1885, he founded and edited the first Jewish nationalist journal in German, and in 1893 published a booklet advocating a solution for the Jewish question along Zionist lines. He also attended the First Zionist Congress (1897) and lobbied briefly on behalf of Zionism. One year later, Birnbaum, recognizing the danger of the Zionist negation of the diaspora, resigned from the World Zionist Organization and advocated diaspora nationalism. In 1908 he was instrumental in convening a conference on Yiddish, which was attended by the leading Yiddish writers of the time and which proclaimed Yiddish as the national language of the Jewish people. After World War I, his views undergoing yet deeper change, he renounced what he termed his atheism and espoused an Orthodox outlook. For the rest of his life he continued to be one of the leading Jewish opponents of Zionism.[13]

It is, of course, difficult to place Ahad Ha'am (Asher Zvi Ginzberg, 1856–1927) in the ranks of the Orthodox, but neither would he feel at home with either the Reform or liberal. He was in many important aspects a Zionist or a Jewish nationalist in the modern, political sense of the word. His whole upbringing in Russia and the limited experience of Jewry there, which was markedly different from the experience of Western Jewry, made him more disposed toward a nationalist outlook. In his sympathetic essay, "Ahad Ha'am: Nationalist with a Difference," Hans Kohn pointed out that the Zionist thinker "could not understand that people of Jewish descent and faith could be, by their cultural roots and free decision, Americans or Italians."[14] Professor Kohn even implied that Ahad Ha'am came very close to the extreme nationalists of the nineteenth century in believing that Judaism was not simply a spiritual tradition but a matter of "biological continuity."[15] Probably this extremism manifests itself in his celebrated essay, "The Transvaluation of Values,"[16] addressed primarily to Jewish Russian youth who defected from Judaism to the philosophy of Nietzsche. In that essay, he tried to appropriate the values and even terminology of Nietzsche's philosophy for Judaism. (He was not an isolated adherent of Nietzsche. Buber and Berdichevsky, as well as many other Zionist writers, also evinced the impact of the German philosopher.) Ahad Ha'am pointed to what he considered the striking similarity between Judaism and the philosophy of Nietzsche. The Jews in Ahad Ha'am's system are a supernation that replaces Nietzsche's superman. It is true that the claim of superiority is predicated on certain moral and spiritual powers the Jews have as a nation, but it is significant that the "agnostic" rabbi[17] from

Russia, very much the son of his time, felt compelled to justify the superiority of the Jews and their chosen-ness in a historical and almost literal sense rather than in a religious and metaphoric sense.

On a more direct plane, Ahad Ha'am's nationalism is manifest in his reply to a letter sent to him by Rabbi Judah Magnes, dated September 18, 1910, about the relation between nationalism and religion. Judaism, Ahad Ha'am said, is the "product of our national spirit—but the reverse is not true."[18] He envisaged the possibility of being a Jew only in a national sense without much reference to the religion. Therefore, it comes as no surprise to know that he participated in "the negotiations of the Zionist leaders with the British government which led to the Balfour Declaration."[19]

Summarizing Ahad Ha'am's reservations about political Zionism, Sir Leon Simon, his Zionist disciple and biographer, said that Ahad Ha'am "rejected the Jewish State as an immediate object of national policy," for what was required was a "truly *Jewish* State" built after long years of preparation and reeducation of diaspora Jews. This process, according to Ahad Ha'am, would rid the Jews of many traits of their diaspora existence, whether these traits are reflected in the stagnation and shiftlessness in Eastern Europe, or "attenuated Jewish consciousness and slavish acceptance of non-Jewish standards and ways of thinking," in the West.[20] Ahad Ha'am is presented by Sir Leon Simon as operating in terms of the quintessential Jew and as advocating more or less an eventual negation of the diaspora. There is undoubtedly some basis for that view, for Ahad Ha'am sometimes viewed the relationship between Jew and gentile as one of natural antagonism (a "lamb among wolves").[21] Such a racist view of the gentiles is usually a corollary of a strong nationalist attitude vis-à-vis the diaspora, viewing it as something doomed to extinction.

The totality of Ahad Ha'am's writings, however, suggests a far more complex outlook. Probably Hans Kohn overstated the case when he said that Ahad Ha'am was "convinced of the permanency of the diaspora."[22] But there is enough evidence in Ahad Ha'am's writings to warrant this view. If the diaspora is a permanent feature of Judaism and Jewry, it necessarily follows that the Jewish state and the ingathering of the exiles are not the one and only way to fulfill Jewish hopes and aspirations, and Jewish destiny ceases to be inextricably woven with the state. Jewish efforts should then be directed toward something more complex and far richer than the construction and defense of a state. Indeed, in many of his writings, Ahad Ha'am viewed the state as a means not an end, the true end being the development of the cultural life of Jewry and the spiritual regeneration of Judaism. Therefore, it was not exactly a cause for jubilation when he saw that all the energies of the Jewish people were to be diverted to the creation "of a little state which would again become football of its strong neighbours,"[23] (or, one might add, its colonial sponsors). He said he sat at the First Zionist Congress as a "mourner at a wedding." It was clear to him, he wrote in a letter to a friend, that destruction exceeded construction: "Who knows whether this was not the last sign of a dying people. I simply cannot get this out of my head."[24]

If Ahad Ha'am's dissent with political Zionist theory was ambiguous, his objections were clear-cut and unqualified when it came to Zionist practice in Palestine. The agnostic rabbi from Russia still felt that the moral values of Judaism were binding on him. He viewed the Jewish prophets not as forerunners of Jewish nationalism but as "prophets of righteousness [who] transcended in spirit political and national boundaries, and preached the gospel of justice and charity for the whole human race."[25] In one of his critical statements on political Zionism, he made a radical break with it when he asserted that "the salvation of Israel will come through prophets, not through diplomats."[26] Responding to the unfolding reality in Palestine as a moralist who called for the "universal dominion of absolute justice"[27] rather than as a diplomat who subjugated means to ends, Ahad Ha'am was one of the first Zionist thinkers to remind the Zionists of the simple yet crucial fact that the Arabs were not "nonexistent." In a letter dated November 18, 1913, he protested against boycott of Arab labor,[28] a practice that was later to be made more systematic through the Histadrut.

In one of his last public utterances, Ahad Ha'am made a pathetic and prophetic protest "against the rumored Zionist murder of an Arab child in retaliation for Arab attacks on Zionist settlements."[29] In an open letter to *Haaretz* (dated September 8, 1922), he expressed his sorrow at the association of "Jews and blood." The teachings of the prophets had saved the Jews from destruction. But the settlers in Palestine do not behave in accordance with these teachings. Toward the end of the letter, Ahad Ha'am asked indignantly: "My God is *this* the end? Is *this* the goal for which our fathers have striven and for whose sake all generations have suffered? Is *this* the dream of a 'return to Zion' to stain its soil with innocent blood?" Then, with words that have the resonance of verses from the Torah, he declared, "And now God has afflicted me to have lived to see with my own eyes that I apparently erred. . . . If this be the 'Messiah' then I do not wish to see His coming."[30]

Ahad Ha'am, it seems, speaks in two voices, one coming out of the nationalist organicist thought of nineteenth-century Europe and the other out of the Jewish religious humanist tradition, which extends back thousands of years and which will presumably survive our time. Zionist historians claim Ahad Ha'am as their own, but non-Zionist Jews make the same claim. Whereas Hans Kohn, for instance, said that Ahad Ha'am called for a "spiritual center,"[31] Sir Leon Simon claimed that the call was for a "national spiritual center."[32] The debate is still going on, but it has lost much of its heat and relevance. Since the issuance of the Balfour Declaration, and much more so since 1948, the argument has become largely academic. All Zionism has become more or less political and practical, with the spiritual and religious overtones reduced to simple elements of diversity within an overall unity. Weizmann claimed to be a disciple of Ahad Ha'am, and even Ben Gurion is considered by some to be one of the heirs of his thought. The Zionists in the diaspora have cast Israel in the role of a cultural center in a crude national sense. Israel, the diaspora Zionists claim, is as much a center for the Jews as Ireland is for the Irish Americans. This is, of course, a simplification, if not a distortion, of Ahad Ha'am's view, but it is undoubtedly a clever distortion. The absorption of Ahad Ha'am's outlook into the political Zionist frame of reference was expedited by the ambiguity of his own statements, utterances, and actions. However, with the growing awareness of the crisis of Zionism and the Zionist state, there is a renewed interest in the work of Ahad Ha'am and the humanist aspects of his thought, especially with regard to the diaspora.

Martin Buber, as indicated earlier, is definitely nationalist in the political Zionist sense, insofar as his theology identifies (no matter how subtly and implicitly) the Jewish people in the religious sense with the idea of the Jewish people in the secular and historical sense. Given this outlook, he felt justified in addressing a letter to Gandhi to secure his sanction for the Zionist project. In an open letter dated 1939, Buber tried to rebut the outrightness of Gandhi's statement that "Palestine belongs to the Arabs." Buber, in a highly mystical manner, glossed over time and history by referring to the Arab "conquest" of Palestine. This argument unintentionally makes Palestine a no-man's-land and fair game for all, thereby lending support to the Zionist efforts at conquest. This seems to be what he says later on in the letter, "The conquered land is . . . only *lent* even to the conqueror who has settled on it—and God waits to see what he will make of it."[33] Knowing Buber's nationalist pantheism and the political bias of his God, it is not very difficult to predict the outcome of this wait-and-see attitude. Gandhi never bothered to reply to this or other letters sent to him by Buber.

Buber, however, classified himself in his open letter to the Indian leader as someone who was striving "for a genuine peace between Jew and Arab."[34] Buber, like Ahad Ha'am, showed breadth of vision and deep moral compassion in matters of practice, for he supported all efforts toward better understanding between the Palestinians and the Zionist settlers and, after 1948, became an advocate of the human and civil rights of the Arabs. At times he tried to distinguish Zionism as a moral ideal and spiritual force, in contrast to Jewish nationalism, which he characterized as a degeneration of the former and mere "collective egoism."[35] But despite all his compassion, Buber's position was ironical: a champion of justice for the Arabs, living in an Arab house whose owners could not go back to dwell in it.

While opposition from the Orthodox wing was strong, Reform liberals proved to be more effective in countering Zionism. Reform Judaism emphasized the universalistic aspects of the faith rather than the more particularistic ones. In the Pittsburgh Platform of 1885, the founders of Reform Judaism (in the United States) recognized "in the era of universal culture of heart and intellect, the approaching realization of Israel's great messianic hope for the establishment of the kingdom of truth, justice and peace among all men." Asserting that the Jews were no longer a nation, the document said further that they therefore expected "neither a return to Palestine, nor a sacrificial worship under the sons of Aaron, nor the restoration of any of the laws concerning the Jewish state." In these unambiguous terms, the incompatibility of Judaism with Zionism's narrow nationalistic interpretation of the faith's ideals was unequivocally stated.

Even in Vienna, Herzl's birthplace, leading Jewish figures expressed their opposition openly. Chief Rabbi Moritz Gudemann refused to lecture on *The Jewish State* after its publication in 1896.[36] He also declined to lend his approval to the concept of a Jewish nation, for he perceived in such a concept "an anti-Semitic label that reduced everything to race and nationalism."[37] In Munich, Jewish opponents of the movement caused the First Zionist Congress (1897), originally scheduled to be held in that city, to be moved to Basel.[38] The Executive Committee of the Association of Rabbis in Germany, on the eve of that Congress, declared its opposition to Zionism on the grounds that the idea of the Jewish national state ran counter to Jewish messianism. The Association proclaimed that it was the duty of Jews as members of a religious community "to serve with complete devotion the fatherlands in which they live."[39]

The two principal Jewish organizations in England, the Board of Deputies of British Jews and the Anglo-Jewish Association, also took similar stands.[40] Dr. Hermann Adler, the chief rabbi of England, and the prominent Jewish philosopher Herman Cohen were both hostile to Zionism. The former believed that since the destruction of the Temple the Jews had been a religious community,[41] and the latter flatly denied the existence of a "Jewish nation."[42]

Several eminent British Jews, especially in the first two decades of the twentieth century, believed that Zionism would encourage anti-Semitism. Laurie Magnus characterized Zionism as a threat to the Jews. He accused the Zionists of being "part-authors of the anti-Semitism they profess to slay."[43] He also considered Zionism detrimental to Judaism, calling it "material messianism,"[44] a phrase reminiscent of Magnus' "pagan Judaism." On the other hand, Claude Montefiore, who preached the "denationalization of Judaism,"[45] felt that the Zionist argument was extremely prejudicial to Jewish interests, and he observed that "anti-Semites are always very sympathetic to Zionism."[46]

The strongest and most articulate opponent of Zionism in England was Sir Edwin Montagu. While recognizing that Palestine was important for the Jews, Montagu believed that it played an equally important role in Christian and Muslim history. A few weeks before the Balfour Declaration was issued, he strongly criticized the document in a memorandum that warned against what he believed to be its anti-Semitic implications. Montagu described Zionism as "a mischievous political creed, untenable by any patriotic citizen of the United Kingdom," and went on to deny the existence of a Jewish nation or a Jewish race linked to Palestine or any territory. He was convinced that the Declaration would lend weight to anti-Semitic demands for the expulsion of the Jews. The "ingathering," according to the Jewish faith, was to be accomplished through "divine leadership," he declared in his memorandum, adding: "I never heard it suggested, even by their most fervent admirers, that either Mr. Balfour or Lord Rothschild would prove to be the Messiah." He said he would rather "disfranchise every Zionist" than deprive British Jews of their nationality, adding that he was "almost tempted to proscribe the Zionist Organization as illegal and against the national interest."[47]

Montagu was equally adamant in his opposition to the formation of the Jewish Regiment, which he said should have been under sovereign command, since it was formed to recruit into the British Army those foreign Jews residing in England who did not know English. Montagu concluded his memorandum on a touching personal note when he declared, "I am waiting to learn that my brother, who has been wounded in the Naval Division, or my nephew, who is in the Grenadier Guards, will be forced by public opinion or by Army regulations to become an officer in a regiment which will mainly be composed of people who will not understand the only language which he speaks—English."[48]

Anti-Zionism among Jews in the United States has an equally long and extensive history. In 1897, the year of the First Zionist Congress, the Central Conference of American Rabbis expressed opposition to the "nationalistic" political Zionist interpretation of Judaism.[49] When the Balfour Declaration was issued, it was immediately disavowed in a petition addressed to the United States Government, signed by 299 American Jews who objected to it on the grounds that it promoted a concept of "dual loyalty."[50]

Opposition came from other quarters. On March 4, 1919, Congressman Julius Kahn of California, along with 30 other prominent American Jews, protested in writing to President Woodrow Wilson against the idea of a Jewish state. The signers expressed their belief that they were "voicing the opinion of the majority of American Jews." To declare Palestine a national home for the Jews, they wrote, would be a "crime against the lofty and world-embracing visions of their great prophets and leaders." The statement went on to say that "a Jewish state involves fundamental limitations as to race and religion, or else the term 'Jewish' means nothing. To unite church and state in any form, as under the old Jewish hierarchy, would be a leap backward of two thousand years." In a happy turn of phrase, very human in its openness, Kahn and the other signers expressed the hope that "what was once a 'Promised Land' for the Jews may become a 'Land of Promise' for all races and creeds."[51]

The American Reform rabbi, Judah Magnes, the first president of the Hebrew University, started off as a political Zionist, then passed through a cultural Zionist phase, and finally arrived at the time when he renounced the idea of the pure Jewish state altogether. In 1904, in a speech at the American Zionist Convention, he set forth the view that "a race cannot give full expression to its genius except in its own home on indigenous soil."[52] In a pamphlet titled *What Zionism Has Given the Jews,* he characterized Zionism as "the conception of the Jews as a people with a national past, a national present and a national future."[53] In 1910, he wrote to Ahad Ha'am about his aspirations to help develop a "national religion" and a "religious nationalism."[54]

The symmetrical juxtaposition of words in these phrases, however, proved troublesome when Magnes had to grapple with the complexity of Jewish existence in the diaspora and Arab existence in Palestine. He resigned in 1915 from the Provisional Executive Committee for Zionist Affairs,[55] and devoted himself to the promotion of Arab-Jewish understanding in Palestine. He called for a system of complete parity of Arabs and Jews, and restrictions on *aliyah.* In an article titled "Like All the Nations," written in 1930, he alerted the Zionists to the fact that Arabs comprised the overwhelming majority in Palestine: "Whereas it may have been in accord with Israelitic needs of the time of Joshua to conquer the land and maintain this position in it with the sword," he said, "that is not in accord with the desire of plain Jews or with the long ethical tradition of Judaism that has not ceased developing to this day."[56] Magnes opposed the Partition Plan and called for the integration of Israel into the Middle East. On April 28, 1948, the Senate of the Hebrew University disavowed him, declaring that anything "bearing the name of Judah Magnes" did not represent its views or those of its academic staff.

As with Ahad Ha'am, the attitude of some prominent Jewish Americans toward Zionism and its goals has been neither simple nor clear-cut. A case in point is Judge Louis D. Brandeis, who once defined Jewishness in terms of a *blood* relationship. Press reaction to his pamphlet, entitled *The Jewish Problem and How to Solve It,* was caustic. *The Los Angeles Times* of June 4, 1915, derided Brandeis' plea that the Jews acquire Palestinian real estate at bargain prices. He was sarcastically advised to "open a real estate office there—and stay there—above all, stay there." Brandeis, in the fashion of latter-day Zionists, described all anti-Zionist Jews as being "against their own people." The *American Israelite* of July 1, 1915, castigated him for "uttering that which is not true" and accused him of being "grossly impertinent."[57]

However, in later years, Brandeis changed his position vis-à-vis Zionism. On one occasion, he asked Judge Julian Mack to speak on his behalf at the Zionist Annual Convention, which was to be held in Cleveland in June 1921, and to assert that "there is no political tie binding together the Jews of the world. . . . The thought of a political status of the Jews of the world was an impossible conception."[58] Brandeis, however, did make a number of pro-Zionist statements after 1921. His vacillation on the issue of Zionism is perfectly understandable. It reflects the untenable position of the diaspora Zionist Jew whose concrete existence is in his real homeland, but who is given to making ideological proclamations about his loyalty to a Jewish homeland, in which he is so reluctant to settle.

Even Albert Einstein was not able to formulate a coherent opinion regarding Zionism. Advancing an argument that is a favorite with Zionists and anti-Semites, he is known to have claimed that a Jew remains a Jew even though he renounces his religion. To illustrate his point of view, he used the image of "a snail [which] remains a snail when it sheds its shells."[59] His views of anti-Semitism, which he expressed in a letter dated April 3, 1920, bring him very close to the Zionist position. Einstein claimed in that letter that anti-Semitism will exist as long as Jews come in contact with gentiles. In a typical Zionist fashion he added that Jews "owe it to anti-Semitism that we can maintain ourselves as a race." He went on to emphasize that he was neither a "German citizen" nor a German of Jewish faith: "I am a Jew and am glad to belong to the Jewish people."[60] Many a time Einstein expressed his sympathy for and lent his support to the Zionist project. After the death of Weizmann, when he was offered the ceremonial post of the President of Israel, he declined to accept, but not for ideological reasons.

However, the attitude of the famous mathematician was far from being one-sided. In 1938, Einstein argued that "the essential nature of Judaism resists the idea of a Jewish state, with borders, an army, and a measure of temporal power, no matter how modest." He even expressed his fears concerning "the inner damage Judaism will sustain" if the Zionist program were implemented. He stated the obvious though overlooked fact that the Jews of the present time are not the Jews of the Maccabee period. Then, in no uncertain terms, he indicated that "a return to a nation in the political sense of the word" is a turning away from the true message of the prophets.[61] That is why, in the same year, he defined his "Zionist" affiliations along cultural lines. The value of Zionism, for him, as he said, lay mainly "in the educational and unifying effect on Jews of different countries," a statement premised on the belief in the permanency of the diaspora and the possibility of coexistence between Jews and non-Jews.[62] In 1946, testifying before the Anglo-American Committee, he expressed his dissatisfaction with the Jewish-state idea, adding that he was *"always* against it,"[63] a forgivable overstatement.

But the thing that disturbed Einstein most was the problem of the Arabs. In 1929, in a letter to Weizmann, Einstein warned against bypassing the Arab question. He counseled that the Zionist settlers should avoid "leaning too much on the English" and should "seek cooperation and honest pacts with the Arabs." Given his awareness of the existence of the Arabs, he foresaw the inherent danger in the Zionist *aliyah.*[64] Einstein's efforts and concern for the Arabs did not wane over the years, even though his Zionist zeal went through different phases. In a letter dated April 1948, he and Rabbi Leo Baeck endorsed the position of Rabbi Judah Magnes, who was advocating the idea of a binational state, adding that he was speaking in "the name of principles which have been the most significant contribution of the Jewish people to humanity."[65]

It should be noted that this was not by any means Einstein's last word on the subject, for he made many pro-Zionist and pro-Israeli statements long after this date. Alfred Lilienthal, in his study *There Goes the Middle East,* referred to what he termed "Einstein's last statement about the state of Israel." This statement, made in an interview with Dorothy Schiff in *The New York Post,* was basically an expression of a deep disappointment in Israel.[66] But the statement is ambiguous, and it does not in any fundamental way question the ideas of Jewish nationalism; it simply decries some aspects of Zionist practice. Einstein's position in this matter is very much like that of Ahad Ha'am and Buber, who equivocated when it came to theory but showed unqualified indignation when it came to practice and injustice inflicted on the Arabs.

THE CENTRALITY OF THE DIASPORA

Political Zionism, despite the adverse response it initially received, became a popular movement, and indeed it enjoys at present the support of a large number of Jews. Many of the erstwhile anti-Zionists and non-Zionists have either moderated or changed their position in the face of a series of Zionist *faits accomplis,* starting with the "Jewish" state and ending with a series of brilliant military victories. Many Orthodox and Reform Jewish groups that earlier took an anti-Zionist position on religious grounds, changed their outlook and theology. The Agudat Israel, for instance, which was launched as an anti-Zionist organization, has now political parties in Israel, some agricultural settlements, and even economic projects subsidized by the Jewish Agency.   The Agudat has also joined many government coalitions.

Reform Judaism has also been retreating from its earlier universalistic attitude to a more ethnic nationalist one. Reform Jewish organizations in the diaspora lobby on behalf of the Zionist state, and there are even "reform" *Kibbutzim* in Israel! This change was not lost on Rabbi Meir Kahane, founder of the Jewish Defense League.   In the summer issue of *Kahane,* a publication dedicated "to the idea of a chosen Jewish people, living in a chosen Jewish land, creating a chosen Jewish society," the nationalist "rabbi" identified many signs of the new trend.   For instance, he pointed out that the new Reform prayer books are "so much more nationalist and particularist and inward looking."[67] Many of the "nationalist" references that were deleted in the nineteenth century were restored, and the humanistic, universalistic line was replaced by a more fashionable one.

But despite all this capitulation to the political nationalist formulations, observers who refuse to take things at face value note that the anti-Zionist or non-Zionist positions are still quite strong, although they do not always take the form of vociferous or organized opposition. Perhaps that is why their effectiveness on the ideological plane is less noticeable, except in the case of some courageous groups and personalities such as the Neturei Karta; Rabbi Elmer Berger's American Jewish Alternatives to Zionism (AJAZ); Dr. Alfred Lilienthal, who publishes *Middle East Perspective* and who has authored many pioneering studies on Zionism; Moshe Menuhin, author of *The Decadence of Judaism in Our Time;* and Edmund R. Hanauer, Executive Director of Search for Justice and Equality in Palestine.

Aside from the "image" of Jews perpetuated by Zionist spokesmen, one finds that most Jewish youth, according to many opinion surveys, "regard themselves as being Jewish by virtue of faith,"[68] not nationality. In a recent article, in the Spring 1976 issue of *Judaism,* Professor Chaim Waxman, a fervent Zionist himself, reported "that most American Jews are *not* Zionists and that Israel is *not* central in their lives." Evaluating the result of various academic studies and surveys, Dr. Waxman came to the conclusion that only 1 percent of the respondents in these surveys would consider settling in Israel or would encourage their children to emigrate. Waxman found that only 13 percent of another sample thought it essential to support Israel, and only 28 percent agreed that "Israel is the center of contemporary Jewish life."   More than two-thirds of the Jewish college students polled "found support for Zionism either irrelevant or unessential to being a good Jew."[69]

This is one clue to an understanding of why, despite all the favorable and supportive reporting on Zionism and its "achievements," the Zionist state's Jewish population is only a fraction of the Jews in the diaspora, and why in New York City alone there are more Jews than in the whole of Israel. As a Jewish-French intellectual has pointed out, the fact is that "five Jews out of six live outside Israel, rooted in their respective diasporas, with their own specific questions that political Zionism cannot answer and cannot even ask." He draws the inevitable conclusion that "a few of them choose or have chosen Israel, but this only throws into greater relief the fact that the majority have chosen the diaspora."[70]

The Jewish-American community is far from dying out, as Ben Gurion opined at the Twenty-Fifth Zionist Congress (1960–1961).[71] It is far from gradually withering away through intermarriage or assimilation, as Rabbi Arthur Hertzberg alleged that it was in the December 1975 issue of *Moment*.[72] Rather, this vibrant community has developed a separate Jewish identity, making distinctly "Jewish" contributions to American culture and history. Its vibrancy and rich variety have been the result of interaction, not with an abstract and purely pan-Jewish culture or history, but with the whole mosaic of American society. Its Jewishness, in practice, does not clash with its American-ness. Rather, the two enrich each other. Like many other Jewish communities around the world, the Jewish community in the United States refuses to conform to the mechanistic Zionist formula, and remains rooted in its own rich and complex historical situation.

The impressive literary achievement of Jewish-American authors deals with the life of Jewish Americans, with their specifically American experience, using an idiom that only Americans can fully grasp. The central figure in Saul Bellow's novel *Henderson the Rain King* has no "organic" link to any territory, except his own country. When he decides to explore his psyche, he flies to black Africa, which serves as an essentially universal and dehistoricized setting for the process of self-discovery. His preoccupations are at once broadly human and distinctly American. Zionism is not relevant to this process, for the hero's perception of himself and his view of reality are not in any way shaped by concepts of Jewish specificity in the national sense. In his other novels, with an explicit Jewish subject, Bellow explores his characters from the standpoint of his own American experience and not with reference to hypothetical promised lands or to a pure Jewish people. That is why a Zionist novelist, Meyer Levin, lashed out at Bellow for his failure to give "descriptions of Jewish meetings, Israeli drives, of the day-to-day absorptions that occupy us on the Jewish scene."[73] Bellow, the winner of the Pulitzer and Nobel prizes in literature, is known to have taken issue with the Zionist concept of the abstract pure Jew, and the Zionist assumption of the need to live in Israel to be a "whole" Jew and not one with a "split personality." He has described himself as "an American loyal to his American experience and culture," whose language and upbringing are American, and who cannot reject 60 years of his life in the United States.[74] For him, the label "Jewish writer" is "intellectually vulgar, unnecessarily parochializing and utterly without value."[75]

Philip Roth is another distinguished American writer who does not fall into the Zionist "collectivist" pattern. The narrator and hero of *Portnoy's Complaint,* which is not exactly an expression of a millennial longing to be ingathered, goes to Israel. He records his personal impressions as his airplane makes "contact with a Jewish airstrip."[76] His feelings are not exactly those of reverence or of dreams fulfilled. With tongue in cheek, he describes the Jewish flag, the Jewish longshoremen, and even "Jewish graffiti."[77] Here in Israel, he sarcastically notes, the Jews are the "Wasps." He even runs into a street gang of Jewish youth and, as if in a dream, he murmurs with frank naiveté, "I am in a Jewish country. In this country, everybody is Jewish."[78] He dutifully visits the Carmel Caves, looks at the Chagall windows, runs into the inevitable ladies from the Detroit Hadassah, then tours the green *Kibbutzim.* He even climbs a "little ways up Massada."[79] Yet at no time does he succumb to the "whole Jew" syndrome.

Philip Roth's character perceives the militaristic and colonialist nature of Israel, a country populated with "the faces of Eastern Europe, but only a stone's throw from Africa."[80] The two women he comes to know in the Promised Land are not the personification of his or any man's dream, each being too much of a she-warrior. The first, a "lieutenant in the Jewish Army," asks him while he is gulping his Jewish beer whether he prefers "tractors or bulldozers or tanks."[81] The second, Naomi, who was born in a kibbutz near the Lebanese border, completed her service in the army, and chose to settle in a kibbutz by the Syrian border, prattles about socialism and the corruption of the American system and way of life.[82] When he makes passes at her, she rebuffs him and ridicules his "*ghetto* humor." By dawn the Jewish-American hero from Newark, New Jersey, has been made to understand that he is "the epitome of what was most shameful in the 'culture of the diaspora.' "

The female warrior-ideologue lectures him on Jewish history, rehashed in Zionist terminology. She bemoans those "centuries and centuries of homelessness" which have "produced just such disagreeable men" as he—"frightened, defensive, self-deprecating, unmanned and corrupted by life in the gentile world." Her view of Jewish history even places the blame for the Holocaust at his doorstep. Yes, it was diaspora Jews, she reminds him, "who had gone by the millions to the gas chambers without even raising a hand against their persecutors, who did not know enough to defend their lives with their blood! The Diaspora! The very word made her furious."[83] It is no wonder that Portnoy's efforts to find a love match in Israel met with dismal failure.

Jewish-American literature and thought in general do not assume the centrality of Israel. When engaged in creative work, even self-proclaimed Zionists or pro-Zionists like Norman Podhoretz fall back on the realities of their own personal experience, casting aside their Zionism. Significantly, even the title of Podhoretz's literary autobiography, *Making It,* is an unmistakably American expression. The main theme of the work is success—how the little Jewish boy from Brooklyn moves to Manhattan and rises from rags to riches and fame. The American odyssey of his soul is primarily a quest for the earthly paradise. The Jewish thread running through the narrative gives his autobiography a specifically East-European flavor, but the overall thrust is unmistakably American. We are reminded that Podhoretz's father is from Eastern Europe and that the author encounters some difficulties in restaurants that do not serve Kosher food. Dominating the autobiography, however, is the theme of success, or trying to "make it" in America. Podhoretz is strongly Jewish-American in his imagination, his creative ability, and his ambitious drive to achieve success. He is American in his life-style and in the way he talks. His pro-Zionist pronouncements and generalizations notwithstanding, Podhoretz is a product of American society, and he uses this society and its values as his main frame of reference.

In his essay titled "The Negation of the Diaspora," Ahad Ha'am characterized the Jewish attitude to the diaspora as "subjectively negative, but objectively positive."[84] This ambivalence characterizes the attitude of the diaspora Zionists and Ahad Ha'am's own outlook. But there are many Jewish intellectuals whose attitude is not characterized by this ambiguity and vacillation. They vigorously argue against the liquidation of the diaspora as a desirable objective, and ardently advocate a multiplicity of centers for Judaism and Jewry. Rabbi Jacob Bernard Agus, a liberal Jewish American who prizes the humanistic and the universalistic aspects of Judaism, is a good representative of that trend. Agus views Jewish identity as determined by a religious rather than an ethnic content. He affirms the importance of the diaspora and points out that Judaism in the United States is not an "exotic cult of quaint and outlandish people, but one of the major faiths of the land."[85] In his global view of Judaism, Jewish Americans are a religious denomination with an ethnic underside, whereas the Israelis are fast becoming "a secular nationality, with the ancient faith as a subordinate reality."[86] Such is the irony of the situation created by Zionist ideology that many observers in both Israel and the diaspora communities argue that the Jewish people will eventually be divided into two distinct groupings—an entirely unexpected consequence of Zionist activism. Rabbi Agus sees Jewish history in terms of an ever-present conflict between a nationalist pseudo-messianism and a universalist messianism. Projecting that conflict on the political plane, he argues that

Zionist Israel is playing a pseudo-messianic role, arrogating to itself "the role of God in disposing of the destinies of Jewish communities," reducing them to the status of "colonies."[87]

Rabbi Jacob Neusner's views are also of interest in the present context. In some of his writings he has suggested an implied common identity between Israel and world Jewry. At other times he has espoused a somewhat different position. For instance, in addressing a conference of the Synagogue Council of America, he once challenged the Zionist concept of Israel as "the national spiritual center of Judaism." It seems that Rabbi Neusner's outlook is based on two definitions of the Jewish people—one religious and cultural, and the other political and national. He claimed a "centrality" for Israel only in "the world-historical existence of the Jewish people." His argument postulated that "so far as Jews live and suffer, are born and die, reflect and doubt, raise children and worry over them, love and work—so far as Jews are human and live within the human condition, . . . Zionism and the State of Israel cannot and do not form the center of their lives."[88] If we accept his thesis that all these activities lie outside the purview of political Zionism, then we are left with none other than narrowly political concerns and the purchase of State of Israel bonds. Rabbi Neusner even asserted emphatically that "to the enduring and eternal issues of life, Zionism and Israel have very little to say," for Zionism, he argued, "never raised the question of Jewish existence as it is phrased by Judaism."[89]

In his book *American Judaism: Adventure in Modernity,* Rabbi Neusner's attitude grew more radical and his views moved closer to those of Rabbi Agus. Zionism is gradually becoming a fake-substitute religion for many Jews, he wrote, and it has appropriated "the eschatological language and symbolism of classical Judaism." As a consequence of that erroneous identification between Judaism and Zionism, Neusner believes that Jewish Americans are not in a position to experience spiritual transcendence, since they "focus their spiritual lives solely on an earthly territory, in which they do not live." Then, restoring the overlooked distinction between a spiritual and a physical Zion, Rabbi Neusner said: "It is one thing for that land to be in heaven, at the end of time. . . . It is quite another to dream of a far-away place where everything is good—*but* where one may go if he wants."[90]

I. F. Stone, one of America's most respected intellectuals, has dealt with the problems facing Jewish Americans in a widely read article in the *New York Review of Books.* Adopting a position reminiscent of Dubnow in some of his statements on the subject, Stone took a dim view of the "Lilliputian nationalism" of the Israelis, which he contrasts with the universalism of the diaspora. Whereas the first is the fruit of a narrow concern with the welfare of one's tribe, he maintains, the second has evolved

naturally from a universalist vision. Stone surveyed the achievements of
the diaspora and found that each period of Jewish creative accomplishment
has been associated with pluralistic civilizations, whether in the Hellen-
istic period, the Arab civilization of North Africa and Spain, or in Western
Europe and America.[91] Recognizing this as a positive phenomenon that is
worthy of being perpetuated and enhanced, he proposed that the problems
of Soviet Jewry be dealt with in a manner diametrically opposed to Zionist
schemes and maneuverings. Instead of Zionist agitation, which has as its
objective an "inevitable exodus" of Soviet Jewry, Stone found that a more
humane and just approach would urge the Soviet Union to "wipe out anti-
Semitism and . . . accord its Jews the same rights of cultural autonomy and
expression it gives to its other nationalities."[92] This argument, free of any
bias or preconceptions about the "quintessential Jew," is based on the
recognition and humanistic acceptance of the plurality of Jewish identities.

Michael Selzer, author of *The Aryanization of the Jewish State,* an
incisive and lucid study of discrimination against Sephardic Jews in Israel,
is yet another proponent of the development of diaspora communities.
Selzer took as his point of departure the Dubnowian premise about a
"Jewish nationhood" with a single but ever-changing center. Like Dubnow, Selzer believed that this center had moved from Europe to the United
States. In his words, Jews in America have been offered "boundless opportunities for free expression and development"—a development that is free
from the insulation of ghetto life and the simplistic secularism of the nineteenth-century assimilationist outlook. In the United States, as Selzer
pointed out, "the Jew can cultivate his Jewishness as fully as he wishes
without thereby impairing his standing as a citizen of this country."[93]
Perhaps what makes the American experiment unique, from the standpoint
of the historical experience or Jewry, Selzer noted, is the fact that there is
no " 'pure' American culture of identity" that excludes the Jews, given the
fact that American society is basically a mosaic of minorities and immigrant communities, each maintaining the best part of its cultural traditions.[94] (In my *Encyclopedia of Zionist Concepts and Terminology,* I
coined the term "neo-Jews" to refer to the post-ghetto Jews of the United
States and their assimilation in a culture relatively free from anti-Semitism
—one that does not force on them either unique economic functions or
specific occupations.)

The Jewish American community, in Selzer's view, has developed its
indigenous traditions to such a degree that the lives and thoughts of Jewish
Americans, including those who evince marked sympathy for Israel, are
hardly "colored or conditioned by anything Israeli." He cited as illustration a symposium on Jewish religious belief to which over "forty of the
most eminent representatives of all the various rabbinical trends in the
United States and Canada contributed." Except for a passing reference

to Rabbi Kook and Martin Buber, both of whom originally formulated their ideas in the diaspora, none of the participants gave any indication that the religious or cultural life in Israel had any impact on his beliefs. This, Selzer declares, is confirmation that a fully Jewish life is possible "with only the most peripheral reference to the Jewish state."[95]

Selzer's diaspora orientation and his awareness of the diversity of the Jewish communities in the world explain his sympathy for the cultural traditions of the Sephardic Jews among whom he worked for several years in Israel. Selzer's ability to shun any fervent commitment to an abstract center of world Jewry makes it possible for him to understand the concrete realities in the Middle East and to formulate his own general principles for an improvement of relations between Israeli Arabs and Jews.

Even though the voices of Jewish dissent from Zionism have hardly ever subsided, Jewish anti-Zionism and non-Zionism are not very strong in the United States at the moment. One reason may be the failure of many Jewish Americans to comprehend the full implications of their Zionist outlook or to come to grips with the contradictions inherent in espousing a Zionist nationalist position while opting to live in the diaspora. However, the very fact that they do not care at present to define their theoretical position is characteristically American in its pragmatism. They prefer to solve their problems one at a time and as they arise.

This pragmatism is dramatically summarized by Michael Selzer. He sees Jewish Americans as leading a full Jewish-American life, yet continuing "to support Israeli fund-raising drives for no other reason than that they view the State as a kind of insurance against renewal of anti-Semitism." According to him, they are "just about as conscious of Israel as a healthy man who sends his premium to the insurance company each month and then forgets all about his policy."[96]

The reluctance of many Jewish Americans to subject their Zionist leanings to scrutiny is hardly helped by the media in the United States, which confuse rather than clarify the issues involved. The Zionist idiom prevails, whether in the Jewish or non-Jewish media of information. Israel is referred to as the "Jewish state," and the Jews as the "Jewish people" with a unique and separate history. They are quite often viewed through Zionist lenses, which can see nothing but pogroms and persecution. Furthermore, there is nearly always the assumed synonymity between Zionism and Judaism, and the concomitant assumption that anti-Zionism is anti-Semitism.

The Arab-Israeli conflict is also projected in Zionist terms and is often described as a *jihad,* or holy war. One hundred million Arabs are pictured as ready to pounce on that "little oasis of democracy, gallantly fighting for its survival." Any news developments that do not support these clichés and stereotypes, or that fail to fit the image, are either dis-

torted or ignored. To cite an example, Saul Bellow's challenge to the
Zionist view of the diaspora hardly made a dent in the American press. A
statement by President Qaddafi of Libya in which he denied that the war
against Israel is perceived by the Arabs as a *jihad,* and even invited the
Jews as a religious community to engage in a dialogue with the Muslims,
was hardly reported at all.[97]

If this is generally true of the American press, it is particularly so of
the Jewish press, which is serviced entirely by the Jewish Telegraphic
Agency. The latter, as is well known, is owned by the Jewish Agency in
Jerusalem. Commenting on this unfortunate state of affairs and on the
total dependence of Jewish-Americans on news favorable to Israel, Selzer
indicated that "no Jewish newspaper in the United States could continue
to exist without the JTA's support in various forms."[98]

Another reason for the relative weakness of the anti-Zionist position
in the United States is the fear of intimidation. It is clear to many Jews
who have tried to argue against the centrality of the state of Israel that their
views will not be tolerated. In fact, one writer who condones this kind of
intolerance went so far as to state in the most unambiguous terms that "in
dealing with those who oppose Israel we are not reasonable and we are not
rational. Nor should we be."[99]

Matters have come to such a pass that some members of the Socialist
Workers Party have recently felt compelled to get a letter from certain
eminent Jewish thinkers and personalities—such as Professor Noam Chomsky, writer Murray Kempton, literary critic Dwight MacDonald, Rabbi A.
Bruce Goldman, *inter alia*—stating that their opposition to Zionism should
not in any way be "equated with anti-Semitism."[100]

In the face of such slurs and attacks, anti-Zionist feelings do not freely
surface in any open or coherent form. The dissenters remain unorganized
and reluctant to form a unified pressure group with a well-articulated
position. This being the case, observers of the Jewish scene are unaware of
the tension that exists within the community. Rather, one is aware only of
the strident vocal Zionist leadership that creates the erroneous impression
that the Jewish communities have uncritically surrendered to a "tribalistic
nationalism."[101]

WHO IS A ZIONIST?

Despite the silence and the intimidation, Israel is still without the vast
majority of "exiles" for whom the state was created. Most Jews do not
show any great enthusiasm "to fly to Israel for anything other than a holi-
day."[102] In 1975, for instance, less than 3,000 Americans (including men,
women, and children) settled in Israel.[103] A vexed prominent Zionist

leader once complained that Jewish Americans view Israel as a Jewish Disneyland or Williamsburg, a marginal place for sightseeing and excitement. Contrary to Zionist proclamations, those diaspora Jews who feel a deep cultural or spiritual link with Zion are not convinced that physical settlement there is at all essential for the fulfillment of their cultural and religious yearnings.

In the Zionist Organization of America, only a handful of the card-carrying members who attend all conferences and parades will emigrate to Israel or send their children to settle there. Many an Israeli ambassador has exhorted a lethargic American Jewry to accept *aliyah* (or immigration) as applying to all Jews—"not merely as an idea, but as a well-organized, efficient, constant process from every city and town, every family."[104]

If one were to give the term "Zionist" its precise political meaning, the true Zionists could indeed be numbered as an infinitesimal minority of Jews everywhere. Various individuals and groups that use that label would turn out to be tenuously related, if at all, to the ideology of political Zionism. A large percentage of those claiming to be Zionist would disavow many of the inherent tenets of the ideology they espouse, were they to be informed of its real goals.

Zionism, claiming to be the only answer to the Jewish question, means, first and foremost, a necessary return to the homeland. Anything short of that is a form of sentimentality parading as Zionism. To ignore this major tenet of Zionism—immigration—and still insist on being called Zionist is "an act of distortion," as Ben Gurion said.[105] He further added that "concepts and names are stubbornly retained long after they have lost their meaning," and the term "Zionist" is no exception. The Zionist leader had the good sense to recognize the obvious, namely, that American Jewry does not consider itself in exile. Given his other observations on Zionism, it is strange that he did not find this fact of life anomalous in any way. It was in fact the vast majority of the so-called Zionists who aroused his resentment, for they stubbornly insisted, and still do, on retaining the term while not showing any desire to emigrate. To Ben Gurion, this was an absurd situation.[106] Another Israeli leader who deplored this phenomenon was Levi Eshkol, a former Israeli prime minister, who once described diaspora Zionism as "an anti-national ideology garbed in 'national' verbiage."[107]

Since the inception of the movement, both philanthropy and political lobbying on behalf of the settlers in Palestine/Israel have masqueraded as Zionism. Philanthropic or monetary Zionism does not go beyond financial aid for nonideological educational, health, or welfare Jewish projects inside and outside Israel. Diplomatic Zionism as well has always lobbied on behalf of the Zionist colonists and later on behalf of the Zionist state. This monetary-diplomatic Zionism, which has been the most prevalent in

"Western democracies," was encouraged since the early days as means of raising funds and peddling influence for the needy and besieged "colonial Zionists"[108] in Palestine. The settlement of the East European Jews in Palestine was to be sponsored by a colonial power and to be subsidized by Jewish funds from West European Jews, such as the Hirsches, the Rothschilds, and other philanthropists who were interested in diverting the East European Jewish migrants away from their own countries.

One can argue that West European and American Zionism has been traditionally of this latter variety, producing funds and political pressure, but practically no immigrants. Interestingly enough, Herzl detected an anti-Semitic strain in this type of philanthropic zeal, since it sought primarily to divert East European Jewish emigrants to another territory and to remove "the paupers as quickly and as far away as possible." As he put it, "many an apparent friend of the Jews turns out, on closer examination, to be no more than an anti-Semite of Jewish origin in a philanthropist's clothing."[109] The joke about the Zionist being a Jew collecting a donation from another Jew in order to send a third Jew to the Promised Land is but an attempt to establish the distinction between two varieties of Zionism and to hint at the unconscious anti-Semitism latent in the monetary-diplomatic variety of that ideology.

Be that as it may, these philanthropic diaspora Zionists are convinced of one thing—that the nationalist goal of settlement in Palestine is not for them. Baron Edmond de Rothschild or some other zealous supporter of the Zionist project was said to have been asked what post he would like to occupy after the establishment of the Jewish state. He jocularly replied that he would certainly choose the post of ambassador of the Jewish state to Paris or London. This form of diaspora Zionism is so common that Ben Gurion was once moved to observe bitterly that after the establishment of the state, there were not even five Zionist leaders "who got up to go to Israel."[110] A few years ago the World Zionist Organization, in deferring to the wishes of American members, did not insist on putting to the vote a resolution making it binding on diaspora Zionist *leaders* to settle in Israel after serving for two terms in the organization.

In a burst of honest anger and protest against this highly diluted version of Zionism, Ben Gurion once tried to draw the line for the Zionists by indicating the incompatibility of "national" Jewishness (that is, Zionism) with American-ness. To him there could be only *one* true "American" Zionist. This person, according to Ben Gurion's purist doctrine, "does not think of himself as an American. He thinks of himself only as a Jew"[111]— a pure Jewish national.

Even though Ben Gurion did not reveal the name of this one worthy exception, Nahum Goldmann may have been the person he had in mind. As head of the World Zionist Organization, Nahum Goldmann had devoted his life to the Zionist cause, but he did become an Israeli citizen in 1962. However, even Goldmann does not at present meet the purist Zionist criterion. In 1968, he was granted Swiss citizenship, which he had applied for "for personal and economic reasons."[112] More important are his views regarding diaspora existence. He does not hold the traditional negative views of the diaspora which other leaders espouse, and he repeatedly emphasizes the necessity of defending the civil rights of Soviet Jews within the USSR, placing the need to defend these rights above the central Zionist goal of settlement in Israel. In his autobiography, Goldmann defined the relationship between the diaspora and Israel in complex terms, describing as "somewhat naive" the Zionist idea that a normal life for the Jews "is possible only in a homeland and that the diaspora is in some way abnormal." Goldmann noted that Jews have spent more years in the diaspora than in the homeland, and therefore their existence, far from being abnormal, is a more characteristic condition of Judaism than statehood.[113] He suggested that there should be more interaction between the diaspora and Israel in order to guarantee the "continued existence of both branches of the people."[114]

Such a sophisticated attitude is a convenient theoretical construct, implying many contradictory premises, which probably only diaspora Zionists can grasp and sustain. The broad Jewish masses in the United States, who consider themselves Zionists because they give generously to the United Jewish Appeal and dutifully buy State of Israel bonds, cannot even begin to grasp such contradictions. More often than not they are unaware of the ideological content of their donations, believing their actions to be simply an expression of their American Jewishness and of their traditional generosity.

A naive diaspora Jew will pay for a university to be founded in Jerusalem out of noble and charitable motives, but for the Zionist this act is an expression of "nationalist renaissance,"[115] as Weizmann observed. Richard Crossman, his British friend, once said that even while pitying and despising fully or partly assimilated Jews, Weizmann was nevertheless always ready "to collect their money for the [national] cause."[116]

One must also exclude from the Zionist category the Jews in the United States who support Israel because they are "good American citizens" and believe that in supporting Israel they are also furthering the interest of their own country. That American and Israeli interests are identical is an argument frequently used by Zionist leaders to win more adherents. As a matter of fact, diaspora Zionists in America have sometimes tried to solve their dilemma as "Zionists in voluntary exile" by capitalizing on the legitimate national feelings of Jewish Americans. Brandeis declared in 1915 that "multiple loyalties are objectionable only if they are inconsistent," and that in the case of Zionism, no such inconsistency exists.

He went further, stating that "loyalty to America demands rather that each American Jew become a Zionist,"[117] liberalism (in his opinion at least) being an underlying premise of both Zionism and American society.

Ben Gurion found it difficult to accept the logic underlying diaspora Zionism. For him it was unthinkable that a Zionist could take pride in his Jewish homeland if he knew "that neither he nor his descendants will ever live there."[118] Such a Zionist is nothing more than a "friend of Israel," no different from other Jews,[119] Ben Gurion believed. One might add that such a Jew is no different, either, from any non-Jew who considers it in the best interests of the United States that it align itself with Israel. His support for Israel is neither specifically Jewish nor Zionist; it is pragmatic and is maintained in light of political considerations. Thus, it can change with changing circumstances. To go on labeling this type of support as specifically Jewish or Zionist is quite misleading.

As for those Jews who are interested in a specifically Jewish cultural or religious revival in their own homelands, neither can they be termed Zionists because their behavior is no different from that of many ethnic or religious groups interested in maintaining their identity and in revitalizing their heritage. For them, Jewish statehood and political peoplehood are not in the least relevant to their interests.

When we consider the Jewish emigrants from the Soviet Union, no one can vouch that the majority among them go to Israel for other than strictly economic reasons. For some of them, Israel is not a "homeland" at all. Many have never learned Hebrew. Others are not Jewish, having left the Soviet Union with Jewish husbands or wives.[120] In an article in *The New York Times Magazine* by Faubion Bowers, titled "Only—and Lonely in America," some of the emigrants described their reasons for leaving the Soviet Union. One saxophone player said he left because "life was so boring," and a professor of algebra explained that he left because he knew it was time "for him to leave." A third emigrant indicated that he left because he wanted to live "better." To underscore this point, he said that he came "not to have a car, but to have a car with a bigger engine." A tailor from Kiev proved to be an exception to the rule, for he found his life as a Jew in the Soviet Union intolerable; yet even he chose to settle in the United States rather than make his home in Israel.[121] It is impossible to know how many Soviet emigrants were like a certain Ivan, who, according to a *Washington Post* article, left Israel after working for one year in a kibbutz because he disliked the religious intolerance and "the hot climate."[122]

The Institute for Jewish Policy Planning and Research describes the typical emigrant as someone who did not flee persecution, but rather was a "migrant of choice," coming for "essentially nonideological motives." The findings of this report are corroborated by another report, issued in

November 1974, by the Synagogue Council of America, which states that the American philanthropic response sees the emigration campaign as an effort to save a remnant of the Jewish people, but that those who choose to emigrate do not share such romantic illusions.[123]

If Soviet Jews lack nationalist or ideological motivation, many American Zionists, despite their protestations to the contrary, also lack such motivation. "Immigration to Israel is a function of absorption," a group of influential Jewish Americans told an Israeli journalist, dropping all their messianic pretensions. The significance of this fact was quite obvious to the reporter from *Maariv,* who wrote that "for so many square metres of housing and such and such salaries and concessions even now, these people would be ready to march in the vanguard of the struggle for Jewish existence."[124]

When the Jewish Agency closed down its immigration offices in several American cities and began to recruit among the ranks of the Jewish unemployed in New York City and around the country, its recruits cannot and should not be labeled "Zionists." Even though the Agency sought them out as "Jews," those who responded did so as "unemployed," looking for economic opportunities elsewhere.

Even huge donations in themselves sometimes prove not to be motivated by any Zionist fervor to support Israel. Doubts as to the motives of United States housing magnate William Levitt were aroused by an article in the January 1, 1975, issue of *Haolam Hazeh* which reported the deal that Levitt had struck with Bar-Ilan University in Tel Aviv, to which he had donated $6 million. Of the $6 million, $5 million were to be deposited with the Anglo-Palestine Bank, in order to be loaned back "to Levitt's own companies, allowing him to deduct six million dollars for tax purposes, while donating only one in his lifetime."[125] This is hardly Zionism.

Yair Bar-am, in the November 1975 issue of Breira's *Interchange,* wrote that "it has suited the Israeli Government to identify Zionism with monetary support for the state and unquestioning support of its policies." He argued that this loose and imprecise definition had allowed traditionally "non-Zionist organizations like the United Jewish Appeal and the American Jewish Committee to call themselves 'Zionist.' "[126] He further accused these organizations of hypocrisy when they assert that "Zionism is the national liberation movement of the Jewish people," because, as he noted, "they certainly do not subscribe to the view that they themselves living in America are 'unliberated.' "[127]

Breira, a new Jewish organization whose emergence is one of the more positive developments on the Jewish-American scene, is itself a mild example of this confusion. Breira, a Hebrew word meaning "choice," sharply contrasts with *ein breira* (no choice), an Israeli slogan adopted by Israeli Foreign Minister Moshe Dayan and other determinist militaristic leaders inside and outside the Israeli establishment. "The alternative toward which Breira is working," explains one of the organization's booklets, "is an independent American-Jewish community capable of revitalizing diaspora Jewish life."[128]   Looking with favor on the diversity of Jewish identities in the world implies an acceptance of the diaspora and its existence as inherently worthwhile. The diaspora in Breira publications emerges as more Jewish, more creative, and far more dynamic than the Israeli community.

The writings of some influential members of Breira offer an insight into their thinking. In an interesting article entitled "Beyond Idolatry: Toward a Transnational Alternative," Arthur Waskow, member of Breira's Executive Board, drew an outline for what he considered to be the ideal relationship between the diaspora and Israel. He advocated a relationship of "loving criticism" between the two sides. Such a relationship does not presume the existence of an "organic link" with Israel, as Zionist literature claims.[129] Waskow even suggested that a transnational Jewish alternative will replace the exclusively national Zionist one that supports Israeli policy unreservedly.[130]

Breira's view of the historical experience of Jewry, if we are to take Waskow's opinions as representative, is diametrically opposed to that of Zionism. Waskow spoke of a "post-ghetto diaspora" characterized by a Jewish creativity that is enhanced through constant "encounter with universalist Christianity, liberalism and radicalism." Such a relationship with the gentiles is not one of eternal hostility and alienation. Rather, it signifies a healthy interaction and reciprocity. "The trade-off," Waskow wrote, "is assimilation—but the pay-off . . . is greater social and intellectual invention within Jewish life."[131]

In Waskow's universalistic approach, reminiscent of the Jewish prophetic tradition in its finest moments, generosity and openness to the world at large reach out to include the Arabs. There is a realization here that "love of the land" is a quality shared by both Jews and Palestinians.[132] If this is Breira's philosophy, it is hoped that it can be translated into wider influence among the Jewish-American community and eventually into meaningful political action.

Waskow's language reminds one of the anti-Zionist reference to Palestine as an open-ended land of promise rather than the Zionist self-enclosed Promised Land. This generous language is in strong contrast to the routine statements enunciated by Menahem Begin, Yitzhak Rabin, Yigal Allon, Moshe Dayan, Shimon Peres, Abba Eban, and many others in Israeli society whose position is that the Palestinians do not exist, or if they do, they have no title to the land.

But despite all these differences, Breira at times labels itself "Zionist." One is at a loss to detect any common attributes between Waskow's humanistic vision and the narrow views implied in some statements by Goldmann, who once described "ghettoization" as "the salvation of the American-Jewish community"[133] and by Golda Meir, who defined Zionism as the force that should "harness all Jews," bringing them to Israel, helping them, if they remain in the *galut,* to have a "meaningful Jewish life." She told Jewish Americans that should they ever yearn for a higher education, it should be "the university in Jerusalem and not any other"; and if they ever "talk of a summer camp, it should be a summer camp in Israel and not any other"; and she called on them to create "a Jewish ghetto in free America," where Jewish children are "brought up in Jewish homes with one goal and one thought, to be in Israel."[134]

Fortunately, the Breira group distinguishes between Zionism and Israel. Bar-am, for instance, viewed the policies of Israel as merely Israeli and not necessarily Zionist. Israel, according to that definition, even though brought into being by the efforts of the Zionist movement, "must stand on its own [as a state], for it can only represent the will of its *citizens,* not the will of Jews or even Zionists living abroad."[135] There is an implied assumption here, namely, that Zionism is an ideology and an ideal, whereas Israel is merely *one* form of Zionist practice, not the only feasible one. Such an interpretation is difficult to accept, given an entire century of Zionist policies and actions that have produced unmistakable patterns with the most adverse consequences for the cause of peace in the Middle East.

Be that as it may, Bar-am's definition of "Zionism" is moral, not national; as such, one can say that Breira's concern with the Middle East and its Jewry, whether in Israel or Morocco, is humanitarian or cultural, not political or nationalistic. The Arabs can appreciate such an attitude as both legitimate and positive, and therefore worthy of encouragement and support. The Zionist state, if we accept *that* definition, has no special significance apart from that attached to any other state. It should be viewed as *a* state, originating under specific historical circumstances, and maintained by virtue of certain military aid and political power.

However, if Breira, in one way or another, endows Israel with any special status that gives it the right to speak for world Jewry and to continue its policy of the "ingathering of the exiles," then it is obvious that this organization, too, is espousing a nationalist position, but is reluctant to face up squarely to its full implications. If that is the case, Breira is superficially moderating its stand by a series of lofty and noble statements.

Regrettably, the history of Zionism is full of thinkers like Martin Buber, whose theology and vision definitely implied a "transfer" of the Jews and therefore an expulsion of the Palestinians—even though Buber did not want to admit it, and despite the fact that throughout his life he called for a moral Zionist policy. All things considered, what holds hope for the future is the fact that there have always been Jews who had the courage to face up to the full implications of their moral commitments and religious convictions, and who were able to reject the narrow nationalist illusion that distorts Judaism and its values.

5

ZIONIST SETTLER COLONIALISM: ORIGINS AND SPECIFIC TRAITS

RESTORING THE JEWS

Political Zionism is indebted for its very origin and success to non-Jewish religio-colonialist ideas and forces. Like anti-Semitism, Western colonialism paved the way for the birth of political Zionism, but above all, it gave it the power to survive and succeed. Long before the idea of the Jewish people as a political entity began to gain credence among Jews, another variety of gentile "Zionism," namely, the Christian restorationist movement, had appeared on the scene. The campaign for restoring the Jews to their Promised Fatherland had mythical sanction in the various eschatological doctrines concerning the Second Coming of Christ to rule the world from Jerusalem for a millennium. Such restorationist movements, particularly in Protestant Europe, flourished in the sixteenth and seventeenth centuries, the age of mercantilism and of the great geographical discoveries, as well as of the early forms of colonialism.

Christian restorationism viewed the Jew primarily as an instrument in its own scheme of salvation. The Jew was to be restored to Palestine in order to expedite the process of his conversion, an essential step for the coming of the millennium and also a sure sign of it. This religious myth was gradually remolded by the political situation in Europe in the early nineteenth century, which emphasized certain aspects of the myth at the expense of others. The religious objectives were conveniently adapted to a program for colonization, predicated on the return and settlement of the Jews. The Jews were perceived within the Christian scheme of salvation and redemption both as members of a religious community and as potential converts. Additionally, they were simply to comprise a community that could be settled in Palestine or elsewhere to serve colonial interests. *Eretz Yisrael* was both the Holy Place of the religious vision and a land at the heart of the Ottoman Empire, providentially lying along the route to India.

In the nineteenth century, the restorationist movement was given strong impetus in England and France by the rise of the Eastern question and the European (Christian) ambition to inherit the Ottoman Empire. The weakness of that dying empire assumed apocalyptic significance in the minds of the restorationists, and many "European statesmen began to view the idea of the Jews' return to Zion as a political means of ousting the Turks from the Middle East," as the author of the entry on the "Restorationist Movement" in the *Encyclopedia of Zionism and Israel* indicated.[1] Even though the restorationists were not a major political force, they undoubtedly helped shape the thinking and political vocabulary of the time, first among the gentiles and then among Jews, especially in the England of that era.

From the very beginning, restorationism generally assumed both an idealistic religious garb and a hard political dimension. It called for the restoration of the Jews to Palestine to fulfill biblical prophecy as well as to open the markets of the East. In his *History of Zionism*, for instance, Nahum Sokolow attributed British sympathy for Zionist aspirations to such lofty reasons as the "Biblical character of the English People," and what he termed "the Bible in English Literature," as well as "the love for Palestine in England." As an afterthought, he added a fourth and last reason, which he called "English Politics in the Near East."[2] Even though Sokolow recognized the colonial dimension basic to British sympathy, he nevertheless gave prominence to the romantic restorationist thought.

When Herzl went to Palestine in 1898 to explore the possibilities for Zionist colonization and to meet with the Emperor Wilhelm II of Germany, someone there took him to be a functionary of the English mission among the Jews to convert them to Protestantism.[3] Such overlapping between the religious and the political aspects endures to this day, for many people still speak of the Zionist settlement in Palestine in religious as well as in political terms. Indeed, after the 1967 war, some Christian missionaries saw Israel's military victory as a literal sign of the approaching millennium, and accordingly intensified their activities in the Zionist state!

The Jewish response to Christian (Protestant) restorationist overtures remained lukewarm for a long time. No Jewish voice was raised to welcome the idea or support it, so the call for terminating the state of "exile" remained largely a gentile pursuit.[4] But toward the mid-nineteenth century, with the intensification of the East European Jewish question, Jewish thinkers began to respond more positively to gentile Zionist formulations.

In a typically Zionist fashion that ignored the complexities of history,

Weizmann harked back to "those greatest soldiers of history [Julius Cae-sar, Alexander, and Napoleon] who recognized the immense importance of Palestine in their Eastern schemes and were markedly pro-Jewish in their foreign policy.[5] Napoleon Bonaparte, the first European invader of the Middle East in modern times, was described by Weizmann as "the first of the modern non-Jewish Zionists."[6] In his April 20, 1799, appeal to all the Jews of Asia and Africa, Napoleon had urged them to follow the French command so that the "pristine splendor" of Jerusalem might be restored. He promised to return the Jews to the "Holy Land," if they would "aid his forces."[7] Despite its romantic language, Napoleon's appeal stemmed from his imperial interests and his desire to block Britain's route to India. Needless to say, the Jews of the East did not heed his call, and they fought alongside their Arab compatriots, under Ottoman leadership, to repel the invading French troops.

Ernest Laharane, the private secretary of Napoleon III in 1860, at a time of increasing French intervention in Syria, argued in favor of the economic gains that would accrue to Europe if the Jews were to be settled in Palestine. Given that European industry was always on the lookout for "new markets as an outlet for its products," Laharane suggested that it was "imperative to call the ancient nations back to life." To him it was not a question of converting them or making them "see the light," but rather of helping to "open new highways and byways to European civiliza-tion." Laharane believed that "all Europe would support Jewish acquisi-tion of Palestine from Turkey."[8] Significantly, Laharane's proclamations predate those of Moses Hess, the proto-"socialist" Jewish-Zionist thinker. Hess' *Rome and Jerusalem*, published in 1862, includes extensive quota-tions from Laharane's brochure, *La Nouvelle Question d'Orient*.[9]

In the eighteenth and nineteenth centuries, Protestant England, the leading colonial power, was a hotbed of restorationist ideas. A typical exponent of British gentile Zionism was Colonel George Gawler (1796–1869), onetime governor of South Australia, who throughout the 1840s advocated Jewish resettlement in Palestine as a means of ensuring un-broken lines of communication between the various parts of the empire.

Political arguments were always presented by the restorationists in such a manner as to reflect a providential view of history. As Gawler saw it, nothing less than Divine Providence had placed Syria and Egypt between England and the most important regions of British "colonial and foreign trade." England, called upon to civilize the world, had already extended its influence to Egypt, and it was time for Syria to be rejuven-ated through a settlement of "the real children of the soil, the sons of *Israel*."[10] Already in these early religio-political arguments one can detect hints of the interlocked destinies of Western imperialism and Zionist colonialism.

Long before the advent of Jewish Zionism, a British gentile colonial "Zionist" evidently had decided to use the Jews as a pawn in the attempt to put down the Arabs. In a letter to the British ambassador in Istanbul, capital of the Ottoman Empire, Lord Palmerston once declared that if the Jewish people were to return to Palestine "under the sanction and protection and at the invitation of the Sultan," who was then the dominant power in the Arab world, they would act as a "check upon any future evil designs of Mehmet [Muhammed] Ali or his successor."[11] Muhammed Ali's accession to power made Egypt the subject of European concern and thereby escalated restorationist ambitions. It should be noted here that Muhammed Ali, though no Arab himself, was the first modernizer in the Arab world. To England and other potential colonial powers, he represented a "threat" to Western colonial ambitions in the region, for he was an early expression of a nascent national power in the Arab East.

Another prominent gentile Zionist was the Reverend William H. Hechler (1845–1931), who spoke of the project of restoring the Jews to Palestine in theological as well as political terms. Hechler, born in South Africa, was the chaplain of the British Embassy in Vienna. There he met Herzl, with whom he developed a life-long friendship, and whom he introduced to various political figures in Europe. Hechler was preoccupied with calculations concerning the end of the world and the eventual much-hoped-for conversion of the Jews. But his religious preoccupations were not without a political colonialist content.

Overlapping theological and political considerations account for the fact that Hechler attended a conference in 1882 which dealt with the settlement of Jewish immigrants from Rumania and Russia. But two years later, when he wrote a pamphlet about the same socioeconomic problem, he used a biblical idiom and talked of the need for "restoring the Jews to Palestine according to the Old Testament prophets." Both the conference and the booklet *predate* the first Zionist congress and Herzl's own *Jewish State*, just as Laharane's proclamations predated those of Hess.

Laurence Oliphant (1829–1888), born in South Africa, also exemplified this type of theo-political thinking. Like Reverend Hechler, he "shared much of the facile anti-Semitism of his time." A leading proponent of the idea of settling the Jews in Palestine, he corresponded with Disraeli and was sent on a trip to Palestine, with official British government backing, to conduct a feasibility study concerning the proposed settlement. He concluded that the scheme of the Jewish state in this region would ensure the "political and economic penetration of Palestine by Britain."[12] In 1880, on his own initiative, Oliphant published a book advocating Jewish settlement, though again the frame of reference was more biblical than political. In 1882, he actually settled in Palestine with his Jewish secretary, Naftali Herz Imber, author of the *Hatikva*, which became the Zionist (and later the Israeli) national anthem. Curiously enough, this Christian Zionist spent the rest of his life promoting Zionist settlement, whereas the author of the Zionist-Israeli national anthem emigrated to the United States and settled and died there.

Colonel J. C. Wedgewood (1872–1943), whose pamphlet *The Seventh Dominion* was published in February 1928, was among the most idiosyncratic advocates of the restoration of the Jews. The people of Moses and the Prophets, he said, could be settled in Palestine "to be of real political and commercial service to the empire." He thought Zionism was a movement that would restore to the Jews that "corporate national confidence they appeared to lack."[13] Wedgewood perceived a basic affinity between the British and the Jews because both are "moneylenders," wanderers among strange people, traders who look down on those with whom they trade. Both Jews and Britishers, Wedgewood asserted, are unpopular, ever willing to use their mutual Holy Books as "conventional justification for all that needs justification in our relations with mankind."[14]

The most dedicated British gentile colonial Zionist was Orde Wingate (1903–1944). Born in India to missionary parents, young Wingate joined the British Army and worked in the Sudan, where he learned Arabic; but he could never overcome his hatred of Islam and its Holy Book the Koran. In 1936 he was transferred to Palestine, where he worked as an intelligence officer for three years. It was during that period that Wingate had the chance to cooperate with the Zionist settlers.

Wingate, like most gentile Zionists, was a fanatical fundamentalist who, according to Ben Gurion, could give a "military interpretation" of the "historic events" of the Bible, "as if they had happened yesterday."[15] Like most gentile Zionists, Wingate was convinced beyond doubt that he "was engaged in a divinely appointed task, charged like Gideon before him, to 'go in this thy might, and thou shalt save Israel.' "[16]

Wingate's sense of mission, coupled with his belief in "elemental power," made him a charismatic figure for the Zionists. His "magnetic hold" over them was such that "all the high officials of the Jewish Agency and the Haganah were ready to do his bidding."[17] He would look at the settlers with "contempt and disbelief" for daring to make their plans without consulting him. Without his advice, he told them, they were "bound to blunder into disaster." As General Dayan recalls, "though he was such a small man, when he was disdainful he could make [one] . . . feel as tiny as a mouse."[18]

The main concern of this overpowering military personality was not merely salvationist or redemptive. Behind his activism on behalf of the Zionists was his concern for British colonial interests. Throughout his life Wingate entertained the notion that a modern, industrial Zionist state under the protection of Britain would watch over the Mediterranean and, in the bargain, represent the best hope for Arab development.

He was called by some "Lawrence of Judea," the absurd assumption, still common in Zionist circles, being that the whole world was purely a British "product." Even though Wingate assumed there was a certain mutuality of interests among British imperialists, Zionist settler-colonists, and Arab nationalists, his real loyalties lay with the first two groups only. He paid mere lip service to the interests of the natives.

Wingate was deeply concerned about the failure of the British regular troops "to protect the [Haifa] pipeline" against Arab resistance in the late 1930s. He pledged that if he were allowed a free hand to organize mixed squads of British soldiers and Zionist settlers, "he could wipe out the [Arab] gangs . . . and see that the oil flows freely once more to the refinery at Haifa."[19]

The British command reluctantly accepted the idea of forming the Night Squad, whose basic doctrine was offensive rather than defensive. Instead of waiting for the Arab enemy to attack, the settlers were to form mobile units and seek out the enemy in his own territory under cover of darkness. Some members of the Haganah objected to Wingate's tactics, fearing that an offensive against the Arabs would further exacerbate the already strained relations between Zionist settlers and their Arab neighbors.[20] Wingate, however, argued that the Night Squad was proof that "the spirit of the Maccabees still lived" in the Jewish youth.[21] This was of great help in overcoming Zionist objections.

In his book, *Gideon Goes to War,* Leonard Mosley gave us a glimpse of one of these squads in operation. The mission usually started with Wingate firing a few shots at an Arab village, thus provoking "a fusillade of fire obviously from the Arabs." The Arabs would converge in search of the attackers, whereupon they were quickly surrounded. In one instance, of the nine Arabs searching for the attackers, five were killed and four captured. Wingate, "calm and serene," praised the members of his squad, assuring them that they were "fine boys" who *would* "make good soldiers."[22]

The interrogation of the Arabs regarding their hidden arms was then begun. When they refused to cooperate, the Mosley account goes, Wingate "reached down and took sand and grit from the ground," forcing it into "the mouth of the first Arab" and pushing it down "his throat till he choked and puked." But the Arabs would not give in, so the gentile Zionist adopted a different approach. He turned to one of the Jews and "pointing to the coughing and spluttering Arab, said: " 'Shoot this man.' " The Jew hesitated, whereupon Wingate said in a tense voice, "Did you hear? Shoot him!" The Zionist settler obediently shot the Arab, and the other prisoners were finally induced to talk.[23]

Writing his memoirs in later years, General Dayan reminisced that many of the men with Wingate "had become officers in the Israeli army which fought and defeated the Arabs." Dayan makes it clear that it was not only Wingate's immediate disciples and collaborators who benefited from his knowledge and tactics. "In some sense, every leader of the Israeli Army even today is a disciple of Wingate. He gave us our technique, he was the inspiration of our tactics, he was our dynamic."[24] This is a view with which Ben Gurion fully concurred, for he believed that Wingate's military doctrines, adopted by the Israelis, were to play an important part in the 1948 war,[25] and that "the Haganah's best officers were trained in the special Night Squad."[26]

Wingate, with his deep sense of mission and his militaristic biblical exegesis, was fully aware of the role he was playing. In a military training course he gave at Ein Harod for "the Haganah's best young officers," Wingate, adopting the theo-militaristic vocabulary of fundamentalism, usually opened the course with the remark, "We are establishing here the foundations for the army of Zion."[27]

PRO-ANTI-SEMITISM

Though it may have appeared nebulous at times, the outlook of the gentile colonial Zionists, even as it overlapped religious motives and concepts, was largely determined by their specific political and economic interests. The core of their argument was mainly political; nevertheless an exclusively political account would probably be incomplete and even simplistic, for behind gentile Zionism there lurks a deep-seated hatred for Jews.

British historian Arnold Toynbee, in *A Study of History,* took note of the link between "subconscious anti-Semitism" and "Christian pro-Zionism."[28] It is in this area that gentile Zionism saw eye to eye with Jewish Zionism, thus forging an enduring alliance between each other.

A good case in point is Anthony Ashley Cooper (1801–1885), the seventh Earl of Shaftesbury, who was a member of the London Society for Promoting Christianity Among the Jews.[29] Out of "love and veneration for the Jews," Cooper, in 1840, pressed a Zionist scheme on Lord Palmerston, suggesting a number of formulas for the establishment of a Jewish homeland. In the same year, he addressed a memorandum to all the Protestant rulers and leaders in Europe and the United States, advocating the return of the Jews.[30] This theme was later to be pursued by Herzl, who expressed the hope that the Zionists would reach their "goal with the aid of the rising Protestant power."[31]

But behind the romantic veneration there lay more negative feelings. The Earl of Shaftesbury himself had earlier objected to the removal of

political restrictions against British Jews as "an insult to Christianity."[32]
The Earl considered Jews nothing more than "voluntary strangers" pos-
sessing no claim to citizenship;[33] hence, his belief in the need to restore
the Jews to Palestine. "If Syria and Palestine," he wrote, are important
for the British Empire, and if this geographical area needs "capital and
population, the Jews can give it both." "England," he said, has a "special
interest in promoting such restoration" or transfer. It must "foster the
nationality of the Jews and aid them."[34] The fundamentals of Shaftesbury's
perception are simultaneously anti-Semitic and Zionist: The Jew is a
trader by nature, an alien outsider, who therefore should be placed outside
gentile Christian society in a little ghetto or a state of his own so that
he may better serve the interests of the gentiles.

Such a perception of the Jews accounts for the recurrence of the
words "gratitude" and "loyalty" in Zionist colonial literature, either Jewish or gentile. For instance, Leopold Amery, a member of the British war-
cabinet secretariat during World War I, once declared that the British were
aware of the temporary nature "of our protectorate in Egypt." Hence,
the Balfour Declaration sought to create in Palestine a "prosperous community bound to Britain by ties of gratitude and interest."[35] Sir Roland
Storrs, the first civilian governor of Jerusalem under the British Mandate,
believed that the Zionist enterprise was one "that blessed him that gave,
as well as him that took, by forming for England 'a little loyal Jewish Ul-
ster' in a sea of hostile Arabism."[36] The quasi-religious overtone in Sir
Roland's statement is quite characteristic of Jewish and gentile colonial
Zionist rhetoric.

Kaiser Wilhelm II sometimes suppressed his religious anti-Semitism
in order to cooperate with the Jewish Zionists, but only to lapse later into a
kind of economic anti-Semitism. He underscored "the immense power [of]
that international Jewish capital," and appreciated the potential advantages for Germany in sponsoring the Zionist program. He thought "it
would be an enormous gain for Germany if the world of the Hebrews
looked up to . . . [Germany] with gratitude."[37]

Many of the leading British statesmen who supported Zionism entertained in one form or another a racist outlook concerning the Jews.
Joseph Chamberlain, as his biographer indicates, was one such anti-
Semite who viewed Zionism as a means of serving British colonial interests and of ridding Europe of the Jewish question. A British colony in
Sinai, according to his line of thinking, would not only extend the British
sphere of influence, but would also ease the pressure represented by
cheap Jewish immigrant labor in Europe.[38]

Lloyd George, the British prime minister who presided over the cabinet that issued the Balfour Declaration, was described by his secretary
as someone who "does not care a damn for the Jews or their past or their

future."[39]   Leonard Stein detected in some of Lloyd George's speeches a "streak of ordinary vulgar anti-Semitism." In his 1904 speech on the East Africa project, and in several others, Lloyd George found it natural to make uncomplimentary remarks about the Jews.[40] Stein, however, in trying to apologize for this gentile Zionist, cited his sympathy for the Jews "in the abstract." What Stein failed to see is the fact that to abstract the Jew, to view him outside any concrete situation, is the very essence of anti-Semitism. Worthy of note also is Stein's distinction between "vulgar anti-Semitism" and an implied natural, clean anti-Semitism. The latter is apparently a more respectable variety, a form of legitimate national self-defense against the foreign Jewish nationals, which Klatzkin and other Zionists accepted and even praised.

Lord Balfour, after whom a *moshav* (a cooperative agricultural settlement) in Israel is named, is another case in point. His contribution to the achievement of Zionist goals needs no elaboration, for the Balfour Declaration, issued while he was foreign secretary, is engraved in the hearts and minds of Arabs and Zionists alike. Significantly, in his capacity as prime minister, Balfour had previously piloted through the House of Commons the Aliens Act, which aimed at restricting the entry of East European Jews into England.[41] Balfour pointedly spoke of the "undoubted evils that had fallen upon the country from an immigration which was largely Jewish."[42] It should be recalled in this context that the years 1903–1905 witnessed both the promulgation of the Aliens Act as well as the project aiming at Zionist settlement in East Africa, both of which were approved by the pro–anti-Semitic Balfour.

In the face of such discriminatory laws, Weizmann proved quite flexible and accommodating, for he considered the anti-Jewish legislation of 1905 to be a perfectly "natural phenomenon." Hostility to Jewish immigration should not be looked upon as "anti-Semitism in the ordinary or vulgar sense of that word, it is a universal social and economic concomitant" of that immigration.[43] Therefore, legislation such as the Aliens Act, Weizmann's argument implied, should be seen as a legitimate act of national self-defense.

Balfour's support of Zionism and the Zionist project stemmed from his perception of the "uniqueness" of the Jew in an abstract sense, as in both Zionist and anti-Semitic literature. In his Introduction to Sokolow's *History of Zionism* he argued against a Buddhist settlement in India and against a comparable Christian settlement. Yet he found it perfectly legitimate to argue *for* Jewish settlement in Palestine because, for the Jews, "race, religion and country are inter-related."[44] His perception of this uniqueness was the basis not only of his pro-Semitic Zionism, but also of his avowed anti-Semitism and his various anti-Semitic acts and views. Balfour admitted to Weizmann that he agreed with some of Cosima Wagner's "anti-Semitic postulates." Weizmann again proved quite accommodating, for his own attitude was that he, too, viewed the assimilated Jews of Germany as "an undesirable and demoralizing phenomenon."[45]

The anti-Semitic postulates of Balfour are obvious in the way he stereotyped the Jew. The Jews were seen as an "alien and even hostile . . . Body" whose existence in Western civilization had caused "age-long miseries," for this civilization could neither *expel* nor absorb that Body.[46] Balfour declared that on account of their mode of existence and their alienation, the Jews' "loyalty to the State in which they dwell is (to put it mildly) feeble compared to their loyalty to their religion and their race."[47]

The argument for the "uniqueness of the Jew" was used by Balfour to justify the Russian persecution of the Jews, as when he declared that "the persecutors had a case of their own."[48] The Jew in the abstract does not belong to any country, and consequently he has either to be transferred to a country of his own or be suppressed, a common premise shared by Jewish and gentile Zionists alike.

A blatant example of gentile Zionist anti-Semitism is Richard Crossman, member of the British Labour Party. In a review of Stein's *The Balfour Declaration*, Crossman cited Weizmann's view that the best gentile Zionists "are drawn from those gentiles who were conscious of their hostility to the Jews."[49] Any reader of Crossman's *A Nation Reborn* will conclude that the gentile Zionist was quite honest in expressing his racist feelings toward the Jews.

Weizmann is in the background of the book, approving and blessing Crossman's racism. The Zionist leader, Crossman told his reader, had "hatred for the assimilated Jew,"[50] an admission that probably eased Crossman's conscience and legitimized his racist feelings, making them seem natural, reasonable, and even respectable. Like Weizmann, Crossman believed in "the basic fact on which Zionism is founded—the essential unassimilable Jewishness of the Jew" and the unavoidable hostility that Jews living in a "foreign community" were bound to arouse. The bacilli would multiply and the epidemic would break out.[51] The only radical cure would be the Jewish state and the only acceptable Jew would be the quintessential Jew, who is a transient resident in a foreign country, on his way out to his own homeland. Crossman told us that the British, or at least the British he associated with, developed a liking for Weizmann because he was an undiluted abstract Jew. "He impressed us," said Crossman, "*because* he was not Western, *because* he had no feelings of double loyalty," because he was "the most Jewish Jew." The absurdity of the process of abstraction takes an amusing turn when Crossman goes on to say that Weizmann "knew only one patriotism, the love of a country that did not yet exist."[52]

The gentile Zionist perception of the Jew still thrives in the West. It is a strange mixture of sympathy and a sense of admiration toward the

Jews, on the one hand, with latent hostile feelings, on the other, indicative of a genuine lack of concern for their fate. To cite an example, Garry Wills' article, "A New Way to Perceive the State of Israel," in *Esquire* of July 1975 purports to be a favorable portrait of the Zionist state. The writer attempts to understand Israel's situation by relating it to the history of the Crusades—an image that (I know) makes many Israelis wince, for it implies that Israel is a foreign body that will eventually be ejected after prolonged warfare. If this is the inescapable logic of the metaphor for the Israelis, its implications for the Jewish communities around the world are not very reassuring. The image in the article suggests that these communities probably share in a hysterical and blind devotion to an impossible chauvinistic ideal which they do not fully comprehend. With such ambiguities in the central image, one begins to wonder: Can this be a subtle attack on the Jews?

The description of Israeli society in the Wills article is marked by the same vagueness, for Israel is seen as a "primitive" society of warriors, "which made war glamorous again." Soldiers jubilantly hunt Arabs and "generals come to join in the sport."[53] The soldiers remember the hunt without nervous pride or shame. Wills noted that not only is Israel a "military state" governed by "the elite fighters, the pilots and tank commanders" who replaced the early Zionist pioneers, but that the army, whose power is growing, is "the principal instrument of the socialization" of "Orientals."[54] Although Amos Elon, the well-known Israeli author, has remarked that the Israelis under the stress of their situation are increasingly becoming "a well-oiled but inhuman machine,"[55] one still cannot view these aspects of Israeli life as admirable. But Wills is full of admiration and praise for Israel's fighting spirit. The Jews, he declares approvingly, are "the last Crusaders."

Such an article should have aroused anger among the Jews and created a furor in any civilized community. Since it did not, one must assume that the Zionist establishment found in this picture nothing that contradicts its own image of the Jew—"the Fighting Jew" who, like Israeli Prime Minister Menahem Begin, adapts the Cartesian *cogito* to the needs of settler colonialism: "We fight, therefore we are."[56]

THE ZIONIST STRATEGY I

The colonial Zionism of the gentiles stems from the complex and not-so-complex assumptions of anti-Semitism, as well as from the colonial interests of Europe in the late nineteenth century. Jewish Zionists, whose ideology is partly derived from anti-Semitic assumptions, found in the gentile Zionists not only a perfect ally but also a sponsor to provide them with the power base they could not create among the Jewish diaspora. As the record shows, it was gentile Zionism that turned Jewish Zionism from the ideology of a small disaffected sector of Eastern European Jewry into a movement of far wider appeal to world Jewry.

From the beginning, the Zionists were aware of the fact that they were powerless, with little or no support among either the Jewish masses or the intelligentsia. In 1927 Weizmann admitted that the Balfour Declaration was "built on air." He was trembling, he related, lest the British government should query him concerning the extent of Jewish support for the Zionist movement. "The Jews, they knew, *were against us*," he wrote. "We stood alone on a little island, a tiny group of Jews with a foreign past."[57] In a secret memorandum to the British cabinet, Sir Edwin Montagu made the point that "Jews of foreign birth . . . have played a very large part in the Zionist movement in England." He then listed a certain Dr. Gaster, a native of Rumania; a Dr. Hertz, a native of Austria; and Dr. Weizmann, a native of Russia.[58]

In the absence of a power base among the Jewish masses, the Zionists had to rely on a non-Jewish superpower. Perhaps one can argue that what the Jewish Zionists finally managed to "conquer" was not the Jewish communities as much as the gentile colonists. The Jewish Zionists posed primarily as brokers for the colonial power structure among the Jews, without the consent of the Jewish communities. But once the Zionists obtained approval for their plan from this or that state, they uniformly turned in triumph to the powerless Jewish community, proclaiming their new legitimacy and prestige.

In 1914 Weizmann confided to a friend of his that the chance for the Jewish people to present their claim for a homeland was finally at hand. But he said that the Zionists could not make any claims because the Jews were "much too atomized for it." So a solution was sought, and Weizmann and other Zionists suggested that an approach *from above* might get them out of the impasse. He outlined the following strategy: Should Palestine "fall within the British sphere of influence, and should Britain encourage Jewish settlement there, as a British dependency, we could have in twenty or thirty years a million Jews out there,"[59] serving British interests.

When a government official expressed astonishment at the anti-Zionist stand of leading British Jews, Weizmann assured him that the plan for attacking from above was certain to succeed. Once Palestine was recognized as a Jewish National Home, the anti-Zionist British Jews, he predicted, would "fall into line quickly enough." In due time they themselves "will claim to be Zionists."[60]

Weizmann's lobbying efforts for the Balfour Declaration are a good illustration of this strategy in practice. To circumvent the opposition of Sir Edwin Montagu, the strongly anti-Zionist Jewish minister in the British cabinet, Weizmann wrote a note to the British Foreign Office for transmission to the war cabinet, expressing the hope that the problem of Zionist settlement "would be considered in the light of Imperial interests."[61] In later years he was to write that if there had been no Palestine, it would have been "necessary to create one in the Imperial interest."[62]

A VASSAL JEWISH STATE

Since both gentile and Jewish Zionists came from more or less the same nineteenth-century European colonial tradition, the most natural thing for both groups was to think in terms of exporting "European tensions" and problems to Africa and Asia. The overproduction of commodities, for example, could be solved through the Indian market, and the lack of raw materials for British factories could be solved by converting Egypt into a cotton plantation. The problem of overpopulation, or the "human surplus," a huge portion of which was "Jewish," could be solved in a similar manner. For overproduction of commodities, conventional colonialism was the answer; for the human surplus, it was settler colonialism.

Max Nordau, even before his conversion to Zionism, was already thinking along such lines. For Europe to solve the problem of unemployed workers, it should turn them into agricultural workers, "and if Europe lacked the space they must emigrate overseas."[63] Though answering two different problems, both types of colonialism rotate within the Western colonial orbit and serve its interests. The settler-colonial pockets would serve not only as human enclaves to absorb the surplus, but also as bases of operations for conventional colonialism.

The Zionist proposal to solve the Jewish question was very much in keeping with the nineteenth-century European colonial formula, which implied that non-Western peoples should foot the bill for Western progress and prosperity. Writing in the *Herzl Year Book,* Oskar K. Rabinowicz, in summarizing Herzl's diplomacy and tactics, stated that the Zionist project aimed at solving the Jewish question by diverting "the stream of Jewish migration from England to Africa and Asia." Furthermore, "through the establishment of a Jewish autonomous center," Zionism would "create . . . an important post for Britain's lifeline: London-Singapore-Melbourne, which would strengthen her position in the Near East."[64]

It was with this European formula in mind that Herzl and the Zionist leadership after him thought of the following territories and at one time or another negotiated for them: the Sinai Peninsula, the al-Arish region, a part of Kenya (known in Zionist histories as "East Africa" or "Uganda"), all of Malagasy, a slice of Cyprus, the "Belgian" Congo, Mozambique, Iraq, Libya, and Palestine.

It was with full awareness of the import of this colonial dimension to the Zionist project that Herzl, in a journal entry dated September 23, 1902, listed some of the colonists he thought he was manipulating as mere figures in his "chess game": Cecil Rhodes, President Theodore Roosevelt, the King of England, and the Czar.[65] Writing to Sir Cecil Rhodes, an advocate of settler colonialism as an antidote to social upheaval in Europe, Herzl invited him to help make history by participating in "something colonial." Then, getting down to specifics, Herzl told him that this something "doesn't involve Africa, but a place in Asia Minor, not Englishmen, but Jews."[66] But why Rhodes in particular? Herzl turned to the famed colonist so that Rhodes might "put the stamp of [his] authority on the Zionist plan" and make a declaration in its favor.[67] Herzl's identification with colonialism was so deep and personal that he took care to note in his diary that he should wear a "cap designed à la Stanley for the future legend."[68]

Herzl at times entertained grandiose imperial notions about the Zionist project. Writing to Max Nordau in 1903 about the East Africa project, he cited the various European nations which had built "colonial empires that are making their fortune," and referred to England, which "pours her excess population into the immense empire she has acquired." Then, in words at once comic and pathetic, he stated that the Zionists, too, should "seize the opportunity offered . . . [to them] to become a miniature England." He outlined the process of implementing the imperial dream: "Let us begin by acquiring our own colonies. On the strength of our colonies we shall conquer our own homeland. Let the territory situated between Kilimanjaro and Kenya become the first colony of Israel. This . . . will establish the foundations of Zion."[69] Nordau was not unresponsive to the idea, for he, too, described the East Africa project as "a night shelter," a colonial stepping stone to the colonial Zion.

But the Zionists, with no Jewish masses behind them and no territorial base to operate from, were in dire need of support from a European imperial force to provide them with the military, political, and economic cover necessary for colonization. This dimension did not have a moderating influence on Herzl, for he envisaged (in the same letter to Nordau) *several imperial patrons* helping *several Zionist colonies in Africa and Asia*: "Other countries will follow the example of England; we will establish new 'reserves of power' in Mozambique, Congo and Tripolitania with the help of the Portuguese, Belgians and Italians."[70] The indomitable Herzl entertained a grand vision of himself, sitting calmly among the leaders of colonial powers—"Englishmen and Russians, Protestants and Catholics"—jealously fighting over him. In that manner, he solemnly said, "our cause will be furthered."[71]

Herzl, intoxicated by his own imperial dreams, envisioned a pan-Jewish, pan-European settler-colonial state, serving imperial Europe as a whole without discrimination: "We should as a neutral state remain in contact with all Europe, which would have to guarantee our existence."[72] But the more sober moments were those in which the Zionist leader addressed himself to *one* colonial power to help him found an "autonomous Jewish vassal state in Palestine," or anywhere else under the "suzerainty"[73] of this or that power.

In his meeting with Victor Emmanuel III, king of Italy, Herzl brought up his project "to channel the surplus Jewish immigration into Tripolitania, under the liberal laws and institutions of Italy." The Catholic monarch did not take Herzl very seriously, and gently told him that the Zionist project would mean building in "someone else's house."[74] On the other hand, Mussolini, in his frequent meetings with Weizmann and Goldmann, proved more sympathetic and understanding, for he gave his approval to the idea of a Zionist state. The Fascist leader even claimed to be a gentile Zionist himself.[75]

Herzl also turned to the Ottoman Empire, pledging that if the Sultan were to give the Zionists "that piece of land . . . in return we shall set his house in order, straighten out his finances, and influence public opinion all over the world in his favor."[76] Other advantages would also accrue, such as the establishment of a university in Istanbul so that Turkish students would not have to go to Europe and be exposed to the influence of dangerous democratic and revolutionary ideas.

With the resurgence of Arab nationalism and opposition to Turkish rule, the Arabs found a temporary ally in England. The Zionists then turned to the Turks and their German allies, suggesting "that a Jewish enclave in Palestine might be highly desirable as a counter-balance to the 600,000 Arabs of Palestine" and to the surrounding Arab countries.[77] For several years, Herzl, in keeping with his Germanic background and his deep admiration for German culture and politics, thought of the Jewish state as a German protectorate. (At a later date the Nazis did develop an interest in the Jewish state, fully cooperated in that project, and even considered three other settlement schemes in Syria, Ecuador, and Madagascar.[78]) The Ottoman Sultan, however, refused to "sell" Palestine to the Zionists, and his successors did not prove any more amenable. The Germans, too, eventually lost interest, partly because of the international situation and partly because of their interest in the German settlers in Palestine. The Zionist leader had to turn elsewhere.

Even while negotiating with other potential colonial sponsors, Herzl directed his gaze "toward England," "from the first moment."[79] His Anglophilia was rooted in the realization that British colonialism was the best established and most expansionist of all varieties known at that time. "The English," he said in a speech in London in 1899, "were the first to recognize the necessity of colonial expansion in the modern world. There-fore the flag of Great Britain is flying across the seas." For that reason the Zionist leader packed up and went to London, where he expected to find admiration for his Zionist vision. He was convinced that "the Zionist idea, which is a colonial idea, must be understood in England easily and quickly."[80]

Throughout his career, Herzl tried to demonstrate the usefulness of the Zionist state to the British Empire. Two years before his death, he wrote to Lord Rothschild in England, telling him that the Zionist project would strengthen British influence east of the Mediterranean by a "great coloniza-tion of our [Jewish] people at a nodal point of Egyptian and Indo-Persian interests."[81] In another context he even suggested that the Zionist state would make "the Empire . . . bigger by a rich colony."[82]

This perception of the Jewish state as a vassal is characteristic of all Zionist schools, whether Labor, General, or Revisionist. Nordau also per-ceived the role of the Jewish state as a "trustee" of Great Britain, and the Jews as "her sentries on the long and dangerous road through the Near and Middle East up to the frontiers of India."[83]

Characterized by his friend Crossman as a firm believer in the "vir-tues of the Empire,"[84] Weizmann viewed the Jewish settlement in Pales-tine as a safeguard for England, particularly "in respect to the Suez Canal."[85] In an undispatched letter to Winston Churchill, written in 1921, the Zionist leader discussed the "identity of interests" and the "natural alliance" between the Empire and the Zionist enclave.[86] The same identity of interests was obvious to Ben Gurion, the Labor Zionist leader, who de-clared at the Nineteenth Zionist Congress in 1935 that "whoever betrays Great Britain betrays Zionism." Elsewhere, he spoke of the enclave as constituting "bases of defense on sea and on land" for the Empire.[87]

In her prophetic essay on Zionism written in 1945, Hannah Arendt viewed this procolonialist Zionist stance as unavoidable. She said that Zionism, as a national movement, "sold out at the very first moment to the powers-that-be" because the slogan of the Jewish state meant actually that the Jews "propose to establish themselves from the very beginning as a 'sphere of interest' under the delusion of nationhood."[88]

Collaboration between Zionism and Western colonialism is perhaps the earliest and most persistent of all Zionist themes in both gentile and Jewish Zionist circles. In the second volume of his *History of Zionism*, Sokolow cited a letter dated 1798 from a Jew to his coreligionists, calling for the return of the Jews to a country stretching from Lower Egypt to the Dead Sea, which would render the Jews the "masters of the commerce of India, Arabia, and the South and East Africa."[89] The writer of the letter added that the Council of the Jews would offer to the French government, if it protected the new Zion, "to share the commerce of India, etc., with the merchants of France *only*."[90]

In his book, *Rome and Jerusalem*, published in 1862, Moses Hess called for the establishment of Jewish colonies founded from "Suez to Jerusalem and from the banks of the Jordan to the coast of Mediterranean," under French patronage. Then he waxed quasi-religious: "Frenchmen and Jews!" he declared, "It seems that in all things they were created for one another."[91]

Almost a century later, an article entitled "The Prostitute of the Sea Ports and Ourselves," published in *Haaretz* on September 30, 1951, reiterated the same idea of the "vassal Jewish state." "Israel," the article said, "has been assigned the role of a kind of watchdog" that "can be relied upon to punish properly one or several of her Arab neighbor states whose lack of manners toward the West has exceeded permissible limits." Even though the title of the piece is harsh, the overall premise has been borne out several times by Zionist statements and policies.

From the outset, the Zionists apparently hoped to harness not only the Jewish community settled in Palestine/Israel, but also all the Jewish communities of the world, in the service of the colonial power sponsoring the Zionist project. In his meeting with Victor Emmanuel III, king of Italy, Herzl used the romanticized rhetoric of restorationism by recalling that Napoleon had once urged that the Jews be restored to Palestine, whereupon the Italian king, politely but firmly replied, "He only wanted to make the Jews, who were scattered all over the world, his *agents*." At that point, Herzl had to admit that Chamberlain, the secretary of state, also had similar notions. The king, probably bored, replied, "It is an obvious idea."[92] This was not exactly a revelation to Herzl, for he himself had promised that if England consented to his plan, it would get "at one stroke . . . ten million *secret but loyal* subjects active in all walks of life all over the world. . . . As at a signal, all of them will place themselves at the service of the magnanimous nation that brings long-desired help. England will get ten million *agents* for her greatness and influence." Then, using a mercantile metaphor common in Zionist literature, he pointed out that "there are values that fall to the share of the one who acquires them at a time when they are esteemed lightly." In a master stroke, the Zionist leader expressed his hope that "the English government [would] recognize what value there is in gaining the Jewish people."[93]

The Herzlian scheme of harnessing a "grateful" Jewish people in the service of the gentile colonial power structure gained strength over the years. In an address in 1920, Max Nordau, Herzl's friend, showed his awareness of the forces that motivated gentile Zionists. British statesmen, according to him, had to "grapple with hard, cold and concrete political problems" and they had to look "for every possible asset in the grand balance." After such calculations, it was concluded by the British that the

Jews were indeed an "asset" and "might be useful" to Great Britain and her allies, whereupon Palestine was offered to them.[94]

Another recurring theme in the writings of Zionist thinkers and leaders was that the *Jewishness* of the state was a sure guarantee of its loyalty to the colonial powers. Nordau, for instance, saw that Britain was threatened by the Soviet Union, the rise of Arab nationalism, and Arab aspirations toward unity. This last trend in particular, he maintained, would jeopardise Britain's control over the Suez Canal. "A reliable ally ought to be more than welcome. Zionism offers to be this ally provided it be given opportunity by Britain to be a strong Jewish state in the land of the fathers," as Nordau's biographer said, summarizing the Zionist leader's view.[95]

Jabotinsky stressed what he considered to be a "well-known truism"— the importance of Palestine from the viewpoint of British imperial interests. However, the validity of this imperialist precept, as he claimed, "depends on one paramount condition, namely that Palestine should cease being an Arab country." He believed that "all England's 'strongholds' in the Mediterranean" are flawed because "they are all . . . inhabited by populations whose national magnetic centers lie elsewhere and who are therefore organically and incurably centrifugal." The inhabitants would, in due time, seek independence and gravitate away from England. This law would apply to Arab Palestine, which would follow "the orbit of Arab destinies— federation of Arab countries, and elimination of all traces of European influences." With that negative vision of an Arab Palestine belonging to a unified Arab world, Jabotinsky contrasted the image of a "Palestine predominantly Jewish,"[96] ever loyal to Britain.

Using the same line of argument, Weizmann warned that the Western colonial powers could not rely "on the dubious Arab loyalty so near the vital communications across the Isthmus of Suez." The Arab movement, he said, "leads one to believe that it is anti-European." For "your loyal element," he wrote in the undispatched 1921 letter, "you will have to rely . . . on the Jews."[97]

Today, over a half-century later, the Israeli Socialist Organization (Matzpen) perceives no change in Israel's role. Because of its own profound conflict with the Palestinians, the Israeli state is "relatively immune to the revolutionary struggle for political and economic independence." Hence, Matzpen contends, it remains a reliable base for an armed force directed against that struggle, in the interests of imperialism.[98]

To maintain Israel in the role of guardian of Western interests has been a relatively cheap venture, Zionist literature has maintained. The shrewd Herzl realized that the revolt of the Egyptian *fellahin* would make Egypt too expensive and too unwieldy to keep under colonial domination. This made the Zionist option more economical and attractive. In his undispatched letter to Winston Churchill, Weizmann used a commercial metaphor when he wrote that "the Palestine Zionist policy, far from being waste, becomes a necessary *insurance* that we *quote* to you at a *lower rate* than anyone else could dream of."[99]

In opting to back the Zionist Organization, British colonialism placed its faith in a group prepared to take "a great deal of the financial responsibility" for colonization, as Weizmann explained. If the cost of the British garrison proved to be high, then the "Jewish colonists" could be organized and armed. "Was a colonization ever conducted under such favorable conditions that a Government found at its elbow an organization with a considerable income ready to take over some of its most costly liabilities?"[100] It was also convenient for the British that they could, after being forced to evacuate from Egypt, "concentrate in the Canal Zone with your army based in Palestine." British-Zionist cooperation was often discussed by Weizmann in terms of hard cash: "If one were paying three times as much on the military garrison of Palestine, one would be purchasing these strategic advantages very cheaply."[101]

Given the colonial frame of reference within which the idea of the Zionist state was conceived and implemented, one can argue that it is by no means a coincidence that the Balfour Declaration and the South Africa Act of Union (1909) were both effected in "large part by the same handful of politicians"—Lord Milner, Lord Selbourne, Lord Balfour, Joseph Chamberlain, and General Smuts. In implanting and backing white settlers in South Africa and Zionist settlers in Palestine, the British Empire was founding two little pockets of settler-colonists who would owe allegiance to the imperial metropolis and would serve as bases of operations when the need arose.[102]

SPECIFIC TRAITS

The Zionist enclave established in Palestine is clearly a settler-colonial enterprise sponsored by the Western powers to solve some economic and demographic problems and to serve as bases for military operations. Basically, all known settler-colonial enclaves have been established as separate and distinct entities, sheltering an alien demographic element which, despite its existence in a distant geographical region, maintains strong ties with a Western power. Perhaps this last characteristic accounts for the fact that almost all settler-colonial enclaves have been implanted in coastal areas so as to maintain ties with the colonial metropolis and to secure supply lines. Settler-colonial enclaves formed a circle around Africa, with Israel occupying the northernmost point, at the gates to Africa and Asia, and the southernmost tip occupied by South Africa. The French *colons* in Algeria and the settlements in Angola and Mozambique completed the circle.

Having been sponsored from the outset by the West, Israel shares a number of common traits with other similarly supported colonial ventures. Yet its historical origins and specific situation have combined to give it four distinctive features that set it apart as a colonialist form.

The first, and most important, of these distinctive features is the fact that in theory as well as in practice Zionist settler colonialism was based on the principle of population transfer. Even though originating in Europe, the Zionist enclave was not meant to serve as an outlet for the European demographic surplus in general, but rather for the Jewish demographic surplus in particular. For various historical reasons pertaining to their distinctly "Jewish" origin, the Zionist settlers did not come to settle in the land merely to exploit its natural and human resources; they coveted *the land itself without its population*. Most varieties of settler colonialism involve usurpation of land, settlement by an alien demographic element, and exploitation of the indigenous inhabitants of the land. However, Zionist settler colonialism—and therein lies its "Zionism"—consists of usurpation of the land, settlement of an alien demographic element, and a "transfer" of the indigenous inhabitants.

In this sense, Zionism in practice is perhaps the most acute form of settler colonialism, for it guarantees the internal racial stability of the settler community while totally deforming the economic and cultural structure of the evicted one. Ben Gurion advocated this "pure" form of settler colonialism when he advised de Gaulle that, as a solution to the Algerian problem, the French should *depopulate* the *coastal* area of Algeria, settle the *colons* there, and declare the enclave an independent state.

This essentially distinctive feature of Zionist settler colonialism has not often been realized. Karl Kautsky hinted briefly at it in his classic *Are the Jews a Race?* He predicted that the Jewish settlers would suffer greatly during the Arab struggle for independence because Jewish colonization of Palestine demonstrated their intent "to remain in it, and not only make the former inhabitants dependent on them but even to drive them out entirely."[103] At present, the socialist-oriented Matzpen is among the few groups in Israel that have noted this trait in Zionist colonialism and have defined its full political and economic implications for both the Palestinians and the Israelis.

The cultural origins of the two forms of settler colonialism are of some interest. The more conventional variety (Algeria and Angola) seems to have originated in Catholic countries, whereas the population-transfer variety (South Africa) had its origins in Protestant countries. This would lead one to wonder whether a literal interpretation of the Old Testament may not be conducive to a state of mind that accepts as "natural" the transfer of people in the name of divinely ordained dictates.

Perhaps the "national church," bestowing a degree of sanctity on the deeds of its members only, provides a religious rationalization for such processes. On the other hand, the "universal church" extends certain rights to the believer regardless of his national or racial affiliation. The religio-national sanction abstracts the self and dehumanizes the "Other," keeping him outside the scheme of redemption and salvation. Not everyone is to be ingathered, and only the elect can have any claims on Zion.

Herzl, for instance, was vaguely aware of a Catholic opposition to his project. But he saw that stand as stemming from competition between what he considered to be two universal churches: Judaism and Catholicism. As for other national churches, Herzl argued that they were not universal and therefore did not need Jerusalem "an an Archimedian point."[104] Be that as it may, there seems to be some basic relation, which deserves further study, between the specific form of a settler-colonial enclave and its cultural roots in Europe.

The *second* specific trait of Zionist settler colonialism is its simultaneous independence from *and* dependence on the West. During one phase or another of their development, settler states are dependent on a Western sponsor. The degree of dependence, its duration, and the form it takes are determined by a complex of historical and political circumstances. Enclaves not based on a population transfer, like Angola and Algeria, remain completely open to the mother country, maintaining strong ties and deriving a sense of identity from it. What the mother country decrees is law, for the enclave is more or less an organic part of it. If a conflict of interest arises between the two and the enclave proves costly or embarrassing, it is uniformly liquidated. The settlers are repatriated to their land of origin and the dispute is resolved in favor of the mother country.

On the other hand, enclaves based on a population transfer gradually develop a degree of autonomy and relative independence from the Western sponsor. Sooner or later the settlers take matters into their own hands, setting up a state of their own, largely closed unto itself as in the case of the apartheid state of South Africa.

The Zionist enclave was originally meant to be of the independent variety. When Cecil Rhodes asked Weizmann about his objections to a "purely French control," the Zionist leader replied that the French, unlike the English, "always interfered with the population and tried to impose on it *l'ésprit français*."[105] As things turned out, however, the Zionist enclave conformed to neither pattern. It has been dependent on a Western superpower while at the same time enjoying a measure of independence. This peculiarity can be traced back to various factors unique to Zionism.

The Zionist settlers did not originate in *one* single European country to which they owed allegiance, and which in turn afforded them protection and shelter in case of decolonization. Unlike other settler colonialists, the

Zionists did not have a "mother" country; instead, they have always had a stepmother who was willing to go only so far. The stepmother used the stepchild as much as the stepchild used her. Since the relation between the Western sponsor and the Zionist agent was a matter of practical convenience and was not the product of deep or *organic* cultural ties, the Zionist enclave came under the temporary protection of several interested sponsors. As a result, the Zionist leadership was always hurriedly moving its headquarters from one center of gravity to another, shifting from Turkey to France, and finally to England, in pursuit of a real or imaginary center of imperial power in the Middle East. In more recent times, the United States has been assumed to be in firm control of world leadership. Therefore, in Ben Gurion's words, "the center of gravity" of Zionist "political work in the international arena" had to be shifted there.

The ambivalent character of the Zionist state was the result of two forces. A sense of relative independence was achieved primarily through the population transfer. But as hostility and resistance by the dispossessed and alienated natives became evident, the instinct for self-preservation led to heavy dependence on a superpower.

Jabotinsky himself believed that "surrounded on all sides by Arab countries," Palestine as a Jewish state would "always seek to lean upon some powerful Empire, non-Arab, and non-Mohammedan." He viewed this isolationism as being "an almost providential basis for a permanent alliance between England and a Jewish (but only a Jewish) Palestine."[106] Being an inveterate empiricist, Jabotinsky could never visualize a time when such an alliance would make the Jewish state particularly vulnerable to demands from the guarantor of its security.

The complex yet endless rhythm of attraction and repulsion, of autonomy and abject dependence, and of alliance and conflict with the sponsor has characterized Western-Zionist relationships from the very beginning. Each side has tried to "use" the other, and has defined the area of "common interests" in a way more favorable to itself. The relationship between England and the enclave is a good case in point.

As indicated earlier, it was the British colonial restorationists who first broached the theme of Jewish settlement in Palestine. The Balfour Declaration, and later the British Mandate, enabled the Zionists to gain a foothold in the Middle East. Under British protection the gates of Palestine were flung open to Jewish immigration. The settlers undoubtedly needed full cooperation with the mandatory government as a *basic* condition for the growth of the Jewish population and for the consolidation of its hold on the land.[107] When Arab resistance in Palestine in the 1930s grew more active, the Zionists were sheltered by the British. Ben Gurion characterized the protective British stand as "the greatest political success since the Balfour Declaration.[108] A military correspondent of *Haaretz*, writing on the military balance in Palestine, attributed the strength of the Zionists after the 1936 Palestine revolt to "the strong support they received from the British government and army in Palestine."[109] It was this favorable military balance that led eventually to the Zionist victory of 1948.

But the relationship between the British and Zionist colonists took a turn for the worse under the pressure of new factors in the situation. Among these was the political pressure on the British from "friendly" Arab governments as well as from the more radical Palestinian resistance. Another cause was the growing British fear that Gestapo agents might infiltrate the ranks of Jewish immigrants. It was believed then (and later confirmed) that the Nazis lent their support to the Zionist *aliyah bet* (illegal immigration) and that they had decided to use it as a means of creating problems for the British in the Middle East.

Given these new factors, the imperial sponsor developed a view of the colonial settlement in Palestine which was at odds with that of the settlers themselves. Thus a number of White Papers and regulations, more favorable to the Arabs, were issued by the British government. Basic concepts such as the absorptive capacity of Palestine, long disregarded by the British, were revived in order to limit Jewish immigration to Palestine. Hostilities developed between the imperial power and the colonial enclave, taking at times extreme forms, as in the case of the blowing up of the King David Hotel.

However, the conflict was contained within recognizable limits. Jabotinsky's remarks concerning imperial England are more realistic than latter-day Zionist liberationist rhetoric, which describes Zionism as "a national liberation movement" of the Jewish people. In a letter to Leopold Amery in 1935, Jabotinsky tried to explain away his "alleged 'anti-Britishness.' " He assured the British colonist that despite his criticism of England, he remained loyal and grateful "so long as the Balfour Declaration stands—it is England, right or wrong."[110]

Ben Gurion too, as his biographer Bar-Zohar indicates, was ready "to swear" at the time of strained relations with Britain that a Jewish state in Palestine would safeguard British interests.[111] Still, the British were apparently beginning to give more consideration to their long-range interests.

Once the State of Israel was established in 1948 and relations with Britain were normalized, the Tripartite Declaration of Britain, France, and the United States guaranteed the enclave's survival. Collaboration with the former imperial sponsor reached new heights in 1956, as demonstrated in the British-French-Israeli invasion of Egypt. With Palestinian resistance and Arab pressure on the rise, and with widening global interests claiming its sponsor's attention, the enclave found itself once more asked to give up some of the very "rights" it had formerly claimed for itself with the full encouragement of the colonial sponsor, such as keeping territories acquired by force. Until today, this has in fact been the main problem facing the Israelis. They have to rely on the United States for their very existence, but this very reliance makes them vulnerable to pressure from a superpower that has wider global concerns and interests.

Compounding the situation is the Jewish diaspora, which, like the Zionist state itself, is at once relatively autonomous yet dependent on a larger structure. American Jewry zealously extends to Israel both financial and political support, but such support can continue only as long as there is a basic identity of interests between the American guarantor and the Zionist enclave. Diaspora Zionism plays a dual role. It lobbies on behalf of the enclave in the United States, obtaining for Israel a degree of freedom and independence much larger than that of any other client state, but (and therein lies the irony of Israel's situation) the diaspora will surely find itself forced to put pressure on the enclave when the United States decides that Israel should change its policies in a way that accords with America's global interests.

The history of Zionism is also a history of tensions, not only between Zionism and the diaspora, but also between colonial Zionism and monetary and diplomatic. diaspora Zionism. These tensions were clearly demonstrated in the Brandeis-Weizmann and Goldmann-Ben Gurion controversies; at the present time they become apparent when some diaspora Zionists oppose the annexationist and expansionist policies of political Zionism, as if such policies were mere aberrations, not an organic part and logical consequence of the political Zionist outlook.

The third trait that sets Zionist settler colonialism apart from other varieties of settler colonialism is its irredentist and expansionist nature. Israel is a state constituted for the Jewish people, the people of the Book. The religious concept, in this case, results not in a limited population transfer but in endless expansion. David Triestsch (1870–1935), the German-born Zionist writer and statistician, and editor and founder of the Berlin weekly *Volk und Land*, told Herzl soon after the First Zionist Congress to consider "the 'Greater Palestine' program before it is too late. . . . You do not get ten million Jews into a land of 25,000 kilometers."[112] William Hechler, Herzl's Christian associate, instructed him on April 26, 1896, to adopt and circulate the following as a slogan for the Jewish state: "The Palestine of David and Solomon."[113] The Zionist leader was obviously impressed because two years thereafter he defined the area of the Jewish state in precise theo-geographical, rather than vague theo-historical terms: "From the Brook of Egypt to the Euphrates."[114] It was a slogan to be echoed on July 9, 1947, by Rabbi Fischmann, member of the Jewish Agency, in his testimony to the United Nations Special Committee of Enquiry. At the hearing, he said that "The Promised Land extends from the River of Egypt to the Euphrates; it includes parts of Syria and Lebanon." But one need not take the Nile-Euphrates formula too seriously. What matters is the fact that it is an open-ended dynamism, a settler colonialism bent on expansion. According to Herzl's diary entries, the boundaries of the state will expand as the Jewish population grows. "The more immigrants, the more land,"[115] he wrote.

On February 12, 1952, Moshe Dayan spoke frankly of establishing an Israeli empire.[116] The Israeli foreign minister views expansion as an ongoing process that has not yet ended. The process of building the homeland started one hundred years ago—"a process of building up . . . of expansion, of getting more Jews and settlements and of colonization, in order to expand the borders here." These were his words to a group of Jewish-American students in the summer of 1968. He also told them: "Let there be no Jew who says that this is the end of the process. Let there be no Jew who says that we are near the end of the road." The fact that these statements were made on the Golan Heights makes them especially significant.[117]

The Israeli writer Eliezer Livneh, associated with the Greater Israel Movement, declared in *Haaretz* of November 12, 1973, his opposition to United Nations Resolution 242 on the grounds that it might result in the strangulation of Zionism "at the height of its impetus." It is "victories" such as those of 1967 which give "tremendous impetus to the desire of immigration from the Soviet Union," he wrote, whereas "the retreat from the liberated [that is, occupied areas] will bring about a Zionist depression." He claimed that it is this "Zionist lever" of liberation/occupation that "gives purpose and sense to Israeli society," and that without it an exodus of settlers might set in.[118] One of the reasons behind Israel's refusal to promulgate a constitution in Israel is to leave the expansionist option open. In a formal constitution the boundaries of the colonial-settler state would have to be precisely drawn.[119]

Because it is open to the diaspora, the Zionist enclave can achieve neither the limitedness of similar enclaves nor their staticism. It should not be thought, however, that Israel expands solely because of its "diaspora" or its religio-national-territorial aspirations, for Israeli expansionism has its hard economic aspects and yields many economic gains, such as the oil fields in Sinai and territories for future separate economic development. Moreover, various strategic and military considerations undoubtedly help determine Israel's policies. But these are aspects Israel has in common not only with other settler enclaves but also with all colonial ventures, whereas the major concern in this context is with the specific aspects of Zionist expansionism. The diaspora, both as a concept and as an economic and political reality, is unique to Zionist settler colonialism.

The fourth and final trait of the Zionist enclave is its racial and cultural heterogeneity. The surplus Ashkenazi European Jews were neither culturally nor racially homogenous. It included Poles, Russians, French, Germans, and even Americans. Each group had its distinct cultural heritage, generating conflicts that at times broke into the open (as was the case with the Language War between the supporters of German and the supporters of Hebrew).

The introduction of a European demographic element into Palestine sparked the exodus of Oriental Jewry from Arab countries, a process that resulted in the inundation of the Ashkenazi state by Oriental Jews. This trait of the Zionist state is unparalleled elsewhere, for the Sephardic (Arab) Jews are drawn from the ranks of the victims and the resistant natives. It might thus be useful from an analytical and political viewpoint to see Israel both as a settler-colonial enclave like South Africa, as well as a secessionist state like Katanga or Biafra.

This aspect of the Zionist enclave is a liability from the standpoint of internal stability. Yet, it can be a positive one if viewed from the standpoint of the future of the *whole* Israeli community. All other traits limit the options for a resolution of the conflict, but racial heterogeneity holds some hope that the process of transition and final integration into the area will not be so painful or disruptive. The implanted demographic element is not totally alien, for a large sector of it has common economic and political interests with the natives of the land.

The specificity of the Zionist enclave not only pertains to its origins or objective traits, but also manifests itself, and probably more pronouncedly so, in its apologetics and the way the claimed rights of the settlers are rationalized. The Israeli writer Amos Kenan said, "The uniqueness of Zionism lies, not in its blossoming of deserts, but in the sweet lie which accompanied that process."[120] This uniqueness of Zionist apologetics calls for a detailed treatment in a separate chapter.

6

ZIONIST SETTLER COLONIALISM: APOLOGETICS

THE WHITE JEW'S BURDEN

Settler-colonial enclaves have developed elaborate arguments to rationalize their anomalous existence in Asia and Africa. Sometimes Zionist apologetics are simply the familiar type that expounds on the purity and the superiority of the white man. At other times, circumstances call for less familiar terms and for an idiom more suited for achieving specific ends. In this chapter, after an analysis of the more familiar rationalizations, the less familiar ones will be explored.

European settler colonialism was predicated on certain racist assumptions concerning the genetic and cultural superiority of Western civilization and the white man. In the eyes of the colonists it was these assumptions that sanctioned the introduction of an alien Western demographic element into the continents of Africa and Asia. Lord Balfour described the process of settler colonialism as being an expression of the "great rights and privileges" of the races of Europe, and he considered the inequality of the races "to be the plain historic truth of the situation."[1]

European settler colonialism, according to Crossman, was launched in terms of the white man's right to bring civilization to the "less civilized 'natives' " of Asia and Africa by physically occupying the two continents even at the cost of "wiping out the aboriginal population,"[2] a curious way of civilizing a people by exterminating them. Even before his espousal of Zionism, in keeping with his *racist* colonialist outlook, Max Nordau suggested the settlement of unemployed European workers, with the European immigrants taking "the place of the 'lower races' who were not surviving in the struggle of evolution."[3]

To prove his innocence during his trial at Nuremberg, Nazi theoretician Alfred Rosenberg advanced a similar argument, underscoring for his judges the organic relationship between racism and colonialism. He pointed out that he had stumbled on the term "superman (*Herrenmensch*)" in a book on the life of Lord Kitchener, a man who "had conquered the world." He also claimed that he had come across the term " 'master race' (*Herrenrasse*)" in the writings of "the American ethnologist Madison Grant and of the French ethnologist Lapouge." He noted further that this kind of ethnology was but a "biological discovery which was the conclusion of 400 years of European research."[4]

With the growing need for markets and territories, and the intensification of Europe's economic and demographic crises, racist theories gained in intensity and depth. The author of the entry on "Race Relations" in the *International Encyclopedia of the Social Sciences* indicated that "the era of race relations can be said to have begun with the overseas expansion of the major European powers from the fifteenth century onward."[5] Gentile Zionism and Christian restorationist views began to flourish at the same time. Nor is it a coincidence that contemporaneous pseudo-messianic movements in Judaism also became more frequent from that time on. The false messiah, Shabettai Tzvi, came from a mercantile background, and his father worked for a British overseas trading company.

But all these myths and ideologies were trial runs for the full-fledged global imperialism and racism of the late nineteenth century. The author of the entry on "Racism" in *The New Encyclopedia Britannica* found it "no accident that racism flourished at the time of the second great wave of European colonial expansion and the scramble for Africa." He added that the ideology of colonialism and the theory of the white man's burden were "often expressed in racist terms."[6]

The fraudulent messiah of the age of imperialism and scramble for Africa was Zionism, and it was in the late nineteenth-century imperialist-racist frame of reference that the Zionist theoreticians conceived of their project and implemented it. In order to benefit from the colonialist formula and to share the privilege and right of shouldering that most onerous burden of civilizing the nonwhite races and of engaging in the noble *mission civilisatrice* of Europe, one had to be a white man.

In his study *The Jews of Today*, published first in German in 1904, Arthur Ruppin sided with a certain von Luschau, one of the many Zionist theoreticians of the "Jewish race," whom he credited with the discovery of "the physical resemblance between the Jews and the races of Asia Minor, especially the Armenians." Ruppin preferred to see the Jews as members of the "white race," and he lauded any theoretical efforts that struck a "blow at the Semitic theory."[7] The racial difference between Jews and *Europeans*, according to him, "was not great enough to warrant an unfavorable prognostic as to the fruits of a mixed marriage."[8]

There is a whole strain in Zionist thought which confines the term "Jew" to the white Jews of Europe, the Ashkenazim. This premise is given its most open expression in Ruppin's *The Jews of Today*, where he discusses the effect of the Zionist movement on the consciousness of many a "Western Jew."[9] Zionist settlement efforts were largely aimed at recruiting European Jews only, and rarely tried to recruit Oriental Jews, Ruppin explained, despite the fact that it would have been "a far easier task to settle Oriental Jews (Jews from Yemen, Morocco, Aleppo [Syria], and the Caucasus) in agricultural colonies."

Ruppin stated that Oriental Jews, nevertheless, were "already *drifting* toward Palestine," presumably without conscious Zionist efforts. This Oriental drift did not please him because "the spiritual and intellectual status of these Jews is so low that an immigration *en masse* would lower the general cultural standard of the [Ashkenazi] Jews in Palestine and would be bad from several points of view."[10] (These are words that Abba Eban was to echo a half-century later in his *Voice of Israel*.)

Ruppin reminded his reader that the Ashkenazi Jews, because of the nature of their life in Europe and the oppression they had been subjected to, had undergone a "long process of selection" and "a bitter struggle for life." In that struggle for survival "only the cleverest and strongest survived," and therefore the "great natural racial gifts" of the Jews were not only preserved but also strengthened. Other factors also contributed to the elimination of "all but the most gifted," ensuring "the mental progress of the race." Then, in unequivocal words, Ruppin alerted his reader in a footnote to the fact that "this severe process of selection," largely through persecution and ghettoization, applies only to the Ashkenazi Jews. Therefore, despite "their common racial ancestry," the struggle for survival rendered the Ashkenazim "superior in activity, intelligence and scientific capacity to the Sephardim and Arabian Jews."[11]

Only pragmatic considerations, however, made a dent in the Zionist white Ashkenazi supremacist outlook. As Ruppin explained, Oriental Jews, provided they come "in small numbers . . . might be extremely useful" by virtue "of their knowledge of Oriental conditions, [and] their small needs."[12] But above all, it was their capacity for "competing in wages with the Arab agricultural laborer" that increased their utility. The problem with the East European Jew was that he could not "possibly live on such [low] wages" as those given to Arabs. Moreover, the European Jew, given the fact that he lives "in Palestine only by work which makes demands on his intelligence and reliability," has to employ Arabs "for purely manual labor."[13] This would have been an acceptable arrangement had it not been imperative from the Zionist standpoint to segregate the Jewish economic system in order to achieve "separate development" through the pure Hebrew labor of the Zionist settlers. The hiring of an Arab would have represented a "breach" of the Zionist closed Jewish system and, therefore, this breach had to be "bridged by the Oriental Jew who can do the rough work at the same price as the Arabs."[14]

In other words, the Zionist claim of racial rights, according to Ruppin's view, applies only to the Ashkenazim. As for the Sephardim, they were to be admitted into the enclave only out of dire economic necessity and pragmatic considerations.

The language of Ruppin's analysis may sound immorally racist and excessively utilitarian, for he speaks of the Sephardic Jews as useful beings with small needs, an *instrumentum vocale,* but such was the language common to Europe at the time. Zionism functioned within that framework, and the ethical values of Judaism apparently did not inhibit the dynamics and orientation of the movement.

In fairness to Ruppin, though, it should be noted that he proved personally far more generous, far most sensitive, than what his ideas implied. When he went to Palestine to supervise Zionist colonial activities there, he developed an awareness of the specificity of the situation as being far more complex than his questionable notion of the rights and superiority of the white Jews.

Theodor Herzl was also part of that white supremacist culture, and he fully realized that his Zionist efforts for colonization had to be coordinated with similar projects so that different "white" rights would not come into conflict with each other. Before meeting "Joe" Chamberlain, as Herzl affectionately called the British colonist, he wrote in his dairy that he had to show the Colonial Secretary "a spot in the English possessions where there were no *white people* as yet" before they "could talk about that"[15] Zionist project for settlement. Israel Zangwill, a leading British Zionist, assumed the whiteness of the Zionist venture as a matter of course. He favored Zionist settlement in East Africa as a way of doubling Britain's "white population" there.[16]

Throughout all the discussions involving Zionist proposals for penetration into Africa and Asia, it was assumed that the white people of the Occident possessed certain rights because of their high level of civilization. Herzl, in the manner of nineteenth-century imperialist thinkers, spoke of imperialism as a noble activity, destined to bring civilization to the benighted members of other races.[17] Viewing the Jewish state through these Occidental binoculars, in 1896 he wrote a letter to the Grand Duke of Baden assuring him that when the Jews returned to their "historical fatherland," they would do so as "representatives of Western civilization," who would bring "cleanliness, order, and the well-established customs of the Occident to this plague-ridden, blighted corner of the Orient." The Zionists, as fervent advocates of European progress, would "build railroads into Asia—the highway of the civilized peoples."[18] Herzl, operating within the context of the myth of the white Jew, asserted that the Jewish state was designed to "form a part of a wall of defense for Europe in Asia, an outpost of civilization against barbarism."[19]

The perception of the Jews not merely as a separate racial entity, but as members of the white race and Western civilization, underlies many statements of the Zionists and their image of themselves. In *Rebirth and Destiny of Israel,* Ben Gurion drew a number of analogies between the Zionists and other colonists, which revealed his strong "white" orientation. In 1917, in an article entitled "In Judea and Galilee," he saw the Zionist settlers in the Land of Israel "as not just working" but rather as "conquering, conquering a land. We were a company of conquistadores."[20] In another piece entitled "Earning a Homeland," and dated 1915, Ben Gurion compared the Zionist settlement to the American settlement in the New World, conjuring up the image of the "fierce fights" the American colonists fought against "wild nature and wilder redskins."[21] It is significant how he reduced the "redskins" to the level of nature, or even lower, for they are "wilder." This process of abstracting man, reducing him to mere natural cycles, which is an extension of the Darwinian outlook to the realm of ethics, renders extermination a more acceptable act and the depopulation of an area a prerequisite for survival. The Nazis later made full use of that logic on a more massive and "scientific" scale. They declared it their duty "to depopulate," as part of their mission of preserving the German population. If "nature is cruel . . . we too must be cruel."[22]

In *Trial and Error,* Weizmann preferred to use the image of the French *colons* in Tunisia and British settlers in Canada and Australia as models,[23] while also demonstrating marked sympathy for the white settlers in South Africa.[24]

In a note Weizmann sent to President Truman on November 27, 1947, the colonial tendency to draw a sharp line between a technologically advanced "European" community and backward natives is evident. Describing the Zionist community in Palestine, Weizmann said that it consisted mainly of "an educated peasantry and a skilled industrial class living at high standards." To this bright image he contrasted the bleak one of "illiterate and impoverished communities [in Palestine] bearing no resemblance to the Zionist community."[25] Weizmann did not bother to explain to the American President the reason for this state of affairs, nor why after 50 years of British and Zionist colonialism and enlightenment, the light of civilization had not yet dawned.

Taking its point of departure from such colonial racial myths, the Balfour Declaration did not hesitate to refer to the Arab Muslims and Christians of Palestine, who made up over 90 percent of the population, as the "non-Jewish communities." In other words, the indigenous majority was already being relegated to the status of a minority in the name of the superior rights of Europe's surplus. In an extraordinary display of imperial-ist disdain, Balfour once wrote (in a memorandum dated August 11, 1919), "In Palestine we do not propose ever to go through the form of consulting the wishes of the present inhabitants of the country, though the American [King-Crane] Commission has been going through the form of asking what they are."[26] As for the public proclamations and liberal safeguard clauses, they were to be dumped: "The Powers have made no statement of fact which is not admittedly wrong and no declaration of policy which, at least in the letter, they have not always intended to violate."[27] The dominant colonial powers made the decisions, and the Zionists settler-colonists took full advantage of the international power structure.

The unplanned drift of Oriental Jews was such that by 1948 they constituted about 22 percent of all Zionist settlers.[28] After 1948, however, the drift became a "flood of primitive, panicky Oriental Jews," who formed the majority of its Jewish population. Maurice Samuel, from whose essay "We Didn't Plan It This Way" the preceding quotation was extracted, left Israel in disgust at the influx of Oriental Jewry, who, in his words, were launching "an attack on the framework of the country and its in-stitutions.[29]

That influx of Oriental Jews was defined as early as April 28, 1949, by a writer in *Haaretz* as "the immigration of a race the likes of which we have not yet known in this country. You will find among them dirt, card games for money, drunkenness and fornication. Many of these suffer from serious eye, skin and venereal diseases; not to mention immorality, and stealing."[30]

Despite the larger number of Oriental Jews, and despite the fact that Israel is situated in the "East," the Ashkenazi Jews have long been trying to maintain the state's Western orientation. Ben Gurion claimed that Israel was only geographically in the Middle East and not *of* it.[31] Pinhas Sapir, in his remarks justifying Israel's application for membership in the European Common Market in 1966, reiterated the same words: "Israel belongs to Europe—culturally, politically and economically—despite her being situated in the Middle East geographically."[32]

Given this line of approach, it was only logical for Ben Gurion to declare that he would like to see more Western Jews settle in Israel, to stop it from becoming a Levantine state.[33] Similarly, Moshe Dayan, at the 1974 annual conference of the South African Zionist Federation, viewed the fact that Oriental Jewish immigrants outnumbered immigrants of European origin as "Israel's biggest problem." He appealed to his au-dience to help solve Israel's demographic problem by immigrating there.[34]

As for the Sephardic majority that drifted into the Zionist state from neighboring backward societies, Ben Gurion stated, in a speech to the Knesset in 1960, that the Oriental Jews should be made "to acquire the superior moral and intellectual characteristics of those who created the State."[35] The same Ashkenazi ethno-centricity is evident in Levi Eshkol's claim that the trouble with the Oriental Jews is not simply a question of their "not knowing Yiddish," but rather "it is a question of their *not knowing anything*."[36] Ashkenazi ethno-centricity in the case of the Israeli founding fathers has sometimes reached ridiculous extremes. Former Israeli Prime Minister Golda Meir, for instance, could not understand how one could be Jewish without knowing Yiddish, the *leshon hakedush,* the holy tongue, of the ethnic Jews of Eastern Europe.

The fullest expression of this attitude appears in Abba Eban's *Voice of Israel.* With his customary eloquence, Israel's former Foreign Minister defined his concept of the ideal relationship that should exist between Israel and her neighbors: "The idea should not be one of integration. Quite the contrary," he said, "integration is rather something to be avoided." Turning to the subject of the Oriental Jews, Eban described "the great apprehensions which afflict" the Ashkenazi Israelis, stemming from their feeling of "the danger lest the predominance of immigrants of Oriental origin force Israel to equalize its cultural level with that of the neighboring world"[37] (that is, Asia and Africa). He then went on to say that "far from regarding our immigrants from Oriental countries as a bridge toward our integration with the Arabic-speaking world, our objective should be to infuse them with Occidental spirit, rather than to allow them to draw us into an unnatural orientalism."[38] Ben Gurion evoked the image of the *conquistadores,* and Weizmann that of the *colons,* but Eban presented that of the Yankee in Latin America. Israel, he said, should work toward establishing a relationship akin to that which obtains between the United States and the Latin American continent.[39]

Although muted for ideological reasons, the myth of Ashkenazi superiority expresses itself in the concrete realities of daily life in Israel. Prejudice exists on many levels as in the *Kibbutzim* where, according to Melford Spiro, the attitude toward the Oriental Jew has "racist" overtones. Arab-Jewish youths living in the kibbutz were "often referred to contemptuously as *'hashechorim,'* the dark ones," and their behavior was considered "primitive."[40] Spiro reports that "some students, for example, refused to eat at the same table with those Oriental Jews who work in the kibbutz. When one of these workers sat down beside her, one student rose and walked away. It made her ill, she said, to sit at the same table with them."[41]

Placing Oriental Jews (and Arabs) in the lower cultural or racial strata justifies discrimination against them, on the political and economic levels, by the "white Jew," who firmly believes that he is engaged in a civilizing mission. In 1970, Amos Elon wrote that with roughly half of the Jewish population of Afro-Asian origin, only 20 percent of the seats in the

Knesset (that is, 22 seats) were occupied by Orientals (though according to *Davar,* in its November 4, 1971, issue, there were only five members of Oriental origin). Since 1948, the Israeli Cabinet has never included more than two ministers of Oriental origin. The leadership of both the Jewish Agency, which is in charge of immigration and absorption, and of the Histadrut, which has a firm economic hold on the society, is largely Ashkenazi. The agricultural "cooperatives" in Israel demonstrate the same racial polarity, with the privileged kibbutz[42] being almost exclusively Ashkenazi, and the Sephardic Jew as a mere transient visitor who sells cheap labor. Of the top jobs in government and in the economy, only 9 percent are occupied by the Sephardim.

The picture is the same in education: While 68 percent of the elementary school pupils are Oriental Jews, on the university level there are only 11 percent.[43] To sum up the worsening condition of the Sephardic community, a Moroccan Jew has indicated that in Fez, Morocco, "there are less than 4,000 Jews. But, in spite of this, that city graduates more Jewish university students in a year than the number of university graduates of North African background who graduate in all of Israel." He pointed out that there are only 500 university graduates in Israel of North African background.[44] According to the *Encyclopedia of Zionism and Israel,* there are more than a quarter-million Israeli citizens of North African extraction.

There is also "white" dominance in housing and various other socioeconomic areas. Suffice it here to point out that the average standard of living for the Sephardic community is about 60 percent of that of the Ashkenazim and the gap between the two communities is widening.[45]

Use of the term "racial" to refer to the conflict between the Sephardic and Ashkenazi Jews might sound less reasonable than a view of the conflict in terms of class distinctions. However, Michael Selzer indicated otherwise in his book, *The Aryanization of the Jewish State,* referred to earlier. He wrote that in one of the prosperous middle-class suburbs of Jerusalem, there is a housing project known as the Anglo Saxon. Despite the name, Central and East European Jews, who do not speak English, live there, whereas a Jewish Indian whose mother tongue is English would be barred, because—as the explanation goes—"We would never admit a black."[46]

This kind of discrimination is obviously racial, and it is on the cultural manifestation of that phenomenon that Selzer has focused most of his attention. Using the term "cultural genocide,"[47] Selzer noted that the State of Israel tries to perpetuate the superior culture of the Ashkenazim and to suppress the specific cultural traditions of the Sephardim. Kol Israel is a "kind of Hebrew language version of the BBC rather than the radio station of what is, after all, a Middle-Eastern Country." When Oriental songs are broadcast they are placed under the heading "songs of the communities."

This implies that there is an Ashkenazi norm[48] and that Sephardic culture is merely the culture of one of many minority ethnic groups, even though in fact the majority of Israel's Jews are Sephardic.

The educational system is also consciously geared to Ashkenazi norms and ideals. A large research project conducted by the Hebrew University some years ago was designed to devise ways and means to get Oriental children to adapt "to the Western orientation of Israel's school program."[49] The school curriculum generally plays down the importance of the historical achievements of the Sephardic communities, including Jewry's Golden Age in Arab Spain.

Selzer described the deep alienation among Israel's Sephardic community, and how some children, under existing social pressures, sometimes claim they are French, rather than of Tunisian descent.[50] Some even change their names "not to 'neutral' Hebrew forms but to distinctively European-Jewish ones."[51]

Ashkenazi ethno-centricity has not gone unchallenged. Leading the opposition to the entrenched system of discrimination against the majority is the Black Panther Party, which was formed for the express purpose of giving expression to the interests of Israel's dark-skinned Jews, who remain to this day outside the Ashkenazi power structure. The name they have chosen for their party has a revolutionary ring to it, meant no doubt to convey a sense of class conflict and identification with the national liberation struggle in the Third World. Significantly, when told by former Prime Minister Golda Meir that the name was ill-chosen and that it gave her sleepless nights, one of the founders of the Black Panther Party replied that he was satisfied because that was precisely the intended purpose.

Tensions between the Ashkenazi and Sephardic Jews in Israel have had a deep impact on the existing contradiction between Israeli Jews and Arabs, for Israeli society encompasses Palestinian Arabs who, as a third community, occupy the lowest rung in the social ladder. Above them are the Sephardim and at the very top are the Ashkenazim. The common social concerns that the Sephardim have with the Arabs should make them more understanding of the Arabs' claims and aspirations. However, this very fact may be a source of worry to them because Israeli society is based on Ashkenazi norms and ideals.

Hostility between Oriental Jews and Arabs in Israel is deepened by the attitude of the Israeli establishment, for such tensions are reassuring to the Ashkenazi. One writer, dealing with the subject of Arab-Sephardic relations, noted that Moroccan Jews "manifest such hostility toward anything labelled 'Arab,'" whereas Iraqi Jews do not manifest "enough" hostility.[52] Is there, one wonders, a required degree of hatred that makes a Sephardic Jew eligible for acceptance? If the answer is yes, then this would account partly for the suppression of Sephardic feelings of solidarity with the Arabs.

Labor is one field that enables the white Ashkenazi establishment to sharpen the conflicts between Arabs and Sephardic Jews. Cheap Arab labor is used to undermine the bargaining power of the already exploited Sephardic workers. When a Jewish construction worker asks for better wages, he is told that he can be replaced by an Arab who will work hard and for less.[53]

Furthermore, the Sephardim see themselves as caught in the middle between the Arab freedom fighters and the Zionist colonists, sensing that they do not belong completely in either camp. Economically, they are part-privileged and part-deprived. Culturally, many of them are Arabs, but religiously, they are Jews. This situation does not encourage a sharpening of consciousness, nor a clear definition of priorities.

The Ashkenazi certainty with regard to the loyalties of the Sephardim is not by any means complete. It is significant in this respect that when it was decided to construct Nazareth Illit (Upper Nazareth) on the hills directly above Arab Nazareth, a "preponderantly European population" was settlee thee as the only guaranteed means of controlling the Arab population. The Sephardim, not deemed completely trustworthy, were kept in the minority.[54] Ashkenazi feeling of insecurity about Arab Jews is in a sense justified, for a cultural and economic community of interests does exist between the two groups, even though they do not realize it at present.

Some members of the Sephardic community now show signs of responding to Arab appeals to return to their countries of origin. *Yediot Aharonot* of May 7, 1976, reported that over 45 Jewish Moroccans, who had settled in Israel, had decided to "return" to their homeland. They indicated that they had nothing "to fear of the Arabs in Morocco," and they noted that "thousands of Jews are living there in peace."[55] When the Israeli-Zionist establishment called on the leaders of the Moroccan community to deny the news, they did not readily oblige, a fact that demonstrates the situation to be "far more serious than publicly acknowledged,"[56] as Shaul Ben-Shimon, Chairman of the World Union of North African Jews, indicated.

While the right of every Arab Jew to go back to the land of his birth should be upheld, one should emphasize that such a "return" provides no overall answer to the Sephardic question. Rather than posit "correct" or utopian solutions that are costly, it might be more realistic, more human, and far more revolutionary to think of the Sephardim as forming "a natural bridge for dialogue with the Arab world," as Black Panther Party Secretary (and Knesset member) Charlie Bitton indicated at a press conference in Paris on March 26, 1975.[57]

It should be pointed out, however, that the white Ashkenazi attitude vis-à-vis the Sephardic Oriental Jews has always been moderated by economic considerations, the need for settlers, and other pragmatic factors. On the other hand, there has been no sign of change in the attitude toward the Palestinians and the Arabs in general. Perhaps Zionist willingness to compromise with the Sephardim at the expense of the Arabs, a typically colonialist tactic, accounts for the fact that so far there has been no coalition between the two oppressed groups, although there exist both objective and subjective bases for such a coalition.

THE PURE JEW'S BURDEN

Though distinct and pervasive, the myth of the superiority of the white Occidental Jew and his right to colonize Palestine is not central to the Zionist outlook. Rather, Zionist apologetics are founded more fundamentally on the image of the Jew in the abstract—the "pure" Jew, a category that cuts across all races and cultures because it is taken to constitute a race or a nation in itself, and is not merely an offshoot of the white race or Western culture.

This pure Jewishness, like whiteness, grants the Jews certain timeless and "sacred rights," unmodified by any historical processes or claims. The source of this timelessness can be either divine or racial, depending on the beliefs of the Zionist, for as indicated previously, one can be a pure Jew in a racial, ethnic, or religious sense. But regardless of the *basis* for the absoluteness of the claimed Jewish rights, *all* Zionists agree that nobody else, not even the Palestinians, can have stronger or even comparable claims on Palestine.

The allegation of an eternal link, resulting in an exclusivist timeless claim, is evident in the words of Israel's first Minister of Religion, Rabbi (J. L. Hakohen Fishman) Maimon, who asserted that the bond between the Jewish people and their *eretz* was a "mysterium of holiness." Others might have at best a "political and secular, external, incidental and temporary" bond, whereas the Jews, even in "their state of destruction," have an "imminent, heavenly and eternal . . . bond."[58]

The Palestinians, in this simple scheme, are nonexistent or, at best, they are Canaanites to be expelled or transferred because they are the "political and secular, external, incidental and temporary" inhabitants in a land allocated to the Jewish people since the beginning of time and till the end of days. The mythical yet nonreligious Aaron David Gordon did not argue against the Palestinians, he simply dreamt them away. "In my dream," he wrote, "I come to the land. And it is barren and desolate and given over to *aliens;* destruction darkens its face and foreign rule corrupts it. . . . And the only link that ties my soul to her, the only reminder that I am her son and she my mother, is that my soul was desolate as hers."[59] A deep subjective, yet timeless, bond is claimed as the only criterion relevant to Palestine, reducing the Palestinians to the status of aliens and their existence to the status of mere "foreign rule."

When the Palestinians resist the view that reduces them to marginality, and strongly or mildly protest, the voice of "the armed prophet" comes out loud and clear. In a "historical and moral sense," Ben Gurion said, Palestine, the Holy Land, is a country "without inhabitants."[60] Ben Gurion, elaborating on that point, said that "the rights to Palestine do not, as in other countries they do, belong to the existing settlers" (natives, that is). Palestine is thus set apart and singled out as *sui generis,* and this determination cannot be questioned by fallible human beings, be they "Jews or Arabs," for the "crux" of the issue of Palestine, as he said, "is the Right of Return of Jewry Dispersed,"[61] an absolute right standing at the beginning of history and at its end, which leaves the Palestinians out in the cold and negates their rights.

Any questioning by the irrelevant victim is considered blasphemy. If the Egyptians protest that Sinai is part of Egyptian territory, or the Syrians claim that the Golan Heights is part of Syria, they hear in answer the prophetic voice of Israel's Chief Rabbi Nissim, telling them that Israel's boundaries are not "a question of law or logic," as the Arabs may think, and "neither is it a matter of human treatment or that sort of thing."[62]

Gentile Zionists, like Garry Wills in his *Esquire* article, cited previously, adopt the same logic. Wills expressed his impatience at those who defend Israel on merely political grounds. "There is something shamefaced about the marginal pragmatic arguments made for [the Israelis], so distant from the mystical first claims upon the land."[63] Long before Wills, Balfour wrote in 1919 with the same sense of awe that "Zionism, be it right or wrong, good or bad . . . is of far profounder import than the desires and prejudices of the 700,000 Arabs who inhabit that ancient land."[64]

The land to the Zionist is ancient, holy, and metahistorical. The historical political claims of the Arabs are consequently mere prejudice compared to the Zionists' timeless claims, which exist beyond good and evil. The whole affair is divine, godly, and mystical, conceived on such a high religious plane that any questioning of Zionist rights or "that sort of thing" becomes mere prejudice bordering on blasphemy.

It was in this context that the Zionists could voice with impunity the slogan: "A land without a people for a people without a land."[65] The Zionists were all well aware that the Palestinians were living in Palestine and that diaspora Jews were living in the lands of their birth. But the timeless link between the *eretz* and the Jewish people is what makes the diaspora Jews rootless wanderers and the Palestinians not a people or, at best, a people with marginal claims. All of this is achieved without even having to evolve theories of racial or cultural superiority or inferiority—it is rather a theory of the religio-ethnic eternal relevance of the self and the total marginality of the "Other."

It was probably in defense of this myth of the eternal Jewish rights that Menahem Begin told some *kibbutzniks* in 1969 to live geographically in Palestine, yet to go on pretending and believing and claiming that it was *Eretz Yisrael:* "If this is Palestine and not the Land of Israel, then you are conquerors and not tillers of the land. You are invaders. If this is Palestine then it belongs to the people who lived here before you came. Only if it is the Land of Israel do you have a right to live in" it.[66]

The myth of the timeless claims of the Jew on the land of Palestine and the marginality of the natives is a form of rationalization more insidious and far more unethical than the settler-colonial myth based on genetic or ethnic claims of supremacy. After all, the conventional varieties of settler-colonial myths recognize the "Other" insofar as they try to prove his presumed inferiority, and insofar as they see him as the object of oppression. The Zionist myth of Jewish rights speaks in lofty terms of the Love of Zion, refusing to admit the existence of any form of oppression.

To view the natives as irrelevant and marginal, rather than as inferior, is a form of rationalization not without its parallels. The polished "separate but equal" slogan, which is a weaker version of the "separate and superior" outlook, is strikingly akin to the Zionist myth. In South Africa, the term "apartheid" itself does not really imply superiority, it just means "separateness." If the Zionist settlers saw the Palestinians as temporary dwellers alien to the Holy Land, the white settlers in South Africa regard "Africans living in urban areas as aliens, temporarily residing in white society."[67] The concept of superiority and inferiority is not pertinent here. As a matter of fact, it seems that the South African regime, to consolidate apartheid, is encouraging political autonomy and sovereignty in the Bantusans (the equivalent of the West Bank and the Gaza Strip).

Rationalizations based on the idea of separateness rather than superiority make it easy to perpetuate the claim of the pure Jew's rights without much embarrassment for the Zionists or their supporters in the West. The notorious and discredited formula of superiority and inferiority could be replaced by the more "moderate" and acceptable slogan of relevance and irrelevance.

More important still is the *limited scope* of the myth of the pure Jew, a feature that renders it harmless to everyone except its direct victims. The conventional, more familiar, racist apologetics, such as Nazi ideology, divided *all races* in *all territories* into "superior" and "inferior." All Semites, Negroids, and Asiatics in all places were inferior, and only Aryans (especially the Teutons) were superior. The scope of Nazi imperialism was global and therefore it required an equally global categorization of races that embraced all mankind. On the other hand, the Zionist claim to the rights of the pure Jew, which was designed to legitimize Zionist settler colonialism, does not take the world as its arena; it simply relates eternal Jewish rights to one territory, Palestine.

Narrowing down Zionist ambitions to the *eretz* of Palestine proved to be the least embarrassing of all rationalizing Zionist claims from the standpoint of diaspora Jewry. This myth of rights, which is related to a faraway place, is placed in a special compartment in the mind of the Jew, leaving him free to deal with any issue he might face in his own homeland according to the dictates of his conscience and his situation. To clarify this point, a comparison of the attitudes of American and South African Jewry might be useful. American Jewry forms an organic part of a relatively open political system and has a liberal outlook; South African Jewry forms an organic part of the closed system of apartheid and generally adopts an attitude that condones, not rejects, this racist policy. Nevertheless, and despite the difference in political outlook, a large number of the members of *both* communities do not hesitate to proclaim their Zionist beliefs and sympathies.

The anomaly of this situation is partly understandable when we observe that neither the liberalism of Jewish-Americans nor the racist traditions of South African Jews figure as factors in determining their espousal or rejection of Zionism's racist premises. American liberalism and South African apartheid merely reinforce or supplant their belief in Zionism because the Zionism of the diaspora Jew, be he a liberal or a racist, relates to his attitude concerning only one territory in the world, leaving unchallenged his views of the world at large. Thus, he is able to formulate positions and adopt attitudes on different issues that are in no way determined by his Zionism. As a liberal American, he opposes his country's involvement in Vietnam, supports the civil rights movement, and calls for separation of church and state; yet, as a Zionist, he lauds Israeli victories and expresses unqualified admiration for a society that dislodged the natives and discriminates against their remnants.

The limited scope of the Zionist myth of the rights of the pure Jew has proved also to be an asset insofar as Westerners are concerned. By relating their eternal rights to a territory in Asia, the Zionists remained in complete harmony with the West. Herzl underscored the "parallelism of interest affecting both Britain" and the Zionists.[68] The British, he surmised, would welcome the Zionist project as long as it diverted Jewish immigration *from* the pure shores of Albion.

A similar marriage of convenience was reached between the Zionists and the Nazis. The Zionists set out to transfer the Jews out of Nazi territory to another territory, and the Nazis tolerated and even cooperated with them. A Nazi directive, issued in Munich on April 13, 1935, by the Bavarian political police, points out that the Zionists' "sincere activity directed toward emigration meets *halfway* the intentions of the Reich Government to remove the Jews *from* Germany.[69] The Zionists in their naiveté, advanced the argument that the "dissimilation" [*sic*] of German Jews and emigration to Palestine "could be a '*mutually fair* solution.' "[70]

The limited territorial scope of this Zionist myth has led many people, especially in the West, to believe that Zionism is not racist. They are right, in a sense; Nazism, for instance, was not racist vis-à-vis the Japanese. From the Western perspective, Zionism is a mere political ideology formulated by Jews, for Jews, relating to Jews, which does not imply any discrimination against gentiles in the United States or England. Some Westerners even make a case for the positive, constructive role played by Zionism among Jewish-Americans, providing them with a sense of cohesion and belonging, which may be a valid argument. However, from the perspective of Asia, it is definitely racism and discrimination. The discrepancy here is not between theory and practice, but rather between theory and *two* kinds of practices, one incidental and temporary, and the other necessary and essential. In the West, the claims of the pure Jew's rights do not hold; and therefore Zionist practice, whether constructive or not, is purely incidental. In Palestine, on the other hand, these claims do hold, and therefore Zionist discriminatory practice is necessary and essential. It is primarily in Palestine and it is among the Palestinians that Zionism has its destructive effect, occupying a land and dispersing a whole community. And it is there that it has to be judged. (Some students of the Jewish-American scene observe though that the gradual Zionization of the Jewish community has also moved it more to the right. *Commentary,* published by the American Jewish Committee, has become one of the main platforms for the advocates of cold war, use of nuclear deterrents, and a more activist American foreign policy. This stance of *Commentary* and Israeli sympathizers, such as Senator Henry Jackson, is logical in view of Israel's heavy reliance on American arms and its need for an activist and even interventionist American policy, as a guarantee for its survival and security.)

Ironically, some spokesmen for the South African apartheid regime, who are not concerned with the incidental Zionist practice in the West, have realistically evaluated Zionist practice in Asia. South Africa's former Prime Minister Verwoerd scored some Zionists who wanted to set up a distinction between Israel's "policy of separate development" on the basis of religion (or "pure Jewishness") and South Africa's comparable policies on a racial basis. "If differentiation is wrong on one score, it is also wrong on another,"[71] he declared. The editor of the *Zionist Record,* official organ of the South African Zionist Movement, fully understood Verwoerd's position. He ridiculed the inconsistency latent in anyone's claiming "the rights of Jews to political power and sovereignty" in Israel and in the next breath supporting the positions "which seek to take away the same hard-won right from the children of the Boers."[72]

THE SOCIALIST JEW'S BURDEN

Zionists have in common with Western imperialists the myth of the white man's superiority, and with some settler-colonists they assume and share the privilege of separate development. Nevertheless, the Zionists have faced problems that other colonists have not had to contend with. Given the historical ambience of nineteenth-century Eastern Europe, many Jewish youths joined the ranks of revolutionary movements. Zionism, as the records show, proposed to the colonial powers that it could divert Jewish youth from the revolutionary course.

To achieve this objective, the Labor-Zionist myth of settlement was evolved. Settlement was to take place not in the name of racial superiority or eternal claims, but rather in the name of human labor and even socialism. This logic was not entirely unique to the Zionists, for there was a whole school of "imperialist socialists" who, in the name of "progress" and internationalism, found it incumbent on them to settle somewhere in Asia and Africa for the purpose of bringing progress and socialism to those places. Some of the Saint Simonists encouraged settler colonialism in Algeria for that reason, and many a Dutch socialist defended his country's civilizing onslaught on the Indonesians. Western imperialism was sanctioned by some socialists who believed that capitalism, and *ergo* imperialism, represented the highest level of development yet reached by man.

The Labor-Zionist myth emerged from this cluster of ideas. The Zionist settlers were not merely Jewish *olim,* they were also socialist *halutzim,* tillers of the land of their forefathers. "Our settlers," Buber wrote to Gandhi, "do not come here in Palestine as do the colonists from the Occident to have natives do their work for them; they themselves set their shoulders to the plow to make the land fruitful."[73] The new Hebrew settlers came to the land burdened by the Jewish past in the diaspora, with all of its abnormalities and parasitism. But through Hebrew labor, so went the Labor-Zionist argument, the new settler could cleanse himself. In redeeming the *eretz* by tilling it and making it bloom, the settlers were also redeeming themselves. As Buber phrased it in a mystical way in his letter to Gandhi, "this land recognizes us, for it is fruitful through us."[74] The whole thing is couched in such innocent cosmic language that one experiences tremendous moral uplift. This not only eases one's conscience, but makes one lose sight of irksome historical details. Amos Elon, the Israeli writer, quoted a line from a charming *halutzic* song, in which the farmers describe themselves as the *first* to arrive "like swallows in spring" on burning fields and on the barren and wasted land.[75]

An insight into this cosmic innocence and faith in the healing power of labor is given by Ben Gurion, the founder of Labor-Zionism. In 1915, while in New York, he said that the true right to a country—as to anything else—does not spring "from political or court authority" (all negligible matters from his Labor-Zionist standpoint), but it comes from "work." Then he unfurled a "red" slogan, quite appealing to any revolutionary audience: "The real and lasting ownership is of the workers."[76]   But transfer of concepts from one level to another produces different results. Such a slogan would be truly revolutionary if used by French workers on French soil; once applied by a French worker to Algeria, it becomes a threat of expropriation. It seems that Ben Gurion was vaguely aware of this transfer of meaning, and therefore he used a more violent and radical language, describing mass immigration as something that "recks not of history," but rather "pours into the place where conditions for its absorption have been made ready in advance."[77] This is not socialist humanism— it is an invasion. Commenting on this type of apologetics, the Israeli writer Amos Kenan expressed his doubt that Zionism could have "accomplished its conquests and achievements without the hypocrisy of socialism. Just as Christianity served as the moral alibi for the Crusaders," socialism served that function for the Zionists.[78]

Another argument for the legitimacy of Zionist settlement is technological superiority, which is closely related to the Labor-Zionist claim. Back in April 1936, Mussa Alami, a Palestinian Arab leader, met with Ben Gurion in the house of Moshe Sharett. Ben Gurion, in his own words, "began with the old tune he had prepared" about swamps being drained, deserts blooming, and general prosperity for all. But the Arab interrupted him, "Listen, listen, *Hawaja* Ben Gurion. I would rather that there be a barren waste here for another hundred years, another thousand years, till *we* can make it flourish and redeem it."[79] Ben Gurion, reminiscing over this statement some years later, could not help commenting that the Arab was telling the truth and that "the old tune" sounded empty and more ridiculous than ever.

So the cosmic innocence of the *halutzim* and their technological superiority were challenged from the outset by a complex reality and by the dissenting voices of the victims. Some Zionists, at the beginning of the century, hearing these angry voices, preferred not to speak of a *halutzic* Adam, and urged the settlers to hurry or else "others will take Palestine." A more prosaic and less cosmic Jewish physician rudely denuded the myth when he said, "No one will take it, the Arabs have it and they will stay the leading force by a great margin."[80]

Ironically enough, the Zionists were not even the first settler-colonists to attempt usurping Palestine in modern times. A group of Christian German immigrants, members of the Temple Society, inspired by religious considerations like those of the Zionists, "had the notion of settling permanent Christian pilgrims in the Holy Land." Like the Jews, they were "primarily committed to agricultural settlements, but unlike the Jews they were excellent farmers."[81] Templar communities in Jerusalem, Jaffa, Haifa, and the Galilee existed all through the period of the Mandate and well into 1948. It was these German settlers, most of them German *sabras,* so to speak, who formed the nucleus of the Nazi party in Palestine.[82]

The flooding of Palestine with Jewish *halutzim* or Christian Templars, Jewish or Christian nationalists, was bound to arouse the natives. When the Palestinian resistance began, *all* settlements were attacked, Zionist and German. Walter Laqueur, an Israeli historian of Zionism, pointed out that during the 1908 Palestinian protest, "the German settlements . . . came in for attacks until Berlin intervened and dispatched a warship to Haifa"[83] to *defend* the German settlers; there was no other alternative.

Despite the thick web of apologetics, despite all the ingenuity, the "less civilized" Arab "natives" regarded the Zionists as " 'white settlers,' " who came "to occupy the Middle East."[84] Like the racial, cultural, or religious apologetics, socialist rationalizations did not deceive anyone, except perhaps the apologists themselves.

In the preceding chapters, the origins of Zionism, its covert yet deep anti-Semitic orientation, its semiorganic link with Western imperialism, and its general and specific traits and apologetics have been dealt with so as to deepen our understanding of Zionist ideology and practice. It is my belief that a just and a permanent solution for the Middle East conflict should be based on an awareness of the distinction between Zionism and Judaism, of the tension between Zionism and the diaspora, and of the latent contradictions between the Ashkenazi power structure in Israel and the Sephardic masses. Such a solution should be premised on the fact that even though the majority of diaspora Jewry and Israelis are, at the present, dominated by the Zionist outlook and intimidated by the Israeli-Zionist power structure, they are still potential allies in a humanist and discriminating anti-Zionist struggle that provides them with intelligent and credible alternatives on which to base a viable solution.

Before trying to draw the general outlines of such a program, it is essential to deal with the more obvious casualty of Zionist practice in the Middle East and the backbone of the anti-Zionist struggle: the Palestinian Arabs. In the subsequent three chapters, different aspects of their situation will be dealt with, such as their expulsion from their land of origin, the discrimination against their remnants in Israel, and their response, as well as that of the Arabs and the Afro-Asian peoples at large, to the Israeli-Zionist onslaught.

7

A LAND WITHOUT A PEOPLE

INTENTIONS

The central Zionist premise of Jewish peoplehood, as noted earlier, implies two transfers, one of Jews and the other of Arabs. The rationalizing myths, whether founded on claims of racial superiority, sacred rights, or Zionist socialist humanism, imply the nonexistence or at least the marginal existence of the Arabs and the need for their physical removal, partially or wholly. The transfer of the Arabs is the *sine qua non* for the establishment of a Zionist state for the Jews.

But the Zionists have the all too heavy burden of the Jewish moral tradition to contend with, and therefore the transfer is projected as having been the result of an innocent oversight. The Zionist founding fathers, so goes the argument, knew very little about the Arabs, and the Arab exodus was a natural outcome of war and conflict. It is even argued that the Zionist leaders and theoreticians, always full of lofty ideals, actually wanted the Arabs to stay; indeed they begged them to do so, but to no avail!

Proponents of this myth cite, as an example, Herzl's "noble optimism" and good intentions regarding cooperation with the Arabs. In his utopian novel *Old-New Land*, Herzl projected an Arab welcome for Zionist settlement because the Arabs would surely benefit from it. In the novel, the leader of the local Arabs in the future Zionist state expresses his loyalty and gratitude to the new Zionist order because "the Jews have made us rich."[1] Herzl is also known to have written an idealistic letter in 1899 to a Palestinian Arab, assuring him that there would be no demographic transformations in Palestine, for who, after all, would think of removing the Arabs from there? "Their well-being and private wealth will increase through the importation of ours."[2]

Max Nordau is often pictured as having been unaware of the presence of Arabs in Palestine. In a touching moment in the history of Zionism, Nordau learned, in the First Zionist Congress (1897) quite by accident, that *Eretz Yisrael* was populated by Arabs. He ran to his friend Herzl in protest. "But then we are committing an injustice," the indignant Nordau is quoted as having said. Nor were Nordau and Herzl the only ones who are said to have voiced such misgivings. Weizmann was also given to making all kinds of moral statements about how the Jewish state would be judged by what it would do to its Arab population.

What is one to deduce from such declarations by misguided or misinformed idealists? In light of historical reality and the tragic events that have taken place since they were made, do such proclamations of innocence and disclaimers of bad intentions have any relevance or value?

Undue emphasis on intentions and motivation has vitiated political analysis. One's intentions do not necessarily lead to the intended results, especially if one is venturing beyond one's personal environment and is attempting to create a new social reality. Though they help us to understand the behavior of the actor, motives and intentions cannot serve as a basis for the full explanation of the phenomenon, nor can they undo the tragedy they may have led to.

The discrepancy between "good" personal intentions and tragic political consequences is clearly detected in the case of Haim Margalit Kalvarisky, who worked for Baron Hirsch's colonization society. By temperament an integrationist, and by intention a man well disposed toward the natives, Kalvarisky was well aware of the need for an understanding with the Arabs. His good intentions notwithstanding, it was precisely Kalvarisky's land purchase in the Tiberias district around the turn of the century that "first provoked Arab resistance on a major scale." When about one-half of the district was acquired in 1899–1902 by Jewish land companies, the Arabs began to fear what they rightly termed "denationalization."[3]

Israeli author Amos Elon attributed lofty motives to the *halutzim* who did not purchase the land, but labored on it. According to him, the Zionist pioneers were colonists in a technical sense, yet by "temperament, motivation, circumstance and choice" they differed from other colonists.[4] But, then, does one's temperament really change one's position, and does one's concept of one's self determine one's acts? Let us take "Hebrew labor," the central *halutzic* concept, which was intended (we are told by many a Zionist apologist) to be a means of avoiding, or at least allaying, "the conflict between the two nations." Once placed in the concrete reality of practice, Hebrew labor served only as a means of arousing and intensifying the very fears it was meant to allay. The inexorable logic of this concept "led from a deliberate partition of the economy to the indeliberate partition of the country in bloodshed,"[5] as Elon himself put it. Once unleashed, it had to take its inevitable course.

From the outset, the situation as it developed between the settlers and the Arabs could not be contained within the limits of a well-intentioned theory; it inevitably led to a relationship of inequality and oppression. Indifference to the Arabs was a most fateful mistake of Zionist policy in the early days, according to some writers. Nevertheless, as one sensible Zionist settler concluded, more attention would not have solved the problem, for the Arabs were hostile and would always be hostile "even if the Jews were paragons of modesty and self-denial."[6] The fact is that the early idealistic Zionist settlers—and there were surely many of them—were nevertheless settler-colonists, usurpers of the land, despite their morally laudable personal behavior and intentions.

The attitude of an Arab friend of Ben Gurion, a certain Yehia Effendi, illustrates the distinction between personal relationships, on the one hand, and socio-political considerations, on the other. In 1915, while Ben Gurion was detained by the Turks as a Zionist agitator, he met his Arab friend who, upon being told the reason for Ben Gurion's detention, said, "As your friend—I'm sorry. As an Arab—I'm glad." The Arab was human enough to respond with compassion to Ben Gurion, the friend. Yet, politically, his national awareness led him to oppose the objectives of the Zionist program that Ben Gurion was promoting. Ben Gurion himself felt that the Arab was telling the truth and that the well-advertised Zionist intentions were mere "verbose fuss."[7]

By the same token, as a foreign-implanted body, the settlers were perceived by the displaced Palestinian peasants as colonists, and resistance was understandably mounted against them. The displaced or threatened Palestinian peasant did not distinguish between a Marxist settler or a capitalist one, between a well-intentioned settler and an ill-intentioned one, between a peace-loving settler and a militant one. To him they were all intruders and usurpers. As for the settlers themselves, their goals as Zionists required them to shelve ideological and moral considerations. At times, they liked to engage in theoretical discussions, but the process of colonization and expropriation went on relentlessly. The motives and ideals of the Zionist settlers may have differed, but the practical goal of colonization was the common objective that bound them together.

THE ZIONIST STRATEGY II

Although, as indicated above, intentions, whether good or bad, cannot form an adequate basis for a full explanation of a social development and structure, when dealing with the issue of the Arab population transfer, motives should be examined. This is necessary in view of the fact that so much Zionist propaganda is predicated on the myth of the transfer of the Arabs *as an accident of war or as an oversight.* One must, therefore, test these allegations, not only against the inner logic of the myth and against later developments, but also in light of the very statements and proclaimed *intentions* of the Zionist leaders themselves.

To begin with, the very idea of a Zionist oversight and inadequate knowledge is debatable. How could a mystic such as Rabbi J. H. Sonnenfeld notice the Arabs' presence, their resentment, and resistance from the very beginning, while the practical Zionists failed to do so? In a letter written in 1898, Rabbi Sonnenfeld referred to "the storm that was aroused among the masses of Arabs and Christians."[8] Using the religious terminology that came more naturally to him, he said that when Herzl entered the Holy Land, "hell entered with him."[9]

There is now a rich and subtle Israeli literature on the subject of Zionist "intentions" that does not rest content with crude Zionist allegations of good intentions. Yeshayahu Leibowitz, the Israeli scientist and thinker, argues that the early Zionists "for obvious psychological reasons, did not want to see the truth and did not realize that they were deluding themselves and their fellows."[10] In an interview with Ben Ezer, Shlomo Avineri gives a similar account. He thinks that the early Zionists sincerely believed that they could accomplish the miraculous feat of making "an omelet without breaking the eggs." This patently ridiculous attempt is explained by him on the grounds that there was "a certain functional element in ignoring the concreteness of the Arab question" and in glossing over the inevitability of a clash between settlers and natives. Most of the founding fathers, so goes Avineri's argument, were idealists and humanists, and therefore a full realization on their part of the fact that the "price of Zionism is removal of the Arabs" would have made them give up the project altogether. "Ignoring the concreteness of the Arab problem was an internal defense mechanism of Zionist consciousness." Only through unconscious self-deceptions were they able to maintain their Zionist outlook.[11] There is undoubtedly some truth to that subtle analysis of Zionist self-delusion, because uprooting a whole people required a form of defense mechanism.

But there are still too many bothersome details that challenge the preceding argument. A careful reading of Zionist literature will reveal that the proclamations of innocent oversight are grossly exaggerated. Herzl's suggestions concerning the "gentle expropriation of [the] private property" of the inhabitants of the territory to be settled by the Zionists, the ways and means "of the expropriation and the removal of the poor," and the use of "the natives" in killing big snakes, and so on, then "giving them employment in transit countries" are by now only too well known.[12] These diary entries were written four years before Herzl's 1899 idealistic letter sent to the Palestinian Arab in which he denied such intentions. Three years after that letter was dispatched, Herzl, writing to Chamberlain about Cyprus as another possible site for Zionist settlement, did not hesitate to outline for him the plan for the depopulation of the said territory. "The Moslems will move away and the Greeks will gladly sell their lands at a good price and migrate to Athens or Crete."[13] It mattered very little from the political Zionist perspective: "Arabs, Greeks, the whole 'mixed multitude' of the Orient,"[14] as Herzl casually described the inhabitants of the settlement site. However, the Zionist leader advised, "not everything in politics is disclosed to the public—only results [*faits accomplis*, in modern Zionist parlance], or whatever may happen to be needed in a discussion."[15]

Even Nordau's remorse and moment of truth were short-lived, for Herzl told him that the matter of the natives would be attended to later, whereupon Nordau resumed his campaigning for the Zionist project. He remained a devoted Zionist long after "ignorance" turned into full knowledge. Nordau's attitude and views were more akin to Jabotinsky's—an "extreme" stance even by Zionist criteria.

As for Weizmann, evidence is not lacking that he, too, was fully aware of the plans for the transfer of the Arabs. Lord Boothby, a close friend of the Zionist leader, stated in a 1964 BBC program that the Balfour Declaration, to which Weizmann had devoted so much energy, "had made provisions for the Arabs to be moved elsewhere."[16] When the statement caused an uproar, Weizmann's widow wrote to Lord Boothby "confirming that he was correct."[17] A senior staff officer of the Weizmann Archives in Israel also stated that "the Arabs were never mentioned in the original draft and, by way of omission, the possibility of a transfer becomes plausible."[18] Much earlier, on August 13, 1937, the *Jewish Chronicle* published a document initialed by Weizmann, indicating that he regarded the whole success of the partition plan as dependent on "whether the Government genuinely did or did not wish to carry out this recommendation" for a population transfer.[19] Though the memorandum was secret, its authenticity "has never been denied [and] the Zionist named as furnishing it to the *Chronicle* was suspended by the Zionist Action Committee."[20] Herzl had said that not everything needs to be revealed to the public. Perhaps it was with this in mind that Weizmann winked at a friend of his when Herbert Samuel, British High Commissioner to Palestine, called "for Zionist-Arab partnership." The friend recorded that "one might as well expect a ferret to cooperate with a rabbit."[21]

The unethical nature of political Zionism was admitted by Arthur Ruppin who, being in charge of Zionist colonization during the 1920s and 1930s, had privileged access to accurate information. In 1928, in trying to face the issue of the native Palestinians without evasiveness, he reached the conclusion that it was difficult "to realize Zionism and still *bring it constantly into line with the demands of general ethics.*" By 1936, "he had to admit it was not only 'difficult' but simply impossible." Describing the very process of the colonization he sponsored, he said, "On every site where we purchase land and where we settle people, the present cultivators will inevitably be dispossessed." Concluding, he remarked that as long as Zionist work in Palestine was carried on against the will of the Arabs, "there is no alternative but that lives should be lost."[22] Ruppin even warned against what he termed Herzl's "imperialist approach," for he felt that the implementation of Herzl's concept of the Jewish state was predicated on disregarding the presence of the Arabs.[23]

Dayan also is capable of similar insights. In discussing the alternatives as he saw them, he fully realized that Zionism was faced with two choices: "either making allowances for the views and desires of the Arabs and putting an end to Zionism," or "carrying on with immigration, land purchase and settlement, while denying the right of the Arabs of Palestine to determine the future of the country."[24]

Ruppin and Dayan opted for the inevitable course leading to more warfare and loss of life. "It is our destiny," said Ruppin, "to be in a state of continued warfare with the Arabs. This situation may well be undesirable, but such is the reality."[25] In fairness to Ruppin, though, one must add that his surrender to the logic of his Zionist position was not complete, and he remained until the time of his death a tormented soul trying to find a humane and just way out. But Dayan's conclusion, to which he reconciled himself a long time ago without any evidence of regret or remorse, was that there was no choice—*ein breira*: Israel will simply have to go on fighting, expanding, and displacing the native people of Palestine.

There is no dearth of evidence that the proponents of Zionism were prepared to follow wherever their nationalist ideology led them. In 1919, Israel Zangwill remarked that the Palestinian Arabs would be gradually transferred and settled in what he called the new and vast Arabian Kingdom, for, as he logically perceived (given his Zionist convictions), "only thus can Palestine become a 'Jewish National Home.' "[26] Zangwill, too, like Ruppin and others, realized later the inherent racism in the Zionist scheme. As he put it in *The Voice of Jerusalem,* published in 1920, the Zionists had either "to grapple with the problem of a large alien population," or drive them out "by the sword . . . as our forefathers did."[27]

Joseph Weitz, who replaced Ruppin as the Jewish Agency representative in charge of settlement, reported in the September 29, 1967, issue of *Davar,* organ of the Histadrut, that in 1940 he and other Zionist leaders concluded that there was "no room for both peoples together in this country." The achievement of Zionist objectives, he realized, required "a Palestine or at least Western Palestine (west of the Jordan river) without

Arabs." He wrote that it was necessary "to transfer the Arabs from here to the neighboring countries. To transfer all of them. . . . And only after such transfer will the country be able to absorb millions of our brethren."[28] The support of top Zionist figures had been secured, Weitz said, and "some preliminary preparations were made in order to put this theory into practice."[29] Similarly in 1912, Leo Motzkin, a member of the Zionist Executive, recognized that the only way out of a Jewish-Arab conflict was resettlement of the Arabs elsewhere. And again in 1914, Motzkin and Sokolow toyed with the same idea.[30]

By 1945, the transfer of the Arab population of Palestine was an accepted goal. In an article written that year, Hannah Arendt pointed out that the transfer of the Palestinian Arabs "was earnestly discussed a few years ago in General Zionist circles."[31] We know that by then the transfer was no longer a subject of debate; it had become, on an earlier date, more or less official Zionist policy espoused by most Zionist schools and trends. Item 2 of the enlarged program of the Zionist Organization, presented in 1943 to General Hurley, President Roosevelt's personal envoy to the Middle East, referred to "an eventual transfer of the Arab population to Iraq."[32]

Vladimir Jabotinsky condemned this Zionist "evacuation prattle" because it was "downright criminal." His Zionist biographer, Joseph Schechtman, went on to say that Jabotinsky was no admirer of the Arabs and that he realized that no *modus vivendi* could be worked out. Consequently, he felt that a Jewish majority had to be "achieved against the wish of the country's present Arab majority,"[33] a presumably less criminal act than evacuation from the Revisionist point of view.

But the temptation of a population transfer was nevertheless too strong. Jabotinsky envisaged the prospect of voluntary and "organized migration" of the Arabs, and a paper written by a Jewish-American "philanthropist" on a population transfer did not fail to impress him deeply. This Revisionist theoretician, even though irritated by the Zionists' "evacuation prattle," worked out a little conspiracy to get the Arabs out. He proposed that the Zionist Organization openly oppose Arab migration from Palestine, thereby putting to rest the fears of the Arabs that the transfer scheme was Zionist-supported. On the contrary, the natives would think that the Zionists wanted them to stay on because they wanted to exploit them. Like obstinate children, they would then opt to leave. The scheme was more simplistic than Machiavellian, for the Arabs proved less ignorant than he had imagined and more suspicious than he had hoped.[34]

Nor was the plan for transferring the natives confined to those who settled in the *eretz* for capitalistic or merely nationalistic reasons; it was also the plan acquiesced in by those who settled in Palestine in order to establish an egalitarian and idealistic society. To cite an example, Dov Ber Borochov (1881–1917), the Russion Zionist and father of the Zionist "left," showed remarkable awareness of the fact that the territorialist solution—that is, the transfer and settlement of the Jews in a territory of their own—could *not* occur "without a bitter struggle, without cruelty and injustices, without suffering for the innocent and guilty alike." In outlining his vision for the future of the natives, he stated that they "will be economically and culturally absorbed by those who bring order to the land and develop its productive forces. The Jewish immigrants will build up Palestine and the native population will in time be absorbed by the Jews, both economically and culturally." The history of Zionist settlement will be "written in sweat, tears, and blood."[35]

But there were some voices of dissent in the background, persistently reminding the Zionists of the injustices that were about to be committed. A leading voice was that of Ahad Ha'am, who declared that "Palestine was not only a small land but [also] not an empty one."[36] In 1920, three years after the Balfour Declaration, he warned once more against the Zionist view of the Arab people as "non-existent," which made some Arabs believe that the Jews were coming to drive them from their soil."[37]

Sir Edwin Montagu argued in 1917 that the Zionist state or homeland meant that the Jews would drive out the present inhabitants of Palestine and would be put in "all positions of preference."[38] In 1920, Israel Zangwill wrote in *The Voice of Jerusalem* that "Palestine proper has already its inhabitants" and Jerusalem "is already twice as thickly populated as the United States."[39] Without a solution to the Arab problem, "he did not see that a Jewish state could arise at all, but only a state of friction."[40]

Some of the early Zionist settlers, whom Nordau and Herzl were probably aware of, were shocked by the basic lack of ethics in the Zionist scheme. They raised their voices in protest against "deluding the Jewish people," declaring that Zionism "promised the people a homeland, but the country has been occupied by another people for generations, and the same country cannot be the homeland of two different peoples."[41]

These may have been prophetic voices offering no alternative program, but there were others with pragmatic ideas. Isaac Epstein (1862–1943) addressed the Seventh Zionist Congress (1905) on what he termed "the veiled issue." He "contended that it was a mistake to regard Palestine as a barren waste," and he drew attention to the fact that the Palestinian peasant was "anxious to add a strip of uncultivated land to his lot."[42] He indicated that the Zionists, in the process of acquiring land for their settlement, forced many Arabs and Druzes from their fields, depriving them of their only source of livelihood. Epstein recognized that the purchase of the land was legally justifiable, "but the political and moral aspect was more complicated."[43] This point has been completely lost on today's Zionists, who argue that the land was "purchased" as if Palestine had been up for sale.

To avoid the exploitation or dispossession of Arabs, Epstein did not lapse into the sentimentalism or simplicities of the segregationist concept of Hebrew labor. He spelled out a plan for integration: "The Jews should open their hospitals, pharmacies, libraries, feeding centers and credit institutions to the Arabs, they should study Arabic, and the proposed Hebrew University should attempt to attract Arab students."[44]

Similar voices of dissent in later years included those of Arthur Ruppin, Y. Thon, Reb Binyomin (pseudonym of the Hebrew essayist Benjamin Feldman-Radler), Martin Buber, and Judah Magnes. But many of the dissenters manifested marked ambiguity and vacillation. The dichotomy of their situation, namely, their being in Palestine building a homeland for the Jews, undermined their very moral vision.

Some of the dissenters tried to coordinate their efforts by setting up an organizational frame. Brit Shalom, founded in 1925, was one such organization that tried to develop Palestine into "a bi-national state in which Jew and Arab should enjoy equal civil, political and social rights, without distinction between majority and minority."[45] Commenting on this outlook, the writer of the entry on Brit Shalom in the *Encyclopedia of Zionism and Israel* noted that this stance implied "a renunciation of the plans for a Jewish state."[46] In a sense, he is right, for the members of Brit Shalom, more committed to the ideals of justice and to the cause of peace between the Arabs and settlers, were willing to forego even the right of free immigration. The Brit Shalom also criticized the policies of the Histadrut toward Arab workers.

Ihud, another group founded in 1942, tried to carry on the cause of peace and justice, but did not meet with a better fate. It continued its struggle long after the establishment of the Zionist state. Brit Shalom and Ihud, however, never had a large following and came under attack from the Zionist parties and settlers (though one should add that Arab indifference to these groups contributed to their isolation and lack of legitimacy).

Likewise, many of the individual dissenters were severely attacked by the Zionists. People like Epstein were reprimanded for their "diaspora way of thinking," and were told that "the main thing we should take into account should be what is good and effective for ourselves."[47] Some of their detractors argued with the dissenters and "arrogantly dismissed the Arabs as 'a negligible quantity.' " One who attacked the position of the Jewish dissenters declared, "Everywhere in the world there is a Jewish problem. And what are people doing about it? Here there is an Arab problem. So what can we do?"[48]

Many of those who expressed doubts were either scoffed at or ignored. The Hebrew writer Moshe Smilansky described a meeting of the much-idealized Jewish *halutzim* in Rehovoth in 1891, at which some questions concerning the Arabs were asked:

> "The land in Judea and Galilee is occupied by the Arabs."
> "Well, we'll take it from them."
> "How?" (Silence)
> "A revolutionary doesn't ask naive questions."
> "Well, then, 'revolutionary,' tell us how?"

The answer came forth in matter-of-fact terms: "It's very simple. We'll harass them until they get out. . . . Let them go to Transjordan." When an anxious voice tried to find out whether this was the end or not, the answer once more was definite and unqualified: "As soon as we have a big settlement here, we'll seize the land, we'll become strong and then we'll take care of the Left Bank. We'll expel them from there too. Let them go back to the Arab countries."[49]

Advice about the danger of Herzl's imperialist approach went unheeded. Ahad Ha'am, in a letter to Smilansky dated February 1914, noticed that the Zionists became quite angry toward those who reminded them that there was "still another people in *Eretz Yisrael*."[50] The Zionist leadership was in no mood to heed warnings. Like the Zionist poet Saul Tschernikowsky (1875–1943), they preferred to see the Arabs as savages to be hunted down.[51] As Ahad Ha'am pointed out, Zionist settlers "think that the Arabs are all savages who live like animals and do not understand what is happening around. This is, however, a great error."[52]

POPULATION TRANSFER II

The native Palestinians, reduced by the Zionists to a subhuman or marginal status, had to be expelled or transferred. Zionism, after all, presupposed a Palestine without Palestinians, "a land without a people"! Nevertheless, when the majority of the Palestinians left Palestine in 1948, Zionist spokesmen claimed that this happened at the instigation of Arab leaders. This allegation was perhaps a Zionist afterthought, concocted when it was discovered that the world's reaction to the Palestinians' exodus could be detrimental to the Zionist image. Walid Khalidi, a Palestinian intellectual, noted that early Zionist writings on the subject of the refugees made no reference to Arab orders for the Palestinians to leave. In August and September of 1948, Moshe Sharett, Israel's first foreign minister, disclaimed any Israeli responsibility for the exodus but did not allude to any Arab orders to evacuate. Weizmann also concluded his autobiography in August 1948, with references to the Arab exodus, but he made no mention of such Arab orders.[53] Not until 1949 was it found convenient to perpetuate the myth of the "orders by Arab leaders."

The Zionist allegations have been rebutted in more than one study by Arab and Western authors alike, the best known being by Walid Khalidi and Erskine Childers, the British journalist. The latter examined "every official Israeli statement," and found that "no primary evidence of [Arab] evacuation orders was ever produced."[54] Khalidi and Childers devoted much time to the search for possible Arab sources (newspapers, radio broadcasts, government archives) that might contain the primary evidence never cited in the Israeli allegations. Khalidi examined the files of the press releases of the Arab League, the minutes of the meetings of the Arab League Council, and the resolutions taken by the League Council and the various committees. Nowhere did he come across any mention or trace of any evacuation order.[55] He then turned his attention to the Arab press. Since it was impossible to read all newspapers, he concentrated on three leading dailies: *Al-Ahram*, the Egyptian daily that is widely read in the Arab world; *Al-Hayat*, a Lebanese newspaper more concerned with Palestinians affairs than any other Arab newspaper outside of Palestine; and *Al-Difaa*, the leading Palestinian newspaper. He examined all the issues published during the war years. There were no reports of any order by official Arab sources, purportedly urging evacuation.[56]

It is claimed that sometimes such orders were broadcast by radio. Again, "no dates, names of stations, or texts of messages were ever cited." Childers, who visited Israel in 1958 as a guest of its Foreign Office, was repeatedly told that he would be shown the proof he sought, but none was produced. On his own initiative, Childers doggedly researched the matter through the records of the BBC broadcasts, covering all radio transmission in and around Palestine in 1948. His findings confirmed that there was no evidence of "a single order, or appeal, or suggestion about evacuation from Palestine from any Arab radio station, inside or outside of Palestine, in 1948."[57]

On the contrary, Khalidi and Childers found radio broadcasts, official memos and statements, newspaper and magazine articles that appealed to the Arabs *not* to flee. In February 1948, the Egyptian weekly *Akhir Saa*, perhaps the most widely read periodical in the Arab world at that time, branded as traitors any Palestinian Arabs who left their country.[58] A message appealing to the Palestinians to stay, praising those who remained for their heroism and endurance, was broadcast by King Abdullah on behalf of the Arab League, as reported by the Sharq Al-Adna radio on May 4, 1948.

Childers cited similar Arab appeals, giving dates and contents of the texts. On April 24, at 1200 hours GMT, Al-Inqaz radio, of the Arab Liberation Army, warned against "certain defeatist elements and Jewish agents" who were spreading news to create chaos and panic among the

Palestinians. It branded as "cowards" those who deserted "their houses, villages or cities," and threatened them with severe punishment.[59] (In *The Evasive Peace*, John Davis cited other evidence indicating that "the Arab authorities continuously exhorted Palestinian Arabs not to leave the country."[60])

Unable to uncover any of the purported "original" eviction orders, either through the assistance of the Israelis or through his own research, Childers also investigated the veracity of some of the secondary Israeli evidence. One such example presented by the Israelis and their supporters is a statement attributed to the Greek Catholic Archbishop of Galilee. It "appears in virtually every official Israeli tract, in most of the annual Israeli statements to the United Nations on the Palestine refugees, and in countless books circulating throughout the world."[61] Abba Eban (former Israeli foreign minister) told the United Nations Special Committee in 1957 that Archbishop Hakim had "fully confirmed" that the Arabs had been urged to flee by their own leaders.[62] Childers took the shortest course of action, and in 1958 wrote to the Archbishop asking for verification. The Archbishop's reply was a flat denial of the Israeli allegation. He wrote as follows:

> At no time did I state that the flight of the refugees was due to the orders, explicit or implicit, of their leaders, military or political, to leave the country and seek shelter in the adjacent Arab territories. On the contrary, no such orders were ever made by the military commanders, or by the Higher Arab Committee, or, indeed, by the Arab League or Arab states. I have not the least doubt that any such allegations are sheer concoctions and falsification.[63]

Having investigated other secondary evidence, Childers reached the same conclusion—that quite often Israeli spokesmen cited quotations out of context, giving them a meaning not originally intended.

It is surely common sense that for a whole people, made up largely of peasants, to be uprooted from their ancient homeland, something stronger than government appeals by radio would have been required. In a letter dated 1899, Ludwig Gumplowicz, the Austro-Hungarian sociologist who brought the writings of the Arab historian Ibn Khaldun to the attention of the modern world, charged Herzl with political naiveté and asked him rhetorically, "You want to found a state without bloodshed? . . . Without force or cunning? Just like that, open and honest—by easy instalments."[64] In these few penetrating remarks, the Jewish sociologist put the hard facts before Herzl.

"Force and cunning" were most certainly instrumental in building the

Zionist state. News of Zionist terrorism reached India as early as 1937, prompting the Congress Party to issue a resolution condemning the reign of terror in Palestine.[65] Mahatma Gandhi, one of the first statesmen to deal with the subject of the Jews and Palestine, wrote in 1946 that the Jews erred grievously by resorting to "naked terrorism" and by depending for the realization of their plans on "American money or British arms."[66] One year later, in a reply to a question by a Reuter's correspondent, he warned the Zionists against the use of terrorism.[67]

There were many eyewitness accounts by those who fought in the 1948 war or by civilian observers. Uri Avnery, former member of the Knesset and editor of *Haolam Hazeh*, has distinguished three phases in the war. In the first phase the Palestinian Arabs, he said, committed atrocities against the Zionist settlers. In the second phase there was no uniform policy but, as a general rule, the Arabs were encouraged to evacuate their towns and villages by both Arab leaders and the Zionist Army. As for the third and last phase (that is, after May 15), "the eviction of Arab civilians had become an aim of David Ben Gurion and his government."[68]

Archbishop Hakim is yet another eyewitness: "As soon as hostilities began between Israel and the Arab states, it became the settled policy of the government to drive away the Arabs out of the localities which its forces occupied, notably, Ramleh and Lydda and all the villages around them."[69]

A forced Arab exodus was a matter of Zionist/Israeli planning, and the policy was implemented through two methods: *terrifying and terrorizing the Arabs and/or subjecting them to actual terror.* Nathan Chofshi, who had been a Jewish settler in Palestine since 1908, wrote to the *Jewish Newsletter* in 1959, giving his version of what he had witnessed in 1948. "The Jews," he said, "forced the Arabs to leave cities and villages which they did not want to leave of their own free will. Some of them were driven out *by force of arms*; others were made to leave *by deceit, lying* and false promises."[70] In a report submitted to the United Nations on September 16, 1948, Count Bernadotte, the United Nations mediator in Palestine, pointed out that "the exodus of the Palestinian Arabs resulted from panic created by *fighting* in their communities, by rumors concerning *real or alleged acts of terrorism* or expulsion."[71] Likewise, Major Edgar O'Ballance wrote that "it was the Jewish policy to encourage the Arabs to quit their homes, and they used *psychological warfare* in urging them to do so."[72]

Naked terrorism was used throughout the war. In the last phase, however, acts of physical violence as well as psychological warfare were resorted to in order to frighten and drive out the inhabitants. This is a matter of mere analytical convenience, for the two methods overlapped and were even complementary elements in the Zionist scheme. In the Deir Yassin massacre, for instance, the Zionists took good care to familiarize all the Palestinians with the event, in order to gain advantages from it by instilling fear in the hearts of the people.

The most common method of terrorizing the Arabs was the use of loudspeakers and radio broadcasts to create an atmosphere of panic in a population that was without leadership, especially after the failure of the 1936 Arab revolt against the British and the Zionists. To cite an example, at 1700 hours, on February 19, 1948, the Haganah radio warned the Arabs that "they would be ignored in the conflict of ambitions between Arab leaders."[73] On March 10, 1948, at 1800 hours, the radio reported that "the Arab states were conspiring with Britain against the Palestinians." On March 14, 1948, at 1800 hours, it reported that "the people of Jaffa are so frightened that they are remaining indoors."[74]

On May 15, author Harry Levin noted in his diary the message he had heard being broadcast from the Zionist loudspeaker vans in Arabic. The Arabs were urged "to leave the district before 5:15 A.M." and were advised "to take pity on your wives and children and get out of this bloodbath. . . . Get out by the Jericho road that is still open to you. If you stay, you invite disaster."[75]

It has often been reported that the Jewish mayor of Haifa asked the Arabs to remain in their homes, but his "appeal was neither backed nor reiterated by any Zionist in a responsible position." On the contrary, the inevitable Haganah loudspeakers toured all over, threatening people and urging them to flee with their families, as reported in Jon Kimche's *The Seven Fallen Pillars*.[76]

Thus, the suggestion of terror and impending disaster, of a complete breakdown, was one of the main themes emphasized by the Haganah radio and loudspeakers in the Arab communities. Another theme was the imminent danger of epidemic diseases. On March 20, at 1930 hours, the Zionist Free Hebrew Radio began a chilling broadcast in Arabic in which it asked, "Do you know that it is a sacred duty to inoculate yourselves hastily against cholera, typhus and similar diseases, as it is expected that such diseases will break out in April and May among Arabs in urban agglomerations?"[77] The same theme was used on February 18, 1948, when the Zionist authorities assured the Arabs by radio that the Arab Liberation volunteers "have brought smallpox with them," and added on February 27, that the "Palestinian doctors were fleeing."[78]

Yigal Allon, former Israeli foreign minister, in "The Book of the Palmach," gives an account of his "original" contribution to terror tactics:

> I gathered all of the Jewish *mukhatars* [mayors], who have contact with Arabs in different villages, and asked them to whisper in the ears of some Arabs, that a great Jewish reinforcement has arrived in Galilee and that it is going to burn all of the villages of

the Huleh. They should suggest to these Arabs, as their friends, to escape while there is time.[79]

"The rumor," Allon explained, "spread in all areas of the Huleh that it is time to flee. The flight numbered myriads. The tactic reached its goal completely. . . . The wide areas were cleaned."[80] The "cleansing" metaphor is quite appropriate to express the state of mind of a purist Zionist colonist who not only wanted the land, but also wanted to depopulate it.

Turning from mere terrorizing to downright use of violence, one is struck by the level of the Zionist creativity displayed. One of the techniques, developed by the gentile colonialist Orde Wingate, was the night raids on Arab villages, referred to earlier. This type of raid was mounted by the Haganah and Palmach during the 1948 war. As the Israeli historian Arieh Ytshaki pointed out, the tactics were simple. They "consisted of attacking the enemy village and destroying as many houses there as possible." The results were equally simple: "A great number of old people, women and children were killed wherever the attacking force faced resistance."[81]

But it appears that the Haganah, especially toward the end of the Mandate, made significant improvements in their tactics. In their attack on Arab villages, "Haganah men would first silently place explosive charges around the stone houses and drench the window and door frames in petrol." Once this preparatory step was accomplished, they would "then open fire, simultaneously dynamiting and burning the sleeping inhabitants to death."[82]

The case of the attack on the village of Deir Yassin, "the first Arab village to be captured by Jewish forces,"[83] and the massacre that followed are well documented. Two hundred fifty unarmed Palestinian men, women, and children were killed by Zionist terrorists on April 2, 1948. The massacre itself was staged by the members of the Irgun, headed by Begin, but at a time when the Haganah was "responsible for all military operations," and when all plans had to be cleared with the military arm of the Jewish Agency.[84] The *Encyclopedia of Zionism and Israel* mentioned the fact that in March 1948 the Zionist Action Committee (the Zionist Executive) "had approved a temporary arrangement maintaining Irgun's separate existence but made its operational plans subject to prior approval by the Haganah Command."[85] William Polk, in *Backdrop to Tragedy,* recorded the little known fact that the Haganah "had assisted in the capture of the village and had entrusted its inhabitants to a group known to be terrorist."[86] One month before the massacre, the Mandate Government of Palestine condemned the Jewish Agency for condoning terrorism, and three days after the massacre, Deir Yassin was handed over to the Haganah to serve as an airstrip. *Background Notes on Current Themes,* published on March 16, 1969, by the Information Division of Israel's Ministry of Foreign Affairs, stated in a most unequivocal manner that what it termed the "battle for Deir Yassin" was "an integral inseparable episode in the battle for Jerusalem."[87] Israeli Prime Minister Menahem Begin, in his book *The Revolt*, also asserted that "the capture of Deir Yassin and holding it were one stage in the general plan," and that the operation was undertaken "with the knowledge of Haganah and with the approval of its commander," despite the latter's equivocation[88] and despite the outrage expressed by Jewish Agency officials and Zionist spokesmen.

Perhaps this coordination of efforts, this neat division of labor, was what Weizmann had in mind when, in a rare moment of moral insight, he expressed his revulsion at "not only the murderous terrorism of Begin's Irgun but also the clean acts of violence [*sic*] undertaken by Ben Gurion's Haganah."[89]

Deir Yassin is mentioned here because it became a prototype for several other "successful" Zionist raids. In *Yediot Aharonot* of April 14, 1972, Ytshaki cited examples of other Deir Yassins that took place in 1948:

—On January 30–31, the Palmach forces attacked the village of Al-Sheikh, under the leadership of Haim Avinoan, killing "sixty of the enemy, mostly civilians" inside their own houses.[90]

—On February 14–15, the Palmach's third regiment attacked the village of Sa'sa', destroying a "total of twenty houses . . . over the heads of the occupants, causing the death of sixty people, mostly women and children." This operation was described as "exemplary."[91]

—Zionist forces mounted "indiscriminate reprisal attacks on the Arab civil transport system causing the death of numerous innocent citizens."[92] The source does not mention the number of casualties.

Ytshaki, however, singled out what happened in Lydda as "the best-known Palmach operation." The Lydda (Lod) operation, known as the Dani Campaign, was mounted to suppress an Arab uprising in July 1948 against Israeli occupation. "Instructions were issued to shoot anyone seen on the streets." The Palmach soldiers "opened heavy fire on all pedestrians and brutally suppressed this insurrection within a few hours. They moved from one house to another, firing at any moving target. As a consequence, two hundred and fifty Arabs were killed, according to the report of the brigade's commander."[93] Kenneth Bilby, a New York *Herald Tribune* correspondent who entered Lydda on July 12, reported that Moshe Dayan led a jeep commando column into the town "with rifles, stens, and sub-machine guns blazing. It coursed through the main streets, blasting at everything that moved . . . the corpses of Arab men, women and even children were strewn about the streets in the wake of this ruthlessly brilliant charge."[94] When Ramleh was seized the next day, "all Arab men of military age were rounded up and penned into special enclosures."[95] Once more the vans toured the two towns and blared out the habitual warnings. Then, on July 13, the loudspeakers gave final orders, naming certain bridges as the exodus route."[96]

From Weizmann's point of view, the Arab exodus was understandably a miraculous simplification of Israel's task. Weitz viewed the outcome of the war as doubly miraculous—a territorial victory and a demographic final solution.[97]

WHAT IS TO BE DONE?

At the present time, regardless of the causes of the Arab exodus or of the circumstances under which the Palestinians were dislodged from their homeland, either by Zionist force and treachery or as a result of Arab exhortation to leave, the right of these Palestinians to "return" cannot be denied. Arnold Toynbee suggested that should we accept what happened as a *fait accompli* and leave it at that, then "We must also justify the Nazi confiscation of the property of the Jews who had a chance to flee from Germany."[98] Moreover, on purely moral grounds, the Zionists cannot, as an Israeli rabbi wrote, oppose the return of the Palestinians to their land, and cannot "continue to assert their own holy right to continue the ingathering of the exiles, as long as the Palestinians are denied re-entry into Palestine." Rabbi Benyamin asserted in the December 1, 1958 issue of the *Jewish Newsletter* that the Jews "have no right to demand that American Jews leave their country to which they have been attached and settle in a land that has been stolen from others, while the owners of it are homeless and miserable. . . . We had no right to build a settlement and to realize the ideal of Zionism with other people's property. To do this is robbery."[99]

But apart from the moral considerations, which are ultimately personal, there are legal, universally accepted laws. Article 13, Paragraph 2, of the Universal Declaration of Human Rights, to which Israel is a signatory, provides that "everyone has the right to leave any country, including his own, and to return to his country," and Article 17, Paragraph 2, stipulates that: "No one shall be arbitrarily deprived of his property."[100]

The United Nations General Assembly, on December 11, 1948, passed a resolution providing "that the refugees wishing to return to their homes and live at peace with their neighbors should be permitted to do so at the earliest possible date." The resolution has been readopted year after year, and the General Assembly has deplored Israel's failure to implement it.

Countless United Nations resolutions, having more or less the same substance, have been compiled in various concordances and studies. All have been defied by Israel.

The December 11, 1948, resolution also stipulates that "compensation should be paid for the property of those choosing not to return and for loss or damage of property." Arab property left behind by Palestinian Arabs is valued in millions of dollars. The Arabs, as Childers indicated, "owned or had inhabited roughly 80 percent of the entire Zionist-occupied land area of Palestine"; they had "raised and owned over 50 percent of all the citrus orchards of the area the Zionists had occupied; over 90 percent of the olive groves; 10,000 shops, stores, and other forms; and dwellings which, as late as 1954, were housing more than one-third of the Israeli population."[101]

Despite these hard economic facts, and the moral and legal considerations involved, Israel's foreign minister submitted a memorandum to United Nations mediator Count Bernadotte on August 1, 1948 (that is, only ten weeks after the founding of the Jewish state), objecting to the return of the Palestinians because economically their reintegration into "normal life, and even their mere sustenance, would present an insuperable problem"[102] One year after the "restoration" of the Jewish state into the *eretz* of Palestine, after 2,000 years of Jewish absence, the Israeli minister of foreign affairs submitted an official memorandum to the Technical Committee of the Palestine Conciliation Committee, demonstrating a sudden yet remarkable Zionist respect for the passage of time. The memorandum stated that "the clock cannot be put back," and that "the individual return of the Arab refugees to their former places of residence is an impossible thing."[103]

Certainly the reasons barring the return of the Palestinians are not purely economic, for the racist-demographic imperative of Zionist ideology extends the right of "return" *exclusively* to the Jewish people. *Their* transfer and "repatriation after 2,000 years" of absence is seen as perfectly legitimate. Ben Gurion, in *Rebirth and Destiny of Israel*, revealed the real reason for the denial of Palestinian rights. "During 1946 [probably what is meant is 1948] and the first few months of 1949, we put right 65,000 houses that had been wrecked in the fighting, and abandoned: in Jaffa, Ramleh, and Lydda, in Beisan, and Migdal, Acco and Haifa. That sufficed for the first inflow."[104] For other *olim*, other lands, other houses were naturally needed. Years later, on June 11, 1967, Moshe Dayan asserted on the CBS program *Face the Nation* that Israel could absorb the Arabs economically, but this, he said, would not be "in accord with our aims in the future. It would turn Israel into either a bi-national or poly-Arab-Jewish state instead of the Jewish State, and we want to have a Jewish State."

The argument that the Arab states and the world at large should absorb the Palestinians is patent racism, disguised as a practical and reasonable solution. A pragmatic American Zionist suggested that "if the refugees were provided with passports and other documents enabling them to move freely, if they were given enough money to find their way where they might reasonably expect to make a living, and were told, so much and no more, ever, self-help and self-rehabilitation would have to start."[105] Such logic presupposes that the Palestinian, with money in one pocket and a plane ticket in the other, is bound to forget his identity and will forego his inalienable rights to his homeland.

If it were possible to adopt a clinical and detached attitude toward the problem, similar to the one being urged upon the Arabs, then a more reasonable solution would be the reabsorption of the Israelis into Western societies. As a demographic element they are less rooted in the Middle East than the Palestine Arabs, and they do not claim to be historically of the region, for they are part of a universal pan-Jewish history, to use the Zionist argument. Moreover, given their cultural orientation, they would fit admirably into Western society. Above all, they are the element whose introduction caused so much conflict and strife.

But, of course, this kind of logic is superficial, for it divorces people from their concrete situations, turning them into abstract and isolated units. It is significant that this practical argument is always proposed to the Arabs, who are assumed to be inferior and less powerful. The Palestinians, however, have so far reacted to the Zionists by demonstrating that the "final solution" of the Palestinian question through another transfer from the camps, as a prelude to a systematic dispersion and eventual absorption, cannot be achieved except through violence.

It is unlikely also that the Palestinians will heed the pragmatic advice of the Western world, which looks with tolerance and even admiration at the Jewish "exiles" going back to their Jewish Homeland. They can sarcastically reiterate the words of H. G. Wells, who argued that "if it is proper to 'reconstitute' a Jewish state which has not existed for two thousand years, why not go back another thousand years and reconstitute the Canaanite state? The Canaanites, unlike the Jews, are still there"[106] in the refugee and *fedayeen* camps. The Palestinians can now look across the border only to see the Hebrew *olim* and *halutzim* rebuilding their Homeland, after two millennia of "temporary" absence. Is it any wonder that the Palestinians, after only two decades of absence, yearn to return to their own homeland?

The currently popular Zionist thesis of a population exchange, trading Arab Jews for Palestinian Arabs, is rejected outright for human beings are not "transferable." Moreover, if some Jews from Arab countries settled in Palestine, this was never part of an Arab "plan," it was the very dynamics of the 1948 war that made their existence in their countries of origin almost impossible, as Shlomo Avineri asserted. "The uprooting of the Oriental Jew is . . . one of the prices of Zionism."[107] Be that as it may, most Arab countries have now recognized the right of all Arab Jews to return to their homeland, and some of them have taken advantage of the new regulation. It is not expected that Israel would take a similar attitude to Palestinian Arabs. A population transfer and exchange fit more in the Zionist scenario.

8

ISRAELI-ZIONIST RACISM

IN CAPTIVITY: THE LAWS OF RETURN AND NATIONALITY

The national ancestral dream was fulfilled, and the two population transfers of the vast majority of Palestine Arabs and of a small minority of diaspora Jews were achieved. Yet these developments did not usher in the beginning of the thousand years of lasting peace and justice. The cleansing of the land was not complete, for a Palestinian remnant was left behind in Zion, casting the Zionist state in the role of the oppressor.

Israel, founded as a state for the Jews and determined to maintain and perpetuate this Jewish identity, has incorporated discriminatory laws into its very legal framework. Israeli-Zionist discrimination as such is not merely a matter of personal bigotry or *de facto* segregation; it is primarily a matter of *de jure* discrimination. This particular trait is what sets the racial discrimination practiced by settler-colonial enclaves apart from racial discrimination in the rest of the world. One of the most discriminatory Israeli laws is the Law of Return. Promulgated on July 5, 1950, it grants automatic citizenship to any Jew upon his arrival in Israel, even though he may never before have set foot in the Middle East. This same right is denied to a Palestinian Arab born and raised in Palestine who wishes to return to his homeland. The law has no parallel in any other country; it is based on the unique Zionist concept of pan-Jewish peoplehood and can be construed as racist in that it denies non-Jews their inalienable rights in their own homeland.

Unlike any other country in the world, with the exception of racially conscious settler states, immigrants to Israel are recruited not on the basis of the skills they may have, and which the Zionist state may need, but on the basis of a unique quality—Jewishness, which is defined as a religious, ethnic, and/or genetic quality. In order to maintain the desired demographic balance, the *olim*—that is, Jews returning to their Fatherland according to the Law of Return—are granted all kinds of economic privileges that are denied to the native Arabs.

During the debate before the Law of Return was approved, an Israeli professor, M. R. Konvitz, expressed fears that such a law might be unfavorably compared with Nazi laws, since it embodies "a principle of exclusion which constitutes religious discrimination." He argued that though the law might offer temporary advantages at a time when large numbers of displaced persons in camps had to be settled, thereafter it would undoubtedly be considered discriminatory.[1] Following its passage, the *Jewish Newsletter* warned in its May 12, 1952, issue that the law "revives a dangerous racist theory that smacks of the slogan of a previous generation. A German is a German wherever he is." Reuven Grass, a religious emigrant from the United States to Israel, compared the amended Law of Return to the Nazi laws as "it gives immigration privileges to anyone who is Jewish under the Nuremberg Laws' definition, i.e., having a Jewish grandparent."[2] In fact, there is at least one recorded case wherein the "religious" authorities in Israel used Nazi records to establish the religio-ethnic racial identity of an Israeli citizen.

The uniquely racist character of the Law of Return can be detected in the rigid and hierarchical terms employed in Israel to distinguish between the various forms of immigration. If a Jew returns to *Eretz Yisrael,* this form of immigration is an *aliyah,* or ascent—something akin to a religious experience, "a fulfillment of an ideal . . . the elevation of one's personality to a higher ethical level," as indicated in the entry on *aliyah* in the *Encyclopedia of Zionism and Israel.*[3] However, if he emigrates *from* the Holy Land, this is a degeneration, for he would then be committing *yeridah,* or descent—an apostasy that denotes a fall from paradise into mere history.

If a Soviet emigrant changes his mind during his *aliyah* to the *eretz* (as many have done), it is a *neshirah,* a cutting of the ascent, or a falling away, which is not so bad as *yeridah* because the Jew had not yet touched the Holy Land. A Soviet Jew, however, may leave Russia with the express purpose of emigrating to the United States. This is a *hegira,* a mere emigration, and no different from any other. When a gentile decides to emigrate to Israel, his is not a noble ascent; it is a mere *le-hesh-takia;* that is, a settlement with no religious aura surrounding it.

Palestinian Arabs who stayed on in that part of Palestine that became Israel had to apply for citizenship under the Nationality Law of 1952. They were considered eligible only after a variety of conditions had been met. An Arab had to prove "he was born in the country; that he lived in Israeli-occupied territory three out of the five years preceding the date of application for citizenship; that he is entitled to permanent residence; that he is

settled or intends to settle permanently in the country; that he has a suf-
ficient knowledge of the Hebrew language."[4]

If the Arab met all of these stringent conditions, the matter was still
left to "the discretion of the Israeli Minister of Interior to grant or refuse
the application."[5] The obvious motive behind these conditions is to prevent
as many Palestinians as possible from acquiring Israeli nationality. An
estimated 60,000 to 70,000 Arabs born in Israel and now living there are
denied full rights of citizenship[6] because, for one reason or another, they
cannot fully meet the provisions of the Nationality Law for non-Jews. The
number of these Arabs is increasing, "since statelessness is inherited."
Some Arabs, born to parents without citizenship, become aware of their
statelessness only when they apply for passports or other documents. Not
all of them know that they "do not acquire Israeli citizenship by virtue of
the fact that they were born in Israel—in villages where their families may
have lived for generations."[7] Palestinian Arabs and their children are
allowed to claim the status of "permanent residents." This permits them
to travel outside Israel only for the strictly limited period of a year and a
day. Overstaying by even another 24 hours forecloses their right to reenter
Israel.[8]

Being a non-Jew in the Zionist state means that one is excluded by
law and by practice from enjoying certain privileges. Housing is an area
where the Arabs know what it means to be a non-Jew in the Zionist state.
When Arabs move into a Jewish area, many residents move away in protest. The inhabitants of Upper Nazareth have threatened "a mass exodus
from the town to neighboring areas—if nothing is done to prevent the influx
of Arab families to that part of the town," the July 20, 1975, issue of *Maariv*
reported, adding that the protestors were willing to use force to prevent
"the transformation of Upper Nazareth into an Arab town." Like most
oppressed minorities, Arabs may be prepared to pay far higher rents than
those offered by Jewish buyers or tenants, yet they cannot rent or buy
apartments in certain areas. This deep fear of the imminent Arabization
of Upper Nazareth was caused by the presence in the town of 400 Arab
families.[9]

It might be of some interest to note in this context the findings of an
Israeli sociologist, who reported in the *American Journal of Sociology* of
May 1971 that 91 percent of the Jewish Israelis he questioned agreed that
"it would be better if there were fewer Arabs" in Israel. Furthermore, 76
percent believed that the Arabs would never reach the level of progress
of Jews, 86 percent would not rent a room to an Arab, and 67 percent did
not wish to have an Arab as a neighbor.[10]

As in other areas, discrimination in housing is not so much a matter of
personal bigotry. Rather, it is a policy generated and reinforced by the very
structure of society and government. Israel Shahak, a vocal Israeli dis-

senter and a civil-rights advocate, wrote that the Israeli Ministry of Housing has "a special unit called 'department for the housing of minorities,' " which deals only with "non-Jews." Such a state of affairs is inevitable, since the laws of the Jewish National Fund stipulate that an Arab cannot lease Jewish land, a ruling that applies even to an apartment in government condominiums. The Ministry encourages Jewish housing inside Jerusalem, but discourages it for the minorities, in order to create new demographic facts. In Israeli parlance, according to Israel Shahak, "populating the Galilee" actually means "Judaization of Galilee." Far from inviting Arabs, presumably part of the Israeli population, to settle in Galilee, the Ministry of Housing tries "to thin them out."[11]

With this exclusivist demographic concept in mind, Abraham Ofer, the former minister of housing who committed suicide after a financial scandal, called on the Israeli Army to remove some Bedouins who were settled in an area that, according to him, belonged "organically" to the "living space" of the new Jewish town of Yamit and to the settlers in the Rafiah Approaches. This was reported in *Al Hamishmar*, in its issue of August 22, 1975. The town was to be populated by over 25,000 Jews; therefore, the "non-Jews" (who, according to the Zionist myth, are nonexistent or mere temporary inhabitants) had to be moved out.[12] *Haolam Hazeh* of July 12, 1973, had published the news of the mysterious and sudden killing of the chief of the evicted tribe. The killing was followed by several acts of intimidation. Rafiah's governor, Ofer Ben-David, invited four tribal chiefs to his office and "made them sign a blank authorization according to which they agree to sell their lands at any price offered them by the Government."[13]

The laws of Return and Nationality should also be seen in relation to the more specific and stringent laws governing the daily life of the Arabs in Israel. The Law of Administration Ordinance, the first Israeli legislative act, subjected all Arabs to various Emergency Regulations, which in point of fact abrogated all their civil rights and placed them under military government. The "legal" bases of the military government are a series of laws and "emergency regulations" promulgated by the British in the late 1930s to suppress Palestinian resistance to colonialism. They were later codified to quell those agitators among the ranks of the Zionists who were against the Mandate government.[14] These laws, known as the Defense Laws (State of Emergency), 1945, consist of 170 articles. Another set of laws known as Emergency Laws (Security Areas), 1949, were issued by the Zionist state to tighten the control of the Israeli military government over the Arabs. The British Defense Laws of 1945 empowered the government to establish "defense areas" within which it could also designate "security zones." Authority within these areas and zones could be delegated to military officers of certain ranks.

The Israeli military authorities took full advantage of the provisions of the 1945 Defense Laws. The area where the majority of the Arabs lived was divided into military zones. No one outside or inside these security zones could enter or leave without a written permit from the military authorities. The permit, printed in Hebrew, usually included restrictions such as:

> "The bearer is permitted to remain outside the closed area between 6 A.M. and 3 P.M. only"; "The bearer may not enter the (Jewish) colonies on route"; "The bearer may travel by such-and-such road only"; "This permit is invalid on Saturdays and on (Jewish) holidays"; "You may only leave the closed area for the purpose mentioned on this permit"; "You may not change your place of residence, as recorded in this permit, without permission from the Military Commander."[15]

The procedure of obtaining such a permit is not simple. Two weeks in advance of his proposed journey, the applicant must go to the nearest police station and submit an application, which is then forwarded to the military commander, who may or may not grant this permit. For instance, an Arab member of the Israeli League for Human and Civil Rights finds it much easier to get a permit to appear in court than to get a permit allowing him to travel to the area where an Israel civil rights group meeting is taking place.[16] This means abrogation not only of his civil liberties, but also of his political rights.

New Outlook, a liberal Israeli monthly, gave us a glimpse of the impact of the permit system on the daily life of the Arabs. In a bus ride from Haifa to Nazareth, for instance, the bus would pull up and military police would go through the aisles checking the Arabs' travel permits, ignoring the Jews completely. Any Arab without the correctly signed and stamped slip of paper would be taken off the bus for questioning.[17] One Arab who obtained a permit to go to the dentist eight times was seen "walking up and down the street," and consequently had his permit rescinded.[18] Some Arab students are on ten-day permits, which means that they have to interrupt their studies and return home to have the permit renewed.[19]

The emergency regulations empower the military authorities in Arab-populated areas to expel or assign residence to any citizen, to enter and search any place, to seize and confiscate any goods and articles, and to bar individuals from making use of their private property or even from looking for a job. The regulations also entitle the military governor to impose a curfew to limit an individual's movement and to detain a citizen permanently without stating any charge more specific than that he constitutes a "danger to security." In the period 1956–1957, for example, 315 administrative orders were issued. These notorious laws were used to impose a Spartan curfew "on all the villages of the Triangle for most of the night for fourteen years."[20]

It should be further noted that the one and "final authority regarding violations of emergency regulations was a military court, whose decisions were not subject to the jurisdiction of the Civil Courts of Appeal."[21] Almost all convictions in these courts were based on confessions that were obtained by torture, and denied by the accused in court.[22]

Jacob Shapira, Israel's former minister of justice, asserted, following World War II when these regulations were applied by the British to the Zionist settlers, that "there was no such laws even in Nazi Germany." At the Conference of the Hebrew Lawyers' Union in 1946, one of the speakers characterized the emergency laws as a form of "official terrorism," and a resolution passed by the conference warned that these laws were "a serious danger to individual freedom," undermining "the foundation of law and justice." But as Emmanuel Dror, in a short study on the Emergency Regulations, noted: These regulations "were incorporated into the legal system of the newly born 'Home of the Jewish People,' supposedly the realization of the prophets' dream of justice and equality."[23]

When the Eshkol government came into power in 1963, it gradually replaced the Military Administration by a civilian police apparatus that was to administer the laws. This process was completed by 1966.[24] However, the emergency regulations remained in full force, unchanged, as the Israeli historian, Aharon Cohen, pointed out in *Israel and the Arab World*.[25] Israel Shahak also explained that what had actually changed was not the military government *per se*, but rather the method of application—the old geographical basis had been replaced by an individual one. In the past, *all* Arabs within one geographical zone were detained; now they are theoretically free, but the "military commander can prohibit the movement of *any* Arab whatsoever," invoking the same Emergency Laws.[26]

When these changes were introduced, "notice was sent to hundreds of people on the Military Commander's Black List." For those individuals, who constitute the leadership of the Arab community, the change meant a deterioration in their status. Before the "liberalization" of the laws, they, like the rest of the population, could move freely, at least in daylight hours, *within* the closed areas. After the change, they were forced to get a permit even for that. Moreover, whereas the punishment for leaving the closed area before the liberalization was usually a fine (up to 3,000 and 4,000 Israeli liras per day), after the passage of the new regulations, this was changed to imprisonment.[27]

Finally, it should be pointed out that the Emergency Regulations were extended to the Arab territories occupied after 1967 and are being enforced there.[28]

JEWISH LAND AND HEBREW LABOR

Since the main objective of the Zionist scheme was a land without a people, once the *eretz* had been emptied of its inhabitants and those who remained behind were subjugated, the land could be "legally" appropriated. By 1948, total Jewish holdings, leased and owned, still represented only "around 7 percent of the total land surface."[29] To enlarge that area, Israel enacted several laws, such as the Abandoned Areas Ordinance (1949), the Emergency Articles for the Exploitation of Uncultivated Lands (1947–1949), the Absentee Property Law (1950), and the Land Acquisition Law (1953). Under the first law, any area could be closed by the authorities for security reasons, and its Arab owners barred from it. It would then be declared "abandoned" or "uncultivated." Under the third law, it could subsequently be handed over to others, usually Jews, to cultivate. Many Arab citizens who had never moved from the part of Palestine that became Israel happened to be away from their lands and homes for a certain period during the process of Israeli occupation, annexation, and population transfer. They were barred from their villages upon their return, thereby becoming absentees, and their property was seized.[30] These Arabs earned the bizarre definition of "absent yet present," while the Palestinian refugees now *outside* Israel are completely "absent."[31]

The Land Acquisition Law consolidates Israel's stranglehold on Arab lands, for it "legalizes" and makes final the seizure of the land under the 1949 and 1950 laws, and empowers the transfer of the land thus seized to other owners.[32]

The laws aiming at the expropriation of the land are not unrelated to the Emergency Laws. Quite often, the military governor would declare an area closed for military maneuvers and prohibit landowners from entering it for security reasons. Then the "abandoned" land would be confiscated. This, as Sabri Jiryis stated, quoting the words of an Israeli, means that the closed area "is being prepared for Jewish settlement, which is becoming more and more urgent, with the increasing waves of immigration."[33] Shimon Peres, as deputy minister of defense, stated in an article in *Davar*, on January 26, 1962, that "by making use of Article 125, on which the Military Government is to a great extent based . . . we can directly continue the struggle for Jewish settlement and Jewish immigration."[34]

Since then, the process has continued unabated, with the result that about 150,000 hectares of Arab land have been expropriated by the Zionist state. Arab landholdings have therefore diminished considerably. The situation is further exacerbated by the high Arab birth rate. So, in Umm el Fahem, Israel's biggest Arab village, Arab landholdings originally totaled about 14,000 hectares of which only 1,200 remain, with an average of 700 births a year. "In the village of Ara and Arara, only 900 hectares remain out of an original 5,000." This is a national phenomenon among Israeli Arabs, whose landholdings originally amounted to 1.5 hectares per family. By 1973, "the average had dropped to only 0.46 hectares per family, and the figure has declined even further since then."[35]

The land appropriated before and after 1948 from the non-Jew was to be worked only by Jews, and the Zionist slogan or ideal of Hebrew labor was tailored to achieve that end. If the *eretz* cannot be redeemed except by the *halutzim*, then, as A. D. Gordon, the Zionist mystic "pacifist" demanded, "every single tree or plant in the Jewish Fatherland . . . [should] be planted only by [Jewish] pioneers."[36] To decode the religious and mystical myth into more political language, we have to turn to Ruppin, who declared at the Eleventh Zionist Congress (1913) that the Zionists wanted to found "a closed Jewish economy" in which "producers, consumers, and even middlemen shall all be Jewish."[37]

The whole Zionist "cooperative" movement was basically the vehicle for the realization of the Zionist separatist vision. The cooperative approach, from the standpoint of practice, was primarily an economic and military tool that the settlers adopted in order to guarantee their own cultural and economic segregation, to check the hostility of the dispossessed native peasants, and to prepare for the peasants' eventual eviction at a propitious moment.

The Histadrut is a good case in point. This "trade union" of the settlers, set up to implement the program for economic segregation, organized demonstrations not so much against the exploitative classes, but against Jews who bought Arab produce or hired Arab labor. To realize their vision, many socialist Zionists had to exhort "Jewish housewives not to buy from Arabs." They felt it their duty to "picket citrus plantations so that no Arab worker could work there." They even poured "petroleum on Arab tomatoes," and went so far as to attack Jewish housewives and "break the 'Arab' eggs in their baskets," as David Hacohen, a member of the Israeli Knesset, stated in *Haaretz* of November 15, 1968.[38] The zeal for pure Hebrew labor reached hysterical extremes at times. When some practical Zionists used cheaper Arab labor to plant the saplings of a bush named after Herzl, the purists demonstrated, uprooted the plants, and then, fired by ideological zeal, replanted them.

Hebrew labor has neither changed nor lost force through the passage of time or with the establishment of the state. In recent times, the "left-wing" Zionists of Moked staged "a demonstration . . . before the farm belonging to [the right-wing] general . . . Ariel Sharon, protesting the fact that he employs Arabs there."[39]

The racism of the Zionist cooperative movement in agriculture is manifest in the theory and practice of the Jewish National Fund, which buys land only from non-Jews and now owns more than 90 percent of Israeli farmland. This land is to be leased only to Jews, and only Jews may be employed to work on it. Article 3 of the constitution of the Jewish National Fund states that "land is to be held as the inalienable property of the Jewish people." "The Jewish Agency shall promote agricultural colonization based on Jewish labor, and in all works or undertakings carried out or furthered by the Jewish Agency it shall be a matter of principle that Jewish labor shall be employed." All Zionist agricultural settlements, including the "socialist" *kibbutzim,* exclude Arabs from their membership.

Israel has passed laws that implement the racial tenets, clauses, and ideology of the Jewish National Fund. The Agricultural Settlement Law, designed to stop the infiltration of the Arabs into the Jewish agricultural sector, prohibits even the subleasing of Jewish National Fund land to Arabs.

There have been official outcries against a few violations of these well-known and stringent restrictions. A report in the July 3, 1975, issue of *Maariv* referred to the launching of "a vehement campaign *to eradicate the plague* of land-leasing and orchard-leasing to Bedouins and Arab farmers in the Western Galilee."[40] The former Israeli Minister of Agriculture made use of the "plague" metaphor describing the domination of Jewish agriculture by Arab workers as "a cancer in our body."[41] To hire Arab labor on Jewish settlements, either directly or through leasing land or renting the orchards, contradicts "the law and the regulations of the settlement authorities," according to Aharon Nahmani, director of the Galilee area for the Jewish Agency, in a note circulated to Zionist settlements.[42]

Should some Israeli, out of moral commitment to a higher ideal or out of sheer economic necessity, hire an Arab, he is "punished" for his "unprincipled" act. The terms of the Jewish National Fund bluntly stipulate in Article 23 that failure to comply with this duty by employment of non-Jewish labor renders the lessee liable to the payment of compensation of a certain sum of money for each default. "The fact of the employment of non-Jewish labor shall constitute adequate proof as to the damages and the amount thereof, and the right of the Fund to be paid the compensation referred to. . . . Where the lessee has contravened the provisions of this Article three times, the Fund may apply the right of restitution of the holding without paying any compensation whatever."[43]

This is not mere posturing, for there are frequent Israeli newspaper reports about agricultural settlements that have been "caught" breaking the law and leasing land for cultivation to non-Jews. *Maariv* of October 26, 1971, told its readers that the Jewish Agency planned to confiscate the land of a settler in *moshav* Nitzarei-Or and that legal action was also taken against *moshav* Etorim for renting land to Arabs.[44] In its November 5, 1971, issue *Maariv* reported cases where the Zionist settlers committed the "criminal" act of renting "land to Arabs who used to dwell on it before"[45]

1948. Some settlements, "caught" redhanded, were solemnly warned that "if a settlement is caught once again leasing land [to Arab gentiles], all form of state support will be interrupted. That settlement will not receive water allotments, will not obtain credit, and will not enjoy development loans."[46]

In 1960 a relative change took place when the Histadrut began admitting Arabs to its membership after 40 years of Zionist immigration, colonization, and settlement. This step, which paralleled the abolition of military government, suggests a moderation on the part of the Israeli authorities vis-à-vis Arab labor. However, it should be pointed out that the full rigor in the implementation of repressive acts is necessary only in the first stage of settler colonialism. Once the settle-colonialist power structure has fulfilled its objectives, such as a demographic majority and expropriation of the land, it can somewhat relax the stringent regulations. Incorrigibly frank, Jabotinsky was of the opinion that "only when a Jewish majority was achieved could parliamentary institutions be introduced so that . . . the Jewish point of view should always prevail."[47]

Such slight easing of restrictions is not unknown in other settler-colonial states and, as a rule, takes effect only after the consolidation of the power structure. For example, the May 2, 1977, issue of *Time* quotes Prime Minister Vorster as saying that "discrimination will be eliminated in South Africa." The *Time* report, however, goes on to say that "he meant merely that the government intends to modify some of the abrasive signs of petty apartheid—like separate facilities (toilets, buses, etc.) for blacks and whites." Vorster even talked of his government's commitment to "creating changes and opportunities" for nonwhites. But all this easing of restrictions is placed clearly within the overall commitment to white supremacy. The prime minister, without much evasiveness, declared that his government "has no intention of trying to create a multi-racial society." Needless to say, this consolidation of power makes it possible to restore the initial repression in full force when and if any significant resistance is mounted.

BODY AND SOUL, PAST AND PRESENT

Appropriation of the land and discrimination against Arab labor are not the only forms of Zionist racism. There is enough evidence to prove that the Israeli-Zionist establishment resorts to terror tactics ranging from physical liquidation to torture and collective punishment in order to subdue the Arab population. The Kafr Kassem massacre is a good case in point. In 1956 on October 29, 47 inhabitants of that Arab village within Israel were machine-gunned by border guards upon reaching the outskirts of their village, to which they were returning after a day's work in the fields.

The victims included seven children and nine women. They were unaware of a curfew that had been imposed during their absence at work.

An Amnesty International Report on Israeli Methods of Torture, dated April 1970, describes instances where "dogs are let loose on prisoners usually handcuffed with hands behind backs," of fingers placed in the door jamb and the door closed on them, of fingernails pulled out with pincers, of prisoners injected with a pepper solution, and matchsticks inserted in the penis, among other barbarities.[48]

Muaid Uthman al Bahash, a high school student, was tortured in Israeli jails and barred from meeting with visitors for six months. By the time he was finally allowed to receive his first visitor, his left hand was completely paralyzed.[49] Abla Taha was placed in a cell with several prostitutes who stripped her naked in the presence of a policeman. After being beaten brutally, she was left naked for 11 days and was kicked by a policeman named Duwayk. Though pregnant and bleeding after the torture, she was nevertheless denied medical treatment.[50]

One of the latest incidents is that of Omar Abdul-Ghany Salameh, accused of being a Palestinian guerrilla. In 1969 Salameh was arrested and put in prison for one and a half years, during which he was tortured. But when he was arrested again on October 3, 1976, the torture he had to undergo surpassed anything he had been subjected to earlier. The story of his arrest and torture, reported by David Southerland in the March 1, 1977, issue of *The Christian Science Monitor*, begins at the "Russian Compound" in East Jerusalem, after a few punches he received on the road. Once there, Salameh was questioned by a man named Uri. When he denied that he belonged to any resistance group, "he was forced to lie face down on the floor while three men beat him on the soles of his feet with sticks." The ordeal, which lasted for five months, "included electric shocks which threw him into convulsions and suspension from the ceiling by a system of chains and pulleys which rendered him unconscious." The torturers "clapped their hands against his ears until his hearing was impaired." He was also forced to "clean a floor full of dirt and glass with his tongue" then "forced to swallow the filth afterwards." When he protested to his Israeli-Zionist torturers and "begged them in the name of God to desist," they said "your God is under [our] feet." The torture was also extended to Salameh's nephew, and one of the torturers threatened him that he might do "whatever he wanted with his wife."

Dr. Ahmad Hamza, chief surgeon and director of the King Hussein Hospital, indicated that Salameh had "difficulty walking and was suffering from fractured ribs, multiple 'contusions,' or bruises, and a general weakness due to a loss of weight." In the June 19, 1977, issue of the *Sunday Times* (London), the Insight Team of that paper, after a five-month inquiry, gave a detailed and thoroughly researched report about the nature and extent of torture in Israel. The report indicated that torture in Israel is not mere "primitive brutality" that can be dismissed as the work of a "handful of 'rogue cops' exceeding orders," it is rather a "methodically organized" torture through "refined techniques" such as electric shocks, "confinement in specially constructed cells," and sexual assaults. All Israel's intelligence services were implicated—ranging from the Shin Beth, which reports to the Office of the Police Minister, to Latam (Department of Special Missions), which reports to the Prime Minister, to the Military Intelligence, which reports to the Minister of Defense. The report mentioned six torture centers in Israel: the prisons of the main occupied towns (Nablus, Ramallah, and Gaza), the Russian Compound in Jerusalem, and two other centers whose "whereabouts are uncertain" (one was said to be inside the military base at Sarafand near the Lod Airport, the other was said to be somewhere in Gaza).

Given the methodical nature of Israeli torture, it seems that every center specializes in one technique. At the Russian Compound, for instance, "interrogators tended to favour assaults on the genitals," whereas the torture center at Sarafand has a marked predilection to blindfold prisoners, hang them by the wrists and assault them with dogs. The Ramallah center apparently specializes in the electric shock technique. The report indicated that the objective of Israeli torture is to obtain information from the Palestinian prisoners and to "pacify" the occupied territories.

Among the more intimidating means of controlling the Arab population is collective punishment. Even though outlawed by the 1949 Geneva Convention, it has been widely used by the Israeli authorities in the occupied territories. Such punishment at times takes ingenious forms, and at other times follows more conventional lines. For instance, after a nonviolent strike in Ramallah and al-Bira, all permits for importing sheep from the East Bank were canceled, and funds raised by the Association of Ramallah Immigrants in the United States were intercepted and denied to the Ramallah municipality.[51] In 1976, after a mass demonstration in the same unfortunate town, its entire population (20,000) "was shut down for eleven days," except for short periods, ranging from one to three hours, as indicated in the May 30, 1977, issue of *Time* magazine.

A more conventional form of collective punishment is the concentration camp. Such camps were set up for the families (women, children, and others) of suspected Palestinian guerrillas who could not be apprehended. Since the term "family" in the extended Arab sense does not simply include parents and children, some of the interned families numbered as many as 200 persons. They are released only when the suspected person has been either caught or killed. On March 1971, the Israeli government openly admitted the existence of Abu-Zuneima, a desert camp in which 30 families had been interned.[52]

Moshe Dayan advanced a new idea for punishment, combining conventional and unconventional techniques of concentration camps and collective punishment. Rather than single out individual families, he suggested that any town on the West Bank that shows signs of resistance should be "placed under blanket interdiction." This procedure was designed to deal a crippling blow to Arab livelihood by heading off food supplies, or "barring sheep from leaving for pasture." It is believed that there is a government plan now under preparation whereby an embargo on electricity, food, and medicine would be imposed on rebellious towns or villages, as reported in the May 31, 1976, issue of *Time* magazine.

Racial discrimination in Israel, far from being confined to the economic sector of society or to conventional forms and methods, reaches out to embrace almost all aspects of "life." Shalumit Alloni, a Knesset member concerned with civil rights, is critical of the fact that even the Israeli Ministry of Health, like that of Housing, is divided into the general office of health, serving Jews only, and the minority health subdepartment serving non-Jews.[53] Israel Shahak observed sarcastically, in describing this anomaly, that "only a separate health of a body of a Jew, and another sort of health of a body of a non-Jew are allowed to exist."[54] To preserve the all-too-important pure Jewish health, immunization of Jews takes priority over that of the minority.[55] The trustee of a Bedouin tribe in Galilee, who had even served in the Israeli Army, complained recently that his tribe was not granted "the right to receive immunization from the Ministry of Health."[56]

Israel's racist campaign is not directed exclusively against the physical existence of the Palestinians; it extends to their very intellectual and cultural life as well. In his book *The Unholy War,* David Waines recalls that the "Mandate administration proposed the establishment of a British University in the city of Jerusalem to serve as the educational apex of the two public systems [Arab and Jewish]." The Zionists rejected the plan because it "constituted a threat to Hebrew culture in Palestine." The only university to be set up had to be a Hebrew university. Actually, the Zionists "refused to have anything to do with any education program where Hebrew was not the *sole* language of instruction."[57]

On November 27, 1970, an editorial in *Haaretz* stated that among 16,000 college and university students in Israel, there were about 200 Arabs, and two of these were under administrative arrest.[58] Uri Lubrani, a former advisor on Arab affairs to the Prime Minister, in a statement made to *Haaretz* on April 4, 1961, gave expression to a Zionist hope frustrated by reality when he said, "If there were no [Arab] pupils the situation would be better and more stable. If the Arabs remained hewers of wood, it might be easier for us to control them."[59] There have been a number of Israeli newspaper articles about the threat and danger represented by the increasing number of Palestinian university graduates both in Israel and in exile.

Frustrated political Zionist hopes uniformly translate themselves into racist attempts to suppress the emergence of an educated Arab leadership. The Israeli establishment has denied freedom of movement and expression to a large number of Arab poets, playwrights, lawyers, and newspaper editors.[60] The establishment has also deported a number of leading intellectuals. One of the more recent deportees is Dr. Hanna Nasr, President of Bir Zeit College, where the faculty and students have been the object of persistent Israeli harassment. Aharon David, an advocate of quick and simple procedures leading to the attainment of the racist dream, has proposed that the Arab intellectual class be annihilated.[61]

The attempt to liquidate the Palestinians physically and intellectually assumes a curious aspect when it extends to traces they may have left behind in their exodus. As early as 1940, for instance, Weitz had reached the conclusion that "not one village, not one tribe should be left behind."[62] Thereby it was hoped that the illusion of an empty *eretz* could be perpetuated, even though Palestine was described by Zionist thinker Ahad Ha'am in 1891 as a country in which it was very difficult to find arable land that was not already cultivated.[63] The Zionist program is being more or less meticulously executed by the Zionist state. Israel has bulldozed whole Arab villages, including their cemeteries and tombstones. Of 475 Arab villages in pre-1948 Palestine, 385 have been destroyed.[64] Israel's armed forces bulldozed more than 10,000 homes of resisting Arab civilians in Gaza and the West Bank in the period from July 1967 to December 1972.

There have been ruthless attempts also to obliterate traces of the past. History books are rewritten to accord with the Zionist vision. The Arabs, the indigenous inhabitants of the land for over 13 centuries, are referred to in an Israeli textbook as invaders who "conquered our country one thousand and three hundred years ago." Even though they settled in the land, "they did nothing to preserve it from the teeth of destruction."[65] It is further claimed that the Arabs of Palestine were in Palestine for hundreds of years, for "they arrived," we are told, "only some tens of years before the arrival of the Zionists." "They arrived in the 1830's and 1840's as refugees from the oppression of Muhammed Ali in Egypt," according to the directives approved by the Minister of Education and Culture.[66] A deliberately distorted vision of history has popularized the idea that the mass of the Palestinians came only *after* the Zionist settlement in search of jobs and to share in the new general prosperity and universal happiness created by Zionist settlement.

Segregating Jews from non-Jews in Israel is a procedure that is followed even in compiling statistics pertaining to infants. We are told that infant mortality among Jewish children is meticulously recorded, but no such records have been kept for non-Jewish children. "Only from 1955 on . . . so far as is known under United Nations pressure, were the non-Jewish babies counted—separately."[67] The Zionist mind can even become obsessed with the thought that the unborn may be of the unwanted variety. Golda Meir, a grandmother herself, complained that she could not "sleep at night, thinking how many Arab babies are being born that same night," as reported in the Israeli press on October 25, 1972.[68]

Discrimination in Israel sometimes takes subtle and devious forms. Ben Gurion believed that financial aid should not be given to all Israeli families indiscriminately, but he also was of the mind that the Israeli government could not *openly* practice discrimination. As a way out, he felt financial aid could be extended to large Jewish, but not Arab, families if the responsibility for distributing the aid was turned over to the Jewish Agency, a nongovernmental worldwide Zionist institution. He believed that the Agency and "not the government, should take care of encouraging a rise in the [Jewish] birth rate."[69]

The notorious "Koeing Memorandum," written sometime in 1976, demonstrates that this line of thinking still prevails in Israel. Like Ben Gurion, Israel Koeing, the northern district Commissioner of the Interior, argued in a secret memorandum to the Prime Minister that the government should stop the payment of "big family" grants to the Arabs by transferring "this responsibility from the national insurance system to the Jewish Agency or to the Zionist organization, so that the grant is paid to Jews only."[70]

A similarly subtle approach prompted the promulgation in Israel of the Discharged Soldiers Law (Reinstatement in Employment, Amend. No. 4). To avoid granting cash subsidies to Arab families with numerous children, the law confines such subsidies to soldiers or members of their families only. This guarantees that aid goes only to Jewish children, since Arabs cannot serve in the Israeli Army. It is hoped that in this way the Arabs will be discouraged from having too many children.[71]

Israeli–Zionist racism can at times go to astonishing extremes. As reported in *Yediot Aharonot* of August 5, 1975, the Eighteenth Congress for Talmudic Studies, held in Jerusalem and presided over by former Israeli Premier Yitzhak Rabin and the former Minister for Religious Affairs, Yitzhak Raphael, decided in one of its recommendations "that a Jewish doctor should not help a non-Jewish woman to conceive."[72]

Probably nothing sums up the Israeli–Zionist attitude toward life and the craving for an unattainable purity better than the words of Israel Shahak: "*Everything* in Israel," the Israeli dissenter says, "is either Jewish or non-Jewish by official standards. A city, land, produce—even vegetables can be 'Jewish.' The very tomatoes and potatoes are tallied officially as 'Jewish' and 'non-Jewish.' "[73]

CHRISTIANS AND DRUZES

Zionist settlement from the outset has entailed the displacement and dispossession of the Arabs, whether Muslim, Druze, or Christian. The population of the two villages of Ikrit and Kafr Biram were Arab Christians. However, like other Arab villagers elsewhere in Palestine, they were displaced in 1948 in the customary Zionist fashion. The villagers appealed the evacuation orders in the Israeli Supreme Court, which issued a decree in 1951 upholding their right to return to their land. However, the government refused to honor the verdict, claiming that Kafr Biram was a "security area," a decision which the court rejected. Be that as it may, Kafr Biram was declared a "closed territory," and on September 16, 1953, the day of the Christian Feast of the Cross, the village buildings were blown up. Ikrit suffered the same fate; its turn came on Christmas Day of the same year.

After a few attempts to resettle the villagers elsewhere, the issue surfaced again. None other than Moshe Dayan declared that in the case of Ikrit and Kafr Biram, the necessity for keeping the two villages as "closed areas" no longer existed. His stand created an embarrassing situation for *Hashomer Hatzair*, the leftist Israeli group, which had set up a kibbutz in the area of the former Arab villages.

The case of the two villages raised issues concerning the legitimacy of Zionist dispossession of Palestinian Arabs, bringing into serious question the fate of other Arab villages that had been taken over. This fact in itself was cited as a convincing argument for the obduracy of the government. If Israel had relented in this particular case, the argument went, the action would have set a precedent for other Arabs to reclaim their lands and property. Writing in the July 14, 1972, issue of *Yediot Aharonot*, Yoram Ben Porath suggested that it was time to reeducate the Israeli masses in the basic tenets of Zionism, the first of these being "the fact that there is no Zionism, settlement, or Jewish state without the eviction of the Arabs and expropriation of their land."[74]

Although Zionism had dispossessed and disenfranchised Arab Muslims, Christians, and Druzes, it is claimed that the latter enjoy some minor privileges in Israel. Zionist propaganda sometimes argues in favor of a future Druze state acting as a buffer zone between Israel and Syria, this being part of the Zionist vision of a balkanized Middle East. But this vision founders on the Zionist structure of oppression, and the Druze finds himself in the same camp with his oppressed fellow Arab Muslims and Christians.

Even though he serves in the army, the Israeli Druze is a gentile, a fact that automatically bars him from certain rights and privileges granted only to the Jews and subjects him to most of the disabilities inflicted on the non-Jews. He faces discrimination in his everyday life in housing, business, and in various other social and institutional contexts. *Al Hamishmar,* the Israeli daily, has reported complaints by Druze Arabs concerning the expropriation of their lands and the nonindustrialization of their villages.

Additionally, such legislation as the Law of Return and other varieties of Zionist laws apply to the Druzes as much as to other Arabs. Some Druze youths have requested that the Israelis be taught in schools that the term " 'Israeli' means not only Jewish but Druze too,"[75] a structural impossibility in the Zionist state.

As far as a Druze state is concerned, one must remember that all Israeli statements are extremely evasive. Such a state would have to be carved out of the organic *Eretz Yisrael.* It came as no great surprise to the Arab world when Israel discovered that Druze Arabs supported Palestinian resistance, or when Sheikh Farhud, a leading Druze tribal chief, asked that the law for compulsory recruitment of Druze youth in the Israeli Army be rescinded. He appealed for recognition of the Druzes as a part of the Arab people. In the 1976 uprisings among the Arabs of Israel in the Galilee and elsewhere in protest of land expropriation and discrimination, many Druze villages participated. The leading Arab poet inside Israel today, Samih al Qassem, is a Druze, a fact that the Zionists would do well to ponder.

A non-Jew in Israeli-Zionist vocabulary, as in the Balfour Declaration, means anyone in Palestine who is *not* Jewish, irrespective of whether he is Christian, Muslim, or Druze.

A FORM OF RACISM AND RACIAL DISCRIMINATION

Despite the fact that Zionist theory and Israeli-Zionist practices are obviously discriminatory, some people still believe that the use of the term "racism" in reference to Zionism is unjustified for a variety of reasons. It has been said, for instance, that victims of racism cannot, by the very nature of things, be racists themselves, an argument not borne out by historical realities. While maintaining compassion for the victims of racism, one should not overlook the fact that to undergo such an ordeal is not necessarily the most purifying or ennobling experience. Racism does not itself teach man love for his fellow men. On the contrary, the victim at times may well be unaware that he himself is developing a form of reverse racism as a defense mechanism.

It is quite possible that the same harsh experience can ennoble one man, but brutalize another, depending on the complex psychological and historical circumstances of each individual. For instance, Menahem Begin, of Deir Yassin fame, and Golda Meir, a woman haunted by the fear of the natural increase of the Arab population, were by their own admission subjected to humiliating racist slurs in their land of origin. Naturally, they have been traumatized by their experience. On the other hand, Israel Shahak, who survived the agonizing Holocaust experience as an inmate of a concentration camp, has been a vocal and fearless advocate of equal civil and political rights for Palestinian Arabs. He is an outspoken critic of Israel's discriminatory laws.

The preceding argument against the use of the term "racist" to describe the actions of victims of racism is but one argument among many that Zionist apologists resort to. Another, which may be called the semantic argument, is far subtler and has wider appeal. When used to describe Zionism, the term "racism" is a misnomer, we are told. "Racism," so goes the counterargument, is a discrimination on the basis of *race*, and since the Jews do not consider themselves a race, then they cannot be racists. For one thing, such logic presupposes eternal immunity of one human group against the charge of racism, regardless of any crimes committed by its members. Furthermore, and more important, the semantic argument is premised on the idea that there is a single definition for the terms "racism" and "race," which is not the case by any means. "Racism" is a complex term. Like other terms used to describe concepts, such as "nationalism" and "romanticism," the term "racism" is elusive and difficult to define. Such terms do not designate something physical or quantifiable; they are conceptual constructs that isolate certain aspects of human behavior in order to analyze and understand them. The elusiveness is further compounded by the fact that the traits we try to isolate are embedded in an infinite number of contexts and specific situations. Thus, each of these traits assumes a particular form that differs from one situation to another. It is restating the self-evident to say that no one expects to find the conceptual constructs "racism" or "romanticism" fully applicable in reality. Above all, the term "racism" is vague because it derives from a relatively undefined concept in anthropology, namely that of "race." There is no universally accepted definition of race. Categories such as the "ethnic" (with its cultural overtones) overlap with racial (genetic). There are definitions of race as simply a matter of genetics, and others into which the idea of genes does not enter at all. Webster's *New International Dictionary of the English Language* defines race in the strict genetic sense, yet also cites this broader one: "a state of being one of a special people or ethnical stock."[76] (Such a definition, incidentally, applies to the Jews as the Zionists see them.)

The writer of the entry on "Interracial Relations" in the *Encyclopedia Britannica* devoted a whole section to "The Problem of Definition." Starting off with the assertion that "the very term race is difficult to define," he suggested that we do away completely with the term and replace it with the term "ethnic group," which may be characterized as having a "particular inherited physical type, *or* culture, *or* nationality, *or* any combination of these."[77]

The author of the entry on "Racism" in the *New Encyclopedia Britannica* did not accept this suggestion. He drew a distinction between an "ethnic group" and a "racial group," in the belief that members of the latter have physical characteristics in common, whereas members of the former share "a common language, a common set of religious beliefs or some other cultural characteristics *without* physical considerations." He added, however, that his distinction is merely theoretical. In practice, the writer went on to explain, the distinction between "race" and "ethnic group" is not always clear-cut, and many groups are socially defined in terms of both physical and cultural criteria. He referred to the Jews as a clear example.[78]

The leading theoreticians and originators of modern Western racism, such as Gobineau and Chamberlain, experienced difficulties with the term "race." Gobineau, for instance, writing in the mid-nineteenth century, admitted that "pure races" could no longer be found. Toward the end of the nineteenth century, Chamberlain, who regarded the Jews "as alien in spirit to the favoured Teutons," admitted nevertheless the difficulty of "distinguishing Jews from Germans on the basis of physical characteristics alone."[79] The Italian fascist minister and theoretician Giacomo Acerbo felt the need to use the racialist term "Aryan" in order to isolate the Jewish minority from the "national organism." Nevertheless, he referred to the looseness of the very term he used.[80]

But if terms used in the social sciences are elusive, the term "racism," as it is usually used, presents additional difficulties. Terms that are largely descriptive and only faintly evaluative, such as "romantic," are used to express an idea which in turn corresponds to an element in reality (an outlook, a mode of behavior, a painting). The term is used as a principle of classification. The scholar who uses it is quite often largely engaged in an endeavor that has no direct bearing on his economic or political interests, and which does not involve him morally in an intense way. Given the descriptive nature of the term, the person so described is not likely to be put on the defensive.

"Racism," on the other hand, is at once a descriptive and evaluative term. It defines an attitude derived not from the findings of scientific research about race but from mythic assumptions largely divorced from reality. Self-defense on the part of a group described as racist is understandable. Not many people would recoil when described as "romantic," but the most notorious racist or anti-Semite, especially in our enlightened days, would resist the definition.

The term "racist" not only refers to the *social structure* imposed through oppressive discrimination, but also to the very *racial apologetics and myths* propounded by the oppressor in self-defense. These apologetics can change according to the racists' needs. If ethnology is respectable and if the "science" of the study of races is universally accepted, as was the case in Europe in the nineteenth and early twentieth centuries, then the racist group develops a racial typology, attaches a value judgment to it, and uses it to buttress an exploitative *status quo*. When such theories are discredited, then the racist group conveniently changes its tune, without a corresponding change in the oppressive reality.

Examples of such switches are common. Apartheid in South Africa in the heyday of racialist thought in Europe was defended on racial grounds. At the present time, such attitudes are frowned upon by the world community. Therefore, the oppressors and beneficiaries of the *status quo* present their arguments in terms of ethnicity and culture. The *South African Observer*, a publication that stands to the "right" of the present South African regime, described itself in its December 1975 issue as "the only established publication that is trying to save a place in the world for the children and grandchildren of the generation now in power in South Africa."[81] This smacks very much of the rhetoric of national liberation movements and has no vestige of the rhetoric of the superior white man and his celebrated burden. The magazine further described South Africa as the Western nation that is undeniably committed to the survival of the West.

Even Nazi Germany diversified its rationalizations. On the wall of some labor camps were inscribed such "ennobling" slogans as "Work will make you free," and on the very gate of the Buchenwald concentration camp was inscribed the motto, "My country, right or wrong,"[82] an obvious attempt to justify extermination on patriotic and national grounds rather than on *openly* racial ones. What has changed in all of these instances is the rationalizing myth, or the ideological claims, not the structure of reality.

The rationalizing myths, like intentions, are a closed system which, if judged in isolation from the concrete structure that gave rise to it, will look undoubtedly noble. There is nothing inherently wrong about keeping a piece of land in the world for children of the Afrikaners, let alone preserving Western civilization. It is when placed in concrete reality that we begin to see the human cost of implementing the myth.

To accept the changing rationalizations as the only frame of reference is to surrender to verbal manipulation by the oppressor. Nazism would then cease to be a form of racism and racial discrimination; it would simply be national socialism. Apartheid would be simply apartheid or probably Christian nationalism. One scholar has solemnly suggested that discrimination in South Africa is based not on *race* but rather on color, and consequently it should not be called *racism* but rather "pigmentocracy."

If we were to accept such reasoning, Fascist discriminatory action against the Jews would cease to be defined as such. After the Manifesto of Fascist Racism was issued on July 15, 1938, a Fascist periodical "stressed the 'spiritual' rather than the biological idea of race." However, "a month later . . . it went along with denying Jews influence in government or education because they had a different spirit," not genes.[83] Fascist discriminatory practices, then, on the basis of the semantic argument, should not be termed "racist." If we reduce the oppressive nature of the structures that racism erects to the very language of those structures, we end up with unrelated fragments of reality. Racism, then, despite all the discrimination and oppression, will simply disappear.

There is really no reason why the victims of racism should accept the distorted logic and verbal acrobatics of their oppressors. The black in the Bantustans knows that he does not have to be there for Western civilization to prosper. The European Jews and the workers in the slave labor camps saw no possible link between inscribed motto and the dismal truth. If it is in the interest of the oppressor to obfuscate reality, it is in the interest of the victim to study the concrete structure of discrimination outside the sphere of the oppressor's logic and rationalizations.

Where Zionism is concerned, the same tendencies can be detected. Ashley Montagu, in the *Bulletin of the American Professors for Peace in the Middle East,* presented a good example of the tendency to confuse defensive arguments with concrete practice. Denouncing the United Nations Zionism-racism resolution, Montagu argued that "racism is the practice of the *view* that members of certain socially defined groups are *biologically* characterized by certain traits which disable them from taking full advantage of political and social equality."[84] In Montagu's view, one of the determining factors in the classifying process seems to be the genetic *view* of race entertained by the oppressor. Therefore, the Israeli refusal to accept the return of the Palestinians to their homeland in 1948 is nonracist, for the Israeli practice was decided on "purely political grounds . . . racial [genetic] considerations were not in the least involved here. Political reality was." It would have been "suicidal" for the Israelis, Montagu asserted, "to have become a minority living among a majority in their own state."[85] The argument here distinguishes between injustice and exclusion rationalized on "racial" grounds and the same injustice and exclusion rationalized on "political" grounds. The former is morally reprehensible and the latter is somehow more acceptable in a world of *realpolitik.*

Montagu's choice of example was not exactly a happy one, for the "political" decisions of the Israelis are based on a demographic imperative which is patently racist. Michael Bar-Zohar, Ben Gurion's biographer, a more knowledgeable man about Zionism than Montagu, admitted that the Zionist demographic imperative of a Jewish majority was among the basic principles of Zionism and that the principle could be called "racialist."[86]

There are two basic weaknesses of the term "racism," as outlined above. The first is its ambiguity, given the ambiguity of the term "race" itself. The second is that the term "racism" defines an objective phenomenon, as well as its rationalizing myth of racial superiority. These weaknesses are not by any means unique to the term. When we run into such difficulties, we realize the limits of human discourse, and therefore a radical break with the term is extremely difficult or even impossible. Despite the nuances that distinguish one phenomenon from another, we retain the term because of its utility in designating certain common traits that would otherwise go undetected or remain unrelated to each other.

Perhaps the most we can hope for under the circumstances is to further clarify the term by adding qualifiers. We can consider "racism" as a generic term, referring to the social phenomenon of exploitative discrimination practiced by one human group, which defines itself on the basis of a trait (other than sex and class), against another that lacks that trait. Actually, this seems to be the implicit definition of the term in concrete practice.

Various international resolutions concerning racial discrimination demonstrate an awareness of the problem of definition. The International Convention on the Elimination of All Forms of Racial Discrimination [resolution 2106 (xx)] Article I defines "racial discrimination" as "any distinction, exclusion, restriction, or preference based on race, colour, descent, or national or ethnic origin which has the purpose or effect of nullifying or impairing the recognition, enjoyment, on an equal footing, of human rights and fundamental freedom in the political, economic, social, cultural, or any other field of public life."

This broad and comprehensive definition relegates apologetics based on "race, colour, descent, or national or ethnic origin" to a secondary status, emphasizing the concrete act of "distinction, exclusion, restriction, or preference" and thus making it the point of reference and the basis of classification. The terms "racism" or "racial discrimination" are to be used to refer to such acts of discrimination even when no genetic apologetics is involved.

But there remains the problem of the rationalizing myth and apologetics, which cannot be overlooked and which can be effectively used as a principle of classification for the subsystems of racism. It is suggested that a qualifier be affixed to the term "racism" as a help to differentiate these subsystems, so that one can cite Nazi racism, South African racism,

Fascist racism, meaning "distinction, exclusion, restriction or preference" based on Nazi, South African, or other interpretations. Or one
could cite "genetic racism," "ethnic racism," and probably "religious
racism," meaning exploitative discrimination on the basis of a theory of
genes, exploitative discrimination on the basis of ethnicity, and so on.

In his book *The Fascist Experience*, Professor Edward R. Tannenbaum was aware of the limits of the term "racism" and the verbal acrobatics of the racists. Using the terms "biological racism" and "ethnic
racism," he referred to the attempt of "Fascist theorists" to graft "biological racism" onto "ethnic racism."[87] His efforts at sharpening the
meaning of the terms are praiseworthy, and they proved adequate for the
context in which they were used, but his definitions have never achieved
universal acceptance. Terms must occasionally be redefined and adapted
to ever-changing human situations.

Turning from the general subject of racism to the more particular
topic of Zionist practice, we can apply the same procedure of separating
the phenomenon of exploitative discrimination from the rationalizations.
In this chapter, the particulars of Israeli-Zionist practice vis-à-vis the
Arabs have been described without dealing with the issue of the appli-
cability of the term "racism" to such practice. Eminent anti-Zionist Jews
are quite explicit on this score. Among the more distinguished Jewish
scholars is Rabbi Elmer Berger, who defined racism as "a form of government or a structure of society in which national rights and responsibilities
are officially legislated upon the basis of creed, color or ethnic derivation."
On the basis of this definition, Rabbi Berger concluded that the Zionist
character of much of "basic" Israeli law qualifies for the term "racist."[88]

While not using the term "racism," Noam Chomsky stated flatly in
his *Peace in the Middle East?* that the Jewish state cannot be democratic,
for it wants to be as Jewish as France is French. This, he pointed out,
"is patently impossible." The reason lies in the inevitable institutional
discrimination that it must necessarily practice: An immigrant in France
becomes French, and any disability he might be subjected to is a matter
of personal or social bigotry. The non-Jewish citizen of the Jewish state,
on the other hand, does not necessarily become Jewish. The disabilities
he suffers because he is non-Jewish are a "matter of principle, not a departure from some ideal norm toward which the society strives." These
disabilities, therefore, cannot be remedied "through slow progress."[89]
The Jewish citizen in the Zionist state, whether he is for or against racism,
benefits from institutional *de jure* discrimination. Again, this is a matter
of an institutional structure that has little to do with his moral principles.
Even if a Jew in Israel protests against discrimination and injustice, he is
treated (with or without his approval) in a manner different from that
reserved for the non-Jewish protestor.

One must now turn to the problem of apologetics in order to modify the generic term "racism" by affixing to it the specific term "Zionist," or "Israeli-Zionist," meaning "distinction, exclusion, restriction, or preference" as practiced in the Israeli-Zionist state against Arabs (that is, non-Jews) on the basis of Zionist apologetics and rationalizations. One can use the more general term "ethnic racism" when referring to Eban's or Herzog's speeches, for instance, and "religious racism" when referring to the ideology of Gush Emunim. The term "Zionist racism," however, is at once more comprehensive and more precise because political Zionism itself is an ideology that rationalizes the alleged exclusive rights and claims of the Jew on racial, ethnic, religious, religio-national, and at times socialist grounds.

It should be borne in mind, however, that the subject of the controversy in this section is not the fact of discrimination against the Arabs in Israel. The discussion centers on the appropriateness of using the term "racism" with reference to specific Israeli-Zionist discriminatory practices. As such, it is primarily a matter of semantics. Efforts toward coining more diversified and precise terminology for the description of varieties of racism, relating the specific form and practice to the general conceptual construct, should be encouraged. The controversy surrounding terminology, however, should not be allowed to cloud our perception of the concrete structure of oppression. Palestinian peasants, and indeed many of the peoples of Asia and Africa, did not rebel against a conceptual construct— they mounted their resistance against real oppression.

9

THE RESPONSE OF THE ORIENT

ETERNAL ARAB HOSTILITY?

The histories of South Africa, Angola, Algeria, and other settler-colonial enclaves have shown that such enclaves are uniformly met with the hostility and resistance of the natives. In the face of such resistance, the settlers in turn had to organize themselves in order to break down the opposition and maintain their supremacy. Zionist spokesmen, however, given to a pseudo-historical rationalization of political Zionism, claimed that Jewish settlers, far from being colonists, were a people returning to its ancestral homeland. In his book *A Nation Reborn,* Richard Crossman suggested that both the British government and Chaim Weizmann expected Jewish settlement to be achieved and the "Western, civilized" Jewish state to be founded, "without upsetting the less civilized 'natives,' "[1] It is hard to imagine how such a feat was thought possible.

In 1967, Ben Gurion claimed that none of the "great thinkers" of Zionism ever believed that the Zionist dream could be achieved "only through military victory over the Arabs."[2] Had the "great thinkers" consulted the writings of Karl Kautsky, the German-Jewish thinker and social analyst, they would have learned that Kautsky had predicted in 1921 that "every attempt made by the advancing Jewry in that country [that is, Palestine] to displace the Arabs cannot fail to arouse the fighting spirit of the latter."[3] Two years earlier, the American historian and journalist Herbert Adam Gibbons, who was intimate with the Middle East, had emphasized that Jewish immigration into and development of Palestine could be "assured only by the presence of a considerable army for an indefinite period."[4]

A writer in the July 1920 issue of the *Atlantic* predicted with remarkable accuracy that, to fulfill their aspirations, the Zionists "must obtain the armed assistance of one of the European powers, presumably Great Britain or the United States of America." He went on to outline the expected consequences of Zionist settlement. The entire Palestinian population, he said, "will resist the Zionist Commission's plan of wholesale immigration of Jews." He further indicated that the displacement of the "Muslim cultivators" from their land at the hands of the Jews would "arouse violent outbreaks against the Jewish minority." Using a religio-racial terminology favored until recently in the Western world, he predicted the development of "fierce Muslim hostility and fanaticism against Western Powers that permitted it"—a hostility the effects of which, he went on to say, "would be felt through the Middle East and would cause trouble in Syria, Mesopotamia, Egypt and India."[5]

Or had Ben Gurion read Herzl's letter to Baron de Hirsch, he would have known of Herzl's grandiose plan to create out of the intellectual Jewish proletariat "the general staff and cadres of the army which is to seek, discover and take over the Land."[6] Nordau, after the death of his friend Herzl, carried on the militaristic tradition, for he, who had been deeply shocked at his "belated" discovery of the existence of the Palestinians, proposed the mobilization of a ridiculously large army of 600,000 Jews to go to Palestine in order to force itself as a demographic majority on the Palestinians and so to found the Zionist state. Jabotinsky, as well, the true heir of the Herzlian line, as Nordau indicated, worked out a plan to create an immediate Jewish majority in Palestine, a plan he dubbed the "Nordau Project."

Jabotinsky, however, never claimed innocence, preferring to face squarely the full consequences of the Zionist settlement project. When a German Zionist named Georg Landauer warned the Twelfth Zionist Congress (1921) that an "all-out war with the Arabs was inevitable," and predicted that this war would eventually be won by them unless some kind of agreement was reached with the Palestinians, Jabotinsky scoffed at him.[7] Citing examples from the history of Western colonization in Africa and Asia, he told the Zionist colonists: "History teaches that all colonizations have met with little encouragement from the natives on the spot; it may be very sad but so it is and we Jews are no exception."[8] The Revisionist Zionist leader pleaded with the Palestine Royal Commission in 1937 to let the Zionists train themselves in the arts of self-defense, just as in Kenya, where "every European was obliged to train for the settlers' Defense Force."[9] One year later, in a meeting of the Polish Betar, a Zionist military organization, Menahem Begin, Jabotinsky's faithful disciple, was instrumental in changing the oath of allegiance of the said organization "to include a vow to conquer the Jewish Homeland by force of arms."[10] The members of Betar were indoctrinated in a view of life that posited two alternatives with no middle ground: conquest or death. In 1939, Begin assumed leadership of that organization.

In a letter to Churchill dated 1921, Weizmann discussed the "arming and organizing [of] the Jewish colonists"—the *halutzim*.[11] However, being far more sophisticated than the candid Jabotinsky or Begin, he suggested in the same letter that "as little as possible" be said about stories of Arab resistance to Zionist settlement. He knew that "things just as bad occur in Egypt and India,"[12] but he was concerned about the public image thus created and about the repercussions that such news of resistance might create among the Jews.

Ben Gurion must have been aware of the realities of the situation in Palestine. At the beginning of this century, young men from the Workers of Zion who settled in Palestine had "to walk armed with big sticks and some of them with knives and rifles."[13] In 1907 there was a secret Zionist military organization whose motto claimed that Judea had fallen by blood and fire and that it was going to rise in the same way. This organization became the *Hashomer* in 1909, only to be transformed into the stronger and better organized Haganah in 1920. However, whereas the scrupulous Haganah, the military arm of the Jewish Agency and the World Zionist Organization, dropped the motto, it was retained by the openly terroristic Irgun (or Haganah Bet),[14] headed by Menahem Begin. The Irgun also adopted as its symbol a "hand holding a rifle over the map of Palestine, including Transjordan, with the motto Rak Kakh (Only Thus)." In 1948 the scrupulous Haganah and the terroristic Irgun were both incorporated into the *Tsahal,* the Israeli Defense Army. (The Knesset in December 1961 instructed the Civil Service Commission to consider service in the Irgun on the same basis as service in Haganah, and veterans of the Irgun participate in official government functions.)[15] All this could not have escaped Ben Gurion, who was one of the main architects of Zionist settlement in Palestine and of Israeli independence and expansion.

In the early years of Zionist settlement, the innocuous agricultural cooperative settlements were fortified with primitive *ad hoc* equipment and fences, which were later developed into the "stockade and tower." As more resistance developed after 1948, Israel was turned into a "fortress state," an "armed ghetto,"[16] surrounded by the impregnable Bar Lev Line, set up for purely *defense* reasons. The search for secure *defensible* boundaries is still under way. Such a state of affairs was openly predicted by Jabotinsky, who believed that an "iron wall" of Jewish armed forces would have to defend the process of Zionist settlement.[17] Leo Tolstoy characterized Zionism as being basically a reactionary, "militarist movement."[18] This militaristic aspect of the Zionist pioneering movement was built into the very concept of *halutziut*. Amos Elon tells us that the term means, among other things, "to pass over *armed* before the Lord into the land of Canaan."[19]

But the Zionists were sometimes fearful that recognition of the obdurate reality would uncover the fact that the fulfillment of their rights in Palestine would necessitate a program of dispossession and even genocide. As a defense mechanism, the Zionists have offered several simplistic formulas to explain away Arab resistance. In the face of the early Arab revolt in 1908 against Zionist settlement, Yitzhak Ben Zvi (1884–1963), who was to become Israel's second President, classified the resistance as "anti-Semitic pogroms," and even suggested that it had been instigated by the Czarist consul![20] In more recent times, the Israeli government has accused foreign TV cameramen of being responsible for the disturbances in the West Bank. These cameramen have been accused of bribing Arabs to stage demonstrations for their benefit.

Responding to warnings that the displacement of the native Palestinians would create trouble for the Jews in Palestine, a Zionist settler insisted at the Seventh Zionist Congress (1905) that Arab peasants would turn against Jews no matter how the Jews behaved, not in retaliation for any concrete grievance, but simply because of the "eternal enmity toward a people which had been exiled from its country."[21] This facile metaphysical explanation is still common in Israel even among the Israeli intelligentsia. Yeshayahu Leibowitz blamed the whole "Jewish-Arab conflict," as he phrased it, not on "incorrect tactics or even on incorrect policy," it is simply "an expression of the essence of the Jewish people's historic tragedy."[22] The Israeli poet Pinhas Sadeh develops a sinister conspiratorial view of Arab hostility to the Zionist settlers. Somehow he starts off with the premise that "the dispute between the Jews and Arabs is a very superficial one." Looking for a deeper reason to account for this incomprehensible hostility, Sadeh sets forth the argument that "the Arabs are the emissaries of the Christian world's need to liquidate the phenomenon of the Jews."[23] Abraham Yehoshuah, the Israeli writer, falls back on cosmic psychological drives to account for the conflict. There is something in the Jews, Yehoshuah argues, that "arouses 'insanity' among other nations," and the Arabs, being no exception, are "motivated" in their hostility "largely by drives which are not at all rational."[24]

Of course the Arab peasants had no immutable, metaphysical motives as those being attributed to them by the Zionist settlers. Like the peoples of Asia and Africa, who were similarly subjected to the Western colonial onslaught, they had no alternative but to fight back, defending their land and their national rights against the Zionist settler-colonists. Even though this act of self-defense has its moral dimensions, for it is ultimately an assertion of man's dignity in the face of violence and physical force, Arab resistance to Zionism has been neither absolute nor metaphysical, although it is real and deep. It springs from recognizable socio-historical roots and has various political manifestations.

Most Arabs have always maintained that the struggle over Palestine is a political one. Palestinian resistance to Zionism dates back to 1919, before the Arabs had even heard of Western public-relations gimmicks and image-building. At its July 2, 1919, session, the Syrian Congress, whose Muslim, Christian, and Jewish representatives were elected by the Palestinians, Lebanese, and Syrians, rejected the Zionist demand for the establishment of a Jewish commonwealth in Palestine. It further opposed "Jewish immigration into any part of the country." The Congress also asserted that the Palestinians did not acknowledge that the Zionist Jews had a title "to this land." Opposition to Zionism had no Koranic or biblical basis; it was grounded in concrete realities. "We regard the Zionists' claim," the 1919 Congress resolution said, "as a grave menace to our national, political and economic life." The conferees, nevertheless, took good care to assert that "our Jewish fellow-citizens shall continue to enjoy the rights and to bear the responsibilities which are ours in common,"[25] a standard of equality yet to be reached by the most idealistic of Zionists. The Arab ideal of "rights," unlike that of the Zionists, at least embraces Jews, Christians, and Muslims.

In this respect it is important to note that in the face-to-face negotiations between Zionists and Arabs, it was the "benighted" Oriental Arabs, not the "enlightened" Occidental Zionists, who advocated the concept of a democratic secular state and who were open-minded and realistic. In 1913, Rafiq Bey al-Azm, an Arab leader, declared himself to be too well aware of the value "of Jewish capital, labor and intelligence" to wish to alienate the Jews. He added that he had not studied the problem of Zionism sufficiently. Eventually, however, he was to assert that the segregated structure that the Zionists were advocating was the reason behind the opposition of Arab youth to Zionism.[26]

The tribal *emir*, Prince Faisal, son of Sherif (King) Hussein I of Mecca, was far more "democratic" in spirit than the Zionists who came, it was sometimes claimed, to found the first democracy in the Middle East. On October 3, 1939, in an interview in the *Jewish Chronicle*, he found nothing objectionable in establishing a Jewish cultural center in Palestine or in the free use of the Hebrew language. But in lieu of the quasi-religious *aliyah,* he proposed in the same interview a "regulated immigration into the country, for conditions in which the Jews will have equal rights with the Arabs" and take part in the government of Palestine. "The Jews," he said, "are cousins and we would willingly make them brothers." As for the Zionist scheme of turning Palestine into a Jewish state "as Jewish as England is English," he vigorously protested against that, saying that "if historical rights as claimed by the Jews had value, the Arabs would claim Spain."[27] It might be of some interest to underscore the fact that there was no basic antagonism between Faisal's attitude on the one hand, and Magnes' and probably Ahad Ha'am's and the cultural Zionist outlook on the other.

In one of the last meetings between Zionists and Arabs, held in Cairo as late as 1921, the Arabs showed a willingness to pacify "the spirits in Palestine, with a view to preventing the outbreak of disturbances." They were even prepared to dispatch a delegation to Palestine to bring about peace, provided the Zionists refrained from violence.[28] The Jews could exist as members of a society established there by Arabs and Jews, and run by a duly elected government. Some Arabs were willing to accept the full consequences of the logic of democracy. It was argued by Arabs that "if . . . [the Jews] form the majority here, they will be the rulers. If they are in the minority, they will be represented in proportion to their numbers."[29]

The Arab viewpoint is not of purely historical interest, for it is still the basic stance adopted by most Arab spokesmen. On the eve of the war in June 1967, James Reston, in the June 5 issue of *The New York Times*, tried to outline the Arabs' perception of Israel and their attitude toward it. The Arabs believed that their struggle was not inspired by the desire to "destroy Israel"—as the Western media insist—but rather was directed toward a state acting as a base for Western interests, serving as a barrier to divide the Arab world. The Arabs, according to Reston, argued that they understood the longing of the Jews for a homeland and sympathized with their suffering in Germany. But the settlement of the Jews in the Arab world, in the homeland of the Palestinians, in compensation for crimes committed against them in Europe, was a grievous error. But above all, as the former editor-in-chief of *Al-Ahram* and Nasser's chief spokesman, Mr. Heikal, said, the Jews in Israel remained a "foreign substance" that could be accepted only if Israel changed fundamentally and if the Jews "become a 'natural part' of the Middle Eastern world, [and] if they abandon their Western beliefs in the dominion of power."

Adopting more or less the same line, Prince Fahd of Saudi Arabia asked President Carter on May 25, 1977, to urge the Israelis not to close the door on a settlement "that would provide a just and lasting peace" for all. In Middle East diplomatic parlance, the phrase "just and lasting" has come to mean a solution not based on annexation of land or on sacrifice of Palestinian national rights. Within that frame of reference, Prince Fahd went on to express his strong hope that the Israelis would be reassured about the inclinations of his country toward protection of their security. The idea of a peaceful coexistence with a Jewish community in the Middle East, within the framework of equality for all, is not empty propaganda or a slogan; it was a proposal advanced when the Arabs constituted a vast majority, and they are still advancing it during their present struggle.

Many Arab spokesmen, in their first encounter with Zionist colonial-

ism, tended to draw a line between Zionist settlement and Jewish migration. For the one, they had nothing but hostility and opposition; for the
other there was sympathetic understanding. George Antonius, the Pales-
tinian-Arab historian, indicated in his book *The Arab Awakening* that
Jewish settlement in Palestine "on humanitarian grounds, subject to the
limitations imposed by a proper regard for the welfare of the political and
economic rights" of the Palestinians, was welcomed.[30] The one thing that
Arabs insisted on all along was that Zionist immigration and settlement
under the aegis of the British Empire, and within the framework of the
Balfour Declaration and the Mandate, could not be tolerated. At that, the
Zionists naturally balked, for without the Balfour Declaration and European colonial support, no Zionist state could have been set up. They rejected the very principle of equality at the outset. Moshe Pearlman reported
that the Arab demand "that the Jews, Christians and Moslems be declared
all equally at home in Palestine" was described by Zionists, rightist and
leftist alike, as a "ridiculous and dangerous scheme."[31]

The discriminatory colonialist practice of the Zionist settlers left no
alternative for the Arabs but to fight back. Many a young Israeli is fully
aware that if he were "an Arab I would do exactly the same thing—I
would be fighting us."[32] The reasons for Arab resistance, which have
many historical parallels, are easily understood by both colonizer and
colonized. "It is not true that the Arabs hate the Jews for personal, religious or racial reasons," said Moshe Dayan in July 1963, "they consider
us—and justly, from their point of view—as Westerners, foreigners, invaders
who have seized an Arab country to turn it into a Jewish state." In another
speech he gave just before the 1967 war, he made it clear that the Arabs
viewed the Israelis as "colonists who transform into a Jewish homeland
the territory they [the Arabs] have lived in for generations."[33] Despite
some of the intentional or unintentional errors—equating the Zionists with
the Jews, speaking of the Zionist enclave as a Jewish homeland, and
referring to the Palestinians as having lived for mere generations rather
than for centuries in Palestine—Dayan's statement captures the essence
of the Arab response and attitude to Zionism and the Zionist invasion,
before and since 1948.

AFRO-ASIAN SOLIDARITY

To view Israel in an exclusively Arab context would be to overlook
the wider impact that the creation of the Zionist state has had on the
Afro-Asian scene. Ben Gurion, Israel's first prime minister, believed that
Israel's loyalties from the standpoint of its survival and security required
it to place its "friendship with European countries" far above the mere

"sentiments that prevail among the Asian people."[34]

The same realistic recognition of this identity of interests underlies a statement by Ishar Harari, member of the Knesset and of Israel's delegation to the United Nations General Assembly in 1955. Writing in the *Jerusalem Post* of January 21, 1956, Harari graphically outlined Israel's achievement at the United Nations, asserting that "the most significant development" in Israel's favor was the 1955 "defeat of the Bandung Conference countries on practically every issue brought before the General Assembly."[35]

In keeping with its realistic view of its Afro-Asian neighbors, Israel has vigorously pursued the colonialist policies originally envisaged for it. Noteworthy is its voting record on decolonization in the United Nations since 1949. In January of that year, when the United Nations discussed the first major decolonization problem—that of Indonesia—Israel abstained from participating in the debate and subsequently withheld its support for Indonesia on the West Irian question. Israel also abstained on the resolution upholding the principle of self-determination, which was adopted by the United Nations General Assembly in 1952.

Among Israel's most notorious votes in the United Nations were those cast against the independence of Tunisia and Algeria. Israel's own *colons*, recognizing their real interests, were opposed to the decolonization process under way in Algeria. During their trial, some of the French generals in the Secret Army, who had attempted to set up a settler-colonial government in Algeria independent from France, admitted that they had obtained pledges from Salazar's Portugal and from South Africa and Israel to recognize their government as soon as it was established.

Israel's stand on the issue of decolonization was further clarified when *Haolam Hazeh* reported in its November 29, 1961, issue that Israel had not only sold machine guns to Portugal but had also supplied it with planes at a time when Portugal was engaged in a colonial war against the peoples of Angola and Mozambique. According to the radical American weekly *The Guardian,* in its issue of May 11, 1968, an Angolan national leader had identified Israel and NATO as the two main sources of military aid for Portugal.

It should be pointed out, however, that in the 1960s, Israel began to assume an anti-colonial posture. During that period, Israel supported the Afro-Asian countries in certain United Nations votes, and even extended aid to some African countries. Israel's motives for her short-lived anticolonial stand deserve further study. Suffice it to state here that even during that anticolonialist interregnum she continued to enjoy the support of all Western countries and former colonial powers, mainly because Israel, from their point of view, served as a backdoor to Africa, and therefore they tolerated and even encouraged her anticolonial posture.

A quick glance at the Israeli position at the United Nations during the Thirtieth and Thirty-First sessions (1975 and 1976, respectively) provides clear indications that Israel has reverted to her more fundamental position. With regard to all the resolutions on decolonization or racial discrimination, Israel voted in the negative, abstained, or absented herself during the voting.[36] That in itself should put the posturing of the past in proper perspective. The increasing collaboration between Israel and South Africa in the political, economic, and military fields helped more than anything else to underline the true orientation of the Zionist state.[37]

Rather than study the complex of socio-historical reasons that prompt the Afro-Asian rejection of Zionism, some Western commentators glibly attribute it to Arab wealth or to blackmail. Such a theory implies that, whether as individuals or groups, human beings and nations can be easily bought off. However, even a bird's-eye view of the Afro-Asian stand will demonstrate that resistance to Zionism has complex historical and moral roots, and that it actually predates by many years the celebrated Arab petro-dollars.

As far back as October 1937, the Congress Party of India passed a resolution opposing the partition of Palestine. The text protested the reign of terror let loose in Palestine to force a partition upon the unwilling Arabs, and expressed the Party's sympathy with the native population in its struggle for national freedom and the fight against imperialism.[38] In September 1938, the Congress Party approved its working committee's resolution, which called upon Britain to "revoke its present policy and leave the Jews and Arabs to settle amicably the issue between them and appeal[ed] to the Jews not to take shelter behind British imperialism."[39]

It was obviously not Arab wealth that led Mahatma Gandhi to condemn, in an editorial in the *Harijan* in 1938, the Zionists who were "cosharers with the British" in "despoiling" the Palestinians, and who attempted to enter Palestine "under the shadow of the British gun," and with "the help of the British Bayonet."[40] When Gandhi condemned the Partition Plan as a "crime against humanity," he was giving expression to his political commitment as an Asian national leader, and to his own moral values as a humanist. "Palestine," he declared, "belongs to the Arabs in the same sense that England belongs to the English, or France to the French. It is wrong and inhuman to impose the Jews on the Arabs. What is going on in Palestine today cannot be justified by any moral code of conduct."[41]

It was not Arab pressure that "forced" Nehru, on March 23, 1947, to refuse to grant permission to representatives of Zionist settlers to speak to his Conference for Asian Relationship. Following one of the sessions, Nehru asserted that India's policy was based on the belief that Palestine was Arab and that it was not possible to make any decisions regarding that part of Asia without the approval of the Arabs.

Most Afro-Asian leaders and their peoples are not easily convinced by Zionist biblical apologetics. For them, Palestine, a country located in Asia and inhabited by an Afro-Asian people, is not an empty *Eretz Yisrael*, available if need be as a refuge for persecuted European Jews. During a visit to the Far East, Israeli writer Amos Kenan discovered "that no intelligent person in that part of the world takes the least interest in the debt the Western world owes to Israel. . . . If you ask them to consider where justice lies in the Israeli-Palestinian conflict, they're not the least bit interested in the persecution of Jews through 1,800 years: it just isn't part of their culture."[42]

Such an attitude does not imply any Afro-Asian indifference to suffering. It is simply a recognition of a basic human principle—that every society should resolve its own human tensions. If the problems of one community can be solved through interaction and cooperation with another, then the community participating in these solutions should not suffer the penalty of losing its distinct character and identity. Nor should any outside decisions affecting the right of self-determination of a society be imposed upon it by the use of force. Failing that, we should discard the moral idiom of rescue, and instead simply adopt the frankly racist idiom of power.

Basically, many Afro-Asian leaders and spokesmen, rightist or leftist, adopt this attitude. If Western Jews suffered at the hands of Western societies, then the societies that inflicted the suffering should compensate for that suffering. Gandhi advanced this argument, as did King Ibn Saud of Saudi Arabia. The latter suggested to President Roosevelt that the oppressed Jews should be given "the choicest lands and homes of the Germans who had oppressed them."[43]

The Jewish question, it is sometimes claimed by Zionists and their Western supporters, is a universal human problem. Even acceptance of this proposition does not necessarily make one view the displacement of the Palestinians as a logical solution. Rather, such a universal problem calls for a solution on a universal human scale and one that does not inflict an injustice on an innocent people. "The responsibility for rehabilitating the victims of Hitler's tyranny devolved upon the entire civilized world," as an Indian memorandum to the United Nations Special Committee on Palestine indicated.[44] In essence, this meant that the Palestinian Arabs alone should not be made to pay for Hitler's crimes. Perhaps the answer lies in a universal liberalization of immigration laws and policies, the memorandum said. It is revealing in this context to note that while some of the Western states sponsoring the Zionist project at the United Nations tightened their immigration policies, making it difficult for Hitler's victims to emigrate to their countries, Afro-Asian anti-Zionists, Nehru among them, urged "the British to facilitate Jewish immigration into India."[45] Earlier, in 1943, Saudi Arabia had adopted a similar line, suggesting "a scheme which would divide the refugees proportionately among the United Nations."[46] None of these suggestions earned the support of the Zionists or Zionist sympathizers because they were all suggestions in direct opposition to the very essence of Zionism—the "ingathering of the exiles."

In 1947, when the United Nations was dominated by Western countries that tried to force the Zionist enclave on the Arabs of Palestine, the few Afro-Asian members put up as much resistance to the scheme as they could. The original 1947 recommendation to create "a Jewish state" in Palestine was approved on the first vote only by the European states, the United States, and Australia. Every Asian and African state (with the exception of South Africa) voted against it.[47]

During the discussion of the Partition Plan in the plenary session, many representatives from Asia expressed vigorous opposition. The chief delegate from the Philippines was particularly eloquent in his speech, for he characterized the Partition Plan as a violation of the fundamental principles of the United Nations Charter and as being "clearly repugnant to the valid nationalist aspirations of the peoples of Palestine." To sanction the partition of Palestine, he said, was to "turn back on the road to the dangerous principles of racial exclusiveness and to the archaic doctrines of theocractic governments."[48] The Pakistani, Indian, and Iranian delegates joined in condemning the proposed plan, and the Chinese delegate found it unsatisfactory.

When the vote was cast in plenary session on November 29, 1947, the Western powers voted their approval. American and Zionist pressure, however, succeeded in prevailing upon the Philippines and Liberia, both of which were especially vulnerable to American pressure, to abandon their declared opposition.[49] Thus, Zionist Israel was imposed on the Arabs and Afro-Asians without their consent mainly because they were powerless to thwart the plan. As the Indian memorandum to the United Nations Special Committee on Palestine had noted earlier, if the Jews really needed a state, why not the state of New York, "which has well over three million Jews already"? But the United States did possess the power to thwart such a plan, had it been proposed, by force of arms if necessary, whereas Palestine could not defend itself against the "forces which the Jews have organized."[50]

Even though the Afro-Asians failed to stop the Western powers from using the United Nations as a tool to force the Zionist state on the native inhabitants of Palestine, they did not abandon all efforts to contain the settler state. For instance, Israel has been refused admission to every interstate conference of Asian, African, Afro-Asian, or Non-Aligned states, and to all conferences held by revolutionary and national liberation movements and organizations. Of particular importance in the Afro-Asian response to Zionism are the resolutions of the First, Second, Third, and Fourth Conferences for the Solidarity of Afro-Asians, held respectively in Egypt in 1958, Ghana in 1960, Tanganyika (now Tanzania) in 1963, and again in Ghana in 1965. The Fourth Conference was attended by delegates from 70 countries.

The conferees attending these meetings agreed that Israel was a base of Western imperialism, serving as a jumping-off point to dominate the emerging Afro-Asian countries. The resolutions of the Third Conference especially stated that Israel was founded to protect the oil interests of the imperialists and to halt Arab socialist and nationalist reconstruction as well. The Second Conference described Israel as an agent of neocolonialism and international corporations. After reviewing Israel's role in Afro-Asian countries, the Third and Fourth Conferences asked all revolutionary forces and parties to fight against Zionist penetration of the African and Asian continents. All conferences condemned the forcible eviction of the Palestinian people in order to make way for the alien state of Israel. The conferees at the Second and Third Conferences condemned Jewish immigration to occupied Palestine, upheld the right of the Palestinian people to return to their land, and praised the heroic determination to achieve this goal.

The resolutions concerning Israel at the First Tricontinental, held in Havana, Cuba, in January 1966 and attended by representatives from 82 countries, were comprehensive. Recalling the resolutions of the Afro-Asian Solidarity Conferences, and taking cognizance of the role that Israel was playing in serving the interests of the imperialists, the First Tri-Continental Conference resolved that world Zionism was an imperialistic movement, expansionist in its goals, racist in its structure, and fascist in its methods; that Israel, the settler state, was a base of imperialism and one of its tools; that the right of the Palestinian people to liberate their homeland was a natural extension of their right to self-defense; that the presence of Israel in occupied Palestine was illegitimate; and that all progressive forces and political parties and committees should sever relations with Israel.

The Conference further denounced United States' backing of Israel, Jewish immigration to Palestine, and the military aid given by Israel to satellite governments in Africa. It also warned against the so-called Israeli technical and financial aid, and considered it a disguised form of imperialism. Finally, the Conference called for support of the Palestinian people in their struggle against Zionism.

Opposition to, and rejection of, Israel increased after the 1967 war.

By 1973, all African states had severed diplomatic relations with the Israeli government, with the exception of Lesotho, Swaziland, and Malawi.

For many years, the West has counseled the Arabs and Afro-Asians to approach the problem of Israel pragmatically. Their reasoning implies that the history of Zionist settlement should be forgotten, Israel should be accepted and should even be regarded a model for all small countries that are seeking ways to develop and achieve progress. This argument and others like it dissociate the Zionist structure from its history and its present orientation, thereby bestowing on it the legitimacy it so sorely needs.

Such logic disregards problems related to the establishment of Israel, its ideology, and its practices. In genesis, Israel originated in Europe and was transplanted into the Middle East, a fact which in itself alienates the Afro-Asian countries. Moreover, Israeli society is probably the most heavily subsidized country on earth. Per capita aid from the outside has reached about $800, which is far above the per capita income in most African and Asian countries. The situation is worsening progressively. An Israeli writer on economic matters indicated recently that in the past "Israel was economically dependent on the United States, today it is subservient." To dramatize this state of affairs, M. Raul Teitelbaum stated that the $500 million cut that former President Ford had planned at the time could mean as many as 80,000 unemployed Israelis," a staggering figure in such a small country.[51]

Western aid continues to flow to a state created by the West and one that has acted ever since its inception as a client that depends for its very survival on that aid. Professor Yeshayahu Leibowitz speaks of "the parasitic nature of the nation in the State of Israel and of its life as a kept woman of vested interests in the world," whether that of American politicians or diaspora Jews.[52] Western financial and technical assistance, it should be noted, has enabled Israel to consolidate her grip on the occupied Arab territories seized in 1967. Significantly, many Afro-Asian countries also receive aid from the superpowers or from richer countries, but none of them rely on that aid as a *sine qua non* for their survival. It is safe to say that the Israeli "model," successful or not, does not deserve to be emulated, since Israeli dependence on astronomical financial input from outside makes such emulation impossible.

Many observers point to the aid Israel gave to some Afro-Asian governments as a basis for cooperation and for acceptance by the Afro-Asians of the Zionist state. Immediate pragmatic considerations naturally determine the course of action of some countries in the short run, but they do not radically change the general orientation. Some African countries cooperate with the apartheid regime of South Africa, and one government has even advocated a "dialogue" with it. Like Israel in the 1960s, South

Africa has of late stepped up its economic aid to a few black regimes, constructing a hotel and low-cost housing projects in a black African country. It is even building the national capital of Malawi, a black African country,[53] and it extended aid to one of the military factions in Angola before independence.

Nevertheless, these pragmatic steps cannot be considered representative of the relation that obtains between the apartheid regime and the African peoples, and could be seen not as a fundamental trait but rather as vestigial remains of a colonial past. Moreover, the amount of Israeli aid is meager, in view of Israel's heavy reliance on Western aid. Israeli "aid," uniformly given to governments, but never to liberation movements, quite often flows into military projects and even into the training of secret police, and in many instances is used to pay high-salaried Israeli experts. If we add to all this the growing economic and military involvement between Israel and South Africa, the image of the little country that is developing itself and even providing aid to underdeveloped countries can be seen for what it is—a public-relations package to expedite Israel's efforts at penetrating the African continent.

It should be clear that the opposition of the Afro-Asian peoples, including the Arabs, to Israel is consistent with the history of these peoples in modern times, which is one of resistance to Western military, economic, and cultural domination. It is this resistance that has weakened the imperialist grip. No settler-colonial enclave that draws its support and strength from outside its borders can survive long enough to crush native resistance. Karl Kautsky predicted as much in 1914 when he wrote that "Jewish colonization in Palestine must collapse as soon as the Anglo-French hegemony over Asia Minor (including Egypt) collapses, and this is merely a question of time."[54]

In a uniquely Hegelian fashion, Herzl's mind was always crammed either with details or with abstract schemes. However, he demonstrated a perceptive understanding of historical processes when he noted in his diary, while in Cairo negotiating for one of his many settlement schemes, "[The Egyptians] are the coming masters here, it is a wonder that the English don't see this. They think they are going to deal with the *fellahin* forever." Then he went on to describe how the very process of colonization creates the germ of its own destruction by "teaching the *fellahin* how to revolt."[55] This is more or less a universal law applicable to Zionist and gentile colonization alike. Since Herzl wondered how the British could not see that, one may wonder why he or the Zionist colonists failed to recognize this fact as applicable to themselves and to their colonial efforts.

It would seem that the Zionist leader never really made up his mind concerning the Western colonial venture and its prospects. As he put it, "The English example in the colonies will *either* destroy England's colonial empire *or* lay the foundation for England's world dominion," a prospect that represented to him "one of the most interesting alternatives of our times.[56]

Herzl must have placed deep faith in the second alternative—a faith that sustained him in his many dark and lonely hours while he was traveling and negotiating, and perhaps even in his last hours on this earth. As he lay on his deathbed, the Zionist leader hallucinated that he was in Palestine buying land from the natives, and was heard to mutter, "We should buy these three acres, take note of that, these three acres."[57]

10

TROUBLE IN THE PROMISED LAND

THE ISRAELI QUESTION

The Zionist State of Israel is the concrete embodiment of the political Zionist vision and the tangible fulfillment of that dream. But the dream, as readers of daily newspapers know, has turned out to be a nightmare for all concerned—for diaspora Jews, for the Arabs, and for the Israelis themselves. For diaspora Jewry, Israel does not serve as their spiritual center, and neither does it provide them with any guarantee against discrimination in their own native lands. As constituted, and as its situation vis-à-vis its neighbors has developed, the Zionist state is a source of embarrassment for those Jews who still identify with the religious and ethical values of Judaism. The image of this little garrison state—equipped with the latest weapons, fighting one war after another, and engaged in quelling demonstrations and uprisings inside its borders and in the lands it has seized from its neighbors—is not exactly appealing or morally uplifting.

This militaristic aspect of the Zionist state is essential for the maintenance not only of the state machinery but also for the promotion of political Zionism as a living ideology. Crisis situations help weld together the multiracial and multicultural polyglot Jewish communities that make up the state (Rabbinical and Karaites, Sephardim and Orientals, Falashas, Bene Israel, Ashkenazim and Occidentals, Orthodox, Conservative, and Reform, with each group speaking one of several tongues: Yiddish, Hebrew, Arabic, English, Ladino, French, German, and a variety of other languages and dialects).

Crises also stimulate the flow of financial donations. An executive vice-chairman of the United Israel Appeal once declared: "When the blood flows, the money flows."[1] In a letter to the Israeli publication *Viewpoint,* Mick Ashley described the British Zionists as Jews who are looking for some kind of moral uplift. They want to "feel good and tall" and a beleaguered Israel, preferably fighting a "heroic" war, answers their emotional needs.[2] Horace M. Kallen is a very good example of such vicarious heroism. In his book *Utopians at Bay,* he praised the Israelis in lyrical, exalted religious terms, extolling their "singularity of spirit" and their very existence, which he compared to a religious ritual.[3] Kallen, however, preferred to experience these heroic feelings from a distance, for he chose *not* to settle in the Middle East and share that sublime religious experience, probably because he was aware that Israel is "a fortress,"[4] and that the "army of Israel is the [whole] people of Israel."[5]

The Israelis themselves have no use for those who wax sentimental about Israel and demonstrate their Zionism merely by paying in dollars or other hard currency while they, the settlers, pay with their blood. In the January 4, 1974, issue of *Maariv* an Israeli citizen expressed his resentment at the fact that he had to shoulder "the burden of Jewish existence and pay for it in sacrifices," whereas the diaspora Zionists played the role of admiring bystanders.[6]

Israeli protest against this kind of Zionism, which keeps the Israelis more or less as hostages, sometimes takes on a more explicit and organized form. Since the creation of the state, there have been various attempts by various groups and personalities to evolve an awareness of new Israeli identity, rejecting the nebulous sentimentalities of Zionism and its hymns to the abstract Jew, and focusing on the realities of the Middle East and the specific Israeli situation. Some of these efforts have been on the intellectual level, while others have been more activist.

An example of repudiation of some of the fundamental premises of political Zionism come from unexpected quarters: Hillel Kook and Shmuel Merlin. These two Israeli businessmen, who were involved in activities leading to the founding of the State of Israel and later became Herut representatives in the Israeli Knesset, circulated privately a report among top government figures. The report, published in the April 29, 1975, issue of the *Jerusalem Post,* is critical of what it calls the dominant "phony post-State Zionist ideology" and suggests that rather than remain an armed Jewish community psychologically and structurally part "of the dispersed world Jewish community," Israel should try to free herself more and more from diaspora Jewish institutions. Emphasis on immigration should be abandoned, the Law of Return should be revised, and the Covenant between the State of Israel and the World Zionist Organization should be annulled.[7]

Another telling example of dissension is the Shinui and Yaad, two small political organizations that operated within the Zionist framework. They, nevertheless, represented an organizational effort at challenging the maximalist Zionist position, proposing instead a minimalist one. Even though these two organizations supported the concept of Jewish peoplehood in a political sense and the need for *aliyah,* their programs diverged from the conventional Zionist approach to the Arabs and the Middle East conflict on many significant points. Some of the figures who joined Yaad were General M. Peled, Shalumit Alloni, a member of the Knesset, and Arie Eliav, former secretary general of the Mapai Party. General Peled is now Chairman of the Israel Council for Israeli-Palestinian Peace, which advocates recognition of the PLO and Arabs, and works for a minimalist Zionist policy.

Some anti-Zionist, non-Zionist fringe groups in Israeli society, experiencing an infinite process of splits and fusions, have of late been gaining more of a hearing both inside and outside Israel. Among these groups are Matzpen, Siah, Rakah, and Uri Avnery's New Force, as well as the Black Panthers. Many such groups disappear, like Yaad and Shinui, only to re-emerge under a new name and a variety of labels. In the 1977 Knesset elections, for instance, Sheli, a *new* Israeli party, was made up of Moked, Arie Eliav's group, a splinter of the Black Panthers, and Uri Avnery's *Haolam Hazeh* movement. Shinui joined with General Yigal Yadin, forming the Democratic Movement for Change.

There are also many public personalities fairly active on behalf of Arab civil and political rights who oppose Zionist theory and practice, such as Israel Shahak, chairman of the Israeli League for Human and Civil Rights; Maxim Ghilan, editor of *Israel and Palestine;* Felicia Langer, Uri Davies, and many others. These groups and personalities are subjected to all kinds of harassment and intimidation on both the official and social levels. The Matzpen and similar groups, given their radical anti-Zionist position, are always a prime target, but even the less militant groups and figures, such as Uri Avnery, have *not* been spared. Uri Avnery survived a bomb explosion in his office in 1952, only to be attacked by a group of Israeli paratroopers in 1953. Two more bombs exploded in May and June 1955 at the office of his periodical, *Haolam Hazeh,* and two years later an editor at the paper was kidnapped. In November 1971, the offices of the magazine was burned down. This was followed, four years later, by a vicious attack during which Avnery suffered "four serious wounds from his assailant's dagger."[8] Such attacks undoubtedly help contain the anti-Zionist forces. However, the presence of these groups, which cover the entire political spectrum from the extreme left to the extreme right, is vital to Israeli Jews seeking a new identity and a new self-definition.

Important as they are on the theoretical level as an alternative, Israeli anti-Zionism and non-Zionism do not carry much political weight. This is understandable in view of the origin and structure of Israeli society. Even though Israel, like other societies, is now relatively independent of the originating ideology, the relationship between the ideology of Zionism and the society of Israel is unique. Practically every society develops its own ideology or ideologies, but Zionism is an ideology that founded a society. Hence, the curious characteristics of Israeli society: the political movement founded the people, not the people the movement; the political parties founded the society and not the society the parties; the Histadrut (the trade union) founded the Israeli working class, not the working class the trade union; and so on. It is like Hegelian dialectics—standing on its head in happy oblivion of the concrete order of reality.

The "Zionism" of the state was not diminished after the latter's establishment, for the state has defined itself along Zionist lines. The Law of Return and the Status Law are Zionist laws unique to the Zionist state. As many Zionist and Israeli-Zionist spokesmen have asserted, these two laws form the very basis of Israeli society.

The citizen in Israel lives in a society that surrounds him with a thick web of symbols and myths, derived by Zionist theoreticians from the Jewish heritage but given nonreligious, "national" content. His flag is white and blue, the colors of the *tallit,* the prayer shawl of the Jews. In the middle is th Star of David, a cabalistic symbol. His national anthem tells of a quasi-messianic "return" to his homeland. Even "Israel," the name of the state, and *Eretz Yisrael,* meaning "the land," are at once religious and national-istic terms. The Knesset and the names of towns and ports have all been changed to conform to the atmosphere of a museum. In his perception of the world and in his view of reality, the Israeli citizen does not have a clear picture of Palestine, the Palestinians, or the Middle East. He uses irrele-vant terms like Samaria and Judea and views the Middle East in terms of absolute biblical rights that cannot be contravened or questioned and which preclude any basis for a dialogue. The Israeli writer Ehud Ben Ezer no-ticed an Israeli tendency (in religious circles and elsewhere) "to identify the Arabs with the Amalek of the Bible." Zionist settlement in Palestine was compared to Joshua's conquest of the land of Canaan, and the Arab inhabitants of the occupied territories sometimes are compared to the "Seven Nations of the Torah commanded to be destroyed."[9]

The political Zionist philosophy, encapsulating the Israelis emotion-ally and mentally, and keeping them insulated from time and historical processes, has a firm economic and political infrastructure. The Histadrut, for instance, is an institution that is unique to the Zionist settler-colonial experiment. Even its name in Hebrew—"General Federation of Jewish Workers in the Land of Israel"—suggests a deep organic link between Zionism and the Histadrut. In describing this institution, Ben Gurion said that it was not merely a trade union, a political party, or even a cooperative; it was, he said, the union of a new people building a new country, a new state, new settlements, and a new culture. Another Zionist spokesman described the main task of Histadrut as the realization of Zionism: immi-gration and settlement.[10]

This trade union, established in 1920 to create a Jewish working class, was charged with implementing the central Zionist and racist concept of pure Hebrew labor. It launched campaigns against Arab labor and Arab produce, and at times used its own funds to pay Jewish capitalists the difference between the more expensive Hebrew labor and the cheaper Arab labor, thus enabling Jewish employers to remain within the pure national fold.[11] Since it was in charge of settlement, it supervised the Haganah, the military arm of the Jewish Agency and the Zionist settlers, and it also served as the main channel through which subsidies and aid were funneled to the Zionist enclave and later to the state.

The Histadrut became the most important single institution, second only to the army when the latter achieved an autonomous status independent of the Histadrut in 1948. It is now a trade union that comprises the vast majority of the Israeli labor force—white collar, blue collar, plant managers, and government employees. One estimate puts the membership at 1.1 million in a total population of nearly 3 million. Strange as this may sound, it owns a large sector of the Israeli economy consisting of a giant industry, banks, shipping, airline companies, and the largest construction firm in Israel. The Histadrut is probably the only "trade union" that has a "department for trade unions" because of its mixed proletarian-capitalist nature as well as its settler-colonial activities.

When Israeli workers organize a strike, they do so against their "union," which often happens to be the sole or partial owner of the plant the workers are striking against. Considering the fact that strike funds are also controlled by the Histadrut, the anomaly of the situation becomes evident. Workers may thus stage a strike against a capitalist enterprise that also runs the trade union and controls the livelihood of the workers, including their very strike funds. A worker who leaves the Histadrut would be faced with indomitable odds, for he would be unable to find employment elsewhere. But looking for a job would not be his only problem, for his exorbitant medical bills would prove to be a crushing burden, since the Histadrut has the most comprehensive health-insurance program in Israel. The Zionist orientation of the Histadrut and its stranglehold on the life of the individual discourage any tendencies toward dissidence on the part of the average Israeli citizen.

Another factor that helps strengthen Zionist domination over Israeli society is its control over the political parties. These parties are subsidized by the World Zionist Organization and by naive contributors abroad who think they are donating money to the needy in Israel. One estimate puts the amount of Zionist funds poured annually into the coffers of Israeli political parties at $3.5 million.[12] Considering the difference in population between Israel and the United States, this would be the equivalent of about $250 million pumped into the American party system. If we allow for the difference in the per capita income between the United States and Israel, the figure would probably be double or triple that amount. It is one of the many anomalies of Israeli political life that most Israeli political parties have "branches" in the diaspora. Shimon Peres, for instance, has made references to the Labor Party as "a Jewish-Zionist world party."[13] The branches in the diaspora function primarily as the monetary arm of the mother colonial party, or as its fund-raising agent.

Some parties take Israeli election campaigns into the United States. The April 3, 1977, issue of *The New York Times* reports that some Israeli politicians, even without registering as foreign agents, engage in fund-raising activities. It is believed that representatives of the new Democratic Movement for Change, headed by Yigal Yadin, gathered about $50,000, and Major General Ariel Sharon, revealed that "a few thousand dollars had been sent to him from the United States" following his two trips there.

By refusing the Zionist premises, the anti-Zionist or non-Zionist parties lose the subsidies and funds necessary for participation in one of the most expensively run elections in the world. These anti-Zionist or non-Zionist parties, because they reject the Zionist concept of Jewish peoplehood and accept that of Israeli peoplehood, cannot address themselves to the diaspora. What exacerbates the situation is that political parties in Israel are not parties in the general sense of the term. They have their own clubs, hospitals, banks, movie theaters, travel agencies, immigrant-recruiting agencies, housing projects, employment agencies, and at times schools.

Most of these projects are subsidized by donations or loans from the Jewish Agency or through direct fund-raising drives abroad. The National Religious Party, for instance, was granted about $1 million by the Jewish Agency in the year 1971–1972. The Zionist parties have a virtual stranglehold on the lives of their members, a grip that can be maintained only through Zionist aid. Amos Elon has painted a picture of Israel as a state made up of more or less separate enclaves, or what he calls "semi-autonomous feudal principalities." Certain rural sections are in fact "one-party enclaves," where most of the "*kibbutzim* and adjacent cooperative settlements are tied to the same party."[14]

Because of the limited funds at their disposal, anti-Zionist and non-Zionist parties cannot run so many extrapolitical projects, making them much less attractive to join and reducing them to a frustrating marginality. *Haolam Hazeh* of May 29, 1974, offered an insight into how the peculiar Zionist structure of the Israeli party system forces a Zionist position on many politicians. For some time, Moshe Kol, the minister of tourism and chairman of the Independent Liberal Party, was known for his dovish attitude. Eventually he was forced to mend his ways. He became more given to making annexationist statements. "Let it be known to all and to our neighbours in the East," he declared, "that we are setting up and militarizing settlements not to dismantle them." *Haolam Hazeh* of May 29, 1974, quoted him as saying, "I am not prepared to move an existing settlement even in exchange for a peace settlement." When the correspondent of *Maariv* asked him about his new hawkish stand, Moshe Kol was constrained to say, "I was never a dove, I am a hawk."[15] The economics of this hawkish stance is rather complex and worth looking into. The cooperative village movement of the Independent Liberals would set up new settlements in occupied territories and then recruit youngsters who want to escape the status of hired labor. The Party then would see to it that the Labor Ministry and the Tourism Ministry invested millions into the new settlements, thereby turning them into profitable enterprises.[16] The settlements then would begin to grow and so would the party. Such a complex process is feasible only if the party is willing to adjust to Zionist annexationist policies.

A glance at the economics of Gush Emunim, the religious annexationist political group, further confirms the above. According to *Maariv* of December 16, 1975, this extreme rightist group has several million Israeli liras in its treasury. The paper identifies the following sources of income for the movement (1 and 2 in Israel, the rest in the diaspora):

1. Wealthy Israeli businessmen.
2. Some Israeli political parties.
3. Members of the Conference of Presidents of Major Jewish Organizations in the United States.
4. United Jewish Appeal.
5. Israel Bonds.
6. Rabbi Fabian Schonfeld, leader of a wealthy congregation in Queens, New York, and President of the Rabbinical Council of America.
7. David Yizelson, head of an international shipping company. (He was the first to give aid to the annexationist group, and he also contributed to the establishment of their first settlement.)
8. Leading Jewish figures and wealthy businessmen in France, England, Switzerland, Canada, and of course South Africa.[17]

The global dimensions of this aid given to a small extremist group inside Israel are indicative of the nature and amount of aid extended to other more influential groups and parties.

The situation of Israel, the Zionist state, and of the Israelis, the new demographic element introduced into the region, is in a sense anomalous and unparalleled. The Israelis live in the Arab Middle East, sustained by an ideology that originated in the Eastern-European ghetto, subsidized and supported by Western aid flowing from both the Western powers and the diaspora. Uri Avnery once wrote that after an air raid on Cairo or Damascus, Israeli pilots would have nightmares, not of Arab children dying, but rather of the sufferings of Jewish children in Eastern-European ghettos during a pogrom. The pilots are usually Western trained and the planes are American-made Phantoms received as gifts from the United States Government. This graphic image sums up more than anything else the anomaly that is Israel.

Perhaps one should, in the context of a political analysis, try to decode the image in more analytical terms. One may advance the argument that Zionism is an ideological superstructure with *three* infrastructures. The *first* infrastructure is the Eastern-European, semiautonomous Jewish enclaves (the ghetto, the *shtetl,* the Pale of Settlement) that produced the Jewish question as well as the general outline of the proposed program for its solution. The large human groups living in these enclaves spoke Yiddish, not Polish or Russian, and they had a degree of cultural autonomy, definite occupational traits, and even a semiautonomous territory. Consequently, some groups among them were open to the idea of a separate Jewish national existence. The ideological atmosphere, created by the pan-Slavic and pan-Germanic movements and by the efforts (in Russia) of the Czarist government to "productivize the Jews" and settle them in arable land in order to turn them into agricultural workers, gave rise to various Zionist slogans, and also gave impetus to the territorialist solution and a population transfer. The Zionist idea was rooted in this limited historical experience, yet it was generalized into *the* solution for the Jewish question, posited as timeless.

Even though the Eastern-European ghetto produced the problem and the proposed solution, it did not have the power or the means to implement it. A population transfer from Eastern Europe and elsewhere into Africa and Asia needed the support and sponsorship of a global power, a European state with a colonial interest in the Orient.

Diaspora Jewry, prestigious and rich, together with the sponsoring colonial power, form the *second* infrastructure. American Jewry plays a very active role in the upbuilding of Israel because the United States Jewish community is an integral part of a superpower that has interests in the Middle East and which condones, even encourages, the flow of Zionist funds to the Zionist state. Tax-exemption privileges, which can be withdrawn at any time, also help. The *third* infrastructure, an outgrowth of the first two, is the Zionist enclave itself, a politically autonomous client state largely dependent on a world power.

One result of this multiplicity of infrastructures is a complexity beyond human control, for each element in the infrastructure is capable of only partially controlling the whole. The diaspora Zionists can control the flow of funds only, the settler-colonial Zionists can decide whether to go to war or not, and the Western sponsoring power can extend or withhold its support according to its own global interests. But none of them can fully control the dynamism and actions of the structure; though in the last analysis, the sponsoring power has more control than the diaspora and the settlers combined.

What has complicated matters further is that Zionist colonial activities were started at a time when Arab nationalism was groping for a sense of direction, thereby creating an illusion of a historical vacuum that corresponded more or less to the Zionist myth. Given the relative weakness of the native nationalist forces, the Zionists gave full rein to their myth-making and took full advantage of the colonial situation. They were able to achieve the colonial Zionist population transfer of Jews and Arabs, only to be faced with growing resistance that has of late assumed proportions never anticipated by the Zionist leadership or the theoreticians.

Evaluating the implications of this complex, abstract structure for the Israelis themselves, one perceives that they exist in a settler-colonial state always faced with the hostility of their neighbors and the natives, who still refuse to accept as final the encroachment on their national and human rights.

Many Israelis, rich or poor, proletarian or capitalist, are the beneficiaries of the Zionist *status quo,* which, after having seized the land for them, guarantees them a high standard of living through aid from diaspora Jewry and Western powers—massive aid that is to continue only if the state is Zionist, serving as a vanguard for the Jewish people and as a base for the West. The aid that supports the Israelis and improves their standard of living isolates them at the same time from their surroundings, subverts their independence, and threatens their very survival.

The Israelis, a population composed of Jews transferred from Europe and the Orient, form a demographic element that replaces the Palestinians. They now find themselves in a situation that is not of their own making, where they are not masters of their own destiny. Those who have a sense of their specific identity as members of a Middle Eastern society, and those who feel dissatisfied with Zionist policies and outlook on history, are entrapped by the Zionist intellectual, economic, and political structure of the state. What has exacerbated the situation even further is the fact that the Palestinian Arabs, just like the Algerian Arabs or Angolans, waged their struggle in generalist, liberationist terms, which did not reckon with the specificity of the Israelis' situation and which offered the Israelis little or no choice between their Zionist state of siege and something more normal. An Israeli writer succinctly summed up the situation in the following words: "I feel myself today to be *a Zionist for lack of an alternative.*"[18] This is the essence of the Israeli question.

A COMPLEX OF LEGITIMACY

Some Israelis evince a remarkable awareness of their complex and untenable situation. The Israeli historian Jacob Talmon quoted Hegel's famous aphorism about the "impotence of victory"[19] as an appropriate description of the Israeli dilemma. He drew a highly unattractive picture of Israel's future if the present *status quo* should continue. More victory, he predicted, would only turn the whole country into a "standing army," for after every victory, as Talmon argues, the Israelis would face still more complicated problems.

Nothing sums up the history of the Zionist settlement better than Hegel's aphorism. The Zionist state is based on a victory, a transfer of the Palestinian population, which cost the victors their peace of mind and incurred the hostility not only of the direct victims but also of the entire Arab people. The second "victory" of 1956 deeply involved the Egyptians, the largest sector of the Arab nations, in the anti-Zionist struggle. Moreover, by collaborating in that war with the two dying colonial powers, the little state discredited herself and her claim to be one of the newly independent nations of the Third World. From that point on, the Afro-Asian states began to suspect the true identity of the Zionist enclave. The "victory" of 1967, the largest of them all, left the Israelis with the Arab demographic problem which they thought they had solved in 1948. It forced them to abandon the subtler Zionist form of colonization and to adopt the more open apartheid form, turning Israeli society into an openly oppressive one and finally landing the Israelis behind the Bar Lev line, where they were to be trapped for six whole years. How did they get themselves into that fix and how were they ever to squeeze out of it? It was, finally, the Egyptian troops that were destined in October 1973 to get the Israelis at least partly out of the fortified ghetto that was of their own making.

There seems to be an inverse ratio between the form of colonialism and the number of options for a peaceful settlement: the more thorough the colonialism, the fewer the options. The same law applies *within* each structure: the more the victories, the fewer the options. A series of wars, begun to root out once and for all the Palestinian "infiltrators," ended up with the victor facing civil disobedience in the West Bank, demonstrations inside Israel, a relatively well-organized, and definitely long-lived Palestinian resistance movement, as well as three Arab states in direct confrontation. The victor is also faced with the hostility of the Arab people, who are supported by the overwhelming majority of the peoples of Asia and Africa. Significantly, the only military confrontation that moved the region toward peace more than any other was the 1973 war, where Israel did not score a complete victory!

Trapped in this spiraling vertigo, the Israelis have developed their specific version of fatalism. The Israeli poet Chaim Guri bitterly observed a few years ago that "this soil [of Israel] is insatiable," ever crying for more graves and more coffins, as if *Eretz Yisrael* were not a piece of land, a territory, but rather an obscene goddess of vengeance.[20] The Israeli writer, Ehud Ben Ezer, observed that young Israelis, serving in the army, "speak of a feeling of a secular 'Sacrifice of Isaac'—they are being sacrificed by their parents and the State without any compensation or consolation of the religious faith in an afterlife."[21] Another Israeli public figure, a paratrooper dropped into Nazi-occupied Europe in 1944, rhetorically asked, "How many wars will our boys fight before they will become animals?"[22] To him, the brutalization of the Israelis and their loss of soul seemed inevitable.

The Zionist-Israeli leadership encapsulated in the *status quo* does not see any end in sight; simply more fighting *ad nauseam,* with funds always flowing, maintaining the Zionist stranglehold on the state and making sure that it remains a ghetto and a fortress. Nothing is more pathetic, more fatalistic, than the words of Moshe Dayan at the burial ceremony of his friend Roy Rutberg, killed by Palestinian guerrillas. Israel's former defense minister and present foreign minister had this to say: "We are a settler generation and without the steel helmet and the cannon we cannot plant a tree or build a house. Let us not flinch from the hatred inflaming hundreds of thousands of Arabs around us. Let us not turn our heads away lest our hands tremble. It is our generation's destiny, our life's alternative, to be prepared and armed, strong and harsh, lest the sword drop from our fist and life cease."[23]

General Andre Beaufre, the commander of the French troops invading Egypt in 1956, visited Egypt frequently in later years as a guest of the Center for Political and Strategic Studies at *Al Ahram,* where he exchanged views with the members of the Center. One day he recounted an episode that left his listeners bewildered. In June 1967, soon after Israel's "victory," he had called on General Rabin, the hero of that war, to congratulate him on his military feat. But Rabin's cryptic remark was, "But what will remain of it all?" Rabin, of course, was right. The lightning victory brought no peace.

Modern Israeli literature is burdened with the sense of the futility of the Israeli situation. Dr. Ibrahim Al-Bahrawi's study of modern Israeli literature,[24] published in Cairo in Arabic, includes a number of representative texts that revolve around the theme of futility. In one poem, by Itzak Shalef, the narrator implores God to grant peace to the souls who live on tranquilizers and sleeping pills. The God of the poem is described as the God of a people whose bodies are enclosed in casts, who breathe through masks, and who are having blood transfusions in a hospital bed. In another poem by Yacov Bassar, the next war is being bred in bedrooms and nurseries, just as if it, too, must be nurtured like a member of the family.

In a short story entitled "Swan Song" by Ran Adlisset, the following conversation takes place between two Israeli soldiers in a trench:

> —Is a bomb about to fall? I heard that the alternate position
> represents real suicide.
> —What then? Are we to remain in this state forever?
> —Are you out of your mind?
> —Shall we withdraw?
> —Are you out of your mind?
> —A new war then?
> —Is the situation that desperate then?
> —Do you know what you want?
> —No, . . . do you?
> —No.
> —Alas . . . let us shift to the alternate position.
> B O O M !!!

A recurrent theme in the texts in this anthology is the Israelis' reluctance to have children, for to give birth in a meaningless world would be tantamount to inflicting an act of injustice on one's own progeny.

This nihilism at times takes a tragi-comic form. Israeli students at times would tell each other "see you in the obituaries" or they would talk of the bargain prices of cemetery plots, "get them while they last," and they would sarcastically inquire whether a new apartment has a "memorial room."[25] During the recession of 1966, with the departing settlers outnumbering the new immigrants, the Israelis often told each other a joke about a sign at Lod Airport which read, "Will the last one out of the country please switch off the lights?"[26]

Another comic comment on the Zionist anomaly is the short poem scribbled by a frustrated Israeli on the wall of the men's room at the Hebrew University:

> Sephardim to Spain,
> Ashkenazim to Europe,
> Arabs to the desert,
> Let's return the country to God,
> He's given us enough trouble by promising it to everyone.[27]

Even the sense of siege, an obsession with the claustrophobic Israelis, is sometimes expressed in humorous terms. At one point, young Israelis used to sing blithely a popular song titled "The Whole World Is Against Us."[28] At the time when hijackings and Palestinian attacks on settlements were common, following the 1967 victory, a writer in *Maariv* sarcastically suggested that each Israeli citizen was in need of a private Bar Lev line to guarantee his own security.   An Israeli poet once noticed sarcastically, and perhaps bitterly, that every people has an air force, whereas in Israel there is an air force that has a people.

The knowledge of the existence of the Arabs and of the claims they put forth is another factor that sometimes shatters the Israelis' peace of mind. The most dedicated Zionist cannot gloss over this issue.   The Israeli Declaration of Independence was by definition the Israeli Expropriation of the Land and the Depopulation of Its Inhabitants.   Perhaps when dutifully recited in London or the Bronx, Zionist apologetics can through sheer sophistry ease some people's conscience.   However, the Israelis who live in the middle of it all, sometimes rubbing shoulders with the oppressed, cannot eschew the questions with similar glibness.   How can they, when even their own children ask about the Arabs?   Amos Elon pointed out that it is impossible for Israeli parents "to offer answers that echo the simple and well-rounded arguments and symmetrical half-truths of the older generation."[29]   The sense of guilt is strong, and there are daily reminders that the victims are not about to go away.   Professor Akiva Ernst Simon, member of Brit Shalom and Ihud and presently an active member of the Peace and Security Movement, went so far as to assert that "the Arab problem can be considered essentially a part of the Jewish problem, just as the Jewish problem was basically a problem of Christianity."[30]

One Israeli soldier, rather than conjure up the Nazi Holocaust in an abstract fashion by using it as a pretext to abrogate the rights of others, turned his experience of tragedy and his memories of suffering into deeper understanding of his situation in Israel/Palestine.   He explained sorrowfully that his only "clear association with the . . . Holocaust . . . was in a certain moment, when he was going up the Jericho-Jerusalem road and the refugees were streaming down (toward the River Jordan)."   He saw himself, the once-persecuted Jewish child, reflected in the expelled Palestinians carrying their children.[31]   Israel Shahak, the prophetic voice always resounding in Israel, also refuses to trade on his suffering under the Nazis. He believes that the crime of the Zionists against the Palestinians is a pressing moral issue.[32]

The sense of guilt about the Arabs, or what Elon calls a "gnawing complex of legitimacy,"[33] is as pervasive as the sense of entrapment in a hopeless situation.   The young Israeli poet, Eli Allon, felt that the "historic resurrection" of the Jewish people, and anything they establish, no matter how beautiful "will be based on injustice to another nation."   Israeli youngsters will go out to fight and die "for something that is based on an act of injustice—this doubt, just this doubt alone, is a difficult basis for living."[34] "Facing the Forest," a short story by the Israeli writer Abraham B. Yehoshuah, is characterized by some critics as both subversive and suicidal.   In a story about a student writing about the Crusades, another fruitless and impotent historical "experiment" haunting the Israeli mind, the hero is reluctantly hired by an official of the Jewish National Fund as a watchman for a forest planted on the site of a destroyed Arab village. The trees carry plaques with the names of diaspora contributors and enthusiasts, such as Louis Schwartz of Chicago. Although the hero is seeking solitude, he encounters an old, mute Arab villager who has been employed as a caretaker. A strange love-hate relationship grows between the Arab and the Israeli, who fears the revenge of the Arab, yet is mysteriously attracted to him. At first the Jewish National Fund watchman finds himself trying to help the Arab set the forest on fire, but fails. Finally, when the Arab succeeds in setting the whole forest afire, the pent-up feelings of the hero are released.[35]

Amos Oz' *Maechel Mine* illustrates a complex of feelings similar to those underlying Yehoshuah's story. Hannah, a native Israeli-born girl in the old city of Jerusalem, is married to a good-natured geologist from a "new" city founded in the mid-1930s. Living in her Jewish European surroundings, her imagination is haunted by her childhood friends, Halil and Azis (probably Khalil and Aziz), who are now Palestinian guerrillas. But her fantasies take on the form of simultaneous fear and the expectation of rape. Toward the end of the book, the two Arabs stage a successful guerrilla attack, which "coincides with and heralds Hannah's reconciliation with herself," a reconciliation described in both apocalyptic and orgasmic terms, for Hannah achieves peace of mind through "a cathartic fantasy of destruction."[36]

Days of Ziklag, S. Yizhar's novel, deals with dreams and visions that have turned into a nightmare. The hero, in the heat of battle, asks himself what he should do when the Arabs come. Should he raise a white flag and scream "Tolstoy, Tolstoy, Gandhi, Gandhi," or should he simply shoot? One thing the hero is sure of, though; he knows very little about what is right and what is wrong.[37] The facile Zionist myth of rights does not correspond to reality, and the Israeli hero is not a simple dupe.

The sense of having committed a sin that should be somehow rectified is pervasive in Yizhar's work. "The Captive," another story by the same author, was published a year after the proclamation of the state. It tells of a "captive" country, taken and imprisoned by the Jewish settlers.[38] The same theme, of a psyche burdened by sin, is central to Yizhar's *Tale of Khirbat Khisa.* The grand Zionist achievement of a modern state is seen as based on an act of rape and robbery. "We house and absorb. We'll open a co-op grocery, a school, perhaps a synagogue. There'll be political parties. They'll discuss lots of things. The fields will be plowed and sown and reaped, and great feats will be accomplished." But unlike our well-intentioned innocent diaspora Zionists, the hero can see through it all to reach to the very foundation of the edifice, and he can therefore sense how weak the structure is. Since the settlers came, shot, burned, blew up, repelled, pushed, and exiled, he knows that the wall will "scream in the ears" of the new dwellers of this Hebrew village.[39]

Guilt feelings and frustrations have led to nihilism and to further militarization. An imaginative moralist such as Ruppin was driven into a state of amoral fatalism. In the face of the violence surrounding him in Palestine, he wrote in his diary, "It seems to me that the whole world is mentally sick, much more so, we Jews. People who have spent their youth in the war and its aftermath must be handled like the insane."[40] Lost in rhetorical abstractions, Ruppin's grip on reality weakened and he found himself in a situation where Jews shoot Arabs or clash with them for no clear reason. It is not surprising to find him turning to the other extreme, advocating the very madness he condemns: "We are doomed to live in a state of permanent belligerency with the Arabs and there is no way to avoid bloody sacrifices,"[41] he wrote. This fatalism reaches a peak in the Massada myth, with the Jews dying heroically on the altar of the state.

Aside from capitulation, there is no way out but eternal and relentless conflict. Survival, cast in political Zionist terms, is predicated on the existence of a purely Jewish state that excludes the Arabs. To preserve that purity, the state must rely on arms and Western support. But having reached that point, there remains only Palestinian and pan-Arab resistance, and the endless cycle of violence.

THE ROAD AWAY FROM MESSADA

After this study and analysis of the Arab-Israeli problem, it is only natural that I should have reached conclusions on which to base a tentative solution of it. (I have tried to define what I consider to be the possible and feasible solutions that satisfy the minimum requirements for cultural survival and autonomy, and for individual human rights.) The reader should realize that what follows here does not have any official sanction, nor does it express recommendations other than my own.

The solution commonly proposed for the Arab-Israeli conflict is usually the pat formula of negotiations and "recognition of Israel." Several solutions for the Palestinian question have been aired and discussed, the most "moderate" among them nowadays being a state comprising the West Bank and the Gaza Strip. It is generally assumed that compromise on the part of the Arabs and the Israelis can turn such a proposal into reality.

It needs to be made clear, however, that the problem between Israel and its Arab neighbors is *not* exclusively territorial, for the territorial aspect is largely a by-product of the conflict. Nor can we consider the Palestinian refugee problem, despite its importance and tragic dimensions, as central. The fundamental cause of the conflict, from the Arab standpoint, was and remains the introduction into the area of a new demographic element that displaced the Palestinian Arab people and that views itself as an autonomous and separate entity, tied to a unitary "Jewish destiny" and a largely Western history, rather than to the historical and political dynamics of the region.

The fact that the Zionist state of Israel is located in the Middle East, yet views itself in an exclusively Jewish context, creates a series of problems and raises a number of questions regarding its relations with the diaspora, with the Arab states and the displaced Palestinians, and finally with its Arab minority.

If Israel is a Jewish state, then the burning issue of apartheid in South Africa, for instance, would no doubt present that state with a great dilemma. It could either remain silent and antagonize all the enemies of apartheid in Africa and elsewhere, or voice opposition and jeopardize the interests of South African Jewry, as Shlomo Aveniri indicated.[42] Israel's relationship with the remaining Jewish communities in the Arab world is another controversial subject, for Jews outside Israel's borders can only be full-fledged citizens of the countries in which they reside, owing no allegiance to any other state. Then, there is also the question of the foreign policy of the Zionist state: Will it forge its international alliances in a way that will accommodate the interests of all Jews the world over, or will it simply act in the best interest of its own nationals?

The relation between the Zionist state and the diaspora creates another problem of a different nature. Some Zionist spokesmen, in order to make Zionism more palatable and acceptable, present the Zionist state as the only permanent haven for all persecuted Jews in the diaspora—whether in the Soviet Union or even the United States, in case of a future American pogrom or a hypothetical holocaust. Such an outlook, however, despite its apparent humaneness, means in essence that Palestine would remain an "open option" for world Jewry. Once more, the colonial formula for solving the racial, demographic, and economic problems of the West would be activated. Once more, Palestine and the Palestinians would find themselves entangled with a timeless Jewish question not of their making, with a unitary Jewish destiny they do not share in, and with the problems of a Western society they do not belong to. Such an ostensibly humane Zionism would simply cause the Palestinians to intensify their struggle.

To turn now to the relation between the displaced Palestinians and the Arab states, on the one hand, and the Zionist state on the other, questions come to mind regarding the immigration laws and borders of this state. Can this Zionist state, no matter how peaceful, modify its immigration laws to accommodate displaced Palestinian Arabs who wish to return to their towns and villages inside pre-1967 Israel, or will its immigration laws be predicated on the Jewish-people concept and geared to its perpetuation and fulfillment?

As for the quest for an Arab recognition of the Zionist state, it will undoubtedly raise the following question: Which Israel? Is it the Israel of 1948, 1956, 1967, or 1973? Is it the Israel of Begin, Ben Gurion, or Buber? Is it a "Greater Israel," ever expanding within its elastic "historical" boundaries? Or is it the Israel of the Partition Plan? Above all, is it a state like any other, constituted for its present citizenry, or is it a state for the "Jewish people," that is, for all the Jews of the world wherever they may reside?

The "Arab left" also argues that a Jewish state provides a "successful" model for those forces of reaction within the Arab world which try to program the future in terms of a glorious past or a religious ideal. Rather than embark on a program of modernization and redefinition of identity, they try to "revive" the past and duplicate it, with the Zionist model as living evidence of the validity of the formula.

Moreover, to bestow legitimacy on itself, the Jewish state would like to see the Arab world divided into a number of small states founded on an ethnic or religious basis. In a unified Arab world, Israel is an anomaly; in a fragmented Arab world, Israel would fit perfectly into a mosaic of ethnic and religious states. Arab fears seem to be substantiated by the actions of the Zionist state and by the statements of many Israeli spokesmen and intellectuals. Yonatan Ratosh, the Israeli "Canaanite" poet, viewing what he calls the "Euphrates country," sees Sunni Muslims, Israeli Jews, Maronites, Druzes, Nuseiris, and only a "scattered minority of Arab Bedouins."[43] Boaz Evron, the Israeli critic and writer, suggested that it is "precisely against Arab nationalism that we have to wage our war."[44] Professor Eri Jabotinsky, son of the Revisionist leader, called for "forging an alliance with other minority groups in the region" against Arab nationalism.[45] But, regardless of Zionist intentions, the Arab left argues that the Jewish state, by the very force of its present orientation and structure, is the potential and actual ally of the forces of reaction and disunity in the Arab world.

One can also argue that the Zionist premise of a unitary and unique "Jewish destiny," which is a rallying cry for the Zionists, forms the basis for colonial-Zionist collaboration, since the Jewish settlers, by segregating themselves and alienating the native inhabitants, have reduced themselves to the necessity of having to rely on a superpower to protect them. The presumed "Jewish" separateness of the state, undoubtedly accentuated by its Ashkenazi sense of superiority vis-à-vis anything that is Arab, is therefore the basis of its policy of colonialism and expansionism that brings it in conflict with its neighbors.

As for the Palestinian Arabs within its boundaries, Israel's situation is not any simpler. The Arab citizens of Israel are barred from the armed services and from some key positions. But if this disability can be remedied others like it have a more structural and permanent nature. The Jewish National Fund's Constitution, for instance, bars Israeli Arabs from tilling or leasing the land, and Israel's *kibbutzim* are closed to non-Jews. Can the Zionist state afford to change this situation? And can the Zionist state guarantee democratic freedom for all its citizens so that the Arabs, if they wish to do so, may enter into political coalitions with Jewish anti-Zionist forces inside Israel? One wonders also what Israel's attitude would be with regard to its "demographic problem" if the Arabs living within its borders attain a numerical majority. In such a situation, will the state, in the name of its *ethnic* Jewishness, expel the Arab surplus and intensify its efforts to replace them with Jewish immigrants? Or will it, in the name of its *ethical* Jewishness, just dissolve itself? In short, how can the Zionist state handle its congenital, chronic, and worsening Arab question?

The Zionist answers to these questions have so far been framed as a perpetuation of the *status quo*—encapsulation in Zionist myths, military confrontation, and increasing reliance on the West. That, in turn, invites growing resistance and deeper rejection on the part of the Arabs.

The Arab attitude to the Zionist settlement is not in any way idiosyncratic. Other enclaves much more impressive and far less dependent on the West than Israel are still the object of the Africans' hostility and rejection. The objection is not to the whites as whites nor to the Jews as Jews. Africa can take in and benefit from more whites, and the Arab world can benefit from Western expertise—regardless of the race, color, or religion of its dispensers. The objection is to an alien political structure that thwarts the political and economic development of the region, that represents and serves external interests, and, by the very force of its structure, displaces and discriminates against the natives.

Zionism, like apartheid, is not an internal Jewish or Israeli issue, it is an ideology that is implemented on the land of the Palestinians in the Arab world and that touches on the destiny of the Arabs. Therefore, in an attempt to formulate a solution, what is needed is not a blueprint for a series of compromises and concessions that keep on changing as the balance of power changes, but a fresh start that goes beyond the *status quo* and the present terms of the debate, and that addresses itself to the very issue of Zionism and the Zionist nature of the state.

Probably the first step toward a solution would be to cast off the hopelessly irrelevant and misleading rhetoric of a timeless and universal Jewish question. If there is a Jewish question in the United States or Peru, and if the Jews of the diaspora suffer from any disability, they must make common cause with other victims of oppression and with the more progressive forces in their society. Their struggle for their rights is properly and more fruitfully conducted in their homelands. Israel/Palestine cannot forever remain a unique and open option. Mahatma Gandhi once asked, "Why should they [Zionist Jews] not, like other peoples of the earth, make that country their home where they are born and where they earn their livelihood?"[46] A Jew, when identified primarily with a universal pan-Jewish history, is also a universal Jew. In that sense he is an eternal alien, whatever his homeland, who can claim no political or civil rights anywhere, and who, when he settles in any land, finds himself rejected because he himself claims that he does not belong.

The assertion of a uniform national identity of the Jews and of unified "Jewish destiny" plays into the hands of the anti-Semites and undermines any intelligent and credible policy for emancipation. The Jewish struggle for freedom in the Soviet Union or in the United States could have taken a radically different and more progressive course if it had been dissociated from the theme of a common national Jewish destiny. As a matter of fact, that theme, and the strategy based on it, encourages the Jews to take the path of least resistance by packing and leaving for Israel.

Paradoxically, the notion of a common destiny implies the need to sacrifice one Jewish community for the sake of another, given the national and/or ideological diversity of world Jewry. American Jewry, whose destiny is that of all Americans, cannot have a common destiny with Soviet Jewry. To say otherwise is to imply that one of the two communities has to become a subservient partner in a spurious unity.

One may argue that there are, at times, even conflicting Jewish destinies, so to speak. The case of Arab Jewry and the Zionist settlers is a good case in point. The "ingathering" of the one necessitated the dispersion of the other. Another case is the destiny of German Jewry. As the latter were being decimated in the 1930s and the 1940s, American Jewry was prospering, or at least did not suffer the same destiny. The Zionist settlement in Israel/Palestine has even profited in monetary as well as in demographic terms from the demise of their German brothers. The Haavra Agreement, which the Nazis were eager to sign with the Zionists so as to break the backbone of the Jewish boycott of their goods, provided for the transfer of Jewish German emigrants and German goods to Palestine. It was during this period that the Zionist enclave in Palestine expanded demographically and economically, and German goods were to be found in abundance in Zion!

The ties between the different Jewish communities are neither political nor economic, for statehood has never been a *sine qua non* for Jewish physical survival or spiritual renaissance. The ties between the Jews—their "peoplehood," so to speak—have always been spiritual and cultural. Such ties can be peacefully maintained and indeed perpetuated as long as they do not carry with them any privileged rights. Viewed in this light, the different Jewish communities of the world are not party to the conflict raging in the Middle East, nor is there an essential or necessary antagonism or conflict between their definition of their selfhood and their "rights," on the one hand, and the selfhood and rights of the Palestinian Arabs, on the other.

Once we view the Arab-Israeli conflict outside the context of an eternal Jewish fate, we can then begin to make a distinction not only between "Jew" and "Zionist," but also between both, on the one hand, and "Israeli" on the other. Probably, it might be quite useful and far more relevant to drop the abstract category "Jewish national," the official designation of Israeli Jews, and replace it by the nonexistent category of "Israeli national." The state of Israel should be reconstituted to be a state neither for Jews nor Zionists but for its *present Israeli citizens* within its pre-1967 borders. Any discriminatory practices, either directly by the government or indirectly through the Jewish Agency, would then have to be discontinued. The new state would necessarily recognize the urgent need to resolve the outstanding problem of the displaced Palestinians. Israeli-Zionist immigration laws, which give preference to Jews living abroad over Palestinians who were born and raised in Acre or Haifa and who still own land there, would have to be adjusted.

A political structure willing to make such decisions would cease to be alien to the region. It might or might not have a "Jewish" majority, but if it did, it would be a Jewish-Israeli majority that is part of the region, sharing the same advantages and suffering the same setbacks. Such a state would not be a "Jewish state" nor even a "state for Jews." It would be a state for its own Israeli citizens, who, regardless of their religious affiliation or cultural or ethnic identity, would define their attitudes in accordance with the dictates of their Middle Eastern situation. Such a state could be readily integrated into the region.

A return to 1948 and to the *status quo ante* would only serve to antagonize the Israeli Jews, thereby unnecessarily prolonging the conflict. In order to win them over in the struggle for a just peace for all, it should be made clear to them that the reconstitution of the Jewish state into a state for its own citizens and within its pre-1967 borders would bring about recognition and normalization of relations with the neighboring states. The human and fundamental *right of belonging to*, as distinct from the colonial and exclusivist *right of settling in*, a land should be upheld as the inalienable right of all Israeli citizens, not of all Jews or Zionists who happen to be citizens of other countries. It should be made clear that the new state, through several constitutional provisions and institutional safeguards, would guarantee the specific religious and cultural identity of the various groups that make it up. This new Israel could probably enter into some kind of federation with the new Palestinian state now being proposed.

Even a reconstituted Zionism could be accommodated within that new proposed frame of reference. If this solution implies that pan-Arabism will have to settle for a less rigorous definition of itself and its goals, while having to coexist with and respect the rights of non-Arab communities existing in its midst, it also follows that Zionism will have to settle for a more realistic view of itself. The present political Zionist approach to Israel and the diaspora in such grandiose terms as the "negation of the diaspora," "ingathering of the exiles," and *Eretz Yisrael* is divorced from any reality, Israel's and the diaspora's, and has succeeded only in arousing Arab fears and plunging the region in an endless conflict. Probably a revival of the abandoned rhetoric of Zionism as a limited rescue operation and of cultural Zionism might provide a ground where pan-Arabism and Zionism might meet with no necessary antagonism. The Israeli writer Abraham Yehoshuah talks of Zionism as a "prosaic rescue movement,"[47] developed "within the Jewish dilemma of a century ago," that is, the Jewish question of Eastern Europe. But above all, he considers "the process practically complete and accepts it as a historical fact." He even goes as far as denying that "the real aim of Zionism" was ever the ingathering of the *entire* Jewish people. Seeking sanction for his view in Jewish history, he refers to the fact that in the period of the Second Temple, there was a large Jewish diaspora "dispersed outside the Land of Israel."[48]

Uri Avnery shares Yehoshuah's viewpoint, preferring to see Zionism as a finished process of historical interest rather than an ongoing dynamism of political relevance or importance. Boaz Evron, the Israeli writer, suggests that the Israeli, in his relationship to Zionism, should be like the American in his relationship to the Puritan outlook. Why the Zionist or Puritan Founding Fathers, or their descendants, settled in the United States or the Middle East should be a matter of historical interest only, not the subject of political debate.[49]

Whether one accepts this view of the origins and nature of Zionism is largely irrelevant from a political standpoint. I, for one, view Zionism differently, but the virtue of the view of Zionism as a limited rescue operation is that it seals off the Zionist process, allays Arab fears about an endless *aliyah* and expansion, and places the whole issue of political Zionism in a historical perspective. Arab and Israeli differences concerning the origins and nature of Zionism would then be of an academic rather than a political-military nature. And since academic differences are far more manageable and far less costly than military ones, this view of Zionism would provide a pragmatic, if not ideological, basis for reconciliation and for a measure of mutual acceptance.

Once legitimate Arab and Palestinian fears are allayed—fears based on their experience with Zionist settlement and statehood—it might not be unrealistic to envisage a creative and positive role for a reconstituted Zionism premised on the nonpolitical concept of religious peoplehood of the Jews, and taking into consideration the rich and specific varieties of their cultural experiences throughout the world. This approach could contribute to the development of the new Hebrew culture in the Middle East, and it could also help the various Jewish communities in the Arab world, Soviet Union, United States, and elsewhere to maintain their respective specificity and to nurture the pride that is essential for their integration into their respective societies. A revival of some of the aspects of Ahad Ha'am's writings and some of the formulas of cultural Zionism might be quite helpful.

All this may seem merely idealistic, visionary, and divorced from reality. But I can at least claim that my proposal is far more realistic and far less ambitious than a Zionism still fantasizing about a Greater Israel, the Ingathering of the Exiles, and a pure Jewish State. It is also far more practical and humane than an Arab myth of rights that excludes or disregards the three million Hebrew-speaking Israelis or that still fantasizes about a pre-1948 or even a pre-1917 Palestine. My proposal is indeed idealistic and visionary insofar as it tries to envisage a relatively rational solution based on a synthesis of all interests and on a recognition of all concrete identities. But I would also argue that it is well rooted in reality. A careful study, bypassing the ideological allegations and political statements that appear in daily headlines, would demonstrate that the dynamics of the situation are already leading into the direction of the proposed frame of reference. Diaspora Jews, including diaspora Zionists, are not very eager to settle in Israel. Their actions as well as their concrete (as distinct from their ideological) view of themselves indicate that they unconsciously operate more in terms of a broad religious or cultural peoplehood than of a national or political one. The theoretical formulations of Breira, even though not yet well articulated, are moving toward that realization.

Israelis who resent diaspora criticism act in accordance with what they consider to be their own specific national interests, outside the dynamics of pan-Jewish nationalism and without much regard for the interests of the various Jewish communities of the world. In his book *The End of the Jewish People?* Georges Friedmann, the Jewish-French sociologist, finds much truth to "the caustic saying that, in Israel, the *olim* are more or less rapidly turned into Israeli patriots, 'Hebrew-speaking gentiles.' "[50] This new community—with its Sephardic majority, its growing Sabra generation, and its substantive Arab minority—is gradually being transformed into a Middle Eastern society, both demographically and culturally. Amos Kenan, the Israeli writer, more or less concurs with some, if not all, of these views. He said that the Israelis "no longer live in a Jewish state but, *de facto*, in a binational one. Those who oppose annexation in order 'to preserve the Jewish character of the State' may rest." Then he warned those who are still encapsulated in their political Zionist vision: "Whoever wants a Jewish state will only have it through oppressing the others or even expelling them altogether."[51]

Even though this fact has commonly been overlooked, many Palestinian and Arab spokesmen, as briefly indicated in the preceding chapter, have often voiced their readiness to coexist with a Middle Eastern state that is willing to solve its Arab question. Arab spokesmen of late have reiterated that position more clearly and less ambiguously than ever. Ambassador Esmat Abdel-Meguid, Permanent Representative of Egypt to the United Nations, in an article (*The New York Times,* July 1, 1977) significantly titled "Egypt's Approach to Peace," declared Arab willingness to accept unreservedly UN resolutions guaranteeing "the security, territorial integrity and peaceful existence of *all* . . . countries in the area." But guarantee of independent existence is rightly modified by the Arabs' right to regain those parts of their homelands occupied by Israel since 1967 and by the right of the Arab Palestinian people to a homeland. "With the implementation of these requirements," Ambassador Abdel-Meguid said, "an end to the state of belligerency will come into effect."

My proposal necessarily requires integrating various United Nations resolutions, such as Security Council Resolution 242 (November 1967), which calls for a withdrawal to the pre-1967 borders and recognition of *all* states in the region, and General Assembly Resolution 3236 (November 1974), which endorses Palestinian national rights. However, this proposal in effect transcends both resolutions in that it raises the fundamental issue of the internal structure and dynamics of the Zionist state and their impact on the very fabric of peace in the region.

If this proposal for the reconstitution of the Zionist state were to be accepted, it would entail sacrifices on all sides. Some Arabs would naturally prefer a restoration of the *status quo ante* of a purely Arab Palestine, and the Zionist-Israelis would rather maintain the *status quo* of a purely Jewish state. Nevertheless, the history of the past 30 years should persuade all parties in the conflict that although purity may be a desirable esthetic ideal, it has questionable value in the realm of politics. Given this fact of life, the proposed reorientation of the peace efforts could provide a broad base for a coalition among Arabs, Israelis, and diaspora Jews interested in a permanent and just peace.

Demilitarized zones, step-by-step diplomacy, and different interim stages and states are not excluded. They could be very useful in bringing active hostility to an end and in giving the warring parties the time necessary to develop a better perspective of the situation and to cultivate concrete relations and common interests. But all these compromise solutions and procedures are acceptable only if they are seen simply as means rather than as an end. If the compromise solution is seen as an end, then it will simply serve, as it did in the past, as a breathing spell during which all the parties rearm themselves and try to tilt the balance of power in their favor. Most compromise solutions to the problem are proposed in either narrow territorialist or in vague humanitarian terms, overlooking the very root of the conflict.

The movement toward the new frame of reference is going to be slow and tentative at first, but it will develop its own momentum, bringing about the desired structural transformations in the region that will benefit all and provide the antagonists with a basis for a lasting peace, lasting because it is based on justice. This *could* be the way to turn Israel/Palestine from the land of strife, bloodshed, and torture into the land of promise envisioned by Congressman Julius Kahn and other Jewish and Arab humanists.

NOTES

CHAPTER 1 (Pages 1–17)

1. Bishop W. Ralph Ward, President of The United Methodist Church's Council of Bishops, *The New York Times,* November 9, 1975.
2. First phrase is from a letter sent by the second annual Christian-Jewish Workshop, sponsored by the United States Conference of Catholic Bishops cited in op. cit. The second phrase is used in the same report with no citation of source.
3. "The Jewish State *(Der Judenstaat),*" in Raphael Patai (Ed.), *Encyclopedia of Zionism and Israel,* Vol. I.
4. "Statement by the Lubbavitcher Rebbe, Rabbi Shulem ben Schneersohn, on Zionism" (1903), in Michael Selzer (Ed.), *Zionism Reconsidered.*
5. Desmond Stewart, *Theodor Herzl,* p. 178.
6. "Notes on Zionism by Max Nordau," selected by Chaim Bloch, *Herzl Year Book,* Vol. VII, p. 34.
7. Richard Crossman, *A Nation Reborn,* p. 23.
8. Amos Elon, *The Israelis: Founders and Sons,* p. 329.
9. Melford E. Spiro, *Kibbutz,* p. 49.
10. Arthur Hertzberg (Ed.), *The Zionist Idea,* p. 321.
11. Ehud Ben Ezer (Ed.), *Unease in Zion,* pp. 150–151.
12. "Statement by the Lubbavitcher Rebbe," in Selzer, *Zionism Reconsidered,* p. 13.
13. Cited in Meir Ben-Horin, *Max Nordau,* p. 199.
14. "A Letter of Ben-Yehuda," dated 1880, in Hertzberg, *The Zionist Idea,* p. 161.
15. *Time,* October 20, 1975.
16. *Yediot Aharonot,* December 20, 1974, cited in *Israel and Palestine,*

March 1975, p. 6.

17.   See "After the War: Chapters of Meditation, Rule and Research," published by the Central Command Headquarters/Israeli Army Chaplaincy. Publication of the booklet and some of its contents were reported in the Israeli papers *Haolam Hazeh,* May 15, 1974, (cited in *Free Palestine,* September 1974 and in *Al Hamishmar,* March 28, 1975, reprinted in *Swasia,* June 6, 1974). The entire passage is cited in *Viewpoint,* July 1974, p. 30.

18.   Cited in D. G. Tendulkar, *Mahatma,* Vol. IV, p. 314.

19.   Cited in Moshe Menuhin, *Jewish Critics of Zionism,* p. 5. Henceforth referred to as *Jewish Critics.*

20.   Horace M. Kallen, *Utopians at Bay,* p. 178.

21.   *The New York Times,* November 23, 1975.

22.   "In Bondage to Our Fellow Jews," in Selzer, *Zionism Reconsidered,* p. 5.

23.   Ibid.

24.   Tendulkar, *Mahatma,* Vol. IV, p. 314.

25.   "My Country,'Tis of Thee?" *Interchange,* December 1975, p. 6.

26.   Bloch, "Notes on Zionism by Max Nordau," *Herzl Year Book,* Vol. VII, p. 32.

27.   Selzer, *Zionism Reconsidered,* p. 13.

28.   Ben-Horin, *Max Nordau,* p. 199.

29.   Raphael Patai (Ed.), *The Complete Diaries of Theodor Herzl,* trans. Harry Zohn, five volumes, Vol. I, p. 133. Henceforth referred to as *Diaries.*

30.   Ibid.

31.   Pinsker, *Auto-Emancipation,* in Hertzberg, *The Zionist Idea,* p. 197.

32.   Ibid., p. 194.

33.   Ibid., p. 197.

34.   Patai, *Diaries,* Vol. IV, p. 1604.

35.   Ibid., p. 1594.

36.   "East Africa Scheme (popularly and incorrectly known as Uganda Scheme)," *Encyclopedia of Zionism and Israel,* Vol. I.

37.   "Uganda Scheme," *Encyclopedia Judaica,* Vol XV.

38.   Patai, *Diaries,* Vol. III, p. 899.

39.   Ibid., Vol. II, p. 500.

40.   Ibid., Vol. I, P. 56.

41.   *The Jewish State,* in Hertzberg, *The Zionist Idea,* p. 222.

42.   Hertzberg, *The Zionist Idea,* p. 418.

43.   Kallen, *Utopians at Bay,* p. 183.

44.   "The Real Issue in the Arab-Israeli-Zionist Conflict," in Garry Smith (Ed.), *Zionism, the Dream and the Reality,* p. 231. Emphasis added.

45. Babylonial Talmud, Ketuvot, 110b, cited by Philip Sigal, "Reflections on Jewish Nationalism," *Issues,* Vol. XV (Fall, 1961), pp. 20–21.
46. Stewart, *Theodor Herzl,* p. 325.
47. Sigal, "Reflections on Jewish Nationalism," *Issues,* Vol. XV (Fall, 1961), p. 21.
48. Patai, *Diaries,* Vol. IV, p. 1599.
49. Jacob Bernard Agus, *The Meaning of Jewish History,* Vol. II, p. 470.
50. Homer A. Jack, "Is Zionism Racism? The 1975 Debate in the United Nations," p. 18.
51. Moshe Pearlman, *Ben Gurion Looks Back,* p. 230.
52. Agus, *The Meaning of Jewish History,* Vol. II, p. 470–471.
53. Ben Ezer, *Unease in Zion,* p. 69.
54. Joseph Nedava, "Herzl and Messianism," in *Herzl Year Book,* Vol. VII, p. 12.
55. Ben Ezer, *Unease in Zion,* p. 157.
56. "Reminiscence" at a banquet at Czernowitz, December 12, 1927, Hertzberg, *The Zionist Idea,* p. 580.
57. Crossman, *A Nation Reborn,* p. 16.
58. Nedava, "Herzl and Messianism," in *Herzl Year Book,* Vol. VII, p. 12.
59. Herzl in an address to the Anglo-Jewish Association, cited in Ahmed El-Kodsy and Eli Lobel, *The Arab World and Israel,* p. 111. All references are to Lobel's section "Palestine and the Jews."
60. Patai, *Diaries,* Vol. II, p. 701.
61. Ibid., Vol. I, P. 27.
62. Ibid., Vol. II, p. 581.
63. Ibid., Vol. I, p. 236.
64. Ibid., Vol. II, pp. 700–701.
65. Ibid., Vol. II, p. 693.
66. Cited in *Viewpoint,* March 1974, p. 46.
67. Menuhin, *Jewish Critics,* p. 5, Book of Amos 9:7.
68. Introductory note to Rabbi Berger's *Prophecy, Zionism and the State of Israel,* p. 3. Rabbi Berger's address was delivered on March 20, 1968.
69. Cited in Elmer Berger, "Theological and Religious Implications of Zionism in Palestine,"in Abdeen Jabara and Janice Terry (Eds.), *The Arab World,* pp. 147–148.
70. Cited in I. Rabinowitch, "Political Zionism and the State of Israel; Moral Issues," *The Jewish Guardian,* February 1975, p. 9.
71. *Interchange,* December 1975, p. 8. Emphasis added.
72. Hertzberg, *The Zionist Idea,* p. 294.

73.   Ibid., p. 159.
74.   Bloch, "Notes on Zionism by Max Nordau," *Herzl Year Book,*
       Vol. VII, p. 29.
75.   Ibid., p. 31.
76.   "Boundaries" (1914–1921), in Hertzberg, *The Zionist Idea,* p. 316.
77.   Selzer, *Zionism Reconsidered,* p. 12.
78.   In Walter Laqueur, *A History of Zionism,* p. 401.
79.   "The Jew in the World" (1934), in Hertzberg, *The Zionist Idea,*
       p. 455.
80.   "Lights for Rebirth" (1910–1930), in Hertzberg, *The Zionist
       Idea,* p. 427.
81.   Ibid., p. 430.
82.   Ibid.
83.   Kallen, *Utopians at Bay,* p. 278.
84.   Ibid., p. 10.
85.   Cited in Sir John Richmond, "Cleaning the Air," *Middle East
       International,* September 1975, p. 9.
86.   "Hope Jewish and Hope Secular," paper read at a religious con-
       ference at St. Xavier College in June 1967, cited by H. Haddad,
       "The Biblical Bases of Zionist Colonialism," in Ibrahim Abu-
       Lughod and Baha Abu-Laban (Eds.), *Settler Regimes in Africa
       and the Arab World,* p. 7.
87.   Elon, *The Israelis,* p. 281.
88.   Ibid., p. 329.
89.   Ben Ezer, *Unease in Zion,* p. 751.
90.   Cited in Menuhin, *The Decadence of Judaism in Our Time,* p. 107.
91.   Menuhin, *Jewish Critics,* p. 38.
92.   Cited in Emile Marmorstein, *Heaven at Bay,* p. 71.
93.   Ibid.
94.   Yermachmiel Domb, "Neturei Karta," in Selzer, *Zionism Recon-
       sidered,* p. 43. Emphasis in the original.
95.   Shlomo Israel, "The First Orthodox Jew Murdered by the Zionists,"
       The Guardians, July 30, 1974, pp. 12–14.

CHAPTER 2 (Pages 19–30)

1.   Nedava, "Herzl and Messianism," *Herzl Year Book,* Vol. VII,
      p. 20.
2.   Arthur Ruppin, *The Jews of Today,* p. 211.
3.   "Boundaries" (1014–1921), in Hertzberg, *The Zionist Idea,* p. 321.
4.   Crossman, *A Nation Reborn,* p. 18.
5.   Weizmann, *Trial and Error,* p. 346.

6. *Brief,* January–February 1965.
7. *Brief,* September 1958.
8. Stewart, *Theodor Herzl,* p. 247.
9. "Israel and the Diaspora," *Encyclopedia of Zionism and Israel,* Vol. I.
10. Cited in Elmer Berger, "After Talbot: Zionism on the Defensive," *Issues,* Vol. XVIII (Fall–Winter 1964), p. 13.
11. Cited by Benyamin Matovu, "The Zionist Wish and the Nazi Deed," *Issues,* Vol. XX (Winter 1966–1967), p. 10.
12. Hertzberg, *The Zionist Idea,* p. 323.
13. Ben Ezer, *Unease in Zion,* p. 72.
14. Hertzberg, *The Zionist Idea,* p. 319. Emphasis in the original.
15. Selzer, *Zionism Reconsidered,* p. xii.
16. Michael Selzer, "The Jewishness of Zionism: A Continuing Controversy," *Issues,* Vol. XXI (Autumn 1967), p. 17.
17. Ibid., p. 5.
18. "Hess, Moses," *Encyclopedia Judaica,* Vol. VII.
19. Stewart, *Theodor Herzl,* p. 178.
20. Patai, *Diaries,* Vol. I, p. 11.
21. "Boundaries," in Hertzberg, *The Zionist Idea,* p. 320.
22. Ruppin, *The Jews of Today,* p. 231, n. 1.
23. Karl Kautsky, *Are the Jews a Race?,* pp. 217–220. Emphasis in the original.
24. Ruppin, *The Jews of Today,* p. 216. Emphasis in the original.
25. Ibid., pp. 227–228.
26. Ibid., p. 228.
27. Morris R. Cohen, "Zionism: Tribalism or Liberalism?," in Smith, *Zionism, The Dream and the Reality,* p. 50.
28. Ruppin, *The Jews of Today,* p. 212.
29. Tahseen Basheer (Ed.), *Edwin Montagu and the Balfour Declaration,* p. 20.
30. Brandeis, *A Collection of Addresses and Statements by Louis Brandeis,* pp. 14–15. Emphasis added.
31. Simcha King, *Nachum Sokolow,* p. 177.
32. Agus, *The Meaning of Jewish History,* Vol. II, p. 427.
33. Leonard Stein, *The Balfour Declaration,* p. 547.
34. "Race," *The New Encyclopedia Britannica,* Vol. XV.
35. King, *Nachum Sokolow,* pp. 176–177.
36. Ibid., p. 177.
37. Stewart, *Theodor Herzl,* p. 210.
38. Jack, "Is Zionism Racism?," p. 5.
39. David Ben Gurion, *Rebirth and Destiny of Israel,* p. 310.
40. Bloch, "Notes on Zionism by Max Nordau,"*Herzl Year Book,*

Vol. VII, p. 34

41. Patai, *Diaries,* Vol. 1, p. 231
42. Ruppin, *The Jews of Today,* p. 217
43. Cited in L. Humphrey Walz, " 'Zionism'? 'Racism'? What Do You Mean?" *The Link,* Winter 1975–1976, p.11
44. Jack, "Is Zionism Racism?" p. 18
45. King, *Nachum Sokolow,* p. 177.
46. "Hess, Moses," *Encyclopedia Judaica,* Vol. VII. Emphasis added.
47. Ruppin, *The Jews of Today,* p. 229.
48. Ibid., p. 228.
49. Cited in Matovu, "The Zionist Wish and the Nazi Deed," *Issues,* Vol. XX (Winter 1966–1967), p. 12.
50. In *The Road to Jerusalem,* cited in Ibrahim Al-Abid, *127 Questions and Answers on the Arab-Israeli Conflict,* p. 31. Henceforth referred to as *127 Questions and Answers.*
51. Hans Kohn, *Living in a World Revolution,* pp. 67–68.
52. Selzer, *Zionism Reconsidered,* p. 241.
53. Richard Korn, "Eshkol's Official Plan for 'Israel and the Diaspora,' " *Issues,* Vol. XIX (Winter 1965–1966), p. 16.
54. Pearlman, *Ben Gurion Looks Back,* p. 245.
55. Ibid., p. 246.
56. Cited in *127 Questions and Answers,* p. 31.
57. A *Haaretz* dispatch dated July 22, 1973, cited in *Viewpoint,* July 1973, p. 31
58. Patrick Marnham, "Is Israel Racist?" *Spectator,* March 6, 1976.
59. *Israel and Palestine,* March 1975, p. 6.
60. Crossman, *A Nation Reborn,* p. 19.
61. Cited in Matovu, "The Zionist Wish and the Nazi Deed," *Issues,* Vol. XX (Winter 1966–1967), p. 10.
62. Ben Gurion, *Rebirth and Destiny of Israel,* pp. 420–421.
63. Pearlman, *Ben Gurion Looks Back,* p. 244.
64. Ben Ezer, *Unease in Zion,* p. 72. Emphasis in the original.
65. *Jewish Daily Forward,* January 9, 1959, cited in Alfred M. Lilienthal, *The Other Side of the Coin,* p. 81.
66. Kallen, *Utopians at Bay,* p. 44.

CHAPTER 3 (Pages 31–54)

1. Basheer, *Edwin Montagu and the Balfour Declaration,* p. 10.
2. Agus, *The Meaning of Jewish History,* Vol. II, p. 468.
3. Ibrahim Al-Abid, *A Handbook to the Palestine Question,* p. 43.
4. Introduction to the 1952 *Israel Government Yearbook,* cited in

Al-Abid, *127 Questions and Answers.*

5. Ibid.
6. Ibid.
7. Ibid.
8. "Israel and the Diaspora," *Encyclopedia of Zionism and Israel,* Vol. I.
9. Ibid.
10. Cited in *Brief,* Spring-Summer 1975.
11. Ben Gurion, *Rebirth and Destiny of Israel,* p. 489.
12. Cited in Lilienthal, *The Other Side of the Coin,* p. 75.
13. "Jewish Survival," *Israel Government Yearbook,* 1953–1954, p. 35. Cited in Lilienthal, op. cit., p. 79.
14. Cited in *Brief,* February 1961.
15. *Brief,* Autumn 1975.
16. *Viewpoint,* July 1974, p. 31. Emphasis added.
17. *Brief,* January–February 1965.
18. W. T. Mallison, Jr., and S. V. Mallison, *An International Law Appraisal,* pp. 26–29.
19. "State Department Says: US Jews Not Linked to Israel," *Issues,* Vol. XIV (Spring 1960), p. 43. Emphasis added.
20. Cited in *Issues,* Vol. XVIII (Fall-Winter 1964), p. 1.
21. *The New York Times,* November 23, 1975.
22. Tendulkar, *Mahatma,* Vol. IV, p. 312.
23. Hannah Arendt, *Eichmann in Jerusalem,* p. 208.
24. Agus, *The Meaning of Jewish History,* Vol. II, p. 397.
25. Hertzberg, *The Zionist Idea,* p. 211.
26. Bar Yochai (pseudonym), "Quotas for the Diaspora," *Israel and Palestine,* April 1975, p. 4.
27. Lilienthal, *The Other Side of the Coin,* p. 47.
28. Jakob I. Petuchowski, "Philanthropy and Politics," excerpt from *Zion Reconsidered,* in Smith, *Zionism, the Dream and the Reality,* p. 155.
29. *Brief,* January–February, 1960.
30. Ben Ezer, *Unease in Zion,* p. 56.
31. "Egypt," *Encyclopedia Judaica,* Vol. VI.
32. The data in this part, unless otherwise indicated, are taken mostly from the following entries in the *Encyclopedia of Zionism and Israel:* "Iraq, Zionism in," Vol. I; "North Africa," Zionism in," Vol. II; and "Egypt, Zionism in," Vol. I.
33. "Egypt," *Encyclopedia Judaica,* Vol. VI.
34. *Brief,* January–February 1962.
35. Elmer Berger, *Who Knows Better Must Say So!,* p. 14.
36. "Egypt," *Encyclopedia Judaica,* Vol. VI.

37. "Marzouk, Moshe" *Encyclopedia Judaica,* Vol. XI.
38. Uri Avnery, *Israel Without Zionists,* pp. 117–118.
39. "Marzouk, Moshe," *Encyclopedia Judaica,* Vol. XI.
40. Amitay Ben-Yona, *What Does Israel Do to Its Palestinians? A Letter from Israel to Jews of the American Left,* Arab-American University Graduates Information Paper Number Two, September 1970.
41. "Marzouk, Moshe," *Encyclopedia Judaica,* Vol. XI.
42. Christopher Sykes, *Crossroads to Israel,* pp. 223–224.
43. Ibid.
44. *The Guardians,* July 1974, p. 15.
45. Sykes, *Crossroads to Israel,* pp. 225–226.
46. Hertzberg, *The Zionist Idea,* p. 325.
47. *The Canadian Jewish News,* cited by *Special Interest Report,* Vol. VIII (April 1977).
48. Ben Ezer, *Unease in Zion,* p. 59.
49. Hertzberg, *The Zionist Idea,* p. 325.
50. Cited in Michael Selzer, "Politics and Human Perfectibility: A Jewish Perspective," in Smith, *Zionism, the Dream and the Reality,* p. 298, n. 30.
51. Korn, "Eshkol's Official Plan for 'Israel and the Diaspora,' " *Issues,* Vol. XIX (Winter 1965–1966), p. 15.
52. Agus, *The Meaning of Jewish History,* Vol. II, p. 469.
53. Hertzberg, *The Zionist Idea,* p. 609.
54. "Boundaries," in Hertzberg, *The Zionist Idea,* p. 324.
55. Jon and David Kimche, *The Secret Roads,* p. 27.
56. "Boundaries," in Hertzberg, *The Zionist Idea,* p. 325.
57. "Our Tasks Ahead," (1920), ibid., p. 382.
58. Cited in Allan C. Brownfeld, "American Jews: Doubts About Zionism," *Middle East International,* September 1974, p. 13.
59. Michael Selzer, *The Aryanization of the Jewish State,* p. 110.
60. Patai, *Diaries,* Vol. I, p. 196.
61. Ibid., pp. 4, 111.
62. Ibid., p. 7.
63. Hertzberg, *The Zionist Idea,* p. 215.
64. Ibid., p. 216.
65. Ibid., p. 185.
66. Crossman, *A Nation Reborn,* pp. 21–22.
67. Hertzberg, *The Zionist Idea,* p. 185.
68. Stewart, *Theodor Herzl,* p. 178.
69. Agus, *The Meaning of Jewish History,* Vol. II, p. 425.
70. Patai, *Diaries,* Vol. I, p. 171.
71. Ibid., p. 181. Emphasis in the original.

72.   Hertzberg, *The Zionist Idea,* p. 224.

73.   Patai, *Diaries,* Vol. I, p. 182.

74.   Ibid., p. 266.

75.   Stewart, *Theodor Herzl,* p. 251, n. Emphasis in the original.

76.   Bloch, "Notes on Zionism by Max Nordau," *Herzl Year Book,* Vol. VII, p. 29.

77.   Yehezkel Kaufman, "The Ruin of the Soul," in Selzer, *Zionism Reconsidered,* p. 121.

78.   "Self-Criticism" (1914), in Hertzberg, *The Zionist Idea,* p. 392.

79.   "Boundaries," ibid., p. 323.

80.   Ibid., p. 184.

81.   Words reported by Issac Bashevis Singer in *In My Father's Court,* cited in Selzer, *The Aryanization of the Jewish State,* p. 35.

82.   Kaufman, in Selzer, *Zionism Reconsidered,* p. 121, n. 7.

83.   Ibid.

84.   Benyamin Matovu, "Zionist and Anti-Semite: 'Of Course,' " *Issues,* Vol. XX (Spring 1966), p. 22.

85.   Chaim Kaplan, *The Scrolls of Agony,* p. 174.

86.   Patai, *Diaries,* Vol. I, p. 84.

87.   Ibid., p. 34.

88.   Ibid., p. 51.

89.   Agus, *The Meaning of Jewish History,* Vol. II, p. 425.

90.   Menuhin, *Jewish Critics,* p. 17.

91.   "Jews and the State of Israel," from *The End of the Jewish People?,* in Smith, *Zionism, The Dream and the Reality,* p. 142.

92.   Ibid.

93.   Selzer, "The Jewishness of Zionism," *Issues,* Vol. XXI (Autumn 1967), p. 18.

94.   Patai, *Diaries,* Vol. I, p. 231.

95.   Selzer, "The Jewishness of Zionism," *Issues,* Vol. XXI (Autumn 1967), p. 18.

96.   Selzer, *Zionism Reconsidered,* p. 128.

97.   Jewish Liberation Project and Committee to Support M. E. Liberation, *Arab-Israeli Debate,* p. 27.

98.   Alfred Lilienthal, *What Price Israel?,* p. 196.

99.   Faubion Bowers, "Only—and Lonely in America," *The New York Times Magazine,* September 25, 1976.

100. Ibid. Emphasis added.

101. Korn, "Eshkol's Official Plan for 'Israel and the Diaspora,' " *Issues,* Vol. XIX (Winter 1965-1966), p. 17.

102. See *The New York Times,* December 12, 1976.

103. *The Washington Post,* September 27, 1976.

104. *The New York Times,* December 12, 1976.

105. *The Washington Post,* September 27, 1976.
106. "Operation Magic Carpet," *Encyclopedia of Zionism and Israel,* Vol. II.
107. "Yemenite Jews in Israel," *Encyclopedia of Zionism and Israel,* Vol. II.
108. Lilienthal, *What Price Israel?,* p. 207.
109. I. F. Stone, "For a New Approach to the Israeli-Arab Conflict," in Smith, *Zionism, The Dream and the Reality,* p. 211.
110. "Iraq, Zionism in," *Encyclopedia of Zionism and Israel,* Vol. I. I am indebted to Ambassador Wessam El-Zehawi, of the Iraqi Mission to the United Nations, for providing information and data about Iraqi Jews.
111. Cited in Mahmud Tarbush, letter to *The Manchester Guardian,* December 21, 1976.
112. Hertzberg, *The Zionist Idea,* p. 188. Emphasis in the original.
113. Douglas L. Greener, "From Babylonian Exile to Ramat Gan," *The Israel Digest,* August 30, 1974, p. 6.
114. "Iraq," *Encyclopedia Judaica,* Vol. VIII.
115. Special correspondent, "How the Iraqi Jews Came to Israel," *Middle East International,* January 1973, p. 18.
116. "Iraq, Zionism in" *Encyclopedia of Zionism and Israel,* Vol. 1.
117. Ibid.
118. Ibid.
119. Lilienthal, *The Other Side of the Coin,* p. 37.
120. Tarbush, letter to *The Manchester Guardian.*
121. Barchas Habas, *The Gate Breakers;* cited in Marion Woolfson, "Pawns in the Zionist Game," *Middle East International,* November 1975, p. 26.
122. Ibid.
123. Berger, *Who Knows Better Must Say So!,* p. 30.
124. Ibid., p. 31.
125. Mendes, "The Iraqi Immigration and the Israeli Government," *Haaretz;* cited in El-Kodsy and Lobel, *The Arab World and Israel,* p. 26.
126. "Iraq," *Encyclopedia Judaica,* Vol. VIII.
127. Special correspondent, "How the Iraqi Jews Came to Israel," *Middle East International,* January 1973, p. 9.
128. Woolfson, "Pawns in the Zionist Game," *Middle East International,* November 1975, p. 25.
129. Special correspondent, "How the Iraqi Jews Came to Israel," *Middle East International,* January 1973, p. 9. Emphasis added.
130. Berger, *Who Knows Better Must Say So!,* p. 33.
131. Special correspondent, "How the Iraqi Jews Came to Israel,"

Middle East International, January 1973, pp. 18–20, 34.

132. Harold Flender, *The Kids Who Went to Israel,* p. 61.
133. Special correspondent, "How the Iraqi Jews Came to Israel," *Middle East International,* January 1973, pp. 20, 34.
134. Ibid., p. 20.
135. Mendes, cited in El-Kodsy and Lobel, *The Arab World and Israel,* p. 122.
136. Hertzberg, *The Zionist Idea,* p. 318.

CHAPTER 4   (Pages 55–82)

1. "Anti-Zionism," *Encyclopedia of Zionism and Israel,* Vol. I. Emphasis added.
2. James N. Rosenberg, member of the Executive Committee of the American Jewish Committee, commenting on a proposal that the Committee support the creation of Palestine as a "commonwealth" only *after* the Jews constitute a majority. Cited in Elmer Berger, "The Old Wolf—in New Sheep's Clothing," *Issues,* Vol. XIV (Spring 1960), pp. 10–11.
3. Cited in *Labour Monthly,* August 1967, p. 342.
4. Patai, *Diaries,* Vol. II, p. 667.
5. Ibid.
6. Ibid., Vol. I, p. 411.
7. Cited in Maxime Rodinson, *Israel, A Colonial-Settler State?,* p. 39.
8. Selzer, *The Aryanization of the Jewish State,* p. 111.
9. Agus, *The Meaning of Jewish History,* Vol. II, p. 371.
10. I. Domb, *The Transformation,* pp. 194–195.
11. Smith, *Zionism, The Dream and the Reality,* pp. 79–80.
12. Ibid., p. 80.
13. See the entry on Birnbaum in *Encyclopedia of Zionism and Israel,* Vol. I, and *Encyclopedia Judaica,* Vol. II.
14. Smith, *Zionism, The Dream and the Reality,* p. 24.
15. Ibid.
16. This essay can be found in any selection of Ahad Ha'am's writings.
17. This phrase is aptly coined by Arthur Hertzberg, *The Zionist Idea,* p. 247.
18. Ibid., p. 262.
19. "Ahad Ha'am," *Encyclopedia of Zionism and Israel,* Vol. I.
20. Ibid.
21. "The Negation of the Diaspora" (1909), in Hertzberg, *The Zionist Idea,* p. 270.
22. Smith, *Zionism, The Dream and the Reality,* p. 32.

23.   Menuhin, *The Decadence of Judaism in Our Time*, p. 61.
24.   Ibid., p. 63.
25.   Menuhin, *Jewish Critics*, p. 5.
26.   Menuhin, *The Decadence of Judaism in Our Time*, p. 62.
27.   Menuhin, *Jewish Critics*, p. 5.
28.   Hans Kohn, in Smith, *Zionism, The Dream and the Reality*, p. 32.
29.   Ibid., p. 36.
30.   Menuhin, *Jewish Critics*, p. 11.
31.   Smith, *Zionism, The Dream and the Reality*, p. 324.
32.   "Ahad Ha'am," *Encyclopedia of Zionism and Israel*, Vol. I.
33.   Hertzberg, *The Zionist State*, pp. 464–465. Emphasis added.
34.   Ibid., p. 463.
35.   Menuhin, *Jewish Critics*, p. 2.
36.   Stewart, *Theodor Herzl*, p. 221.
37.   "Anti-Zionism," *Encyclopedia of Zionism and Israel*, Vol. I.
38.   Ibid.
39.   Ibid.
40.   Ibid.
41.   Stein, *The Balfour Declaration*, p. 81.
42.   "Anti-Zionism," *Encyclopedia of Zionism and Israel*, Vol. I.
43.   Cited in Matovu, "The Zionist Wish and the Nazi Deed," *Issues*, Vol. XX (Winter 1966–1967), p. 4, n. 9.
44.   "Anti-Zionism," *Encyclopedia of Zionism and Israel*, Vol. I.
45.   Ibid.
46.   Stein, *The Balfour Declaration*, p. 526.
47.   Basheer, *Edwin Montagu and the Balfour Declaration*, pp. 7–11.
48.   Ibid.
49.   "Anti-Zionism," *Encyclopedia of Zionism and Israel*, Vol. I.
50.   Ibid.
51.   Menuhin, *The Decadence of Judaism in Our Time*, pp. 70–78.
52.   Norman Bentwitch, *For Zion's Sake*, p. 53.
53.   Ibid., p. 61.
54.   Hertzberg, *The Zionist Idea*, p. 261.
55.   Bentwitch, *For Zion's Sake*, p. 71.
56.   Hertzberg, *The Zionist Idea*, p. 449.
57.   Cited in Sami Hadawi and John Robert, *The Palestine Diary*, Vol. I. pp. 71–72.
58.   Menuhin, *Jewish Critics*, p. 22.
59.   Cited in Sanford Fox, "One Man's View of the Soundness of Zionism's Ideology," *Issues*, Vol. XXI (Autumn 1967), p. 24.
60.   Ronald W. Clark, *Einstein*, p. 379.
61.   Albert Einstein, *Out of My Later Years*, p. 263.
62.   Clark, *Einstein*, p. 381.

63. Lilienthal, *There Goes the Middle East,* p. 328. Emphasis added.
64. Clark, *Einstein,* p. 402.
65. Lilienthal, *There Goes the Middle East,* pp. 239–240.
66. Ibid., p. 243.
67. *Special Interest Report,* Vol. VII (October 1976).
68. Agus, *The Meaning of Jewish History,* Vol. II, p. 474.
69. *Brief,* Spring 1976.
70. Cited in "Personal Variations on Middle Eastern Themes." *Middle East International,* October 1975, p. 24.
71. *Brief,* February 1961.
72. *Brief,* Winter 1975–1976.
73. *Home News,* December 19, 1976.
74. *Jewish Flordian,* March 5, 1976, and *Chicago Tribune,* February 28, 1976, cited in the *Special Interest Report,* Vol. III (April 1972).
75. *Time,* November 1, 1976. Bellow's new book *To Jerusalem and Back* (New York: Viking, 1976) appeared too late to be discussed in this study. However, nothing in it would make me change my judgment. This travel book is not quite representative of Bellow's concrete imagination as manifested in his literary output. It might be of some relevance to underscore the fact that Levin's remarks were made on December 19, 1976, *after* the publication of Bellow's book. Levin found nothing in the book to "rehabilitate" Bellow the novelist.
76. Philip Roth, *Portnoy's Complaint,* p. 244.
77. Ibid., p. 253.
78. Ibid., pp. 253-254.
79. Ibid., p. 252.
80. Ibid., p. 253.
81. Ibid., p. 256.
82. Ibid., pp. 260–261.
83. Ibid., p. 265.
84. Hertzberg, *The Zionist Idea,* p. 271.
85. Agus, *The Meaning of Jewish History,* Vol. II, p. 477.
86. Ibid., p. 483.
87. Ibid., pp. 471, 474.
88. "Israel Not Spiritual Center: Jacob Neusner," *The Jewish Post,* September 13, 1974.
89. Ibid.
90. Review by Allen Brownsfeld, *Brief,* Autumn–Winter 1972.
91. Smith, *Zionism, The Dream and the Reality,* p. 211.
92. Ibid.
93. Selzer, *The Aryanization of the Jewish State,* p. 112.
94. Ibid., p. 117.

95.   Ibid., p. 115.
96.   Ibid.
97.   "Islamic/Christian Dialogue: Tripoli, Libyan Arab Republic, February 1976," *The Link,* Spring 1976, p. 2.
98.   Selzer, *The Aryanization of the Jewish State,* p. 114.
99.   Michael Rosenberg, "Israel Without Apology," cited in Smith, "Introductory Note," *Zionism, The Dream and the Reality,* p. 11.
100.   Peter Seidman, *Socialists and the Fight Against Anti-Semitism,* p. 6.
101.   Menuhin, *Jewish Critics,* p. 24.
102.   A letter by Mick Ashley to *Viewpoint,* March 1974, p. 48.
103.   *Brief,* Spring 1976.
104.   Israeli Ambassador to the United Nations; cited by Elmer Berger, "Theological and Religious Implications of Zionism in Palestine," in Jabara and Terry, *The Arab World,* p. 146.
105.   Pearlman, *Ben Gurion Looks Back,* p. 240.
106.   Ibid., pp. 238–239.
107.   Korn, "Eshkol's Official Plan for 'Israel and the Diaspora,' " *Issues,* Vol. XIX (Winter 1965–1966), p. 15.
108.   "Colonial Zionism" is Nordau's term.   See Bloch, "Notes on Zionism by Max Nordau," *Herzl Year Book,* Vol. VII, p. 27.
109.   "The Jewish State," in Hertzberg, *The Zionist Idea,* p. 212.
110.   Lilienthal, *What Price Israel?,* p. 192.
111.   *The New York Times,* May 18, 1961.
112.   "Goldmann, Nahum," *Encyclopedia Judaica,* Vol. VII.
113.   N. Goldmann, *The Autobiography of Nahum Goldmann,* p. 313.
114.   Ibid., p. 315.
115.   Petuchowski, "Philanthropy and Politics," in Smith, *Zionism The Dream and the Reality,* pp. 150–151.
116.   Crossman, *A Nation Reborn,* p. 19.
117.   "The Jewish Problem and How to Solve It" (1915), in Hertzberg, *The Zionist Idea,* pp. 519–520.
118.   Ibid., p. 520.
119.   Cited in Joachim Prinz, *The Dilemma of the Modern Jew,* p. 145.
120.   *The Washington Post,* September 18, 1974.
121.   *The New York Times Magazine,* September 26, 1976, p. 25.
122.   *The Washington Post,* September 18, 1974.
123.   Cited in *The New York Times Magazine,* September 26, 1976, p. 34.
124.   Cited in *Viewpoint,* March 1974, pp. 47–48.
125.   Cited in *Israel and Palestine,* April 1975, p. 11.
126.   "Israel-Diaspora Relations: Who is a Zionist?," *Interchange,* November 1976, p. 3.
127.   Ibid.

128.   Arthur H. Samuelson (Ed.), *Israel and the Palestinians,* p. xii.
129.   "Beyond Idolatry," *Interchange,* November 1975, p. 7.
130.   Ibid.
131.   Ibid., p. 1.
132.   Ibid., p. 6.
133.   *Brief,* September 1958.
134.   Cited in Fayez Sayegh, "The Encounter of Two Ideologies," in *Collected Essays of Palestine,* p. 103.
135.   "Israel-Diaspora Relations: Who is a Zionist?," *Interchange,* November 1975, p. 8. Emphasis added.

CHAPTER 5   (Pages 83-108)

1.   *Encyclopedia of Zionism and Israel,* Vol I.
2.   Sokolow, *History of Zionism,* Vol. I, p. xxviii.
3.   Patai, *Diaries,* Vol. II, p. 759.
4.   Stein, *The Balfour Declaration,* p. 9.
5.   Letter written, but never sent, by Weizmann to Churchill; cited in Crossman, *A Nation Reborn,* p. 130.
6.   Ibid.
7.   Sokolow, *History of Zionism,* Vol. I, p. 63.
8.   From *The New Eastern Question* (1860), cited in Stephen Hal-brook, "The Philosophy of Zionism: A Materialist Interpretation," in Abu-Lughod and Abu-Laban, *Settler Regimes,* p. 22.
9.   Stein, *The Balfour Declaration,* p. 11.
10.   Sokolow, *History of Zionism,* Vol. I, p. 138.
11.   The letter is dated August 11, 1840, cited in Jabbour, *Settler Colonialism in Southern Africa and the Middle East,* p. 22. In a study on the origins of Zionism published in the March 1977 issue of *El-Arabi,* the Kuwaiti monthly, Dr. Mohamed Hassan El-Zayat, former foreign minister of Egypt, deals with the gentile colonial origins of political Zionism and gives a detailed account of the efforts of the British officer Colonel Charles H. Churchill.
12.   David M. Stamler, "Jewish Interests in Palestine," in William Polk, *Backdrop to Tragedy,* p. 137.
13.   N.A. Rose, *The Gentile Zionists,* p. 74.
14.   Ibid., p. 73.
15.   David Ben Gurion, "Our Friend: What Wingate Did for Us," *Jewish Observer and Middle East Review,* September 27, 1963, pp. 15-16; reprinted in Walid Khalidi, *From Haven to Conquest,* p. 382.
16.   Leonard Mosley, "Orde Wingate and Moshe Dayan, 1938," from

Chapter 4, *Gideon Goes to War;* reprinted in Khalidi, *From Haven to Conquest,* p. 380.

17. Ibid.
18. Ibid., p. 376.
19. Ibid., p. 379.
20. Ben Gurion, "Our Friend," in Khalidi, p. 384.
21. Ibid., p. 385.
22. Mosley, "Orde Wingate and Moshe Dayan, 1938," in Khalidi, p. 377.
23. Ibid., pp. 377–378.
24. Ibid., pp. 381–382.
25. Ben Gurion, "Our Friend," in Khalidi, p. 385.
26. Ibid., p. 387.
27. Ibid., p. 386.
28. Arnold Toynbee, *A Study of History,* Vol. VIII, p. 308. Cited in Matovu, "Zionist and Anti-Semite: 'Of Course,' " *Issues,* Vol. XX (Spring 1966), p. 26.
29. Stein, *The Balfour Declaration,* p. 10.
30. "Restoration Movement," *Encyclopedia of Zionism and Israel,* Vol. II.
31. Patai, *Diaries,* Vol. III, p. 1186.
32. Stein, *The Balfour Declaration,* p. 11.
33. Ibid.
34. Sokolow, *History of Zionism,* Vol. I, pp. 206–207.
35. *My Political Life,* cited in B. Matovu, "Rhodesia and Israel: Parallels and Progress," *Issues,* Vol. XX (Autumn 1966), p. 20.
36. Moshe Machover, "Reply to Sol Stern," *Israca,* January 5, 1973, p. 30.
37. Alex Bein, "Herzl and the Kaiser in Palestine," excerpt from *Theodor Herzl, A Biography,* reprinted in Gordon Levin (Ed.), *The Zionist Movement in Palestine and World Politics,* pp. 76–77.
38. Stewart, *Theodor Herzl,* p. 304.
39. Weizmann, *Trial and Error,* p. 151.
40. Stein, *The Balfour Declaration,* p. 143.
41. Ibid., p. 149.
42. Ibid., p. 79.
43. Crossman, *A Nation Reborn,* p. 27.
44. Sokolow, *History of Zionism,* Vol. I, p. l.
45. Stein, *The Balfour Declaration,* p. 154.
46. Sokolow, *History of Zionism,* Vol. I, p. liv.
47. Ibid., p. li.
48. Stein, *The Balfour Declaration,* p. 164.
49. *Spectator,* February 24, 1961; cited in Matovu, "Zionist and Anti-

Semite: 'Of Course,' " *Issues,* Vol. XX (Spring 1966), p. 26.
50. Crossman, *A Nation Reborn,* p. 17.
51. Ibid., p. 21.
52. Ibid., p. 41.
53. Garry Wills, "A New Way to Perceive the State of Israel: A Holy War Continued," *Esquire,* July 1975, p. 75.
54. Ibid., p. 128.
55. Elon, *The Israelis,* p. 236.
56. Menachem Begin, *The Revolt,* pp. i, 26.
57. Weizmann at a banquet in 1927; cited in Hertzberg, *The Zionist Idea,* p. 579.
58. Basheer, *Edwin Montagu and the Balfour Declaration,* p. 13.
59. Cited in Stevens, "Smuts and Weizmann: A Study in South African-Zionist Cooperation," in Abu-Lughod and Abu-Laban, *Settler Regimes,* p. 183.
60. Weizmann, *Trial and Error,* p. 179.
61. Ibid., p. 205.
62. Cited in Crossman, *A Nation Reborn,* p. 131.
63. Stewart, *Theodor Herzl,* p. 192.
64. "Herzl and England," *Herzl Year Book,* Vol. III, p. 45.
65. Patai, *Diaries,* Vol. III, p. 1179.
66. Ibid., p. 1194.
67 Ibid.
68 Ibid., Vol. I, p. 91.
69. El-Kodsy and Lobel, *The Arab World and Israel,* p. 116.
70. Ibid.
71. Patai, *Diaries,* Vol. I, p. 333.
72. *The Jewish State,* in Hertzberg, *The Zionist Idea,* p. 222.
73. Patai, *Diaries,* Vol. II, p. 501.
74. Ibid., Vol. IV, p. 1600.
75. Goldmann, *The Autobiography of Nahum Goldmann,* pp. 160–163; and Weizmann, *Trial and Error,* pp. 368–372.
76. Patai, *Diaries,* Vol. I, p. 363.
77. Moshe Pearlman, "Chapters of Arab-Jewish Diplomacy, 1918–1922," *Jewish Social Studies,* Vol. VI (April 1944), p. 128.
78. Karl A. Schleunes, *The Twisted Road to Auschwitz,* pp. 182–184.
79. Letter to the founding conference of the English Zionist Federation, dated February 28, 1898, cited in Rabinowicz, "Herzl and England," *Herzl Year Book,* Vol. III, p. 38.
80. A speech in London in 1899, cited in Rabinowicz, pp. 42–43.
81. Patai, *Diaries,* Vol. IV, p. 1309.
82. Ibid., p. 1366.
83. Address at the Albert Hall, London, July 16, 1920, *Max Nordau*

to His People, p. 209.
84.   Crossman, *A Nation Reborn,* p. 36.
85.   Weizmann, *Trial and Error,* p. 192.
86.   Crossman, *A Nation Reborn,* p. 125.
87.   Ben-Herman, "Zionism and the Lion," in Hal Draper (Ed.), *Zionism, Israel and the Arabs,* p. 27.
88.   Selzer, *Zionism Reconsidered,* p. 247.
89.   Sokolow, *History of Zionism,* Vol. II, p. 221.
90.   Ibid., p. 222. Emphasis in the original.
91.   Stein, *The Balfour Declaration,* p. 12.
92.   Patai, *Diaries,* Vol. IV, p. 1600. Emphasis added.
93.   Ibid., p. 1367. Emphasis added.
94.   Address at the Albert Hall, London, July 16, 1920, *Max Nordau to His People,* p. 208.
95.   Ben-Horin, *Max Nordau,* p. 201.
96.   Cited in Ben-Herman, in Draper, *Zionism, Israel and the Arabs,* p. 27.
97.   Cited in Crossman, *A Nation Reborn,* pp. 131–132.
98.   Arie Bober (Ed.), *The Other Israel,* p. 193.
99.   Crossman, *A Nation Reborn,* p. 132. Emphasis added.
100. Ibid., p. 131.
101. Ibid.
102. Stevens, "Smuts and Weizmann," in Abu-Lughod and Abu-Laban, *Settler Regimes,* p. 175.
103. Kautsky, *Are the Jews a Race?,* p. 212.
104. Patai, *Diaries,* Vol. III, p. 899.
105. Weizmann, *Trial and Error,* p. 191.
106. Ben-Herman, in Draper, *Zionism, Israel and the Arabs,* pp. 31, 27.
107. Michael Bar-Zohar, *Ben Gurion, The Armed Prophet,* p. 39.
108. Ibid., p. 56.
109. El-Kosdy and Lobel, *The Arab World and Israel,* p. 68.
110. Joseph B. Schechtman, *Fighter and Prophet,* p. 297.
111. Bar-Zohar, *Ben Gurion,* p. 89.
112. Cited in Menuhin, *Jewish Critics,* p. 9.
113. Patai, *Diaries,* Vol. I, p. 342.
114. Ibid., Vol. II, p. 711.
115. Ibid., pp. 701–702.
116. Cited in Sami Hadawi, *Palestine in the United Nations,* p. 36.
117. Reported in *Maariv,* July 7, 1968; cited by Machover, "Reply to Sol Stern," *Israca* January 5, 1973, p. 28.
118. Noam Chomsky, *Peace in the Middle East?,* p. 28.
119. Emmanuel Rackman, *Israel's Emerging Constitution,* p. 148.
120. "Between Gaza and Tel Aviv, De Facto, We Already Live in a

Bi-national State," in Smith, *Zionism, The Dream and the Reality,* p. 189.

CHAPTER 6   (Pages 109–126)

1. Stevens, "Settler States and Western Response," in Jabara and Terry, *The Arab World,* pp. 167–168.
2. Crossman, *A Nation Reborn,* p. 58.
3. Stewart, *Theodor Herzl,* p. 192.
4. *Trial of the Major War Criminals Before the International Military Tribunal: Nuremberg, 14 November 1945–1 October 1946* (Nuremberg, Germany: 1947), Vol. XI, p. 450. (Official text in the English Language, Proceedings April 8, 1946–April 17, 1946.)
5. "Race Relations," *International Encyclopedia of the Social Sciences,* Vol. XIII.
6. *New Encyclopedia Britannica,* Vol. XV.
7. Ruppin, *The Jews of Today,* pp. 213–214.
8. Ibid., p. 227.
9. Ibid., p. 296.
10. Ibid., pp. 293–294.
11. Ibid., p. 217.
12. Ibid., p. 294.
13. Ibid.
14. Ibid.
15. Patai, *Diaries,* Vol. IV, p. 1361. Emphasis added.
16. Address to the Sixth Zionist Congress (1903), cited by Jabbour, *Settler Colonialism in Southern Africa and the Middle East,* p. 28.
17. "Interracial Relations," *Encyclopedia Britannica,* Vol. XII.
18. Patai, *Diaries,* Vol. I, pp. 343, 338.
19. Hertzberg, *The Zionist Idea,* p. 222.
20. Ben Gurion, *Rebirth and Destiny of Israel,* p. 9.
21. Ibid., pp. 5–6.
22. Agus, *The Meaning of Jewish History,* Vol. II, p. 386.
23. Weizmann, *Trial and Error,* p. 277.
24. Ibid., *passim.* See especially Chapter 31.
25. Harry S. Truman, *Memoirs,* Vol. II, p. 159.
26. Stein, *The Balfour Declaration,* p. 649.
27. Ibid.
28. Selzer, *The Aryanization of the Jewish State,* p. 50.
29. Ibid., p. 66.
30. Ibid., p. 69.
31. Ben Gurion, *Rebirth and Destiny of Israel,* p. 489.

32. Selzer, *The Aryanization of the Jewish State*, p. 70.
33. Sigal, "Reflections on Jewish Nationalism," *Issues*, Vol. XV (Fall 1961), p. 21.
34. *Third World Reports*, Vol. V, No. 7 (September 1974).
35. Selzer, *The Aryanization of the Jewish State*, p. 65.
36. Ibid., p. 67. Emphasis in the original.
37. Eban, *Voice of Israel*, p. 76.
38. Ibid.
39. Ibid.
40. Spiro, *Kibbutz*, pp. 108–109.
41. "The Sabra and Zionism," *Social Problems*, Vol. V (May 1957); cited in Selzer, *The Aryanization of the Jewish State*, p. 78.
42. Elon, *The Israelis*, pp. 316, 307.
43. "The Origin and Development of the Israeli-Black Panther Movement," interviews with Shalom Cohen in April 1976, *Merip Report*, No. 49 (July 1976), p. 20.
44. *Maariv*, March 19, 1971.
45. "The Origin and Development of the Israeli-Black Panther Movement," *Merip Report*, No. 49 (July 1976), p. 20.
46. Selzer, *The Aryanization of the Jewish State*, p. 55.
47. Ibid., p. 68.
48. Ibid.
49. Ibid., pp. 75–76.
50. Ibid., p. 78.
51. Ibid., p. 71.
52. Kallen, *Utopians at Bay*, p. 87.
53. *Merip Report*, No. 49 (July 1976), p. 20.
54. Selzer, *The Aryanization of the Jewish State*, p. 91.
55. *Swasia*, June 4, 1976.
56. Jewish Telegraphic Agency, *Daily News Bulletin*, June 8, 1976.
57. *Le Monde*, March 28, 1975, cited in "News Out of Israel," *Middle East International*, May 1975, p. 22.
58. Written in 1937; cited in Ben-Horin, *Max Nordau*, p. 199.
59. Elon, *The Israelis*, p. 115. Emphasis added.
60. Ibid., p. 156.
61. Ben Gurion, *Rebirth and Destiny of Israel*, p. 38.
62. *Hayom*, June 7, 1968; cited in Haddad, in Abu-Lughod and Abu-Laban, *Settler Regimes*, p. 11.
63. "A New Way to Perceive the State of Israel," *Esquire*, July 1975, p. 120.
64. Cited in Stein, *The Balfour Declaration*, p. 650.
65. Even though this statement is always attributed to Israel Zangwill (see his article "The Return to Palestine," *New Liberal Review*,

Vol. II [December 1901, p. 627] he is not by any means the origina-
tor. The slogan was freely bandied around among Zionists at the
beginning of the century.

66.   *Yediot Aharonot*, October 17, 1969; cited in Bober, *The Other
        Israel*, pp. 77–78.
67.   "Apartheid," *Encyclopedia Britannica*, Vol. II.
68.   Rabinowicz, "Herzl and England," *Herzl Year Book*, Vol. III, p. 41.
69.   Kurt Grassmann, "Zionists and Non-Zionists Under Nazi Rule in
        the 1930's," *Herzl Year Book*, Vol. IV, p. 341. Emphasis added.
70.   Arendt, *Eichmann in Jerusalem*, p. 54. Emphasis added.
71.   *Contemporary Links Between South Africa and Israel*, cited in
        Al-Abid, *127 Questions and Answers*, p. 136.
72.   *Israel and Southern Africa: A Comparison of the Roles of South
        Africa and Israel in the Third World* (Madison Area Committee
        on Southern Africa, n.d.), pp. 13–14.
73.   Hertzberg, *The Zionist Idea*, p. 465.
74.   Ibid.
75.   Elon, *The Israelis*, p. 112.
76.   Ben Gurion, *Rebirth and Destiny of Israel*, p. 5.
77.   Ibid.
78.   Smith, *Zionism, The Dream and the Reality*, p. 189.
79.   Ben Ezer, *Unease in Zion*, p. 83.
80.   Laqueur, *A History of Zionism*, p. 213.
81.   Polk et al., *Backdrop to Tragedy*, pp. 51–52.
82.   H. D. Schmidt, "The Nazi Party in Palestine and the Levant
        1932-9," *International Affairs*, Vol. XXVIII (October 1952),
        pp. 461–462.
83.   Laqueur, *A History of Zionism*, p. 221.
84.   Crossman, *A Nation Reborn*, p. 58.

CHAPTER 7   (Pages 127–146)

1.   Elon, *The Israelis*, p. 161.
2.   Ibid., p. 160.
3.   Laqueur, *A History of Zionism*, p. 220.
4.   Elon, *The Israelis*, p. 111.
5.   Ibid., p. 171.
6.   Laqueur, *A History of Zionism*, p. 214.
7.   Ben Ezer, *Unease in Zion*, pp. 82–83.
8.   Marmorstein, *Heaven at Bay*, p. 80.
9.   Ibid.
10.   Ben Ezer, *Unease in Zion*, p. 183.

11. Ibid., p. 54.
12. Patai, *Diaries,* Vol. I, see entry dated June 12, 1893, pp. 88–90, and again on the same day, p. 98.
13. Ibid., Vol. IV, p. 1362.
14. Ibid., Vol. II, p. 702.
15. Ibid., Vol. IV, p. 1361.
16. Childers, "The Wordless Wish: From Citizens to Refugees," in Ibrahim Abu-Lughod (Ed.), *The Transformation of Palestine,* p. 171.
17. Ibid., p. 172.
18. Ibid.
19. Ibid., pp. 175–176.
20. Ibid., p. 176, n. 39.
21. Ibid., p. 175.
22. Machover, "Reply to Sol Stern," *Israca,* January 5, 1973, p. 27. Emphasis added.
23. Elon, *The Israelis,* p. 178.
24. Tony Thomas, "Roots of the Middle East Conflict," in Dave Frankel et al., *War in the Middle East,* p. 10.
25. Machover, "Reply to Sol Stern," *Israca,* January 5, 1973, p. 27.
26. Stevens, in Jabara and Terry, *The Arab World Today,* p. 170.
27. Cited in Al-Abid, *A Handbook to the Palestine Question,* p. 22.
28. Machover, "Reply to Sol Stern," *Israca,* January 5, 1973, pp. 27–28.
29. Rodinson, *Israel: A Colonial-Settler State?,* p. 16.
30. Laqueur, *A History of Zionism,* p. 231.
31. Selzer, *Zionism Reconsidered,* p. 219.
32. United States, *Foreign Relations of the U.S.: Near East and Africa,* Vol. IV, pp. 776-777; cited by Al-Abid, *A Handbook to the Palestine Question,* p. 81.
33. Schechtman, *Fighter and Prophet,* p. 34.
34. Ibid., p. 325.
35. El-Kodsy and Lobel, *The Arab World and Israel,* p. 119.
36. Menuhin, *The Decadence of Judaism in Our Time,* p. 63.
37. Kohn, in Smith, *Zionism, The Dream and the Reality,* p. 35.
38. Basheer, *Edwin Montagu and the Balfour Declaration,* p. 8.
39. Cited in Al-Abid, *A Handbook to the Palestine Question,* p. 22.
40. Laqueur, *A History of Zionism,* p. 232.
41. El-Kodsy and Lobel, *The Arab World and Israel,* pp. 120-121.
42. Pearlman, "Chapters of Arab-Jewish Diplomacy, 1918-1922," *Jewish Social Studies,* Vol. VI (April 1944), pp. 123-124.
43. Laqueur, *A History of Zionism,* pp. 215-216.
44. Pearlman, "Chapters of Arab-Jewish Diplomacy, 1918-1922," *Jewish Social Studies,* Vol. VI (April 1944), p. 124.

45.   Laqueur, *A History of Zionism*, p. 251.
46.   "Brit Shalom," *Encyclopedia of Zionism and Israel*, Vol. I.
47.   Chomsky, *Peace in the Middle East?*, p. 13.
48.   Elon, *The Israelis*, p. 175.
49.   El-Kodsy and Lobel, *The Arab World and Israel*, p. 120.
50.   Cited in Kohn, in Menuhin, *The Decadence of Judaism in Our Time*, p. 65.
51.   See the poem titled "On Guard," cited in Abdelwahab Elmessiri, *Judaism, Zionism and Israel* (in Arabic), p. 199.
52.   Cited in Kohn, in *Living in a World Revolution*, p. 64.
53.   Walid Khalidi, *Why Did the Palestinians Leave?*, p. 1.
54.   Childers, "The Other Exodus," *Spectator*, May 12, 1961.
55.   Khalidi, *Why Did the Palestinians Leave?*, p. 2.
56.   Ibid., p. 3.
57.   Childers, "The Other Exodus," *Spectator*, May 12, 1961.
58.   Khalidi, *Why Did the Palestinians Leave?*, p. 6.
59.   Childers, "The Other Exodus," *Spectator*, May 12, 1961.
60.   John H. Davis, *The Evasive Peace*, pp. 56–57.
61.   Childers, in Abu-Lughod, *The Transformation of Palestine*, p. 196.
62.   Childers, "The Other Exodus," *Spectator*, May 12, 1961.
63.   Childers, in Abu-Lughod, *The Transformation of Palestine*, p. 197.
64.   Elon, *The Israelis*, p. 161.
65.   Tendulkar, *Mahatma*, Vol. IV, p. 207.
66.   Ibid., Vol. VII, pp. 158–159.
67.   Ibid., p. 390.
68.   Uri Avnery, *Israel Without Zionists*, pp. 196–197.
69.   Childers, in Abu-Lughod, *The Transformation of Palestine*, pp. 197–198.
70.   "The Bitter Truth About the Arab Refugees," *Jewish Newsletter*, February 9, 1959. Emphasis added.
71.   Childers, in Abu-Lughod, *The Transformation of Palestine*, p. 184. Emphasis added.
72.   Ibid., p. 185. Emphasis added.
73.   Ibid., p. 182, n. 60.
74.   Ibid.
75.   *Jerusalem Embattled*, cited in Al-Abid, *127 Questions and Answers*, p. 72.
76.   Cited in Al-Abid, *A Handbook to the Palestine Question*, p. 84.
77.   Childers, in Abu-Lughod, *The Transformation of Palestine*, p. 183.
78.   Ibid., p. 182, n. 60.
79.   Cited in Al-Abid, *127 Questions and Answers*, p. 72.
80.   Ibid.
81.   Ibid., p. 65.

82. Childers, in Abu-Lughod, *The Transformation of Palestine*, p. 182.
83. Begin, *The Revolt*, p. 162.
84. David Waines, *The Unholy War*, p. 107.
85. "Irgun Tz'vai L'umi (Etzel)," *Encyclopedia of Zionism and Israel*, Vol. I.
86. "The Arabs and Palestine" in Polk et al., *Backdrop to Tragedy*, p. 292.
87. "Irgun Tz'vai L'umi (Etzel)," *Encyclopedia of Zionism and Israel*, Vol. I.
88. Begin, *The Revolt*, pp. 162–163.
89. Crossman, *A Nation Reborn*, p. 76.
90. Al-Abid, *127 Questions and Answers*, p. 65.
91. Ibid.
92. Ibid.
93. Ibid., p. 65–66.
94. *New Star in the Middle East*, cited in Childers, in Abu-Lughod, *The Transformation of Palestine*, p. 194.
95. Kimche and Kimche, *Both Sides of the Hill;* cited in Childers, in Abu-Lughod, *The Transformation of Palestine*, p. 194.
96. Ibid.
97. Machover, "Reply to Sol Stern," *Israca*, January 5, 1973, p. 28.
98. "The Jews and Arabs," *Encyclopedia Britannica, Year Book 1959*. Cited in Al-Abid, *A Handbook to the Palestine Question*, p. 36.
99. Cited in Hadawi, *Bitter Harvest*, p. 189.
100. Cited in Al-Abid, *A Handbook to the Palestine Question*, p. 36.
101. Childers, in Abu-Lughod, *The Transformation of Palestine*, p. 195.
102. Ibid.
103. Cited in Fayez Sayegh, *The Record of Israel at the United Nations*, p. 16.
104. Ben Gurion, *Rebirth and Destiny of Israel*, p. 537.
105. Kallen, *Utopians at Bay*, pp. 121–122.
106. Cited in Frank C. Sakran, *Palestine Dilemma*, p. 204.
107. Ben Ezer, *Unease in Zion*, p. 56.

CHAPTER 8   (Pages 147–170)

1. Rackman, *Israel's Emerging Constitution*, p. 155.
2. Maxim Ghilan, *How Israel Lost Its Soul*, p. 178.
3. *Encyclopedia of Zionism and Israel*, Vol. I.
4. Hadawi, *Bitter Harvest*, p. 199.
5. Ibid.
6. Adnan Amad (Comp. and Ed.), *Israeli League for Human and*

Civil Rights (The Shahak Papers), p. 35. Hereafter referred to as *The Shahak Papers.*

7.   Chomsky, *Peace in the Middle East?,* pp. 127–128.

8.   *The Shahak Papers,* p. 35.

9.   Reprinted in *Free Palestine,* October 1975.

10. Yochanan Peres, "Ethnic Relations in Israel," *American Journal of Sociology,* Vol. LXXVI (May 1971), p. 1041.

11. "The Racist Nature of Zionism and of the Zionist State of Israel," in *American Jewish Alternatives to Zionism,* Report No. 25, December 1974/January 1975, p. 20.

12. Cited in *Free Palestine,* October 1975.

13. Cited in *Viewpoint,* July 26, 1973, p. 27.

14. Bober, *The Other Israel,* p. 134.

15. Sabri Jiryis, *The Arabs in Israel,* p. 21, n. 1.

16. *The Shahak Papers,* p. 32.

17. Cited in Hadawi, *Israel and the Arab Minority,* pp. 8–9.

18. *The Shahak Papers,* p. 32.

19. Ibid., p. 223.

20. Jiryis, *The Arabs in Israel,* p. 25.

21. Don Peretz, *Israel and the Palestine Arabs,* p. 96.

22. *The Shahak Papers,* p. 18.

23. Cited in Bober, *The Other Israel,* pp. 123–135.

24. Ibid., p. 140.

25. Cited in Al-Abid, *127 Questions and Answers,* p. 148.

26. *The Shahak Papers,* p. 57. Emphasis added.

27. Jiryis, *The Arabs in Israel,* p. 25.

28. Al-Abid, *127 Questions and Answers,* p. 148.

29. John Rudey, "Dynamics of Land Alienation," in Abu-Lughod, *The Transformation of Palestine,* p. 134.

30. Al-Abid, *127 Questions and Answers,* pp. 158–159.

31. Amnon Kapeliouk, "Less Land for More People," *Manchester Guardian,* June 20, 1976; reprinted in *Swasia,* July 2, 1976.

32. Al-Abid, *127 Questions and Answers,* pp. 158–159.

33. Cited in Jiryis, *The Arabs in Israel,* pp. 45–46.

34. Ibid., p. 46.

35. Kapeliouk, "Less Land for More People," *Swasia,* July 2, 1976.

36. Cited in Shahak, "The Racist Nature of Zionism . . . ," *American Jewish Alternatives to Zionism,* Report No. 25, December 1974/January 1975, p. 17.

37. Childers, in Abu-Lughod, *The Transformation of Palestine,* p. 169.

38. Cited in Al-Abid, *127 Questions and Answers,* p. 125.

39. Cited in Shahak, "The Racist Nature of Zionism . . . ," *American Jewish Alternatives to Zionism,* Report No. 25, December 1974/

January 1975, p. 15.

40. Ibid., p. 18. Emphasis in the original.
41. Ibid., p. 19.
42. Ibid., p. 18.
43. Al-Abid, *127 Questions and Answers*, p. 29.
44. Cited in *The Shahak Papers*, p. 226.
45. Ibid.
46. Cited in Shahak, "The Racist Nature of Zionism . . . ," *American Jewish Alternatives to Zionism,* Report No. 25, December 1974/ January 1975, p. 19.
47. Esco Foundation of Palestine, *A Study of Jewish, Arab and British Policies,* Vol. II, pp. 609–612.
48. UN Document E/CN.4/1016/Add. 1, p. 20, February 11, 1970.
49. *The Shahak Papers*, p. 23.
50. Ibid., p. 24.
51. Ibid., p. 13.
52. Ibid., p. 50.
53. Shalumit Aloni, "Discrimination Against Arab Settlements," *Yediot Aharonot,* October 10, 1975; reprinted in *Swasia,* November 14, 1975.
54. Shahak, "The Racist Nature of Zionism . . . ," *American Jewish Alternatives to Zionism,* Report No. 25, December 1974/January 1975, p. 21.
55. Aloni, *Swasia,* November 14, 1975.
56. Ibid.
57. Waines, *The Unholy War,* p. 79.
58. Norton Mesvinsky, "The Zionist Character of the State of Israel," in Smith, *Zionism, The Dream and the Reality,* p. 252.
59. Jiryis, *The Arabs in Israel,* p. 155.
60. *The Shahak Papers*, p. 82.
61. Shahak, "Israeli Statistics," *Israel and Palestine,* September/ October 1975, p. 6.
62. Machover, "A Reply to Sol Stern," *Israca,* January 5, 1973, p. 28.
63. Cited in Menuhin, *The Decadence of Judaism in Our Time,* p. 63.
64. From a press release issued by Israel Shahak, published in *Viewpoint,* May 1973, pp. 17–18.
65. Companion to the history of the State of Israel, titled *Israel's Independence,* cited in Al-Abid, *127 Questions and Answers,* pp. 118–119.
66. *Haaretz,* September 9, 1974; reprinted in *Swasia,* October 18, 1974.
67. Shahak, "Israeli Statistics," *Israel and Palestine,* September/ October 1975.

68.   Statement carried by several Israeli newspapers cited in op. cit.
69.   Cited in Bober, *The Other Israel,* pp. 164–165.
70.   *Al-Hamishmar,* September 7, 1976, reprinted in *Swasia,* October 15, 1976. The first part of the memorandum is dated March 1, 1976.
71.   *The Shahak Papers,* p. 232.
72.   *Israel and Palestine,* September/October 1975, p. III.
73.   Shahak, "Israeli Statistics," ibid, p. 6.
74.   All data from Mahmud Darwish, "Kafr Biram and Ikrit," *Shu'un Falstiniya,* September 1972.
75.   *Maariv,* May 3, 1974, cited in *Viewpoint,* July 1974, p. 5.
76.   "Race," *Webster's New International Dictionary of the English Language.*
77.   *Encyclopedia Britannica,* Vol. XII, Emphasis added.
78.   *The New Encyclopedia Britannica,* Vol. XV. Emphasis added.
79.   *Encyclopedia Britannica,* Vol. XII. Emphasis added.
80.   Edward R. Tannenbaum, *The Fascist Experience,* p. 78.
81.   *South African Observer,* December 1975.
82.   Rodinson, "A Humanistic Perspective," in Jabara and Terry, *The Arab World,* p. 179.
83.   Tannenbaum, *The Fascist Experience,* p. 78.
84.   "The UN Resolution on Zionism," *Bulletin of the American Professors for Peace in the Middle East,* December 1975, p. 5. Emphasis added.
85.   Ibid.
86.   Bar-Zohar, *Ben Gurion,* p. 103.
87.   Tannenbaum, *The Fascist Experience,* p. 78.
88.   The letter, dated November 14, 1975, published in *The New York Times* on November 23, 1975.
89.   Chomsky, *Peace in the Middle East?, p. 127.*

CHAPTER 9   (Pages 171–186)

1.   Crossman, *A Nation Reborn,* p. 58.
2.   Elon, *The Israelis,* p. 151.
3.   Kautsky, *Are the Jews a Race?,* p. 209.
4.   Stevens, "Zionism as a Phase of Western Imperialism," in Abu-Lughod, *The Transformation of Palestine,* p. 52.
5.   Stevens, in Jabara and Terry, *The Arab World,* p. 174.
6.   Patai, *Diaries,* Vol. I, p. 28.
7.   Elon, *The Israelis,* p. 174.
8.   Ben-Herman, in Draper, *Zionism, Israel and the Arabs,* p. 31.
9.   Hertzberg, *The Zionist Idea,* p. 565.

10.   "Begin, M'nahem," *Encyclopedia of Zionism and Israel, Vol I.*
11.   Crossman, *A Nation Reborn,* p. 131.
12.   Ibid., p. 127.
13.   Laqueur, *A History of Zionism,* p. 219.
14.   "Irgun Tz'vai L'umi (Etzel)," *Encyclopedia of Zionism and Israel,* Vol. I.
15.   Ibid.
16.   Ben Ezer, *Unease in Zion,* p. 202.
17.   Schechtman, *Fighter and Prophet . . . The Last Years,* p. 234.
18.   Laqueur, *A History of Zionism,* p. 384.
19.   Numbers 32:32, in Elon, *The Israelis,* p. 112. Emphasis added.
20.   Ibid., p. 172.
21.   Laqueur, *A History of Zionism,* p. 216.
22.   Ben Ezer, *Unease in Zion,* p. 183.
23.   Ibid., p. 245.
24.   Ibid., pp. 324–325.
25.   Cited in George Antonius, *The Arab Awakening,* p. 441.
26.   Pearlman, "Chapters of Arab-Jewish Diplomacy, 1918–1922," *Jewish Social Studies,* Vol. VI (April 1944), p. 127.
27.   Interview in the *Jewish Chronicle,* October 3, 1939; cited in Pearlman, ibid, p. 144.
28.   Ibid., pp. 148–149.
29.   Ibid., p. 138.
30.   Antonius, *The Arab Awakening,* p. 285.
31.   Pearlman, "Chapters of Arab-Jewish Diplomacy, 1918–1922," *Jewish Social Studies,* Vol. VI (April 1944), p. 143.
32.   Ben Ezer, *Unease in Zion,* p. 302.
33.   *Le Monde,* weekly selection, July 9–16, 1969; cited in Chomsky, *Peace in the Middle East?,* pp. 53–54.
34.   Cited in J. Artusky, "The Tragedy of Israeli Chauvinism," in Draper, *Zionism, Israel and the Arabs,* p. 191.
35.   Cited in Al-Abid, *127 Questions and Answers,* p. 130.
36.   Israel's voting pattern in the Thirtieth and Thirty-First United Nations General Assemblies was brought to my attention by Mahmoud Farghal, director of the United Nations Division at the Arab League Office in New York.
37.   Richard Stevens and Abdelwahab Elmessiri, *Israel and South Africa.*
38.   Tendulkar, *Mahatma,* Vol. IV, p. 207.
39.   Ibid., p. 276.
40.   Ibid., p. 314.
41.   Ibid., p. 312.
42.   Samuelson, *Israel and the Palestinians,* p. 20.

43. Cited in Morroe Berger, *The Arab World Today*, p. 51.
44. Cited in Agwani, "The Palestine Conflict in Asian Perspective," in Abu-Loghod, *The Transformation of Palestine*, p. 455.
45. Resolution of the All-India Congress Committee, ibid., p. 449.
46. Henry Feingold, *The Politics of Rescue*, p. 217.
47. Fayez Sayegh, *Twenty Basic Facts About Israel*.
48. Cited in Agwani in Abu-Lughod, *The Transformation of Palestine*, p. 453.
49. Sayegh, *Twenty Basic Facts About Israel*.
50. Cited in Agwani, in Abu-Lughod, *The Transformation of Palestine*, p. 455.
51. "Why Israel Needs the 500 Million Dollars Ford Does Not Want to Give," *Interchange*, June 1976, p. 6.
52. Ben Ezer, *Unease in Zion*, p. 181.
53. "Vorster: Man on a Wagon Train," *Time*, June 28, 1976.
54. Kautsky, *Are the Jews a Race?*, p. 211.
55. Patai, *Diaries*, Vol. IV, p. 1449.
56. Ibid. Emphasis added.
57. Cited in Abdelwahab M. Elmessiri, "Theodor Herzl: Between the Secular Allegations and the Ghetto Mentality," in *Judaism, Zionism and Israel*.

CHAPTER 10 (Pages 187–210)

1. Cited in Elmer Berger, in Jabara and Terry, *The Arab World*, p. 146.
2. *Viewpoint*, March 1974, pp. 48–49.
3. Kallen, *Utopians at Bay*, p. 278.
4. Ibid., p. 213.
5. Ibid., p. 214.
6. Cited in *Viewpoint*, March 1974, pp. 47–48.
7. Cited in *Brief*, Spring/Summer 1975.
8. *The Guardian*, May 14, 1976.
9. Ben Ezer, *Unease in Zion*, pp. 313–314.
10. Muenzer, "Labor Enterprise in Israel," cited in Al-Abid, *A Handbook to the Palestine Question*, p. 46.
11. Bober, *The Other Israel*, p. 109.
12. The Shinui Report, cited in *The New York Times*, June 21, 1975.
13. Bober, *The Other Israel*, pp. 163–164.
14. Elon, *The Israelis*, pp. 292–293.
15. *Viewpoint*, July 1974, p. 32.
16. Ibid.

17. *Interchange,* January 1976, p. 5.
18. Ben Ezer, *Unease in Zion,* p. 202.
19. Talmon, *New Outlook,* June–July 1969, cited in Al-Abid, *127 Questions and Answers,* p. 115.
20. Elon, *The Israelis,* pp. 230–231.
21. Ben Ezer, *Unease in Zion,* p. 199.
22. Elon, *The Israelis,* pp. 230–231.
23. *Davar,* May 2, 1956.
24. Al-Bahrawi, *Modern Israeli Literature.*
25. Ben Ezer, *Unease in Zion,* p. 316.
26. Elon, *The Israelis,* p. 248.
27. Cited in *Viewpoint,* July 1973, p. 23.
28. Ben Ezer, *Unease in Zion,* p. 332.
29. Elon, *The Israelis,* p. 261.
30. Ben Ezer, *Unease in Zion,* p. 302.
31. Elon, *The Israelis,* pp. 263–264.
32. Menuhin, *Jewish Critics,* p. 36.
33. Elon, *The Israelis,* p. 268.
34. Ben Ezer, *Unease in Zion,* p. 133.
35. Elon, *The Israelis,* pp. 268–271.
36. Ibid., pp. 272–273.
37. Ibid., pp. 275–276.
38. Ibid., p. 278.
39. Ibid., pp. 276–277.
40. Ibid., p. 179.
41. Ibid., p. 180.
42. Ben Ezer, *Unease in Zion,* p. 58.
43. Ibid., p. 211.
44. Ibid., p. 159–160.
45. Ibid., p. 162.
46. Tendulkar, *Mahatma,* Vol. IV, p. 312.
47. Ben Ezer, *Unease in Zion,* p. 327.
48. Ibid., pp. 321–322.
49. Ibid., p. 155.
50. Excerpt in Smith, *Zionism, The Dream and the Reality,* p. 140.
51. Ibid., p. 192.

BIBLIOGRAPHY

Note: Although this bibliography includes very few references to Arab sources, I am deeply indebted to the writings of many Arab authors, particularly Dr. Fayez Sayegh, the Palestinian author and Counselor of the Permanent Mission of Kuwait to the United Nations, and Mr. Ahmed Bahaa El-Din, the Egyptian author and editor-in-chief of the Kuwaiti monthly, *Al-Arabi.* As I indicated in the Preface, I have confined myself, as much as possible, to sources written in English, since this study is addressed to an English-speaking audience.

BOOKS

Abu-Lughod, Ibrahim (Ed.). *The Transformation of Palestine: Essays on the Origin and Developments of the Arab-Israeli Conflict.* Evanston, Ill.: Northwestern University Press, 1971.

Abu-Lughod, Ibrahim, and Abu-Laban, Bahaa (Eds.). *Settler Regimes in Africa and the Arab World: The Illusion of Endurance.* Wilmette, Ill.: Medina University Press, 1974.

Agus, Jacob Bernard. *The Meaning of Jewish History* (2 vols.). London: Abelard-Schuman, 1963.

Al-Abid, Ibrahim. *A Handbook to the Palestine Question: Questions and Answers.* Beirut: Palestine Liberation Organization Research Center, 1969.

———. *127 Questions and Answers on the Arab-Israeli Conflict.* Beirut: Palestine Research Center, 1973.

Al-Bahrawi, Ibrahim. *Modern Israeli Literature.* Cairo: Dar el Helal, 1972. In Arabic.

Amad, Adnan (Comp. and Ed.). *Israeli League for Human and Civil Rights (The Shahak Papers)*. Beirut: Palestine Research Center, 1973.

Antonius, George. *The Arab Awakening: The Story of the Arab National Movement*. New York: Capricorn Books, 1946, 1965.

Arendt, Hannah, *Eichmann in Jerusalem: A Report on the Banality of Evil*. New York: The Viking Press, 1963.

Avnery, Uri. *Israel Without Zionists: A Plea for Peace in the Middle East*. New York: The Macmillan Company, 1970.

Bar-Zohar, Michael. *Ben Gurion, The Armed Prophet*. Englewood Cliffs, N.J.: Prentice Hall, 1967. Trans. Len Ortzen.

Basheer, Tahseen (Ed.). *Edwin Montagu and the Balfour Declaration*. New York: Arab League Office (n.d.).

Begin, Menachem. *The Revolt,* with a Foreword by Rabbi Meir Kahane. Los Angeles: Nash Publishing, 1972.

Ben Ezer, Ehud (Ed.). *Unease in Zion,* with a Foreword by Robert Alter. New York: Quadrangle/The New York Times Book Co., 1974.

Ben Gurion, David. *Rebirth and Destiny of Israel*. New York: Philosophical Library, 1954.

Ben-Horin, Meir. *Max Nordau: Philosopher of Human Solidarity*. New York: Conference of Jewish Social Studies, 1956.

Bentwitch, Norman. *For Zion's Sake: A Biography of Judah L. Magnes*. Philadelphia: Jewish Publication Society, 1954.

Ben-Yona, Amitay. *What Does Israel Do to Its Palestinians? A Letter from Israel to Jews of the American Left*. Arab American University Graduates Information Paper Number Two (September 1970).

Berger, Elmer. *Prophecy, Zionism and the State of Israel*. New York: American Jewish Alternatives to Zionism (n.d.).

———.*Who Knows Better Must Say So!* New York: The Bookmailer, 1955.

Berger, Morroe. *The Arab World Today*. Garden City, N.Y.: Doubleday, 1962.

Bober, Arie (Ed.). *The Other Israel: The Radical Case Against Zionism*. Garden City, N.Y.: Doubleday, 1972.

Brandeis, Louis, *A Collection of Addresses and Statements by Louis Brandeis,* with a Foreword by Mr. Justice Felix Frankfurter. Washington, D.C.: Zionist Organization of America, 1942.

Chomsky, Noam. *Peace in the Middle East? Reflections on Justice and Nationhood*. New York: Vintage Books, 1969.

Clark, Ronald W. *Einstein: The Life and Times*. New York: The World Publishing Company, 1971.

Crossman, Richard. *A Nation Reborn: The Israel of Weizmann, Bevin and Ben Gurion*. London: Hamish Hamilton, 1960.

Davis, John H. *The Evasive Peace: A Study of the Zionist Arab Problem*.

London: John Murray, 1968.

Domb, I. *The Transformation: The Case of the Neturei Karta.* London: Hamadfis, 1958.

Draper, Hal (Ed.). *Zionism, Israel and the Arabs.* Berkeley, Calif.: Independent Socialist Clippingbooks, 1967.

Eban, Abba. *Voice of Israel.* New York: Horizon Press, 1957.

Einstein, Albert. *Out of My Later Years.* New York: Philosophical Library, 1950.

El-Kodsy, Ahmed, and Lobel, Eli. *The Arab World and Israel.* New York: Monthly Review Press, 1970.

Elmessiri, Abdelwahab M. *Encyclopedia of Zionist Concepts and Terminology: A Critical View.* Cairo: Center for Political and Strategic Studies, Al-Ahram, 1975. (In Arabic.)

——. *Judaism, Zionism and Israel.* Beirut: Arab Publishing House, 1975. (In Arabic.)

Elon, Amos. *The Israelis: Founders and Sons.* New York: Holt, Rinehart and Winston, 1971.

Esco Foundation of Palestine. *A Study of Jewish, Arab and British Politics.* New Haven: Yale University Press, 1947.

Feingold, Henry. *The Politics of Rescue: The Roosevelt Administration and the Holocaust, 1938–1945.* New Brunswick, N.J.: Rutgers University Press, 1970.

Flender, Harold. *The Kids Who Went to Israel: Autobiographical Sketches of Young Immigrants.* New York: Simon and Schuster Pocket Books, 1973.

Frankel, Dave, et al. *War in the Middle East: The Socialist View.* New York: Pathfinder Press, 1973.

Ghilan, Maxim. *How Israel Lost Its Soul.* Middlesex, England: Penguin Books, 1974.

Goldmann, Nahum. *The Autobiography of Nahum Goldmann: Sixty Years of Jewish Life.* New York: Holt, Rinehart and Winston, 1969. Trans. Helen Sebba.

Hadawi, Sami. *Bitter Harvest: Palestine Between 1914–1967.* New York: The New World Press, 1967.

——. *Israel and the Arab Minority.* New York: Arab Information Center, 1967.

——. *Palestine in the United Nations.* New York: Arab Information Center, 1964.

Hadawi, Sami and John, Robert. *The Palestine Diary.* Beirut: Palestine Research Center, 1970.

Hertzberg, Arthur (Ed.) *The Zionist Idea: A Historical Analysis and Reader.* Westport, Conn.: Greenwood, 1959.

Jabara, Abdeen, and Terry, Janice (Eds.). *The Arab World: From Nationalism to Revolution.* Wilmette, Ill.: Medina University Press, 1971.

Jabbour, George. *Settler Colonialism in Southern Africa and the Middle
East.* Beirut: Palestine Liberation Organization Research Center,
1970.

Jack, Homer A. "Is Zionism Racism? The 1975 Debate in the United
Nations," WCRP (unpublished) Report. New York: World Conference on Religion and Peace (n.d.).

Jewish Liberation Project and Committee to Support Middle East Liberation. *Arab-Israeli Debate: Toward a Socialist Solution.* New York:
Times Change Press, 1970.

Jiryis, Sabri. *The Arabs in Israel.* Beirut: The Institute for Palestine
Studies, 1969.

Kallen, Horace M. *Utopians at Bay.* New York: Theodor Herzl Foundation, 1958.

Kaplan, Chaim A. *The Scrolls of Agony: The Warsaw Diary of Chaim A.
Kaplan.* New York: The Macmillan Company, 1965.

Kautsky, Karl. *Are the Jews a Race?* New York: International Publishers,
1926. (Translated from the second German edition.)

Khalidi, Walid. *From Haven to Conquest.* Beirut: Institute for Palestine
Studies, 1971.

———. *Why Did the Palestinians Leave? An Examination of the Zionist
Version of the Exodus of 1948.* New York: Arab Information Center
(n.d.).

Kimche, Jon, and Kimche, David. *The Secret Roads: The "Illegal" Migration of a People, 1938-1948.* London: Secker and Warburg, 1954.

King, Simcha. *Nachum Sokolow: Servant of His People.* New York:
Herzl Press, 1960.

Kohn, Hans. *Living in a World Revolution: My Encounter with History.*
New York: Trident Press, 1964.

Laqueur, Walter. *A History of Zionism.* New York: Holt, Rinehart and
Winston, 1972.

Levin, Gordon. *The Zionist Movement in Palestine and World Politics,
1880-1918.* Lexington, Mass.: Heath, 1974.

Lilienthal, Alfred. *The Other Side of the Coin: An American Perspective
of the Arab-Israeli Conflict.* New York: Devin-Adair, 1965.

———. *There Goes the Middle East.* New York: Devin-Adair, 1957.

———. *What Price Israel?* Chicago: Henry Regnery, 1953.

Madison Area Committee on Southern Africa. *Israel and Southern Africa:
A Comparison of the Roles of South Africa and Israel in the Third
World.* Madison, Wis.: Madison Area Committee on Southern Africa
(n.d.).

Mallison, W. T., Jr., and Mallison, S. V. *An International Law Appraisal of the Juridical Characteristics of the Resistance of the People of Palestine: The Struggle for Human Rights.* Beirut: Near East Ecumenical Bureau for Information and Interpretation, 1973.

Marmorstein, Emile. *Heaven at Bay: The Jewish Kulturkampf in the Holy Land.* London: Oxford University Press, 1969.

Menuhin, Moshe. *Jewish Critics of Zionism: A Testamentary Essay with "The Stifling and Smearing of a Dissenter."* New York: Arab Information Center (n.d.).

——. *The Decadence of Judaism in Our Time.* Beirut: Institute for Palestine Studies, 1969.

Nordau, Max. *Max Nordau to His People: A Summons and a Challenge* (Introduction by B. Netanyahu). New York: Scopus Publishing Society; 1941.

Patai, Raphael (Ed.). *The Complete Diaries of Theodor Herzl* (5 vols.). New York: Herzl Press and Thomas Yoseloff, 1960. Trans. Harry Zohn.

Pearlman, Moshe. *Ben Gurion Looks Back in Talks with Moshe Pearlman.* New York: Simon and Schuster, 1965.

Peretz, Don. *Israel and the Palestine Arabs.* Washington, D.C.: The Middle East Institute, 1958. With a Foreword by Roger Baldwin.

Polk, William, et al. *Backdrop to Tragedy: The Struggle for Palestine.* Boston: Beacon Press, 1957.

Prinz, Joachim. *The Dilemma of the Modern Jew.* Boston: Little, Brown, 1962.

Rackman, Emmanuel. *Israel's Emerging Constitution, 1948-1951.* New York: Columbia University Press, 1955.

Rodinson, Maxime. *Israel: A Colonial-Settler State?* New York: Monad Press, 1973.

Rose, N. A. *The Gentile Zionists: A Study in Anglo-Zionist Diplomacy, 1929-1939.* London: Frank Cass, 1973.

Ruppin, Arthur. *The Jews of Today.* London: G. Bell and Sons, 1913. Trans. Margery Bentwitch.

Sakran, Frank C. *Palestine Dilemma.* Washington D.C.: Public Affairs Press, 1948.

Samuelson, Arthur H. (Ed.). *Israel and the Palestinians: A Different Israeli View.* New York: Breira, 1975.

Sayegh, Fayez. "The Encounter of Two Ideologies," in *Collected Essays of Palestine.* Beirut: Arab Cultural Club, 1965.

——. *The Record of Israel at the United Nations.* New York: Arab Information Center, 1967.

——. *Twenty Basic Facts About Israel.* New York: Arab Information Center, 1960.

Schechtman, Joseph B. *Fighter and Prophet: The Vladimir Jabotinsky Story—The Last Years.* New York: Thomas Yoseloff, 1961.

Schleunes, Karl A. *The Twisted Road to Auschwitz: Nazi Policy Toward German Jews, 1933-1939.* Urbana, Ill.: University of Illinois Press, 1970.

Seidman, Peter. *Socialists and the Fight Against Anti-Semitism: An Answer to the B'nai B'rith Anti-Defamation League.* New York: Pathfinder Press, 1973.

Selzer, Michael. *The Aryanization of the Jewish State.* New York: Black Star, 1968.

—— (Ed.). *Zionism Reconsidered: The Rejection of Jewish Normalcy.* New York: The Macmillan Company, 1970.

Smith, Gary V. (Ed.). *Zionism, The Dream and the Reality: A Jewish Critique.* New York: Barnes and Noble, 1974.

Sokolow, Nahum. *History of Zionism, 1600-1918* (2 vols.). New York: KTAV Publishing House, 1969.

Spiro, E. Melford. *Kibbutz: Venture in Utopia.* Cambridge, Mass.: Harvard University Press, 1956.

Stein, Leonard. *The Balfour Declaration.* London: Vallentine, Mitchell, 1961.

Stevens, Richard, and Elmessiri, Abdelwahab M. *Israel and South Africa: The Progression of a Relationship.* Rev. Ed. New Jersey: North American, 1977.

Stewart, Desmond. *Theodor Herzl.* Garden City, N.Y.: Doubleday, 1974.

Sykes, Christopher. *Crossroads to Israel.* Cleveland: The World Publishing Company, 1965.

Tannenbaum, Edward R. *The Fascist Experience: Italian Society and Culture 1922-1945.* New York: Basic Books, 1972.

Tendulkar, D. G. *Mahatma: Life of Mohandas Karamchand Gandhi* (8 vols.). New Delhi: Patalia House, 1961.

Truman, Harry S. *Memoirs* (2 vols.). Garden City, N.Y.: Doubleday, 1955.

Waines, David. *The Unholy War: Israel and Palestine, 1897-1971.* Wilmette, Ill.: Medina University Press International, 1971.

Weizmann, Chaim. *Trial and Error: The Autobiography of Chaim Weizmann.* New York: Harper, 1949.

ENCYCLOPEDIAS AND DOCUMENTS

Encyclopedia Britannica (23 vols.). Chicago: Encyclopedia Britannica, Inc., 1968.

Encyclopedia Judaica (17 vols.). Cecil Roth (Ed.). New York: The Mac-
     millan Company, 1971.
Encyclopedia of Zionism and Israel (2 vols). Raphael Patai (Ed.). New
     York: Herzl Press and McGraw-Hill, 1971.
International Encyclopedia of the Social Sciences (17 vols.). David Sills
     (Ed.). New York: The Macmillan Company and the Free Press, 1968.
New Encyclopedia Britannica (19 vols.). Chicago: Encyclopedia Britan-
     nica, Inc., 1974.
*Trial of the Major War Criminals Before the International Military Tri-
     bunal: Nuremberg, 14 November 1945—1 October 1946* (Nuremberg,
     Germany: 1947). Vol. XI (Official text in the English Language, Pro-
     ceedings April 8, 1946—April 17, 1946.)

PERIODICALS, NEWSPAPERS, AND YEARBOOKS

American Jewish Alternatives to Zionism, published by the American
     Jewish Alternatives to Zionism, Inc., New York.
Brief, newsletter of the American Council for Judaism.
Bulletin of the American Professors for Peace in the Middle East.
Daily News Bulletin, published by the Jewish Telegraphic Agency.
Davar (Tel Aviv).
Free Palestine (London).
The Guardian.
Haaretz (Tel Aviv).
Herzl Year Book.
Interchange, newsletter of the Breira organization.
International Affairs.
Israca (London).
Israel and Palestine (Paris).
The Israel Digest, published by The Jewish Agency, New York.
Issues, a quarterly formerly published by the American Council for Judaism.
The Jewish Guardian. The first issue of this publication appeared under
     the title *The Guardian,* the second issue was titled *The Jewish Guard-
     ians,* and ever since it has appeared under its present title, *The Jewish
     Guardian,* published by the Neturei Karta in Brooklyn, New York.
Jewish Social Studies.
Labour Monthly (London).
The Link, published in New York by Americans for Middle East Under-
     standing.
Maariv (Tel Aviv).
Manchester Guardian (London).
Merip Reports, published by the Middle East Information and Research
     Project, Washington, D.C.

Middle East International (London).

Le Monde.

The New York Times.

Shu'un Falstiniya, in Arabic (Beirut).

Special Interest Report, published in New York by the American Council for Judaism.

Spectator (London).

Swasia, published weekly by the Middle East and Europe Working Groups, Division of Overseas Ministries of the National Council of Churches, New York.

South African Observer (Pretoria).

Third World Reports.

Time.

Viewpoint (Jerusalem).

Washington Post.

INDEX

Abandoned Areas Ordinance (1949) 153
Abdel-Meguid, Esmat 209
Abdel-Nasser, Gamal: *see* Nasser, Gamal Abdel-
Absentee Property Law (1950) 153
Acerbo, Giacomo 165
Adler, Hermann 62
Afro-Asian resistance to Zionism xiv, 177-185
Afro-Asian Solidarity Conference: *see* Conferences for the Solidarity of Afro-Asians
Agricultural Settlement Law 155
Agudat Israel 66-67
Agus, Jacob Bernard 11, 70-71
Ahad Ha'am (Asher Zvi Ginzberg) xv, 58-61, 64, 66, 70, 134, 136, 160, 176, 208
Alami, Mussa 125
Algeria 37, 38, 101, 102, 103, 171, 178
Aliens Act 91
Aliyah 64, 66, 75, 148, 175, 189, 207
Aliyah bet (illegal immigration) 105
Allon, Eli 199
Allon, Yigal 52, 80, 140, 141
Alloni, Shalumit 159, 189
American-Arab Relations Committee 6
American Council for Judaism 34
American Jewish Alternatives to Zionism 67
American Jewish Committee 55, 79, 123
Amery, Leopold 90, 105
Anglo-American Committee 66
Anglo-Jewish Association 62
Angola 101, 102, 103, 171, 178, 184
Anti-Semitism xiv, 23, 26, 35, 36, 40, 43, 44, 45, 46, 47, 48, 49, 50, 62, 63, 65, 72, 73, 76, 86, 89, 90, 91, 92, 93, 174, 205

Antonius, George 177
Apartheid 103, 121, 122, 123, 156, 166, 183, 184, 196, 204
Arab Jews: *see* Sephardim
Arab League 137, 138
Arab League Council 137
Arab Liberation Army 137, 140
Arabs
    attitudes of the Zionists 129-136, 160-161
    discriminated against in Israel xiv, 111-119, 147-156, 159-161, 204
    evacuation from Palestine xiv, 136-143, 147, 160, 162, 195, 196, 202, 206
    initial response to Zionism 175-176
    resistance in Palestine 104, 105, 118, 126, 128, 163, 170, 172-177, 195, 201
    return to Palestine prevented 144-146, 153, 162, 167, 203
    terrorism in Palestine 139
    see also Nationalism, Arab; Palestine; and individual Arab countries
Arendt, Hannah 27, 98, 133
Ashkenazim 37, 47, 108, 111, 112, 114-119, 126, 187, 198, 203
Assimilationists (assimilation of Jews) xiv, 19-20, 22, 30, 35-36, 39, 42, 44, 80, 92; *see also* Diaspora
Association of Rabbis (German) 62
Association of Ramallah Immigrants 158
Avineri, Shlomo 37, 130, 145, 202
Avnery, Uri 40, 139, 189, 193, 207
Azm, Rafiq Bey al- 175

Baeck, Leo 66
Balfour, James Arthur 23, 63, 91-92, 101, 109, 114, 120

Balfour, Declaration (1917) 11, 23, 31, 34, 37, 55, 61, 63, 90, 91, 94, 104, 105, 113, 131, 134, 163, 177
Bandung Conference 178
Bantustans 121, 167
Bar Lev Line 173, 196, 199
Bar-Zohar, Michael 105, 168
Beaufre, Andre 197
Begin, Menahem 93, 121, 141, 142, 163, 172-173, 203
Bellow, Saul 68-69, 74
Ben Ezer, Ehud 130, 190, 197
Ben Gurion, David 11, 20, 21, 25, 27-29, 32-34, 36, 40-42, 61, 68, 75, 76, 78, 87, 89, 98, 102, 104-106, 113-115, 120, 125, 129, 139, 142, 144, 161, 168, 171, 172, 173, 177, 190, 203
Ben Porath, Yoram 162
Ben Schneersohn, Shulem 3, 7
Ben Yehuda, Eliezer 4, 8, 14
Ben Zvi, Yitzhak 174
Bennet, Max 40
Bentwich, Norman 23
Berdichevsky, Micah 14, 58
Berger, Elmer 10, 35, 39, 52, 67, 169
Betar 172
Bible 87
Birnbaum, Nathan 7, 21, 58
Bitton, Charlie 118
Black Panther Party 53, 117, 118, 189
Borochov, Dov Ber 133-134
Borowitz, Eugene B. 15
Brandeis, Louis D. 23, 64-65, 77-78, 106
Breira 7, 14, 79-81, 208
Brenner, Joseph H. 19, 45, 46
Brit Shalom 135, 199
British Mandate (1923) 37, 48, 56, 90, 104, 126, 141, 150, 177
Buber, Martin xv, 15, 16, 58, 61, 66, 73, 81, 124, 135, 203
Bund (Polish) 57

Carter, Jimmy 176
Central Conference of American Rabbis 63
Chamberlain, Joseph 22, 90, 99, 101, 112, 131, 165
Childers, Erskine 137, 138, 144
Chofshi, Nathan 139
Chomsky, Noam 56, 169
Chrisitianity (Christians) xiii, xiv, 6, 10, 15, 17, 30, 63, 80, 83, 84, 89, 90, 113, 125, 126, 130, 162, 163, 174, 177, 199
Churchill, Winston 98, 100, 173
Cohen, Herman 62
Cohen, Morris 23
Concentration camps in Israel
  Abu-Zuneima 158

Colonialism xiv, 38, 40, 42, 55, 70, 75, 76, 83, 84, 85, 86, 87, 94, 96, 97, 98, 99-101, 104-105, 109-110, 113, 121, 171, 172, 174, 178, 182, 196; see also Zionism
Conference for Asian Relationship (1947) 179
Conference of the Hebrew Lawyers' Union (1946) 152
Conferences for the Solidarity of Afro-Asians 182
Congress for Talmudic Studies (1975) 161
Congress Party 139, 179
Cooper, Anthony Ashley 89, 90
Council of the Jews 98
Crémieux Decree (1870) 37
Crossman, Richard 43-44, 77, 92, 98, 109, 171

Dani Campaign (Lydda operation) 142-143
Davies, Uri 189
Dayan, Moshe 16, 25, 79, 80, 87, 88, 89, 107, 114, 132, 142, 144, 159, 162, 177, 197
de Gaulle, Charles 102
De Haan, Jacob 17
Decalogue 56
Defense Laws (1945) 150, 151
Deir Yassin massacre 139-142
del Val, Merry 8
Democratic Movement for Change 189, 192
Diaspora (diaspora Jewry) xiv, xv, 3, 20, 24, 30, 31, 32, 33, 34, 36, 39, 41, 42, 43, 44, 45, 46, 47, 48, 49, 50, 56, 57, 58, 59, 61, 64, 65, 66, 67, 68, 69, 71-72, 73, 75, 77, 80, 94, 106, 107, 120, 122, 124, 126, 135, 147, 183, 187, 188, 192, 193, 194, 195, 200, 202, 204, 207, 208, 209
Discharged Soldiers Law 161
Disraeli, Benjamin 86
Druzes 134, 162-163, 203
Dubnow, Simon 43, 56-57, 71, 72
Duhring, Eugen 43

East Africa Project (Uganda Project) 8-9, 91, 95, 96, 112
Eban, Abba 80, 111, 115, 138, 170
Egypt 13, 37, 38, 49-50, 51, 52, 53, 85, 86, 90, 98, 100, 101, 105, 106, 107, 120, 160, 182, 184, 196, 197
Einstein, Albert 65-66
Eliav, Arie 189
Elon, Amos 93, 115-116, 124-125, 127-128, 173, 192, 199
Emergency Articles for the Exploitation of Uncultivated Lands Law (1947-1949) 153
Emergency Laws (1949) 150, 152, 153
Epstein, Isaac 134-135

Eretz Yisrael 6, 7, 9, 32, 39, 84, 121, 128, 136, 148, 163, 180, 207
Eshkol, Levi 27, 42, 49, 75, 115, 152
European Common Market 114
Evron, Boas 16, 203, 207

Fackenheim, Emile L. 13
Fahd, Prince 176
Faisal (Iraqi king) 51
Faisal, Prince 175-176
Flinker, David 41
Friedmann, Georges 47, 208

Gandhi, Mahatma 5, 7, 35, 61, 124, 139, 179, 180, 205
Gawler, George 85
Gaza Strip 121, 160, 201
Ghetto 1, 4, 22, 31, 72, 193-194
Ghilan, Maxim 189
Ginzberg, Asher Zvi: *see* Ahad Ha'am
Golan Heights 107, 120
Goldmann, Nahum 20, 23, 29, 47, 76, 77, 81, 97, 106
Gordon, Aaron David 42, 119-120, 154
Great Britain 31, 37, 40, 62, 63, 84, 85, 86, 87, 88, 90, 91, 94, 95, 97, 98, 99-100, 101, 104, 105, 113, 122, 140, 172, 177, 184; *see also* Balfour Declaration
Greater Israel Movement 107
Gudemann, Moritz 20, 62
Gumplowicz, Ludwig 138
Guri, Chaim 197
Gush Emunim 5, 170, 193

Ha'am, Ahad: *see* Ahad Ha'am
Haavra Agreement (1933) 35, 205
Haganah 39, 41, 87, 88, 89, 140, 141, 142, 173, 191
Haganah Bet: *see* Irgun
Halutzim: *see* Palestine (Zionist settlers)
Hanauer, Edmund R. 67
Hebrew Immigration Aid Society (HIAS) 49
Hebrew labor 124, 128, 135, 153-156, 191
Hechler, William H. 86, 106
Heikal, Mohamed H. 176
Hertzberg, Arthur 14, 68
Herzl, Theodor xv, 2, 8, 9, 10, 11, 12, 19, 21-22, 24, 25, 35, 38, 43, 44, 45, 46, 47, 53, 55, 56, 58, 76, 84, 86, 89, 95, 96-98, 99, 100, 103, 106-107, 112-113, 122, 127, 130-131, 132, 134, 138, 154, 172, 184-185
Herzog, Chaim 11, 24, 25, 170
Hess, Moses 21, 26, 85, 86, 99
Histadrut 21, 32, 46, 60, 116, 132, 135, 154, 156, 190-191
Humphreys, F. 50-51

Ibn Khaldun 138

Ibn Saud (Saudi Arabian king) 180
Ihud 135, 199
Imber, Naftali Herz 86-87
Immigrants, Jewish: *see Aliyah; Aliyah bet;* Israel (Jewish immigration) Union of Soviet Socialist Republics; United States of America (Jewish immigration)
Imperialism: *see* Colonialism; Zionism.
Independent Liberal Party 192-193
India 5, 87, 91, 98, 139, 179-180, 181
Indonesia 124, 178
Iraq 9, 37, 39, 50-52, 53, 117, 133
Irgun (Haganah Bet) 141, 142, 173
Islam 6, 10, 87; *see also* Muslims
Israel
    as a godless theocracy 16, 17, 71
    diaspora view 67-68, 69-70
    intelligence services 39, 158
    Jewish immigration 10, 33, 38, 40, 48, 52, 56, 74, 78-79, 105, 107, 108, 111-112, 134, 147-149, 172, 175-177, 180, 182, 188, 190, 202-203, 206
    military 88-89, 161, 188, 196
    Western orientation 114, 145, 177-178, 181-183, 184
    Zionist use of the term "Israel" 14-15, 16, 17, 24, 57, 60
    see also Haganah; Hebrew labor, Palestine; Zionism
Israel Council for Israeli-Palestinian Peace 189
Israel Defense Army 41, 173
Israeli Declaration of Independence 16, 199
Israeli League for Human and Civil Rights 151, 189

Jabotinsky, Eri 203
Jabotinsky, Vladimir 15, 100, 104, 105, 131, 133, 156, 172, 173
Jackson, Henry 123
Jerusalem 74, 83, 90, 99, 103
Jewish Agency 39, 40, 41, 67, 74, 79, 87, 116, 132, 141, 142, 155, 161, 173, 191, 192, 206
Jewish Board of Deputies 62
Jewish Defense League 67
Jewish Legions 37
Jewish National Fund 32, 150, 154, 155, 200, 204
Jewish Telegraphic Agency 74
Jews
    dual loyalty 20, 27-30, 34, 77-78
    ethnic and religious definition 23-27, 70
    "restoration" to Palestine 84-89
    Zionist racial definition 21-24, 26, 27, 110-111

see also Judaism; Orthodox Jews; Reform Jews
Jiryis, Sabri   153
Jordan   99
Judaism   xiii, xiv, 2-4, 10, 11, 12, 13, 16, 17, 19, 21, 43, 57, 58, 59, 61, 63, 65, 70, 71, 73, 77, 82, 112, 187

Kafr Kassem massacre (1956)   156-157
Kahane, Meir   67
Kahn, Julius   62, 210
Kallen, Horace Mayer   15, 29, 188
Kalvarisky, Haim Margalit   128
Kaplan, Chaim   46
Kaplan, Mordechai   34, 35
Katzenelson, Berl   19
Kautsky, Karl   22, 102, 171, 184
Kenan, Amos   108, 125, 180, 208
Khaldun, Ibn: *see* Ibn Khaldun
Khalidi, Walid   136, 137
Kibbutz and *Kibbutzim*   2, 32, 67, 69, 115, 162, 204
King-Crane Commission   114
Kissinger, Henry   33, 54
Klatzkin, Jacob   3, 14, 20, 21, 22, 28, 29, 34, 41, 42, 44, 46, 47, 53, 91
Knesset   114, 115-116, 118, 139, 154, 159, 173, 178, 188, 189, 190
Koeing, Israel   161
Koeing Memorandum (1976)   161
Kohn, Hans   26-27, 58, 59, 60
Kol, Moshe   192-193
Kook, Isaac   4, 9, 15, 73
Kook, Zvi Yehuda Hacohen   34
Koran   87

Labor Party (of Israel)   192
Laharane, Ernest   85, 86
Land Acquisition Law (1953)   153
Landauer, Georg   172
Langer, Felicia   189
Lavon Affair   39-40, 54
Lavon, Pinhas   40
Law of Administration Ordinance   150
Law of Return (1950)   32, 33, 147-148, 150, 163, 188, 190
Law of the Status of the World Zionist Organization/Jewish Agency (1952)   33, 190
League of Nations Mandate (1922)   34
Lebanon   107
Leibowitz, Yeshayahu   130, 174, 183
Libya   38, 51, 74
Lilienthal, Alfred   66, 67
Lloyd George, David   90-91
Lydda operation: *see* Dani Campaign.

Maccabiah   28
Magnes, Judah   16-17, 59, 64, 66, 135, 176
Magnus, Laurie   62
Manifesto of Facist Racism (1938)   167
Mapai Party   40, 189
Marranos (Spanish Jews)   46
Marzouk, Moshe   39, 40
Massada   40, 41, 69, 201
Matzpen (Israeli Socialist Organization)   100, 102, 189
Mehmet Alu (Muhammed Ali)   86, 160
Meir, Golda   33, 36, 54, 81, 115, 117, 161, 163
Menuhin, Moshe   5, 67
Messiah, messianism, and pseudo-messianism   4, 10-12, 14, 17, 36, 54, 56, 58, 61, 63, 70-71, 79, 110
Moked   189
Montagu, Edwin   31, 63, 94, 132
Montefiore, Claude   62-63
Morocco   38, 81, 111, 116, 118
Motzkin, Leo   133
Mozambique   101, 178
Muslims   xiv, 17, 51, 63, 74, 113, 162, 163, 172, 175, 177, 203: *see also* Islam
Mussolini, Benito   97

Napoleon   85, 99
Nasr, Hanna   160
Nasser, Gamal Abdel-   38, 176
National Religious Party   192
Nationalism, Arab   37, 97, 100, 195
Nationality Law (1952)   148-149, 150
Nazis   xiii, 24, 35, 42, 97, 105, 109-110, 113, 121-122, 123, 126, 143, 147, 152, 166, 168, 199, 205
Nehru   179-180, 181
Neshirah   148
Neturei Karta   6, 57, 67
Neuser, Jacob   71
New Force   189
Night Squad   88, 89
Nissan, Rafi   51
Nissim, Isaac   16, 120
Nordau, Max   xv, 2, 3, 7, 8, 14, 22, 25, 43, 44, 45, 95, 96, 98-100, 109, 128, 131, 134, 172

Oliphant, Laurence   86-87
Operation Magic Carpet   50
Oriental Jewry: *see* Sephardim
Orthodox Jews   57, 58, 62, 66
Ottoman Empire   56, 84, 85, 86, 97, 104
Oz, Amos   200

Palestine
    Arab natives expelled by Zionists   17, 31,

102, 133, 136-143, 144, 145, 182, 201-202
Arab population 64, 80, 97, 100, 102, 104
  105, 114, 119, 120, 121, 123, 125, 126,
  127, 128, 131, 132, 133, 134, 135, 136,
  137, 143, 144-145, 147, 153, 159, 160,
  162, 163, 171, 172, 174, 175, 176, 179,
  181, 190, 200, 201, 202, 209
establishment of Israel 1, 32, 137, 147,
  167
Jewish religious identification with the
  land of Palestine 6, 7, 10, 35, 80, 106,
  119-120, 121, 122, 190
Jewish reluctance to emigrate 36, 40, 48,
  56, 62, 63
Partition Plan 64, 179, 181
"restoration" of Jews xiv, 25, 83, 84, 86,
  87, 90, 143
Zionist plans for settlement xvi, 8, 20
  22, 38, 40, 42, 51, 61, 85, 86, 87, 91, 94,
  97, 98, 99, 101, 104, 119, 125, 128, 132,
  133, 134, 135, 137, 139, 171, 172, 174, 185
Zionist settlers (Halutzim) 2, 5, 9, 48,
  60, 61, 75, 76, 101, 102, 105, 108, 113,
  124, 125, 128, 129, 135, 139, 145, 154,
  159, 173, 177, 199, 205
Palestine Conciliation Committee 144
Palestine Liberation Organization (PLO)
  189
Palestine Mandatory Government 141
Palestine Royal Commission (1937) 172
Palestine War (1948) 89, 104, 139-143,
  144, 145
Palestinian refugees: see Arabs (evacuation
  from Palestine); Palestine (Arab natives
  expelled by Zionists)
Palmach (elite corps of Haganah) 140, 141,
  142; see also Haganah
Palmerston, Viscount 86, 89
Patria incident 40-41
Peled, Mattityahu 189
Peres, Shimon 40, 80, 153, 192
Petuchowski, Jacob I. 36
Pinsker, Leo 8, 43, 44, 46, 50
Pioneers (Halutzim): see Palestine (Zionist
  settlers)
Piron, Mordechai 41
Pittsburgh Platform (1885) 62
Podhoretz, Norman 70
Prinz, Joachim 26
Protocols of the Elders of Zion 29, 46
Provisional Executive Committee for Zionist
  Affairs 64
Pseudo-messiah, pseudo-messianism: see
  Messiah, messianism, and pseudo-mes-
  sianism

Qaddafi, Mu'ammar 74

Qassem, Samih El- 163

Rabin, Yitzhak 7, 80, 161, 197
Rafi Party 40
Rakah 189
Raphael, Yitzhak 161
Ratosh, Yonatan 203
Reform Jews 57, 58, 62, 66-67
Refugees, Palestinian: see Arabs (evacua-
  tion from Palestine); Palestine (Arab
  natives expelled by Zionists)
Rhodes, Cecil 96, 103
Rosenberg, Alfred 109-110
Roth, Philip 43, 69
Ruppin, Arthur 19-20, 22, 23, 25, 26,
  110-112, 131-132, 135, 154, 201

Sadeh, Pinhas 174
Samuel, Herbert 131
Sapir, Pinhas 114
Sasson, Aharon 51
Saudi Arabia 176, 180, 181
Search for Justice and Equality in Palestine
  67
Selzer, Michael 72, 73, 74, 116-117
Sephardim 16, 37, 39, 72, 73, 108, 111, 112,
  114-118, 126, 145, 187, 198, 208
Shahak, Israel 17, 149-150, 152, 159, 161,
  164, 189, 199
Shapira, Jacob 152
Sharett, Moshe (Shertok) 39, 125, 136
Sharon, Ariel 12, 154, 192
Sheli 189
Shinui 188-189
Siah 189
Simon, Akiva Ernst 199
Simon, Leon 59, 60
Singer, Israel Joshua 46
Six-Day Middle East War (1967) 15, 152,
  176, 177, 182, 183, 196, 197, 198
Smilansky, Moshe 135-136
Smuts, Jan Christian 101
Sokolow, Nahum 23, 26, 84, 91, 98, 133
Sonnenfeld, Joseph Hayyim 57-58, 130
South Africa 86, 102, 103, 113, 121, 122,
  123-124, 156, 166, 168, 171, 178, 179,
  181, 183, 184, 202
South Africa Act of Union (1909) 101
South African Zionist Federation 114
South African Zionist Movement 123
Spiro, Melford 2, 115
Status Law: see Law of the Status of the
  World Zionist Organization/Jewish
  Agency
Stein, Leonard 91, 92
Stone, I. F. 50, 71-72
Storrs, Roland 90

Synagogue Council of America 71, 79
Syria 25, 37, 85, 90, 97, 111, 120, 162
Syrian Congress 175

Talbot, Phillips 35
Talmon, Jacob 196
Talmud 5, 6, 10, 43
Tekoah, Yosef 33
Teschernikowsky, Saul 136
Tolstoy, Leo 173
Torah 2, 3, 6, 13, 14, 16, 60
Toynbee, Arnold 13, 89, 143
Tri-Continental Conference (1966) 182
Triestsch, David 106
Tunisia 37, 38, 39, 113, 178
Tzvi, Shabbetai 11, 110

Uganda Project: *see* East Africa Project
Union of Soviet Socialist Republics (USSR)
    48-50, 58, 72, 78, 92, 107, 148, 194,
    205, 208
United Israel Appeal 187
United Jewish Appeal 79, 193
United Nations Resolutions
    1947 Resolution partitioning Palestine
    1, 34, 179, 181
    1948 Resolution affirming the right of
    Palestinian refugees to return to their
    homes and to live at peace with their
    neighbors 143-144
    1952 Resolution upholding the principle
    of self-determination 178
    1967 Resolution 242 calling for withdrawal
    to pre-1967 borders 209
    1947 Resolution 3236 on the Question of
    Palestine 209
    1975 Resolution equating Zionism with
    racism 1, 28, 167
United States of America 172, 181, 182, 205
    aid to Israel 106, 183, 192, 194
    American Zionism 76
    Jewish community 48, 49, 67-70, 72-73,
    74, 75, 80, 81, 208
    Jewish immigration 56, 57, 77-79, 87
    Jewish opposition to Zionism 63-64,
    73-74
    Jewish support of Israel 77, 106, 194
Universal Declaration of Human Rights 143

Verwoerd, Hendrik F. 123
Victor Emmanuel III (Italian king) 10, 97, 99
Vorster, Balthazar John 156

Wagner, Cosima 91
Wars
    1948 Palestine War 89, 104, 139-143,
    144, 145
    1956 War 38, 196, 197

1967 Six-Day Middle East War 15, 152,
    176, 177, 182, 183, 196, 197, 198
1973 October (Yom Kippur-Ramadan) War
    196
Waskow, Arthur 80
Wedgewood, J. C. 87
Weitz, Joseph 132-133, 143, 160
Weizmann, Chaim 1, 11, 20, 28, 34, 43, 44,
    61, 65, 66, 77, 85, 91-92, 94-95, 97, 98,
    100, 101, 103, 106, 113, 115, 131, 136,
    142, 143, 171, 173
West Bank 121, 159, 160, 174, 196, 201
Wills, Garry 93, 120
Wingate, Orde 87-89, 141
World Jewish Congress 20
World Union of North African Jews 118
World Zionist Organization (WZO) 20,
    32-33, 38, 58, 76, 101, 133, 173, 188, 191

Yaad 188-189
Yadin, Yigal 16, 189, 192
Yehoshuah, Abraham B. 174, 199, 207
Yemen 50, 111
Yeridah 148
Yizhar, S. 200
Yom Kippur Ramadan War (1973) 196

Zangwill, Israel 9, 24, 112, 132, 134
Zionism
    Afro-Asian resistance xiv, 177-185
    anti-Semitism xiv, 23, 43-48, 62-63, 65
    anti-Zionism xiv, 10, 14-15, 16-17, 20,
    39, 55-66, 73-74, 80, 94, 169, 181, 189,
    192
    attitudes toward Arabs 129-136
    diaspora Zionism 78, 106
    distinguished from Judaism xiii, 2-4,
    16-17, 71
    espionage and propaganda 39-41, 51-54
    fund raising 37-38, 73, 75-77, 79, 183,
    187-188, 191-192, 193
    gentile Zionism xiv, 23, 83-93, 94, 97,
    99, 110, 120
    historical roots xiv, 1-4, 8-9, 12, 26, 27,
    83-101, 110-113
    ideology 1-12, 19-30, 41-48, 50, 75-76,
    81, 119-120
    Labor Zionism 1, 98, 124-126
    nationalist outlook 2, 5-6, 7, 14, 15, 16,
    19-20, 26-27, 28, 31, 33-34, 41, 44, 46,
    48-49, 58-60, 64, 66, 67, 71, 74, 77, 80,
    81, 132, 205, 208
    non-Zionism 17, 55, 66, 73, 189, 192
    political Zionism xiii, xiv, xv, xvi, 1-6,
    11-12, 14, 15-17, 27-30, 31-36, 58-59,
    60-61, 68, 71, 75, 83, 106, 131, 171,
    187-190, 201, 207

racism   59, 110-118, 123, 132, 144-145,
    147-156, 159-161, 163-170, 196, 203
Religious Zionism   1, 4-9, 10-12, 15-16,
    27
settler colonialism   25, 37, 85, 93-108,
    121, 128, 176-177, 178, 196
Territorial Zionism   9
terrorism   88, 138-143, 156-159, 189
see also Arabs (resistance in Palestine);
    Balfour Declaration; Ben Gurion, David;
    British   Mandate;   Herzl,   Theodore;
    Nordau, Max; Weizmann, Chaim
Zionist Action Committee (Zionist Executive)
    33, 131, 133, 141
Zionist Annual Convention (1921)   65

Zionist Commission   172
Zionist Congress
    First (1897)   58, 60, 62, 106, 128
    Fourth (1900)   8
    Sixth (1903)   8-9
    Seventh (1905)   9, 134, 174
    Eleventh (1913)   154
    Twelfth (1921)   38, 172
    Thirteenth (1923)   51
    Nineteenth (1935)   98
    Twenty-Fifth (1960-61)   68
    Twenty-Sixth (1964-1965)   20
Zionist Federation of France   38
Zionist Federation of Tunisia   37, 38
Zionist Organization of America   75